SECRET AND SUPPRESSED II

BANNED IDEAS AND HIDDEN HISTORY
INTO THE 21ST CENTURY

Edited by Adam Parfrey and Kenn Thomas

Contributors

Mike Bara
Mark Bruback
Joan ·D'Arc
Joseph P. Farrell
William W. Flint
Adam Gorightly
Douglas Hawes
Craig Heimbichner
Harry Helms
Al Hidell
Paul Krassner
Jim Marrs
David Martin
Robert Sauder
Jerry E. Smith
Robert Sterling
Jay Weidner
Adam Weishaupt
Robert Anton Wilson

Feral House

Feral House
1240 W. Sims Way Ste. 124
Port Townsend, WA 98368
Send S.A.S.E. for free catalogue of publications

info@feralhouse.com
www.feralhouse.com

10 9 8 7 6 5 4 3 2 1

TABLE OF CONTENTS

DEMONS FROM THE FAR SIDE OF TRUTH

by Kenn Thomas and Adam Parfrey

The term "conspiracy theorist" has a trifecta of propagandish intent: it deprives of credibility any perspective not directly approved by academic and political authorities; it implies that conspiracies don't really exist; and it promotes a subgenre of *DaVinci Code*-type print and media entertainments.

When Jim Keith assembled volume one of the now out-of-print *Secret and Suppressed* in 1993, he and publisher Feral House were keenly aware of the institutional disapproval of non-sanctioned views of political assassinations, financial manipulations and the secret operations of military and intelligence black-ops.

Keith did not live to see an American president assume office as the result of a court decision, nor did he witness the 9/11 horrors and the US march to war over imaginary weapons of mass destruction. He did, however, with that first volume of *Secret & Suppressed*, help create the attendant popular culture of *X-Files* TV shows, Mel Gibson-styled *Conspiracy Theory* movies and a conspiracy-obsessed internet.

An *X-Files* offshoot program called *Lone Gunmen* used in its pilot episode concepts that explored in a Feral House book Keith co-wrote with Kenn Thomas called *The Octopus*, based on the conspiracy research of a writer named Danny Casolaro. The *Lone Gunmen* pilot episode included a "back door" computer system, called "Octium" in the show but identical to PROMIS in Casolaro's research, that stopped a plane from crashing into Manhattan's twin Trade towers. This aired in the March preceding the actual events of 9/11, making the show more known for its eerie predictive quality than for its connection to Casolaro and *The Octopus*.

Keith had died by then, and mysteriously so, from a knee injury he suffered at the Burning Man event in Black Rock, Nevada in 1999. Shortly thereafter, a scandal in the medical world caused a temporary suspension of knee surgeries when patients began dying from cartilage transplants tainted with clostridium bacteria. Keith had previously written about the CIA's stockpiles of the same bacteria. Shortly after the knee-surgery scandal,

Keith's publisher Ron Bonds, whose IllumiNet Press published many conspiracy-oriented books, also died of clostridium poisoning from food he ate at a Mexican restaurant near his home in Atlanta, Georgia. In the end, the tainted cartilage samples from the hospital scandal were tracked to a tissue bank near Atlanta.

So Jim Keith became an odd footnote to the bizarre circumstance of the prediction of 9/11 by a TV show in a genre he helped create and popularize in part by editing the first volume of *Secret and Suppressed.*

And though Jim fully believed in *Secret and Suppressed's* sinister shadow histories, he was not above putting on his publisher with the inclusion of an article called "Secrets from the Vatican Library" which purported to have been written by a "member of the Franciscan order." It became clear that this piece was actually written by a prisoner named "Wayne Henderson" who had been (he and justicedenied.org says) falsely convicted of murder. As it turns out, this was not Jim Keith's sole intentional inside joke. He also wrote a couple UFO books under the pen name "Commander X." As Robert Sterling of The Konformist puts it, "many in the conspiracy field have long believed that Commander X was some sort of fascist Nazi propaganda, where good light-skinned aliens battle evil, large-nosed alien monsters. When looking at the work as satire rather than a disinformation vehicle, however, Commander X is quite a hoot."

When dressed down for the conspiratorial put-ons by his Feral House publisher, Keith begged forgiveness by comparing his style to Robert Anton Wilson in which "factions" become more stimulating and illuminating than cautious articles with obsessive academic sourcing.

Keith entered the annals long after the ascendance of stalwart champion conspiracy theorists—more rightly known as parapolitical scholars—Mae Brussell and Robert Anton Wilson, both of whom are represented in this second *Secret and Suppressed* volume. The hard data they harvested needs to be acknowledged by and before new readers.

Satirical factions and dismissible kookiness are not included—at least not intentionally—among *Secret and Suppressed II's* lineup of under or non-reported articles about America's shadow-side operations.

In the last piece of expository prose from his career, Wilson presents one final personal take at Adam Weishaupt, overlord of a central conception to many conspiracy-oriented readers: the Illuminati. "Perhaps Tom Jefferson got it right when he said that secret societies seemed necessary in Europe, haunted by monarchy and Papism, but not in the United States. Certainly when the Constitution remained the law of the land—before the Supremes selected Dubya—no sane person would feel the need for secret societies here. Do I dare add, "but now with the Constitution in cryonic suspension...?"

During George W. Bush's tenure, as conspiracies were happily pushed much more into the face of the American public than they had ever been, the very idea of their secrecy and suppression almost itself seemed to become history, or at least just the stuff of popular entertainment. At the end of Bush's presidency, conspiracy issues seem no less threatening and new shadows gather.

Secret and Suppressed II explores the current parade of cryptocracies, cults, secret societies and international Nazified elites. It examines what the periodicals and electronic media still refuse to take seriously: debates about the nature of evolution that offer more than a dumb show of crypto-Christians and pseudo-skeptics; details about occult themes running in the background of today's space program; symbolic resonances in popular cultures from Nashville to Santa Cruz; weather warfare technology, fusion reactors; and the technology of political disenfranchisement; unsettled arguments about historical conspiracies and just tidbits of oddball and underreported information that Keith called "demons from the far side of the Truth."

NEWSPEAK

SEVENTEEN TECHNIQUES FOR TRUTH SUPPRESSION

By David Martin

Strong, credible allegations of high-level criminal activity can bring down a government. When the government lacks an effective, fact-based defense, other techniques must be employed. The success of these techniques depends heavily upon a cooperative, compliant press and a mere token opposition party.

1.) Dummy up. If it's not reported, if it's not news, it didn't happen.
2.) Wax indignant. This is also known as the "How dare you?" gambit.
3.) Characterize the charges as "rumors" or, better yet, "wild rumors." If, in spite of the news blackout, the public is still able to learn about the suspicious facts, it can only be through "rumors." (If they tend to believe the "rumors" it must be because they are simply "paranoid" or "hysterical.")
4.) Knock down straw men. Deal only with the weakest aspects of the weakest charges. Even better, create your own straw men. Make up wild rumors (or plant false stories) and give them lead play when you appear to debunk all the charges, real and fanciful alike.
5.) Call the skeptics names like "conspiracy theorist," "nutcase," "ranter," "kook," "crackpot," and, of course, "rumormonger." Be sure, too, to use heavily loaded verbs and adjectives when characterizing their charges and defending the "more reasonable" government and its defenders. You must then carefully avoid fair and open debate with any of the people you have thus maligned. For insurance, set up your own "skeptics" to shoot down.
6.) Impugn motives. Attempt to marginalize the critics by suggesting strongly that they are not really interested in the truth but are simply pursuing a partisan political agenda or are out to make money (compared to over-compensated adherents to the government line who, presumably, are not).
7.) Invoke authority. Here the controlled press and the sham opposition can be very useful.

8.) Dismiss the charges as "old news."

9.) Come half-clean. This is also known as "confession and avoidance" or "taking the limited hangout route." This way, you create the impression of candor and honesty while you admit only to relatively harmless, less-than-criminal "mistakes." This stratagem often requires the embrace of a fall-back position quite different from the one originally taken. With effective damage control, the fall-back position need only be peddled by stooge skeptics to carefully limited markets.

10.) Characterize the crimes as impossibly complex and the truth as ultimately unknowable.

11.) Reason backward, using the deductive method with a vengeance. With thoroughly rigorous deduction, troublesome evidence is irrelevant, e.g., we have a completely free press. If evidence exists that the Vince Foster "suicide" note was forged, they would have reported it. They haven't reported it so there is no such evidence. Another variation on this theme involves the likelihood of a conspiracy leaker and a press who would report the leak.

12.) Require the skeptics to solve the crime completely, e.g., if Foster was murdered, who did it and why?

13.) Change the subject. This technique includes creating and/or publicizing distractions.

14.) Lightly report incriminating facts, and then make nothing of them. This is sometimes referred to as "bump and run" reporting.

15.) Baldly and brazenly lie. A favorite way of doing this is to attribute the "facts" furnished the public to a plausible-sounding, but anonymous, source.

16.) Expanding further on numbers 4 and 5, have your own stooges "expose" scandals and champion popular causes.

17.) Flood the Internet with agents. This is the answer to the question, "What could possibly motivate a person to spend hour upon hour on Internet news groups defending the government and/or the press and harassing genuine critics?"

THE MIND OF MAE BRUSSELL

Is she just a paranoid housewife
who likes to clip newspapers?

by Paul Krassner

> *Nothing just happens in politics. If something happens you can*
> *be sure it was planned that way.* — Franklin D. Roosevelt

There she is, the Bionic Researcher. Every day she feeds herself ten newspapers from around the country. This diet is supplemented with items sent to her by a network of conspiracy students. She also consumes magazines, underground papers, unpublished manuscripts, court affidavits, documents from the National Archives, FBI and CIA materials obtained through the Freedom of Information Act and hundreds of books on espionage and assassination. "About 80 percent of all CIA intelligence information comes from printed news," she says, "so I am doing what they are doing but I'm using all the material." Each Sunday, she sorts out the week's clippings into various categories as though she were conducting a symphony of horror. Yet she is cheerful. She almost sways in counterpoint to the rhythms of hypocrisy. For, while there are those who try to discredit her by saying she's crazy, Mae Brussell remains high on her responsibility.

Mae has been our nation's Number One, self-appointed conspiracy freak since the day Jack Ruby shot Lee Harvey Oswald. She has written hundreds of articles detailing the unpleasant connections between what most people consider diverse chapters in American history — like Oswald and Francis Gary Powers, the Kennedy murders and Watergate. For the past seven years, the housewife-turned-crusader has shocked and dismayed listeners of her syndicated radio program, *Dialogue: Conspiracy* (KLRB-FM, Carmel, California), uncovering choice tidbits about everything from Chappaquiddick to Chowchilla. She unabashedly calls herself the country's best researcher.

At 54, she is plump and energetic; she wears long peasant dresses patchworked with philosophical tidbits, and her favorite adjective is "cute." Occasionally, she slurs her words — information overload — but her eyes seem to reveal the deep sense of compassion permeating every fact she shares. One senses a touch of appropriate incongruity about this white, upper-middle-class, twice-divorced mother of a talented brood, who is knitting a sleeve while calmly describing the architecture of a police state in progress.

I first met Mae Brussell when she provided me with leads for a story I did on Charles Manson. Then, a few months after the break-in at Democratic Party headquarters in the Watergate Hotel, Mae rang me up. She recognized names and methods of operation from all her assassination research. For example, she knew that Watergate burglar James McCord had crossed paths with Lee Harvey Oswald when both had been working for CIA intelligence, and that Frank Sturgis had been interrogated by the FBI in Miami the day after JFK was assassinated. She also had a possible tie between McCord and a "secret army" of police who allegedly had planned to disrupt the 1972 Republican Convention with riots and possible assassination attempts on Nixon, would then be blamed on leftist radicals and hopefully result in a further shift to the right — possibly under the figurehead leadership of Spiro T. Agnew.

And then there was L. Patrick Gray, who as acting director of the FBI would later burn evidence from the files of E. Howard Hunt and deep-six numerous documents. Mae recalled the murder of a Los Angeles reporter, Ruben Salazar, at the first Chicano-sponsored antiwar protest. U.S. Attorney Robert Meyer was later pressured by Gray into halting his investigation and resigning from his post. Mae called Meyer, asking if he would help with her research. She wanted to find out why the Justice Department in Washington was stopping an attorney in Los Angeles from investigating the simple killing of a reporter. A month or so later, ex-U.S. Attorney Meyer was found dead "of an apparent heart attack" in a parking lot in Pasadena.

Three weeks after the Watergate break-in, while the Establishment press was calling it "a caper" and "a third-rate burglary," Mae Brussell completed a manuscript titled "Why Was Martha Mitchell Kidnapped?" She named names — John Mitchell, L. Patrick Gray, Richard Nixon, the FBI, the CIA — and I published her first by-lined article in *The Realist*.

"The CIA that killed President Kennedy and Robert Kennedy," she wrote, "did a test case in Greece on canceling elections. Andreas Papandreou, often compared with John Kennedy, appeared to have a good chance of winning the Greek election in 1967. The U.S. Army, the CIA and government agencies helped replace their elections with a coup d'etat... . The significance of the Watergate affair is that every element essential for a political coup in the United States was assembled at the time of the arrests."

Mae Brussell contends that Nixon's own Watergate plumbers, and the entire intelligence network they represented, were prepared to overthrow Nixon whenever it was deemed necessary by the true powers.

Ultimately, she believes, the same men who brought Nixon to power via the Kennedy assassinations were also pulling the strings at Watergate.

Papandreou wrote to her from exile in Canada: "I am overwhelmed by the amount of work you have done and the documentation you bring to support your thesis. I have tried myself for a long time to bring out the conspiratorial aspects of the Greek coup of 1967. People are now beginning to understand how it happened that Greece went under a dictatorship. Your work is tremendously important. You have understood the framework in which these events take place, but more than that, you have dug out the facts..."

Five days before Richard Nixon's would-be adversary, Robert Kennedy, was assassinated in Los Angeles, Mae Brussell handed a letter to Rose Kennedy, expressing her fear of imminent danger to his safety. A month before Mary Jo Kopechne died at Chappaquiddick, Mae warned Teddy Kennedy of "the nest of rattlesnakes" that wanted to abort his presidential possibilities. A few weeks before the SLA kidnapped the media as well as Patty Hearst, she told a Syracuse University audience that the SLA shooting of a black school superintendent in Oakland was merely the preliminary to a main event yet to come.

"A lot of stuff comes to me psychically and then the documents follow," Mae explains. "After Jack Ruby shot Lee Harvey Oswald, I found it very interesting that one of the first things Ruby said was: 'I wanted to show them that a Jew had guts.' Well, the most anti-Semitic man in Dallas was H.L. Hunt, and he was publishing *Lifeline* and was meeting with Reverend Billy Hargis and all these neo-Nazi groups and the Minutemen down in the Dallas-Fort Worth area. A radio script from a Hunt-owned station about being a 'hero' was found in Jack Ruby's car. No one ever asked him to explain how he got it. The Wednesday before the assassination, Ruby took a young woman to Hunt's office, trying to get her a job. Suddenly the whole plot of the Kennedy assassination began to open up in front of me. Here was this Jew, Jack Rubinstein, being used to kill Lee Harvey Oswald. When the Warren Report came out, the very first witness I pulled to, the most important of the 552, was Oswald's friend George de Mohrenschildt, a man surrounded by neo-Nazi oil people, who was also suspected of being a Nazi during World War II. De Mohrenschildt had set Oswald up with his oil-industry contacts in Texas. He also helped arrange for Oswald to get his job at the schoolbook depository and at the printing office where he learned all the details of the Dallas motorcade."

In 1977, shortly before he was to undergo more questioning, De Mohrenschildt purportedly "shot himself" to death with a shotgun. According to the report in the *Dallas News*, just prior to his death he had been under the impression — or delusion — that the FBI was out to "get him" and therefore had been in a mental ward at Parkland Hospital.

Mae Brussell spent eight years cross-filing the Warren Commission report on the assassination of John F. Kennedy. She cross-filed every single minute of Jack Ruby's life that doubly fatal weekend, from Thursday (the day before Kennedy was killed) through Sunday (the day Ruby shot Oswald). She was able to account for his whereabouts totally, except for two hours in the afternoon on Saturday. Although she cannot prove it, she is convinced he was at the home of H.L. Hunt.

."And then there was the testimony of Bernard Weissman. He was only one of twelve military intelligence people that were brought from Germany to Dallas for the assassination. He testified that Lamar Hunt and twenty members of the Birch Society used his name on that inflammatory 'Wanted for Treason' ad in the *Dallas Times Herald* about Kennedy because he was Jewish and they wanted a Jewish name on it. Somehow, on November 24, 1963, the Nazi link, the oil Nazis, the American military from Munich and the two Jew patsies, Rubinstein and Weissman, were all right there in Dallas. As I collected every possible document, the world picture began to get clearer to me, and my interest in the Kennedy assassination became more involved with the Nazi links than with the anti-Castro Cuban links. My disagreement with researchers at large is that they want to stop with the Bay of Pigs operation, and I think it's bigger."

But why the Nazis? Racism, for one thing, says Mae. The Bormann Brotherhood, still dedicated to the establishment of the Fourth Reich, did not appreciate Kennedy's drive to educate Southern blacks and register them to vote. Nor did they care for the fact that he was Catholic and stood in opposition to the neo-Nazi oil interests.

Mae Brussell's ascension to the throne as the queen of conspiracy investigations began with a harsh dose of culture shock during her childhood. Raised in Beverly Hills affluence, she was unhurt by the Depression (her grandfather founded the posh I. Magnin department stores), and her family's house-guests ranged from Jack Warner and Louis B. Mayer to Thomas Mann. Her father used to go bike riding with Albert Einstein. "I grew up," she recalls, "thinking this is the way life was." Then, in her early teens, the family took a trip around the world, and her awareness of suffering expanded in the process. In Bombay, she saw people sleeping in the streets. They had no homes or possessions, let alone memberships in tennis clubs. In Shanghai, their boat hit a sampan and split it in half. Other people came out in boats to get the clothes off the victims' bodies. Some lived and died on their sampans, never getting to shore. She was not used to seeing such overwhelming poverty. In Egypt, it was the same. In Tel Aviv, the hotel her family stayed at was bombed. They were the last Americans out of Spain in 1936.

"We were happy little tourists," she muses. "But it always bothered me. I never felt the same again. I was haunted by the imbalance. I wanted to help people, but I didn't know what form it would take." In a few years, she would attend Stanford University, majoring in philosophy. "I think the discipline of it helped me with my research later."

Then there was the influence of Henry Miller during Mae's forties. "Henry freed me from a lot of hang-ups that I was brought up with. He opened up the whole field of sex as being normal as the air you breathe. He also helped me realize that freedom of the press, freedom to live and to love is what the struggle is all about. It's simply rhythm. People gotta shake their bodies — and relate to each other in their minds and hearts."

A turning point in her comprehension of the global aspect of conspiracy occurred when she came across the story of a Heidelberg professor named E. J. Gumbel, in the book *Inspection for Disarmament* by Seymour Melman. Gumbel was forced to resign from his academic post during the Nazis' rise to power, because of his unpopular stance as a pacifist and anti-fascist. He wrote three books between 1919 and 1922: *Four Years of Lies, Two Years of Murders*, and *Four Years of Political Murders*. In these, Gumbel documented over 400 political assassinations, most of which were admitted to by the Minister of Justice in 1924.

Mae Brussell began to study the pattern of Nazis coming to the United States after World War II and patterns of murders identical to those in Nazi Germany. It was as if an early Lenny Bruce bit — on how a show-bit booking agency, MCA, chose Adolf Hitler as dictator — had actually been a satirical prophecy of the way Richard Nixon would rise to power. The parallels were frightening.

"How much violence was there in Nazi Germany," Mae asks rhetorically, "before the old Germany, the center of theater, opera, philosophy, poetry, psychology and medicine, was destroyed? How many incidents took place that were not coincidental before it was called Fascism? What were the transitions? How many people? Was it when the first tailor disappeared? Or librarian? Or professor? Or when the first press was closed or the first song eliminated? Or when the first political science teacher was killed coming home on his bike? How many incidents happened there that were perfectly normal until people woke up and said, 'Hey, we're in a police state!'

"Hitler was gassed in World War I and they took him to the hospital and, according to a U.S. Navy Intelligence report, they brought in a Dr. Forster, a hypnotist, and they groomed him. They told him that he would have troops that would someday invade Russia and kick the Communists out. They hypnotized him so that he would always believe that he'd be a great leader, like Joan of Arc.

"Now, take a man like Nixon, a man who is going to be President of the United States. He's known for his poker playing, his straight face. He already has a proclivity for intelligence. He wrote to Hoover, asking to join the FBI. After World War II, the great poker player of the South Pacific was assigned to the Navy Bureau of Aeronautics, negotiating settlements of terminated defense contracts, where he helped escalate the importation of 642 Nazi specialists into the U.S. defense and aerospace industry — Project Paperclip. Then he gets a call from Murray Chotiner, who works with Howard Hughes and the Bank of America, inviting him to run for Congress against Jerry Voorhis. What did he have besides a poker face? In 1951, Senator Nixon introduced a bill to bring Nikolai Molaxa into the U.S. Molaxa was a former head of the Iron Guard and was allegedly involved in Nazi atrocities. Nixon set him up in an office of his own."

Another turning point in Mae's research occurred when she attended the trial of Hugo Pinell, who had been charged with killing a Soledad prison guard. "A public defender was assigned on Friday to begin the case on Monday, and none of his witnesses could appear. The whole trial was rigged, and I was just outraged. It was then that I decided not only to study who killed John Kennedy, but also to find the relationship between the corruption of the courts, political prisoners in this country and the political assassinations and conspiracies. When you think of Hitler, you think of prisons like Auschwitz and Dachau. And when I thought about the killing of Kennedy and all the Nazis involved, I realized that the prison system had to be directly related to it. And that's when I began to correspond with prisoners and make friends with them and get more information about prison deaths and mind-control experiments. I found there were incidents identical to what occurred in Nazi Germany, where the innocent were locked up or killed and the guilty were allowed to go free.

"Instead of just researching the deaths of John Kennedy, Robert Kennedy, Malcolm X, Martin Luther King, Mary Jo Kopechne, and the George Wallace shooting, I began collecting articles about the murders of people involved in those cases. And I began paying attention to the deaths of judges, attorneys, labor leaders, musicians, actors, professors, civil rights leaders — studying what I considered to be untimely, suspicious deaths."

In preparation for an upcoming campus lecture in Seattle, Mae spends a day and a half cross-filing one ten-year-old article — "The Murder of Malcolm X" by Eric Norden — into some 30 different subjects. The actual motives behind the assassination. Collusion between Federal intelligence and local police. Involvement of bodyguards. Prime witnesses killed. Perjured testimony that doesn't fit the evidence...

Sometimes Mae's theories seem like they've been pulled from the pages of a James Bond — or perhaps an E. Howard Hunt — spy thriller. "I found it interesting that the Cuban Watergate burglars — who were later given a $200,000 payoff by the CIA — were looking for the air-conditioning plans for the hotels in Miami, when later it was discovered that Legionnaire's Disease may have come through the air-conditioning ducts. There is the capability to use germs to neutralize people. The CIA has the germs. Legionnaire's Disease has the exact symptoms of a disease they were experimenting with at Fort Detrick, Maryland. When you hear of weapons control, you think of guns, tanks, planes, but you don't hear that they're selling germs, or that Nixon ordered Richard Helms to destroy the germs at Fort Detrick and Helms didn't. Nixon was put out as a bad man, isolated and ridiculed, but Helms went on to become ambassador to Iran and is immune to perjury charges."

And now the Bionic Researcher is rolling her big wax ball of conspiracy at full speed.

"Jimmy Carter and the Pentagon can talk about disarmament, but the real tragedy is the chemical weapons used for mind control. Some people are programmed and have lost their minds. What we call the motiveless crime or senseless killings are actually people being trained as zombies."

She zips out the Congressional Record from February 24, 1972, and reads the testimony of Dr. Jose Delgado from Yale University, who was arguing against the proposed discontinuation of research into psychosurgery:

We need a program of psychosurgery for political control of our society. The purpose is physical control of the mind. Everyone who deviates from the given norm can be surgically mutilated. The individual may think that the most important reality is his own existence, but this is only his personal view. This lacks historical perspective. Man does not have the right to develop his own mind. This kind of liberal orientation has great appeal. We must electrically control the brain. Someday armies and generals will be controlled by electric stimulation of the brain.

"So these are not just feelings I have," says Mae. "That speech was greeted by Congress with thundering silence — and money — government-funded programs paid for with our tax dollars. We are witnessing pockets of violence, because they are now able to electronically, surgically and hypnotically kill citizens. The army alone spent $26 million in projects to alter human behavior, and they not only did it with electrode implants but with LSD plus electrodes. They alter minds so that people act without knowing why. They can make someone murder a whole family and then kill himself."

And that is where the prison system comes in. It is like a farm team to develop "talent" for the outside world. "You can't just take anybody off the street and make him decide to walk up and shoot people," Mae insists. "But take people who have had no love or affection, who are in prison, who in adolescence broke a school window and the court put them away. You lock them up — heterosexuals with homosexuals — you break their spirit, dehumanize them, take away chances for education, increase their feelings of inferiority. If you have hostility combined with this lack of opportunities, you begin nurturing a situation where children or young adults like Charles Manson or Gary Gilmore — people with high intelligence but a lot of misery — sit smoking and watching TV, covering up their anger, and become very ripe for indoctrination.

These are the people that they select for electronic or hypnotic control. Hitler was gassed and told his mother had cancer, that a Jewish doctor let her die ... so he transferred his various hatreds.

"The case of Donald DeFreeze is identical to Adolf Hitler's. Colton Westbrook, a mind-control expert who worked with [CIA Director William] Colby in Southeast Asia, helped DeFreeze with the Black Culture Association at the Vacaville prison in California. DeFreeze was told he would be a new black leader to replace Malcolm X and Martin Luther King. Later, he was shot and burned to death with all-white associates, no blacks, in the company of agents from the Defense Department — no different from Hitler or Lee Harvey Oswald."

If, indeed, we each create our deities as extensions of our own personalities, then the first thing that Mae Brussell's version of God would have done was to make a list. She can spew out a ticker tape with names of dead witnesses — literally hundreds of deaths she finds not exactly above suspicion.

Labor leaders: Waiter Reuther, Joseph Yablonski, Saul Alinsky, Jimmy Hoffa, Sam Bramlet — "And there was a contract to kill Cesar Chavez, from the Treasury Department no less — the Alcohol, Tobacco and Firearms agency. Meanwhile, Argentine, Chilean and Brazilian police squads are killing off labor people."

Mafia leaders: Sam Giancana, Jimmy Hoffa, John Roselli — "It was just a fluke that he bounced up; his legs were cut off and his torso put in an oil drum. Carlo Gambino — given a shot of swine flu inoculation when he had a heart disease. Sheffield Edwards was killed and William Harvey was killed—the CIA contacts with the Mafia people — and the CIA agent Guy Bannister was killed. He worked with Robert Maheu and with Lee Harvey Oswald, and he flew out a window. The same people who were behind it are alive today, and they're sweeping away the bodies. It's at the highest levels that these conspiracies are planned, not just with a few Cuban exiles."

Musicians: Otis Redding, Janis Joplin, Jimi Hendrix, Brian Jones, Jim Morrison, Mama Cass Elliott, Jim Croce, Tim Buckley — "And almost thirty other fine musicians have died under mysterious circumstances. Rock musicians had an ability to draw together youth at a time when protest meetings were being broken apart, and the hippie, antiwar youth became too visible with their own, unique art form at Woodstock. The Senate investigation documented that persons seeking 'racial harmony' and 'social protest' were defined as enemies of the state. Only people like Sonny and Cher, the Osmonds, John Denver and the Captain and Tennille make it as role models. They either have to tame you or kill you."

And then there's Freddie Prinze. "He was an active Democrat, entertained by the president at the White House, a symbol for the Chicano. He had a deep concern about who killed Kennedy. He had a copy of the Abraham Zapruder film, and he kept playing it over and over. *Time* magazine says he had an intrigue about death because he kept watching Kennedy die. Well, you could say he was worried about how Kennedy was killed.

"I know researchers who've played that film over two hundred times. It's not because they are preoccupied with death, but because it's perfectly obvious that the government is lying, that Kennedy's head is going back. And here's a guy, Freddie Prinze, who every time somebody comes over, he shows the film to them and talks about it. He tells a psychiatrist he's suicidal, who takes his gun, and then when he leaves, he hands it back to him. Then Freddie goes to Vegas and picks up a hundred Quaaludes from another doctor. The removal of Freddie Prinze means one less visual person from that stratum of society. They lose a symbol for the Puerto Rican kids sitting on the steps in New York. There are no positive visual images of Chicanos on the screen. No encouragement for the young ones, because this one's heavily doped and has blown his brains out."

In lieu of the frightening conclusions she's made, does she have any basis for optimism?

"No, I'm not optimistic now — not when government agents work with germ warfare and genocide, and those who put Hitler into power are still at it. Instead of having low-cost housing, there are SWAT teams for food riots when there's no shortage of food.

"I see pockets of fascism. You can still read about a Jewish butcher in Miami having his window broken every night, and in San José a bookstore broken into like in Nazi Germany, and *Mein Kampf* coming out all over Latin America. Those Nazis were brought there and now they're surfacing. The Rockefellers' attorney, Allen Dulles, consulted with Reinhard Gehlen, the Nazi intelligence chief, to form our own CIA. George Ball writes about getting rid of people by the millions. Patrick Buchanan writes an article justifying the use of torture. Zbigniew Brzezinski, head of our National Security Council, writes that 'with the use of computers, human behavior itself will become more determined and subject to deliberate programming,' and that 'it will soon be possible to assert almost continuous surveillance over every citizen.'

"I believe that the Nazis and the Minutemen and the Christian movement are going to get very strong, and at the same time there's going to be a massive depression. I see large masses of people around the world being deliberately starved every day. I see terrible things happening to reduce the population of this earth, so that those who control the corporations don't have to provide for the needs of the poor."

At KLRB one Monday, somebody called and asked Mae the question that she is asked most often: "How come you're still alive?"

"Well, I'm not," she chuckled. "I'm a robot."

But it is a question that Mae Brussell has obviously considered. If she knows so much, why haven't they killed her?

"The way they handle you is to ignore or discredit. But if I were at Madison Square Garden and had that big an audience, then I wouldn't be alive. I don't want to meet large masses of people. My role is mostly to educate people and let them figure it out for themselves. Tell them books to read and sources of information. The main contribution that I've tried to make with my research is to study things individually and then find the connecting links. I'm not a movement or organization, because if I had five people, one would probably be an agent. The ratio is four to one."

She pauses to count her stitches. Mae is knitting sweaters for each of her children.

"That's why the CIA works on a basis of need-to-know. Because if you know too much, you may not do what you're supposed to do. If you know that the end result is that somebody's going to be blown up twelve miles away — and all you're supposed to do is deliver an envelope — you may think about it. One man who called me had killed ten people—a number of the murders were chemically induced 'apparent heart attacks' — for the CIA. But when he was ordered to kill a congresswoman, he refused. Another CIA agent then tried to kill him by cutting his jugular vein, but he had it sewn up and survived. Now he's vowed vengeance against them. He told me that agents listen to my show, *Dialogue: Conspiracy*, and I asked: 'What do they think about it?' He said they think it's right on, that they can understand.

That it's also a safety valve for them, something that lets them know just how far things are going." And so we are left with the bizarre possibility that the intelligence community allows the Bionic Researcher to function precisely because she knows more than any of them do.

Despite her obsession, Mae Brussell claims she has not had to sacrifice her family because of her work. "It's not my whole life," she says. "It's important to find out who killed Kennedy, but not at the expense of your own humanness. I don't lose anything if they never find out who killed him. I still have my self-respect. And I like having children and preparing meals and mastering everything having to do with the home. In fact, my initial concern over who killed John Kennedy was basically a selfish one. I wanted to find out if there had been a coup, if the United States was going fascist. Would I be like Anne Frank's father, who told his family that things were okay and that people were basically good while they were living their last days? They never fought Nazism, but just watched it all go by and hid in the attic until their time came around to be taken away. With a family of five children, my husband and myself, I had an obligation to understand the world outside my home.

"When Hitler failed, his officers were brought to the U.S., from inside Rockefeller Center, and to the Bahamas and Southern states to build that dream of the Fourth Reich. It is in this context that the Kennedys, Malcolm X, Martin Luther King, labor leaders, judges, entertainers, reporters, authors, students, Black Panthers, Indians, Chicanos and hippies are being slain, and why the masses are being doped into control."

In December 1970, Mae's daughter, Bonnie, was killed at the age of 15 in a suspicious auto accident.

The driver of the other car — a soldier in the U.S. Army at Fort Ord — went AWOL two weeks after the crash, returned to his home and was not sought by authorities. Barbara Brussell, another daughter, was also in that accident. Her legs were severely injured; she also suffered from a broken back, face injuries and a broken nose and arm, but now dances with graceful agility. She took a course called "American Assassinations" that Mae taught at Monterey Peninsula College.

"Mom combines being a researcher and a mother," Barbara says. "They have to overlap at times. Mom tends to doubt almost everything; that's her first instinct — especially as events are described in the news — instead of taking any chances of agreeing first, then having to go back later. It's a way of perceiving things that adds a little negativity to events — worrying or being suspicious if a person is an agent or not. But it's her world."

Her mother is casually devouring the obituary page for clues. A neighborhood pharmacist has died at the age of 81 of "natural causes." The clipping triggers no conspiratorial connections in Mae's computer.

"Here," the Bionic Researcher laughs, "I'll give you this one ..."

(Originally published in *OUI* magazine, May 1978)

THE EVIL FEEDBACK LOOP & EMERSON'S LAW OF CONSERVATION

Mae Brussell Interview (1978)

Conspiracy Digest: Personally, I no longer have any firm prescriptions for social betterment. The study of conspiracy seems to indicate that the laws of reality give the dedicated conspirators the upper hand against anyone with any version of social reform in mind. Another way of looking at it is that evil has a better feedback loop than good. The loot gained by conspiracy puts power in the hands of a few conspirators who then can undertake even vaster conspiracies to further enhance their power. The fruits of "good" movements, on the other hand, are widely dispersed among the people rather than being concentrated and available for further success. Perhaps this would be a good question. Do you have any reaction?

Mae Brussell: There are also philosophical, literary and historical examples where evil does not have a better feedback loop than good. The laws of reality do not guarantee that power gained from force and monopoly will be lasting or of any long-range value to those who have struggled to obtain that power. "Compensation," Ralph Waldo Emerson's essay, describes my views on evil, power and the attempted manipulations of mankind and nature: The farmer imagines power and place are fine things. But the President has paid dearly for his White House. It has commonly cost him all his peace and the best of his manly attributes. To preserve for a short time so conspicuous an appearance before the world, he is content to eat dust before the real masters who stand erect behind the throne. This law (of compensation) writes the laws of the cities and nations. It is in vain to build or plot or combine against it. Things refuse to be mismanaged for long. Though no checks to a new evil appear, the checks exist and will appear. If the government is cruel, the governor's life is not safe. If you tax too high, the revenue will yield nothing. The dice of God are always loaded. Every secret is told, every crime punished, every virtue rewarded, every wrong redressed in silence and certainty. David, the poet, was able to halt Goliath, the giant.

Remember Achilles' heel? Children love Popeye and instant spinach. Power comes from many sources to counteract evil. Evil has never had a better feedback loop than good. The popularity of *Star Wars* has to do with the longing for heroes, the triumph of good over evil, the forces of good winning. The CIA spent $26-million in tax revenue over a 25-year period with the express purpose of altering human behavior, starting as early as 1947. This budget was not only for defensive purposes, but to erase memories and to create apathy at home. Dr. Jose Delgado at Yale University, funded by Naval Intelligence (our tax money again), specialized in electronically controlling human beings. We are preparing for future warfare robots. If power and evil provide such a good feedback, why the necessity to worry about emotions such as anxiety, guilt, or conscience?

Power is temporary and illusive. It can be shattered by one leak or scrap of evidence. One slip of scotch tape placed on the door-latch at the Watergate Hotel in Washington, D.C. was responsible for removing the president, vice president, attorney general, secretary of commerce, top presidential aides and attorneys. The kinds of conspiracies I am talking about pertain to political assassinations and their cover-ups. The fruits of good movements are too widely dispersed. They receive no assistance from the federal government. The FBI COINTELPRO and the CIA's Operation Chaos have been breaking up leftist organizations and social-cultural activities with a purposeful vengeance (again with our tax dollars). Divide and conquer is the rule, whether inside the prisons or at charitable meetings. Anywhere people get together, they are infiltrated. The ratio of agents and informants has been about one provocateur to five members of any given group. There has been a systematic effort to kill all leaders whose awareness or activities interfere with international oil interests or narcotics traffic. It has been alleged that the CIA-FBI combine, in conjunction with the Defense Industrial Security Command, has supported a school in Oaxaco, Mexico, for professional assassins. This religious academy, disguised as a missionary, was exposed in 1970. Albert Osborne, alias John Howard Bowan, director and head "missionary," accompanied Lee Harvey Oswald on his trip to Mexico in September, 1962. Oswald, not an assassin, was a patsy for the men who killed President John F. Kennedy. The killing of Kennedy was only one of dozens or possibly hundreds of murders of leaders around the world, or potential future leaders. With this kind of worldwide organization in operation, how can any movement or leader ever serve the people?

C.D.: Do you think, then, that centralization of power can be a good thing as long as the power is held by persons selected by the people and dedicated to what you consider to be a valid program of social reform? Doesn't power always corrupt? Aren't the worst always attracted by the prospect of centralized power? Wouldn't extreme decentralized power be the solution to conspiracy?

M.B.: Centralization of power is always dangerous. What is valid social reform to one group, such as Hitler's Germany, is genocide for others. I have to agree with Thomas Jefferson's thoughts about power: "I have never been able to conceive how any rational being could bring happiness to himself from the exercise of power over others." You have to understand that my views about power and happiness are not realistic or even possible. Utopian dreams of a world without fear, killings and unnecessary pain is only a goal that makes every day a challenge and every hour worthwhile. Yes, power corrupts. The worst are attracted by centralized power. The solution is for parents and educators to avoid subjecting children to power trips, the church to avoid the lure of power, the government to halt dividing economic and ethnic groups against each other. Conspiracies are possible when people have been conspired against from birth. If parents, schools, church and government divested themselves of the games that increase their power, new sources of energy and production would take their place and do a much better job of it.

C.D.: What is your attitude on the right-left dichotomy? From your writing, I would presume that you have a "left-wing" background and probably are favorably disposed to socialism or "true" communism. Could you describe your social-political ideals? Everyone knows what Mae Brussell is against — your positive philosophy, on the other hand, would be news to many of our readers.

M.B.: My attitude on the right-left dichotomy should not enter into or affect my research. When a biologist looks at cancer cells in a microscope, they are not Republican or Democratic or Socialist cells. There is no right-left distinction in diseases. I examine autopsy reports, sworn testimony under oath, Congressional Hearings, FBI, CIA and other government documents, witness testimony, police reports, books, articles and unpublished manuscripts along with newsletters. My conclusions about assassinations and their cover-ups are cross-referenced and constantly checked for changes or new information. The FBI and Los Angeles Police Department have photographs labeled that prove ten or more bullets were fired in the Ambassador Hotel the night Sen. Robert Kennedy was killed. Sirhan Sirhan's weapon only fired eight shots. There is no indication that any of Sirhan's bullets went into Kennedy. The fatal shot came from behind the Senator, into his head. A guard from Lockheed, Thane Cesar, fired his gun that night. Kennedy's coat sleeve was cut off and is missing. The bullet-ridden ceiling panels are gone. Sirhan Sirhan's weapon was "sold" and is out of the state, probably destroyed. If the Republicans and the right-wing did the killing and cover up, we should know. If the Democrats or Communists did the killing or cover-up, we should know. L.A. Chief of Police Ed Davis, and former District Attorney Evelle Younger, were both running for governor of California at the time of the cover-up. The voters should be informed if Davis and Younger were engaged in a conspiracy to cover up the murder of a senator and presidential candidate. The voters must be informed. This has nothing really to do with right-left. Documents exist to prove that the CIA and FBI planned the murder of Richard Nixon in 1972. Conservative George Wallace was eliminated from the 1972 election due to a near-assassination. I want to know who is killing Republicans or Conservatives as much as I want to know who is killing President John F. Kennedy, Sen. Robert Kennedy, Malcolm X, Reverend Martin Luther King or hundreds of others less known. Everyone doesn't know what Mae Brussell is against. If I tell you what I am against, you can deduce or know what I am for. I am against planned political assassinations by our intelligence and defense agents. The CIA, FBI, DIA and DISC (Defense Industry Security Command), were set up originally to protect citizens of the USA. They became their own judges and juries, private servants of corporations with investments at home and abroad. I am against the constant destruction of evidence in criminal cases and political assassinations. Prime witnesses are murdered before or after testifying. Diaries are forged and planted in obvious places. Doubles are created to confuse. Police departments manipulate facts in cooperation with conspirators. I am outraged that our judicial system since 1947 has been patterned after Nazi Germany. Patsies are dead or locked away. The assassins walk the streets or leave the country, "home free." I am against using Earl Warren, chief justice of the Supreme Court, to cover up the assassination of President Kennedy. When the highest court is corrupt, there is no hope at local levels. I am against allowing the CIA to spend millions since 1947 for the express purpose, as stated before, to alter our behavior. Is the State supreme over individuals? Who owns or controls our minds? Why was CIA Director Allen Dulles allowed to order 100 million LSD tablets? Were half the U.S. population going to receive their doses? What gives the CIA and Pentagon the right to define normal, or to determine what is national security? Are we being drugged through food, water, and supplied with chemicals so we become slaves and robots? Where is all the cancer coming from? Why the preoccupation with death? Why is the government in the business of creating a "psycho-civilized" world? Who is ordering the ultrasonic waves to lower brain waves of cities' populations to an alpha state, leaving citizens susceptible to mass propaganda and hypnotic suggestion? These facts have been confirmed by researcher Walter Bowart in 1977. I learned about the project years ago. I am against the using of CBS, ABC, NBC, UPI and AP by Washington D.C. since WWI, and by the CIA since WWII as propaganda tools. The so-called "liberal" New York Times and Washington Post would make Adolf Hitler proud. Notice that in all the Washington Post accolades concerning Watergate exposures, the newspaper never delved into the massive evidence surrounding the murder of Mary Jo Kopechne, the shooting of George Wallace, the Howard Hughes connections, the murder of J. Edgar Hoover, the planned riots for Miami in 1972, the assassination plans for Richard Nixon through both the San Diego Secret Army Organization and the Andrew Topping arrest in New York. The media are cover-up artists. They allow assassins or would-be assassins to fade away. One thing is certain about all these matters: The laws of nature are such that certain truths are going to come out. It is only a matter of time. There is no den in the wide world to hide a rogue. Commit a crime. You cannot recall the spoken word, you cannot wipe out the foot track, you cannot draw up the ladder as to leave no inlet or clue.

Some damning circumstance always transpires.

The laws and substances of nature become penalties to the thief. My positive philosophy is very simple. I believe there is in each of us a potential for peace and harmony. A few power-mad perverts dictate orders that must be challenged. They are in violation of the laws of nature. A society that does not care for its infants with love and affection will create mad bombers. The source of this peace and harmony is within the family unit, not government agents or law enforcement. Without love in the home, there is never quiet in the community, cities or around the world. There are ways to counteract the evil being purposely planned. Study history. Separate fears and prejudices from facts. Recognize facts from propaganda. Invest energy in fighting for what you believe in. Analyze harder where we are going and what you are doing about it. What do you really believe in? How much do we care?

C.D.: Where can our readers get information on Walter Bowart's research on the mind-control uses of ultrasonics and microwaves?

M.B.: Walter Bowart's book, *Operation Mind Control*, will be published in the Spring, 1978. Bowart's allegations about the CIA using ultrasonic waves on the human brain to control the behavior pattern of entire cities confirm information I received in 1974 about the same project. A reliable source of information told me that a radio tower and a tall bank tower in San Francisco were going to extend a beam to have virtual radio control of that entire city. He informed me that the radio frequencies would make meditation impossible. The radio towers were being utilized for future control of our minds. The same week that I received this information, an article in the *Los Angeles Times* appeared mentioning the use of radio beams over large cities to control the population.

C.D.: *Conspiracy Digest* has often propounded the theory that the right-left political-economic spectrum is an artificial concoction of the ruling class that creates a "heads I win, tails you lose" situation for the ruled class. Isn't the choice between communism and fascism only a choice in style of tyranny? Are you familiar with Antony Sutton's Wall Street series of books that documents that both Nazism and Soviet Communism were financed largely by the same Wall Street cabal whose interest was in creating conditions for big government favoritism as opposed to laissez-faire competition?

M.B.: The choices between fascism and communism are not our ONLY alternatives. Tyranny, by any name, isn't the only solution. I am familiar with Antony Sutton's books and own a few. Nazism and Soviet Communism were financed by Wall Street cabals. They were NOT funded to support communism. Money was poured into the USSR and behind the Iron Curtain for the purpose of funding future uprisings and encouraging dissidents. Nazi agents are behind part of the KGB and MKD. Just as Wall Street poured money in Russia after WWI, Allen Dulles, attorney for the Wall Street cabal, then Director of the CIA, funded Adolf Hitler's chief of Nazi-Eastern Intelligence with $200 million (our tax revenue again). Gehlen was paid for placing agents behind the Iron Curtain, and for cold war/hot war purposes. This money does not support communism, but anti-communism. Marina Oswald's background was White Russian aristocracy. Marina has overwhelming links to the CIA, defense industry and General Reinhard Gehlen's agents through the CIA/Greek Orthodox Church. Her membership in the communist Komsomol organization, a leftist front, didn't bother the State Department or violently Anti-Communist Rescue Commission that met Lee and Marina in New York City. The right-left political and economic spectrum is a farce. Howard Hughes' Summa Company, the South Korean KCIA, Hughes Medical Institute and other funding front operations have bought our Congress, Republicans as well as Democrats. Those that can't be bought are blackmailed.

C.D.: On numerous occasions you have mentioned that the Buckley school of conservatives and his youth wing, Young Americans for Freedom (YAF), are connected to CIA/ruling-class dirty tricks and even the Kennedy Assassination. Few conspiracy buffs would dispute the CIA-Buckley-Establishment connection. Of course, Buckley is death on conspiracy theory. His favorite target is "paranoids." What do you think of the conspiracy-minded conservatives, such as the Liberty Lobby and the John Birch Society? No doubt you disagree with their theories, but do you think they are largely sincere? Or are they black propaganda outlets for the Establishment? Or like many other organizations are they simply infiltrated and used from time to time in specific black propaganda campaigns? In one of your tapes you seemed to imply that George Schuler's *American Opinion* attack on Malcolm X contained outright lies and was timed to coincide with Malcolm's assassination. Comments?

M.B.: Paranoia is a psychological diagnosis applied to a disease of the mind. Buckley is hardly a psychiatrist. He is a useful media showcase and propaganda machine. When Buckley states his opinions in writing or on the air, he never prefaces remarks or articles by providing facts about his CIA days with E. Howard Hunt. Few people know that Buckley's family fortune came from Pantipec Oil Company. E. Howard Hunt and George DeMohrenschildt, Oswald's CIA babysitter, both worked under Warren Smith. Smith was President of Buckley's Pantipec Oil.

Buckley not only worked with E. Howard Hunt in the CIA, but formed the notorious YAF with Douglas Caddy, co-worker in the CIA office of Mullen and Co. of Watergate fame.

Members of the YAF were brought from U.S. Military Intelligence in Germany to the Dallas-Ft. Worth area in the fall of 1962. Their object was to infiltrate and take over this conveniently formed new organization. Orders went from Larry Schmidt, first to arrive, that all members had to be in Dallas before JFK arrived ... for their briefings and roles to be played. There is more to the Buckley-CIA-YAF-Caddy connections than time allows here. Liberty Lobby and the John Birch Society accumulate interesting facts. Their numbers are correct, but the conclusions can't be proven and are in error.

Jimmy Carter sent a message into the new spacecraft. He wrote that "we human beings are still divided into nation states, but these states are rapidly becoming a single global civilization." The Birch Society and Liberty Lobby would claim this is proof of "one world" conspiracy of communism and the communists are winning their goals. On the other hand, my assessment forces me to believe the Bormann Brotherhood exists. Hitler's goal to rule the world through satellites and weapons is working. We are moving into the Nazification of Planet Earth. Carter's Human Rights issue is a sham. He scolds the USSR. We support and fund South Africa, Argentina, Chile, Brazil, South Korea, Nicaragua, Iran, feudal Middle-East countries with no trials and much torture. George Schuler's attack upon Malcolm X, published in *American Opinion*, Feb. 1973, argues that it would be better to memorialize Benedict Arnold, a known traitor, than Malcolm X. Malcolm X was never a traitor to the USA. Schuler's put-down on Malcolm begins by stating Malcolm X was once a pimp, dope peddler, an ex-convict who served ten years for robbery. He fails to mention the murder of Malcolm's father, the causes of his hatred and poverty, the reasons blacks get into crime. Schuler doesn't praise Malcolm X for changing his ways, for his eloquent self-education, for his published lectures and writings, for his ability to raise himself above the gutter to become an inspiration for many people. White racists use black fools and Jewish apologists for much of their dirty work. The anti-semitic YAF — John Birch Society wanted to place an ad, "Wanted for Treason," with a black border, in the newspapers the day JFK was assassinated in Dallas, Texas. Birch Society members paid for the ad. Neo-Nazi Christians wrote the ad. Whose name was at the bottom, in the newspaper Nov. 22, 1963? Jew boy Bernard Weissman. Why his name? Weissman testified before the Warren Commission that they wanted his name "because he was Jewish." Why did they need a Jewish name identified with the death of JFK? Because another Jew, Jack Rubenstein (Ruby), who worked with oil millionaire anti-Semites and wanted their approval, was going to silence the patsy. No other members of the YAF were asked to come before the Warren Commission. Why not?

C.D.: A number of conspiracy researchers are suspicious of the U.S. Labor Party and NCLC, funded by powerful governments or private interests. They seem to promote some of your conspiracy theories, such as your interpretation of the Symbionese Liberation Army kidnapping of Patty Hearst. What do you think, is Lyndon LaRouche for real? We find it suspicious that a new world Central Bank is the linchpin of his program. Central Banks and their power to create money (power) by slapping ink on paper have always been the primary tool of ruling classes. What is your opinion of the money question?

M.B.: The U.S. Labor Party always blames the CIA and Rockefeller for everything that is wrong. Maybe they are hitting the top dogs. It is hard to argue that one. However, the CIA and the Rockefellers can't do it alone. The USLP praises Gerald Ford as a fine man. Ford was a cover-up artist for the Warren Commission. His crime of lies about Oswald in his book and the cover-up of hard evidence make him guilty of crimes worse than Nixon was charged with. Ford covered up the killings of Kennedy, Officer J.D. Tippit, and the murder of Lee Harvey Oswald. Ford brought neo-Nazi G. Gordon Liddy to Washington, D.C. to work in the Treasury Dept. Ford pardoned Nixon because he was guilty of the same charges, cover-up of conspiracies.

The NCLC never uses documents that prove the Defense Industry Security Command, Division V of the FBI and other agencies had a part in the assassinations and conspiracies.

They were and are not interested in assassinations inside the USA. Political murders determine who will become head of the Pentagon, Marines, Air Force, Navy, FBI, CIA, Treasury Dept., etc. Financial policies, national and international, are controlled by corporations and individuals to make up multinational nation-state empires. It is the systematic and always planned murders that control their financial investments. I want to know who is murdering. The NCLC speak of the condition. They can't make a proper diagnosis without examining the deaths. I agree with the NCLC that terrorism is funded by the right. This has been a historical truth, a technique used by the Czar then brought to Germany for the Nazis. The SLA was formed by the CIA to infiltrate Bay Area left-wing movements and test mind-control drugs. Lyndon LaRouche never writes about Ronald Reagan, Robert Maheu, Howard Hughes, Paul Laxalt, the Summa Company, the Hughes Medical Institute in Florida or others who are the opposite side of the Rockefeller coin. There is a battle going on between the warfare industries and war machine and the Eastern Wall Street gang. The NCLC knows the names of some of the players. They conspicuously omit others. Chase Manhattan Bank is named. Bank of America is never fingered. My opinion on the money question could fill your entire issue. Profits are obtained by monopolizing what we need; oil, coal, water, transportation, minerals, gas, food, health, homes, entertainment, and communications (phones). Profits are made from what we don't need; drugs, chemicals, tobacco, narcotics, gambling, prostitution, kidnapping, bank robberies, white collar crimes, hijacking, weapons, overcosts, guns, warfare machinery. Murders and assassinations that I study pertain to those killings that served a purpose involving future financial gains that would not have occurred without those deaths. If the electoral system were REALLY FREE to allow people to vote for those representatives who could alter their lives and pocketbooks, the profits in the hands of a few would be considerably reduced. If the Judicial system really worked, there would be fewer crimes and payoffs for murdering. Is money the root of all evil? It comes pretty close. For a given salary, the head and fingers of SLA leader Donald DeFreeze were cut off before his body was sent to Ohio. Who paid for the injections that Jack Ruby and Martha Mitchell received? What laboratory manufactured the substance? What profits were made from the LSD given to Patty Hearst while locked in a closet for 45 days? How were the car accidents of Murray Chotiner and Clay Shaw financed? What did it cost to cover up the fatal plane crash of CIA money bagwoman Dorothy Hunt at the height of Watergate? How much was the telephone bill from New York City to Chicago when CBS ordered the cremation of Michelle Clark, victim on Dorothy Hunt's plane, along with 45 others? Were Jack Ruby's debts of $40,000 to IRS before the Kennedy assassination automatically paid when he obliged and shot Lee Harvey Oswald?

How much tax money went to fund doubles for Lee Harvey Oswald, Sirhan Sirhan, Donald DeFreeze and James Earl Ray? Where are the bankers who are funding violence? Are we paying for all this, the murders, the expensive, lengthy trials and hush money? Who paid the hospital bills in Colorado for Dita Beard, ITT secretary, when she embarrassed President Richard Nixon? The important crises in America are what we are doing and what we are allowing to happen. Fascism isn't found in bank names or bank titles. It is what they are doing to people in front of our eyes. According to New York City Health Department figures during 1976, murder was the number one cause of death for ages between 15–24. MURDER IS WINNING OVER DRUG ABUSE, CANCER, DISEASES OR ANY OTHER CAUSE. I don't care as much about the banking houses as I do about where money is abused and wasted. If we were ever to solve these crimes, we could locate which banking houses were funding the plans.

C.D.: From listening to your tapes, I detect that you believe that the Bildeberger-CIA-CFR "free world" Establishment ruling class is Anglo-Saxon/White Racist. How do you square this theory with the apparent pro-minority attitude of the Establishment's kept liberals and think tank/foundations? Left-cover? Incitement to backlash? How do so many of Jewish descent become prominent in government and finance if the ruling class is still White Racist? How do you account for the Rothschilds, Warburgs, Schiffs, Kissingers, etc.?

M.B.: The Bildebergers, CIA, CFR establishment ruling class is basically Anglo-Saxon White Racist. There are a few Jewish showpieces allowed on the fringe for entertainment or media coverage. Racism in the USA is everywhere, in every prison, police department, and so-called peacemaking organizations. *The Control of Candy Jones* by Donald Bain tells how a New York model was taken by the CIA, injected with sodium pentathol, and hypnotized. Candy was then taught to hate blacks, Jews and Italians. Why? Why were our tax dollars (I keep repeating this because it makes me furious that we are funding these crimes) used to further hatred? How many more Candy Joneses were taught to hate? Candy joined the CIA to deliver messages and ended up with two personalities inside her head. There is no pro-minority attitude on the part of the Establishment. That is so foolish that I wonder what kind of vacuum you are coming from. Blacks, Mexicans, Jews and Indians are not part of the mainstream of white USA. They are on the lowest fringes. A few Jews such as the Rothschilds, Warburgs and Schiffs are always the token names for a gentile society. They do not represent assimilation or a symbol of Jewish-Christian solidarity. Henry Kissinger is a different story. Kissinger was developed by U.S. Army Intelligence following World War II. Kissinger worked in counterintelligence. Many Christian agents were assuming names of Jews killed in the concentration camps.

How is it possible that Jewish Henry Kissinger became the darling protégé of Rockefeller, Exxon, Standard Oil? Kissinger has been photographed kissing Anwar Sadat in Egypt. Sadat was in league with Hitler's Nazi brotherhood. Would oil magnates with their anti-Semitic clubs and multi-million-dollar investments allow Jewish Kissinger to make deals and sign contracts with oil giants in the Middle East? Why does the Shah of Iran, a Moslem, work with Kissinger so well? Kissinger put Nazis into power in Greece, Brazil, Chile — they love him. When Hitler's $400 million in cash went to Argentina, did they know that Kissinger would be heading our State Department and National Security Council? No Jew would be in charge of the Pentagon. The CIA is a racist organization. All of this is impossible!!! Kissinger's Jewish cover conceals the Rockefeller and Wall Street bankers directing him.

C.D.: Isn't it possible that all racial-ethic issues are simply manipulated to keep the ruled class fighting among themselves? It seems incredible to me that men (or women) with the intelligence (if evil intelligence) to conspiratorially rule nations (and maybe even the world) would be so petty-minded as to be racists. What is your reaction?

M.B.: Racism is taught from an early age. White men and women fear they will lose their jobs, and also lose their possessions in a competitive market with minorities. There must have been a lot of black anger after slavery, a rage that the white man feared. The way to control this situation was and is by nurturing hatreds, hiring more police, rigging the courts to keep minorities locked up, sending narcotics to the ghetto, exclusion from labor unions and labor market, and many other techniques. You know what they are.

C.D.: I agree that race prejudice exists to one degree or another at most levels of U.S. society. However, it seems to me that the majority working classes are the most racist because they fear competition for jobs from blacks and Mexicans. The ruling class, especially the Eastern Wall Street gang that controls the "liberal" CBS/ABC/NBC/*New York Times*/*Washington Post*, really seems to take the side of minorities. Is this just fake propaganda to rake in minority votes?

M.B.: Competition for jobs between Indians, blacks and Chicanos is caused by a racist power structure in this country that refuses to allow jobs in the first place. Labor Unions exclude minorities. Medical schools and law schools could be increased by the hundreds instead of bickering over a particular student's grades.

IQ tests have been proven to be racist, thereby dropping off otherwise qualified students. By keeping minorities out of the professions, except entertainment and athletics, the white community can keep their residential areas white, their schools white, their churches white, perpetuate the racism. There is no need for fences or ID cards. Law enforcement and government agencies, such as the FBI, CIA, NSA, DIA, DISC, are predominantly white. We could write an entire issue of *Conspiracy Digest* about our differences regarding CBS, ABC, NBC, *New York Times* and *Washington Post*. Where do you ever get the label "liberal" for these people? How can you possibly say they take the side of minorities? When? Where? How? I subscribe to these newspapers and want to puke. I have boycotted major network news coverage since I studied political assassinations because of their lies, distortions, half truths, insinuations and massive cover-ups. The United States press doesn't fake propaganda. They don't even appeal to minorities. To hell with minority votes. These maniacs support military dictatorships and fascism, instituted by the USA since World War II. They treat the CIA and heads of state as if they were some kind of royalty, not the war criminals they really are.

C.D.: Several right-wing authors have theorized that the main conflict in the world is or was the battle between WASP and Jewish financiers. Or, more simply, that the history of the 20th century is primarily the Rockefeller (Standard Oil) vs. Rothschild (Royal Dutch Shell) battle to control governments and resources. Do you think there is anything to these theories? What do you think about *The Cowboy-Yankee War* [sic], by Carl Oglesby? Your research would seem to support the theory that Nixon was an agent of new wealth, the "Cowboy" capitalist faction (Hughes?), finally done in by the old wealth, "Yankee" capitalist faction (Rockefeller-Rothschild) at Watergate?

M.B.: The main conflict in the world is not between WASP and Jewish financiers. The battle of Cowboy vs. Yankee, Carl Oglesby's theories, are oversimplified. There is no way to mark off geographical boundaries or to separate fighting factions into such categories. What we are experiencing is a series of revolutions taking place at the same time. Some of them are political. Others are cultural and social. While these changes have been occurring in the 20th century, the old feudal monopolies, economically dependent upon empires, have been grasping for control of sources of power and wealth (listed earlier as sources of profit). Three good books that describe the origins for our current moral and financial bankruptcy are *The Great Conspiracy* by Michael Sayers and Albert E. Kahn, *Merchants of Death* by H.C. Egglebrecht, and *Weimar Republic, Clandestine Rearmament*, by E.J. Gumbel. Following World War I, the allied armies were afraid to disarm German militarism, fearing that Bolshevism would spread throughout Europe. The solution was secret, clandestine armies, the secret SS, a series of over 400 murders that altered the face of Germany. U.S. Corporations and Wall Street, along with France and England, armed Germany. World War I mobilized 66,103,164 men. 37,494,186 were killed. Indirect costs were $151 million. Direct costs were $208 billion.

The propaganda myth of the "menace of Bolshevism" put Nazis in power. Adolf Hitler, hypnotized front man for the warfare industries and corporations, was to rid Europe of Bolshevism. When World War II was over, and the communists were still very much alive, the same corporations and multinational companies that armed Germany after WWI sent the Nazis and war criminals with their loot, counterfeit or otherwise, to the USA, Middle East, Asia, Africa and South America. Allen Dulles, Wall Street attorney, made arrangements for the Nazis' exit. He became the first director of the CIA in 1947. The divisions and decoys we fall into, all the categories of conflict, never follow history or documents day-by-day to understand why we have so many assassinations and cover-ups. Over 600 Nazis were brought to our defense industries, universities and hospitals from 1945–1952 under Project Paperclip.

World War II cost 80 million lives. The cost went up. The rearming for World War III began as early as 1945, when the decision was made to protect doctors and scientists under Hitler to continue their human experimentations and weapons systems research in the United States. The real battle now is whether or not it is too late to stop this country from going fascist.

If Arab investors, funded by the Nazis, withdraw their savings from U.S. banks, the country will be instantly bankrupt. Nazi General Reinard Gehlen had the solution for conquered USSR territory. Gehlen was going to turn 50 million Russians into slaves "in accordance with Aryan racial principals, to become sub humans." Some "40 million Soviet Citizens would be eliminated by natural means, namely famine." This is the same Gehlen that Allen Dulles provided $200,000,000 of our tax dollars. Yes! Add it up. Are we getting our money's worth? (See *Reinhard Gehlen, Spy of the Century*, E.H. Cookridge) It is easier to understand droughts, famines, terrorism, new kinds of diseases, rare cancers, mind-control experiments, stock manipulations, labor strikes and other unpleasant "accidents" of nature in the USA after studying the history of Nazism.

C.D.: How much conflict do you see in the ruling class? Some conspiriologists think it is all fake, a diversion.

M.B.: The conflict in the ruling class is between those who are elected and appointed to rule, and those who are acting illegally to condition us for the next war or series of wars. We are identical to Germany in 1932. Salvadore Allende had to put up with strikes and the raging of the Chilean citizens who turned out to be paid by the CIA (over $8 million was spent to disrupt his country). Nothing is natural today. Billions are going into creating divisions, terror, to make headlines, to spread confusion and fear. If any officials come along with independence or suggestions, they are killed, blackmailed, ignored, surreptitiously drugged, paid off or bugged. To make change today is to enter into an obstacle course. The intelligence community and the people doing all this manipulating to enhance power and wealth are moving against the laws of nature. Something must give. Our institutions should be re-examined. Individuals must come forward with enough courage to support investigators like myself, who are armed with facts and information. As Emerson said, "That form of government which prevails is the expression of what civilization exists in the population which permits it."

C.D.: Many conspiriologists point the finger at David Rockefeller as the most powerful financial conspirator in America and possibly the world. Do you agree? What about Hughes, H.L. Hunt? Others? Is Chase-Manhattan really going broke?

M.B.: David Rockefeller might be the most powerful financial conspirator in America. Howard Hughes and H.L. Hunt are dead. Daniel Ludwig is hiding. Rockefeller managed to keep their boy Kissinger running all our foreign policies in every country while their Exxon stayed on top, the ranking corporation for profits. Nice arrangement!! That is power. The Bildebergers select our presidents. The power is in a silencer, secret weapons. It comes in many forms. This is a battle royal between two kings, the Rockefeller Dynasty and the weapons-warfare, clandestine government the Rockefellers created originally for their own power.

Can the Rockefellers survive? Are they part of a dying era, identical to Kaiser Wilhelm? Is the ammunition industry ready to take over the USA? That is where the power struggle is taking place. The Wall Street-based international banks created spies to march in protection of their profits. The armies turned against their masters. They decided they could create their own wealth and power. New York is crumbling. The Pentagon is stronger than ever. Yale, Harvard, Princeton and the top eastern universities haven't produced a new idea or a constructive change for all their classical education. They have been swallowed by the Pentagon and spy contracts.

The USA looks like a dance of death in every major city.

C.D.: Unless I am misreading you, you seem to have deep respect for John F. Kennedy. Is there any reason to believe that his idealistic line was for real? Wasn't he just another glib gangster who lost? Do you agree with Oglesby that he was an agent of the old Wall Street establishment (as was his Nazi-leaning father), and that his assassination was plotted by Southern Rim upstarts?

M.B.: Yes, I do have a respect for John F. Kennedy. If you don't believe his idealistic line was for real, just add up what he was doing when he was killed. JFK asked his brother, Attorney General Robert Kennedy, to break up organized crime. Nobody high-up in government has tangled with the Mafia. J.E. Hoover, the hired hands of FBI and CIA, ran the assassination teams. They have been used since World War II. JFK was attempting to end the oil-tax depletion rip-offs, to get tax money from oil companies. JFK instituted the nuclear test ban treaty, often called "the kiss of death," to oppose the Pentagon. JFK called off the Invasion of Cuba. He allowed Castro to live, antagonized narcotics and gambling, oil and sugar interests, formerly in Cuba. JFK asked his brother, Attorney General Robert Kennedy, to break up the CIA, the "hidden government behind my back." Allen Dulles was fired. Dulles, the attorney for international multinationals, was angry. JFK planned to withdraw troops from Vietnam after the 1964 elections. Nov. 24, 1963, two days after JFK's burial, the Pentagon escalated the Vietnam war ... with no known provocations, after JFK was gone. There was no chance Kennedy could survive antagonizing the CIA, oil companies, Pentagon, organized crime.

He was not their man. The assassination of JFK employed people from the Texas-Southwest. It was not a Southern plot. Upstarts could not have controlled the northern CIA, FBI, Kennedy family connections. This was a more detailed, sophisticated conspiracy that was to set the pattern for future murders to take place. The murder was funded by Permindex, with headquarters in Montreal and Switzerland. Their stated purpose was to encourage trade between nations in the Western world. Their actual purpose was fourfold:

1) To fund and direct assassinations of European, Mid-East and world leaders considered threats to the Western world, and to Petroleum Interests of their backers.

2) Provide couriers, agents for transporting and depositing funds through Swiss Banks for Vegas, Miami and the international gambling syndicate.

3) Coordinate the espionage activities of White Russian Solidarists and Division V of the FBI, headed by William Sullivan.

4) Build, acquire and operate hotels and gambling casinos. See: *Nomenclature of an Assassination Cabal*, by William Torbitt.

THE
ILLUMINATED

WHO WAS ADAM WEISHAUPT?

By Sir Mark E. Bruback, Knight Templar

Born on February 6th, 1748 in Ingoldstadt, Bavaria of Jewish parentage, Adam Weishaupt was orphaned at an early age due to his parents' untimely death, and educated and raised by a Jesuit order who held Adam in as much contempt as he them. His youthful ideals and free spirit upset the priests and gained the admiration of his fellow students.

In 1772, at the age of 24, he received his professorship of law. Three years later, he became a Professor of Natural and Canon Law at the University of Ingoldstadt. This advancement embittered the clergy as the post had only been previously held by an ecclesiastic.

Weishaupt's liberal views enraged the clergy, yet drew favor and support from other staff, students and faculty. Supporters began to meet in his private apartment where they would discuss philosophy, religion and topics of the day while drinking wine, listening to music and smoking. These parties soon turned into a formal society, named The Enlightened or Illuminati, a term Weishaupt bestowed upon members when they showed proficiency in intelligence and moral virtue. The Order was first called 'The Perfectibilists' yet subsequently gave way to the name by which it is now universally known.

The Illuminati was divided into three classes:

I. *The Nursery*
   1. *Novice*
   2. *Minerval*
   3. *Illuminatus Minor*
II. *Symbolic Masonry*
   1. *Illuminatus Major*
   2, *Illuminatus Dirigens or Knight*
III. *The Mysteries*
   1. *Presbyter or Priest*
   2. *Prince or Regent*
   3. *Magus*
   4. *Rex or King*

The Order also gave its members coded names of a classical nature, Weishaupt was known as Spartacus. The major cities were also encoded: Ingoldstadt was Eleusis, Austria was Egypt, Munich was Athens and Vienna was Rome. There was even a cipher calendar and all correspondence between members were made to be unintelligible to non-members (known by brothers to be "the profane").

Two years later Weishaupt was initiated into Freemasonry at Theodore of Good Council Lodge in Munich and soon he promoted his own system within Masonry. Here he met Baron Knigge (a.k.a. Philo) who aided in writing and expanding upon the degree system that Weishaupt had created. The modern detractors' claims of a closer Illuminati/Freemasonry connection is primarily based on slander promoted by the Catholic church's contentious secret society, the Jesuits. Though the Jesuit order was officially abolished some years earlier, that didn't stop their power at influencing a new act that, on June 22, 1784, abolished all secret organizations by royal decree. The following year, Weishaupt lost his professorship at the University and was banished from the country.

Leaving Bavaria, he found safety and patronage with Duke Ernst in Gotha. Here in this free town, Weishaupt wrote a number of books, some of which were never published. Most focused on promoting the ideals of Illuminism or Enlightenment. In 1786 alone, he published *A Picture of the Illuminati, History of the Persecutions of the Illuminati, An Apology for the Illuminati* and *An Improved System of the Illuminati.* In 1787 he wrote *Diogenes' Lamp.* And in 1811, Weishaupt passed from this earth at the age of 63 to the Great Architect above. Spoken of highly by his peers, pupils and fellow Illuminists, Weishaupt was regarded as a scholarly genius and outstanding advocate for human rights.

Considering the monarchical climate of the time, there's no wonder that the Catholic Church tried everything in their power to destroy Weishaupt's Illuminism. The Illuminati's stated mission of human liberation while increasing moral virtue was an underground battle in Europe that played itself out in America as the Revolutionary War.

Those who continue to vilify Adam Weishaupt claim to be carrying the flag of freedom by using the propaganda of the past institutions of slavery. This excerpt from the first English translation of *Diogenes' Lamp* by Amelia Gill in this conspiratorial compilation proves that Weishaupt was not some evil Luciferian magician but a kind-hearted scholar who wished to improve the world through philosophical conversations.

Let us close with Dr. Weishaupt's own words:

Whoever does not close their ears to the lamentations of the miserable, nor their heart to gentle pity; whoever is the friend and brother to the unfortunate; whoever has a heart capable of love and friendship; whoever who is steadfast in adversity, unwearied in the carrying out of whatever has been engaged in, undaunted in the overcoming of difficulties, whoever does not mock and despise the weak, whose soul is susceptible of conceiving great designs, desirous of rising superior to base motives, and of distinguishing itself by deeds of benevolence, whoever shuns idleness, whoever considers no knowledge as unessential which they may have the opportunity of acquiring, regarding the knowledge of mankind as their chief study; whoever, when truth and virtue are in question, despising the approbation of the multitude, is sufficiently courageous to follow the dictates of their own heart, such a one is a proper candidate.

Occult Theocrasy

by Lady Queenborough
(Edith Starr Miller)

Edith Starr Miller wrote two books: the first, Common Sense in the Kitchen, *in 1918; the second,* Occult Theocrasy, *was published posthumously in France in 1933.* Occult Theocrasy *relies heavily on the published works of the freemason, Domenico Margiotta; the hoaxers Dr. Karl Hacks and Leo Taxil, and their creations, Diana Vaughan and Dr. Bataille; the imaginary Miss Vaughan's promoter, Adriano Lemmi; anti-mason Samuel Paul Rosen (1840–1907); theosophist Alice Bailey (1880–1949); Taxil's supporter, Clarin de la Rive; Nesta H. Webster and the once anonymous "Inquire Within." Though Lady Queenborough's publication was intentionally published to warn against the anti-Christian concepts of secret societies, a number of Masons have publicly accepted her work as largely accurate though viewed through a hostile and anti-Semitic lens.*

The following excerpt, the third chapter of the book, describes the revolutionary workings of Weishaupt and secretive Masonic lodges.

The Gospel of Revolution

Apart from the Rosicrucians already mentioned, we see the foundation and growth of such societies as:

1. The Strict Observance of the Baron Hund and the notorious Jew Leucht who had assumed the name of Johnson, and several other aliases. It recruited its members in the Lodges and went from occultism into political intrigue, later even formulating a plan of economic and financial rule.
2. The Martinists, which, founded by a Portuguese Marrano Jew, Martinez Depasqualy, united political intrigues, fomented for the overthrow of the monarchy, together with magical

practices. It numbered among its members the chief politicians
who prepared the French Revolution. These were Savalette de
Lange, William Law and Mirabeau.
3. The Scottish Rite.
4. The Moravian Brothers.
5. The Alta Vendita.
6. The Egyptian Rites of Cagliostro (Mizraim).

The adepts of all these different rites knew but little beyond the fact that
they had shaken off the yoke of Christian principles which were replaced
by the cult of nature, and in almost all cases licentiousness. They were but
mere puppets manipulated by unseen men whose sinister aims were the
destruction of Christianity and disruption of States and to whom all the above
named orders or organizations were but so many recruiting grounds. It was
only when each and all had gathered sufficient strength that the "Invisible
Masters "attempted to unite them all under one supreme sway, namely that
of Illuminism at the Convent of Wilhelmsbad in 1782.

Illuminism represented the efforts of the heads of the powerful Jewish
Kabal which has ever striven for the attainment of political financial, economic
and moral world dominion. The movement had been founded in 1776 by
Adam Weishaupt. Bernard Lazare, himself a Jew, has written that "There
were Jews behind Weishaupt," and upon a close study of Illuminism, we
find that the destructive forces which culminated in the French Revolution
were of three kinds; financial, intellectual and anti-Christian.

In the first class, we come upon the names of Jewish Financiers such
as: Daniel Itzig, Friedlander, Ceerfbeer, Benjamin and Abraham Goldsmid,
Moses Mocatta, Veitel Heine Ephraim. In the second category, we find Moses
Mendelssohn, Naphtali Wessely, Moses Hersheim — who are the inspirers of
Lessing — Frederic Nicolai, Weishaupt, Mirabeau, l'Abbe Grégoire, the Duke
of Brunswick-Wolfenbuttel and Anacharsis Clootz. Lastly, the third class is
composed mostly of the group known as the Encyclopedists: d'Alembert,
Diderot, Rousseau, Voltaire and of all the Cabalists practising magic and
among whom we find: Martinez Depasqualy, Leucht, the enigmatic Count of
Saint Germain, Falke and Joseph Balsamo surnamed Cagliostro. The objects
of this powerful organization of the Bavarian Illuminati, were:

1. The destruction of Christianity and of all Monarchical
   Governments;
2. The destruction of nations as such in favour of universal
   internationalism;
3. The discouragement of patriotic and loyal effort branded as
   narrow minded prejudice, incompatible with the tenets of
   goodwill to all men and the cry of "Universal Brotherhood";
4. The abolition of family ties and of marriage by means of
   systematic corruption;
5. The suppression of the rights of inheritance and property.

Moses Mendelssohn, himself the head of the Haskalah (Jewish Illuminati), cooperated with the Bavarian Illuminati of Weishaupt and with the prominent members of the other revolutionary secret societies aspiring to political power, but, in 1784, the Elector of Bavaria made an abortive effort to stamp out the conspiracy which, being international, was necessarily impervious to local measures. The poison of subversion was working in France where on January 21, 1793, it culminated in the death on the scaffold of Louis XVI, an event that in masonic jargon is known as "The second cannon shot." The capture of Rome by Cadorna in 1870 was the third.

As a further confirmation of concerted masonic action let us bring yet another illustration:

In the first days of the French Revolution (1848), 300 Freemasons, with their banners flying over brethren of every rite representing French Freemasonry, marched to the Hotel de Ville, and there offered their banner to the Provisional Government of the Republic, proclaiming aloud the part they had just taken in the glorious Revolution.

M. de Lamartine made them this answer, which was received with enthusiasm by the Freemasonry Lodges: "It is from the depths of your lodges that the ideas have emanated, first in the dark, then in the twilight, and now in the full light of day, which have laid the foundations of the Revolutions of 1789, 1830, and 1849."

Fourteen days later, a new deputation of the "Grand Orient," adorned with their Masonic scarves and jewels, repaired to the Hotel de Ville. They were received by A. Crémieux, and Garnier Pagès, attended by pages, who also wore their Masonic emblems. The Representative of the Grand Master spoke thus: "French Freemasonry cannot contain her universal burst of sympathy with the great social and national movement which has just been effected. The Freemasons hail with joy the triumph of their principles, and boast of being able to say that the whole country has received through you a Masonic consecration. Forty thousand Freemasons in 500 lodges, forming but one heart and one soul, assure you here of their support happily to lead to the end the work of regeneration so gloriously begun." Brother Crémieux, a Jewish brother, member of the Provisional Government, replied: "Citizens and brothers of the Grand Orient, the Provisional Government accepts with pleasure your useful and complete adhesion. The Republic exists in Freemasonry. If the Republic do as the Freemasons have done, it will become the glowing pledge of union with all men; in all parts of the globe, and on all sides of our triangle."

If the wielding of power and their national political economic and financial strength over the peoples by a few hidden hands can result in such calamitous upheavals as the French Revolution, the World War of 1914 and the Russian Revolution of 1917, were it not wise to apply the lesson of experience to ascertain whether the supposed harmless Masonry of today does not again serve as a screen or curtain behind which thrive secret societies no less subversive, revolutionary and demoralising than those which we have just so briefly sketched?

We know that most of them such as the Martinists, the Illuminatis, the Scottish Rite and the Egyptian Lodges of Memphis and Mizraim still exist today, so, on what grounds can we base our assumption of a change of their revolutionary and anti-Christian principles? In the face of late events, namely, the Peace Conference, the creation of the League of Nations, the amalgamation of international resources, the confiscatory inheritance taxes, the development of international finance, the proposed establishment of an international non-Christian cult, have we the right to refrain from lifting the veil of Masonry behind which subversive movements are so conveniently hidden?

Weishaupt Meets Wilson

by Robert Anton Wilson

Robert Anton Wilson re-introduced the historic figure of Adam Weishaupt to a new generation of readers and students of parapolitics in 1975 with his remarkable satirical trilogy, Illuminatus!, *co-authored with Robert Shea. By the time of his death in January 2007, Wilson had taken Weishaupt on a journey of many years through the sensibility of a conspiracy-obsessed subculture, blurring the line between the accepted canon of normal history and a more animated subtext best described as tongue-in-cheek. Factions of those cognizant of this subtext at various times declared both men as the head of the Illuminati, that ages-old conspiratorial secret society responsible for the world's evil, putting each on a par with Satan himself.*

Weishaupt first appears in Illuminatus! *as part of Illuminati Project memo #7:*

This is from a small left-wing newspaper in Chicago (The RogerSPARK Chicago, July 1969, Vol. 2, No. 9): "Daley Linked With Illuminati," no author's name given: No historian knows what happened to Adam Weishaupt after he was exiled from Bavaria in 1785, and entries in '[George] Washington's' diary after that date frequently refer to the hemp crop at Mount Vernon. The possibility that Adam Weishaupt killed George Washington and took his place, serving as our first president, is now confirmed... The two main colors of the American flag are, excluding a small patch of blue in one corner, red and white: these are also the official colors of the Hashishim. The flag and the Illuminati pyramid both have thirteen horizontal divisions: thirteen is, of course, the traditional code for marijuana... and is still used in that sense by Hell's Angels among others. Now, 'Washington' formed the Federalist party. The other major party those days, The Democratic Republicans, was formed by Thomas Jefferson [and] there are grounds for accepting the testimony of Reverend Jedediah Morse of Charleston, who accused Jefferson of being an Illuminati agent. Thus, even at the dawn of our government, both parties were Illuminati fronts..."

After the publication of his satire, Wilson went on to build a career as an essayist, philosopher and futurist that grabbed the attention of a full-spectrum of left-wing and right-wing aficionados. As with Adam Weishaupt himself, much of his readership came to regard Wilson as the keeper of secrets and perhaps a mastermind plotter bent on world domination.

Wilson championed an almost deliberately naïve prescription for human betterment that borrowed from his friend, the LSD guru Timothy Leary. The two futurists summarized their "plot" for the future with the motto Space Migration, Intelligence Intensification and Life Extension (abbreviated SMI2LE). As much as that appealed to stoner science fiction fans, it essentially summarized the more widely held, if not so well articulated, philosophy of mainstream scientific humanism. Wilson characterized himself as a cheerleader for the space program, for scientific advances that could expand the human life span and in general whatever promoted people becoming smarter, funnier and able to grasp the cosmic humor of the conspiracy that had entangled his name with Weishaupt's. In an age of true conspiracies, with authentic electoral process subverted by the schemes and scams of the ruling elite connected to still dimly understood power blocs that do include secret alliances and societies, Wilson's simple philosophy came off as Enlightenment to his readers.

Weishaupt, too, was a product of Enlightenment. He opposed strictly religious authority in favor of the rationalism of the Enlightenment. The domination of the Catholic Church in his time made such an inclination something that only could be encouraged in secret, and the idea of the secret society became much in vogue for the intelligentsia of the period. Weishaupt founded the historical Illuminati at the University of Ingolstadt in south Germany in May 1776 patterned after the Freemasons. It conscripted wealthy young men into a program of self-confessionals, study and secret fraternity, creating a network of contacts that advanced their public careers—a kind of invisible college that actually did bring progressive ideas into some staid institutions. So much so, in fact, that the Bavarian government banned the Illuminati in 1784. In the following years, the brotherhood of secret enlightenment became accused of everything from the Reign of Terror in France to overthrow plots against all religion and government in Europe.

What impact Robert Anton Wilson's lifetime of Illuminist provocation will remain to be seen. On January 6, 2007, he sent a final note to his internet "group mind":

Hi there,

Various medical authorities swarm in and out of here predicting I have between two days and months to live. I think they are guessing. I remain cheerful and unimpressed. I look forward without dogmatic optimism but without dread. I love you all and I deeply implore you to keep the lasagna flying. Please pardon my levity, I don't see how to take death seriously. It seems absurd.

RAW

As fitting that a last ironic chuckle comprised Wilson's final personal communication to his readers, so too that his last bit of expository prose, the following essay on Adam Weishaupt, concerned the enlightenment figure resurrected for them in his satire. (Kenn Thomas)

CHORUS

Rarely is the question asked: Is our children learning? — George W. Bush

The only book you've got to read is The Godfather. *That's the only one that tells how the world is really run.* —Roberto Calvi, President, Banco Ambrosiano; stretched, London, 18/6/1982; quoted by Gurwin. (See *Recommended Reading*.)

Adam Weishaupt founded — or revived — the secret Order of the Illuminati on May 1,1776; that much seems like Historical Fact. All else remains disputed and heatedly controversial.

Most historians believe the Illuminati originally recruited only high degree Freemasons, and every generation since 1785 — when the Bavarian government discovered and outlawed the Illuminati — Freemasons have faced the charge that they remain "under Illuminati control."

They all deny it, of course.

Well, not all of them; a Scotch Freemason, John Robison, in his *Proofs of a Conspiracy* [1801], claimed the damned Illuminati had taken over Continental European Masonry; he wrote chiefly to warn the lodges of England, Scotland and Ireland against a similar coup.

Ever since Robison, the Masonic/Illuminati debate has included those who think the Weishauptians have taken over all Freemasonic lodges, those like Robison who think they've only infiltrated some, and those, including the *Encyclopedia Britannica*, who see Illuminism as a "short-lived movement of Republican free thought" which never had a major influence on Masonry — or on anything else.

But the Illuminati debate covers a lot more ground than that.

For example: Kris Millegan in his *Fleshing Out Skull & Bones* presents that Yale society as a branch of the Illuminati. In case you don't know, some prominent Bonesmen have included Bush I, Bush II, Henry Luce of *Time*, Justice Potter Stewart, an all-star cast of the Captains of American banking, publishing and politics, and most of the directors of the C.I.A.

Sure you really want to know more about this?

From another angle, Akron Daraul, in his *History of Secret Societies*, argues that Weishaupt did not invent but only refurbished the Illuminati, which he relates to earlier movements known as the Holy Vehm (Germany),

Allumbrados (Spain), Roshinaya (Persia) etc.; while the more exuberant John Steinbacher in *Novus Ordo Seclorum* traces them all the way back to the Garden of Eden! They were founded, he says, by Cain, the son not of the holy marriage of Adam and Eve but of an illicit and Satanic coupling between Eve and the Serpent.

How's that for Hot Stuff? Bestiality, Satanism and all the themes for a new *X Files* movie...

Meanwhile, Eliphas Levi's *History of Magic* traces the Illuminati back to Zarathustra and claims its secret docrine came down to Weishaupt via Manicheanism, the Knights Templar and Freemasonry. This places them as part of the same occult tradition as Giordano Bruno, Dr. John Dee, Aleister Crowley and the Sufis of Islam.

But on the fourth or fifth hand, a British researcher named Nesta Webster sees the Illuminati as the brains behind socialism, communism, anarchism, and the Prussian government from 1776 to 1918. (She wrote shortly after England's first war with the latter.)

On the sixth hand, J.F.C. Moore argues that the Illuminati, a secret source of fascist occultism, inspired such odd birds as Aaron Burr, Adolf Hitler and J. Edgar Hoover; but Philip Campbell Argyle-Smith clams they are extraterrestrial invaders from the planet Vulcan. They call themselves "Jews" on this planet, he adds.

Whether that means all Jews are Vulcans, or only some of them, seems unclear to me, but the most famous Vulcan, Mr, Spock, is Jewish insofar as being performed by a Jewish actor makes one at least partially "Jewish," whatever that means.

Maybe Argyle-Smith has looked at too many *Star Trek* movies.

He also credits the Illuminized Vulcans with managing the Thugs of India, the Zionists in Israel, the Rothschild banks, the Communist International, the Theosophical Society, Freemasonry and the Assassins of medieval Agfhhanistan. I don't know why he left out George Bush and Al Qaeda; maybe he just wrote too soon.

Another Cosmic Illumiinati theory appeared in the *East Village Other* June 1969; it included Skull & Bones, the Rothschilds, the Nation of Islam ["Black Muslims"], Richard Nixon, the Black Panthers, the Bank of America, the Rosicrucians, the Holy Vehm, the Federal Reserve and the Combine's Fog Machine. That one must contain some hidden jokes [I hope].

According to the *RogerSpark*, a radical Chicago newspaper [July 1969] Weishaupt actually murdered George Washington and served in his place for his two terms as president. (Then who wrote *Diogenes' Lamp*? Hegel maybe; it sounds like him at times....)

The John Birch Society, of course, has a different slant on all this. According to Gary Allen, the editor of their news magazine, *American Opinion*, Adam Weishaupt was a "monster" but the Illuminati only got really monstrous after its capture by English adventurer/billionaire Cecil Rhodes, who used it to establish British domination of the world. The Council on Foreign Relations acts as its most important "front" in the U.S. today, according to Allen.

Sandra Glass, however, thinks of the Illuminati as a group of clandestine pot-heads [cannabis abusers] which included the medieval Assassins, Weishaupt, Goethe, Washington, the first mayor Richard Daly of Chicago and Ludwig van Beethoven.

"Beethoven?" you may gasp. Well, oddly enough, a recent, scholarly and non-conspiratorial biography of the great Ludwig van, by Maynard Solomon, says Mr. B wrote some of his music under commission from the Illuminati and had many friends in the Order itself. Solomon doesn't mention the pot, though; maybe Ludwig, like a recent president with a perpetual hard-on, didn't inhale.

Then again, Adam Gorightly in *The Prankster and the Conspiracy* claims that all recent Illuminati research [post-1960s] has become confused and chaotic because of a hoax conspiracy, also called the Illuminati, founded by one Kerry Thornley, a man accused of involvement in the JFK assassination by New Orleans D.A. Jim Garrison. According to Gorightly, this neo-Illuminati aims to bedevil and mock the efforts of sincere conspiracy researchers, and he even accuses the author of this essay [me, R.A.W.] of involvement in this Fiendish Plot!

I, of course, refuse to dignify this absurd charge with a denial, which nobody would believe anyway. Besides, as Rev. Ivan Stang of the Church of the Sub-Genius says in *Maybe Logic*, "Well, if I was a member of the Illuminati, I wouldn't say so, would I?"

ANTICHORUS

We are not victims of the world we see, we are victims of the way we see the world. — Dennis Kucinich

I think God is sending us a message: "If you can't take a joke, go fuck yourselves."— Woody Allen

What does *Diogenes' Lamp* reveal about the "real" Adam Weishaupt and the "real" Illuminati?

A book works like a mirror, somebody said once: when a monkey looks in, no philosopher looks out. I can only tell you what this book seems to me; others, I feel certain, will find other things in it — including coded references to Vulcans, Skull & Bones, Zarathustra, the Holy Vehm, communism, Mary Magdalene, the Federal Reserve, the Combine's Fog Machine et al.

To me, this book seems to support the most cautious and conservative of my sources, the Encyclopedia Britannica, and old Adam looks much like a weary defender of "Republican free thought," 18th century-style. In other words, he seems a distant relative, philosophically speaking, of Adam

Smith, Hume, Voltaire, Jefferson, Franklin, Tom Paine — i.e. of all those libertarian ideas currently as unfashionable in this country as in the Bavaria in Weishaupt's day. I know why he seems weary to me: trying to teach liberation to people who feel reconciled to their slavery can really grind you down, in 1804 or 2006...

I also think I see an influence of Kant, and perhaps a foreshadowing of Hegel, in the semantic structure used continually by Weishaupt — "X seems true; not-X also seems true; we'll have to think more about that." Aquinas did the same trick, but always comes down on the side of safe orthodoxy, Papist flavor. Weishaupt throws the ball back to the reader, although you may not always catch him doing that.

I do not see any conclusive proof that the Illuminati plotted anything nefarious or even illegal, except insofar as free thought itself remained illegal in southern Europe. But I also don't see any conclusive proof that they wouldn't and couldn't and didn't do nasty things. As a secret society hidden inside the secret society of Freemasonry, the Illuminati will always remain somewhat mysterious, and pedants and paranoids will argue about it until the last galoot's ashore.

Perhaps Tom Jefferson got it right when he said that secret societies seemed necessary in Europe, haunted by monarchy and Papism, but not in the United States. Certainly, when the Constitution remained the law of the land [i.e. before the Supremes (s)elected Dubya] no sane person would feel the need for secret societies here. Do I dare add "But now with the Constitution in cryonic suspension —"?

No: I better not ... better safe than sorry....

On the other hand, not just secret societies but secrecy itself or even privacy seem increasingly impossible under the reign of George III.

They have hidden cameras everywhere.

They bug our phones.

If they want to, they can "read" every keystroke on my computer, including this one: >>.

They can even pry into the contents of our bladders, in random tests explicitly forbidden by that wonderful, moribund Constitution. Sweet grieving Jesus, there's no place we can escape or hide or feel alone, is there?

Sometimes, tossing and trying to sleep in the wee hours, I explore the ideas rejected by my skeptical waking mind. Maybe the most paranoid fantasies about the Illuminati contain some truth... maybe....

Maybe the All-Seeing Eye on the dollar bill does represent the fascist state those bastards want.

Maybe all those Internet rants about Skull & Bones serving as a recruiter for the Illuminati have some foundation in fact, after all.

Maybe we should really worry when the choice in a presidential election remains limited to two rich Bonesmen... What is it Weishaupt wrote? "Whoever is rich — very rich — can do anything...."

Maybe we should regard "Illuminati" as a generic term, or a metaphor?

Maybe every Power Structure acts a lot like the most paranoid fantasies

about the Illuminati, especially when it feels threatened?
No, no — that way lies madness, schizophrenia and Usenet trolls. After
some sound sleep, I wake, the shadows flee, and I remember that "all's for
the best in this best of all possible worlds."
Voltaire didn't intend that as sarcasm, did he?

Robert Anton Wilson
Deep Underground
Somewhere in Occupied U.S.A.

Recommended Reading and Viewing:

Argyle-Smith, Philip Campbell — *High IQ Bulletin*, Colorado Springs, 1970, IV, 1

Bauscher, Lance — *MaybeLogic*, http://www.maybelogic.com

Daraul, Akron — *History of Secret Societies*, Citadel Press, NY, 1961.

Ellul, Jacques —*Violence*, Seabury Press, NY, 1969.

Glass, Sandra — "The Conspiracy," *Teenset*, March 1969.

Gorightly, Adam — *The Prankster and the Conspiracy*, ParaView Press, NY, 2003.

Gurwin, Larry — *The Calvi Affair*, Pan Books, London, 1984.

Knight, Stephen — *The Brotherhood*, Grenada, London, 1984

Levi, Eliphas — *History of Magic*, Borden Publishing, Los Angeles, 1963.

Millegan, Kris — *Fleshing Out Skull & Bones*, Trineday, Walterville, OR, 2003.

Moore, J.F.C. —"The Nazi Religion," *Libertarian American*, August 1969.

Morals, Vamberto — *Short History of Anti-Semitism*, Norton, NY, 1976.

Robison, John — *Proofs of a Conspiracy*, Christian Book Club, Hawthorn, CA, 1961.

Solomon, Maynard — *Beethoven*, Schirmer Books, NY, 1977.

Vankin, Jonathan — *Conspiracies, Cover-Ups and Crimes*, IllumiNet Press, Lilburn, GA, 1996.

Webster, Nesta — *World Revolution*, Constable, London, 1921.

Wilgus, Neal — *The Illuminoids*, Sun Press, Albuquerque, NM, 1977.

From *Diogenes' Lamp*

Or, an Examination of Our Present-Day Morality and Enlightenment.

by Adam Weishaupt

Translated by Amelia Gill

Edited by Andrew Swanlund

> But, Lords, we hear this fearful tempest sing,
> Yet seek no shelter to avoid the storm:
> We see the wind sit sore upon our sails,
> And yet we strike not, but securely perish,
> Wee see the very wreck that we must suffer;
> And unavoided is the danger now
> For suffering so the causes of our wreck.
>   *Richard II*, Act II, Sc. 1

Our knowledge is a Whole. If our first principles and ideas are flawed, this error will spread to all branches of our knowledge. They even give our individual actions their unmistakeable character. So, if we remain in the dark today about certain main questions upon which our welfare or woe depends, then it is solely because there is not enough respect for the higher principles, because we are considering a subordinated Purpose to be the chief Purpose, and consequently are not unifying the varying points of view into a Highest and Final point of view, as we ought to be doing. For this reason, despite our supposed Enlightenment, we do not know with certainty whether the world is heading toward Evil or toward Improvement, and this fact is the source of the most harmful results, as I have proven above. Even more harmful, we know equally little about whether we ourselves are good or evil, what the purpose of our existence is, whether we are in fact ruined, and whether our ruin is incurable. Likewise, we know not whether Reason and Enlightenment are Good or Evil things that ought to be encouraged or impeded. We even appear to think that a government's strength rests on the blindness and ignorance of its subjects. This leads one to the conclusion that we still have very inadequate ideas about even the foundations of the highest authority.

Before these questions are resolved, no one can be surprised if we are the same today as we were centuries ago. But they cannot be resolved before the point of view has been fixed.

To place this point of view beyond doubt and thus to determine whether the world is good or evil, our ruin incurable, to determine the true foundation of the highest authority, whether ignorance is a lasting foundation for the same, whether Reason should be encouraged or suppressed—my goal in this treatise is to prove all these things.

This subject appears vast to me. To me, it seems the most important but also the unhappiest subject a writer could choose.

It seems important to me because it goes to the single and true core of the matter and grasps Evil by its roots. If anything can still be done to abet humanity's ennoblement and happiness, it can only be done in this way.

But I tell you it is also the most unhappy way that can be selected by a writer, and I could wish that I had erred in my judgment. Success will prove me only too right, however. This subject is an unhappy one to take up. For the examination itself is a thankless task and can do aught else but make hateful the writer.

It is a thankless subject. For it interests no one. Everyone already has their own system for dealing with this matter, and those who lack a system would prefer not to have one. Books of this sort are never read, or people read them to be able to refute them.

Men read no morals now: It was a custom.
But all are to their fathers' vices born
And in their mothers' ignorance are bred.
If you have children, never give them knowledge,
'Twill spoil their fortune, fools are all the fashion.
If you've religion, keep it to yourselves.
Atheists will else make use of toleration
And laugh ye aut on't.
  Ottway, *The Orphan*, Act III

But it is also a dangerous subject because it cannot be dealt with without disparaging humanity's moral conceit and administering a telling blow to our own self-love. Our egoism will not refrain from exacting revenge and repayment in kind. It has more than one false ground to choose from as justification for such intentions. Such enterprises awaken the suspicion however that people consider themselves wiser and better than everyone else. People seldom reprimand the errors and transgressions of others without betraying a certain maliciousness and proud schadenfreude.

I must leave it to my readers to decide what they will be pleased to think about me in this regard. Any excuses on my part would only add weight to their suspicions. To this end, I have nothing better to say than what Rousseau declares at the start of his *Confessions*:

> *Je ne suis fait comme aucun de ceux que j'ai vus; J'ose croire n'être fait comme aucun de ceux qui éxistent. Si je ne vaux pas mieux, au moins je suis autre. Si la nature a bien ou mal fait de briser le moule, dans lequel elle m'a jetté, c'est ce dont on ne peut juger qu'après m'avoir lu.*

So much is certain: My way of seeing things is quite different from others' ways. I do not deny that my way could be false. But anyone who wishes to disregard it completely is undeniably wrong. Precisely because it deviates greatly from their ways of seeing things, my way's great contrast can enable anyone who truly desires further perfectioning to uncover many an unused aspect and find results that they never would have found in any other way. My work provides much food for thought and for comparison. I dare to vouch for this.

It is true that this sort of thing rarely occurs free of pretensions and vanity and for the most part can be interpreted to mean nothing more than that I think people are no good because they are not as I am or as I require them to be. They would be better if they were as I need them to be to further my own intentions. But should this be grounds for eliminating all instruction and leaving people to their own devices with no further guidance? Should this be grounds for all writers to fall silent? Show me the writers who would consider themselves incapable of teaching others and thus less wise then their readers. What would be their purpose in writing if they did not believe that other people were not in need of a lesson in something, a lesson that, according to the writers' personal delusion, no one would be as capable of delivering as themselves. We authors are thus permitted our vanity, and we in turn allow our readers to judge our labors for themselves, according to their preferences; we only ask them to remember that the delusion that one can do without all instruction betrays no lesser an arrogance and is much more harmful.

Because we humans have too many reasons to wish that we never be recognized for what we in fact are; because we cannot be more painfully insulted then when someone takes the trouble to destroy the illusions in which our vanity has veiled itself, which happens when the baselessness of our virtues is demonstrated—for such reasons alone it is very easy to comprehend that a moral writer could not do more to spoil his relationship with his readers than by touching on this area they despise so much. Unfortunately, that is what occurs in this book; it is even this book's primary and most especial objective. The natural consequence is that everyone closes their minds and accuses anyone dealing with such topics of deliberate viciousness. Such people are thus feared and hated and lose any ability to successfully influence others. I concede quite freely that this is not the way to win people's hearts, and that it is even less suited for finding one's fortune in the world. No vanity could be more foolish than the wish to be known as a good judge of human nature. Everyone judges people who praise themselves, as Caesar praised Cassius, whether rightly or no

> He is a great observer, and he looks
> Quite through the deeds of men.—
> Such men as he be never at heart's case.
> Whilst they behold a greater than themselves;
> And therefore are they very dangerous.
> *Julius Caesar*, Act I, Sc. 2

Anyone who knows people knows their weaknesses, and these weaknesses are precisely what people least want to be known, which would force people to be rather than to merely appear. Thus not only is their self-love disturbed, but also their lethargy and laziness, which they feel is a great, irreconcilable crime. For this reason I very much understand how a practiced and clever man of the world might be obliged to feign ignorance and inexperience and create the illusion that he does not notice many a thing that is right before his eyes.

But what do we reap from this for mankind's true benefit? Only that our deception be everlasting, that people always act as they did before, and that humanity remain a mystery to itself forever and thus never achieves its potential. The question thus arises: Ought we to improve ourselves, or not? If yes, then it is the moralist's duty to track down the sources and discover the basis of the evil. And this basis can always be found in the driving forces motivating our actions.

For no matter how much we humans differ in our opinions, I do believe the more reasonable of us recognize as a general truth that our greatest good and our greatest woes on this earth all stem from people's way of acting, which in turn is based on something else, on the fundamental beliefs inspiring the actions. But because these convictions themselves are the result of certain ideas and principles, all humanity's happiness and misery thus depend the prevailing ideas and principles prevailing in each age. Which have no choice but to be false when moral decline is great and the manner of acting is wrong.

Be that as it may, we now know what matters. We are going to have to keep to what is before our eyes and, as the visible portion is incontradictable, to our contemporaries' manner of acting, and the reasons that motivate our contemporaries, examining the ideas and principles that produce similar behaviors.

So much remains undeniable: if our era is as corrupted as people say, it is impossible for our Enlightenment today to be True and of the Highest nature. Our ideas about the most important things in life cannot but be wrong, and in studying humanity we must run into results everywhere that our own self-love would very much like to hide away.

Consequently, if progress is to be made in the moral world, all our energies must be focused on waking people up from their dozings and stimulating them to better examination of themselves and others. To this end, we must get to know the true forces driving our actions. This cannot occur without the most rigorous examination of our prior reasons and development of our inadequate ones. For all human beings act as they do because they are firmly convinced no one could behave more reasonably. You could reliably count on them to renounce their former behavior if they could be fully convinced that it was impractical and unreliable. For this reason, it is absolutely necessary that people be neither flattered nor supported in the delusion that they have achieved culmination. This sort of behavior is high treason to human nature. People too inclined to think themselves better than they truly are absolutely have to be taught to adjust their opinion downwards, and consider themselves weak and imperfect. Wherever people believe they are acting for the most sublime reasons, they must become acquainted with their self-deception and be brought to the point where they can see the commonplace game of propped-up, small-minded *amour propre*.

For these reasons alone my readers will already have concluded that my aim in this treatise could not possibly have been to eulogize our virtues. The purpose of this treatise is in fact to expose the vanity and emptiness of our virtues. I will seek out every weakness and conceal none. But I will also in no way keep silent about the goodness in us. Even my rebukes will be in protection of the excellence of our nature. Not I, but others declare our ruination incurable; only these others believe that force is the only thing will have an effect upon us; they alone are the ones who despise and blaspheme mankind. I for my part am developing the inadequate aspects of our behavior; I look for them in my own behavior, as the closest source with which I am best acquainted, to discover the causes of these flaws; to prove that not everything has happened yet that is capable of happening; to show that despite all our persisting flaws we humans have something great and splendid at our core; that even our greatest defects have an innocent source; that it will be impossible for us to change and improve while certain conditions and causes remain in existence. I for my part shall prove that we are as good as we can be under such circumstances; that it is true that we are not what we ought to be on the strength of our destiny; but that everyone who ever requires more from us before the sources have been eliminated does not understand human nature and is demanding sheer impossibilities. People should therefore refrain from calling things malicious that are in fact the true and unfeigned love of mankind and the result of a more rigorous and natural observing spirit.

I am malicious, if this way of being different deserves to be called malicious, because I am neither a flatterer nor blind; because I distinguish between the better driving forces and the worse ones; because no one could wish more for things to be better than they are; and because at the same time I am convinced that things cannot be better until people stop failing to recognize the true forces driving their actions. If using a higher standard to determine people's true value indicates maliciousness, then I cannot deny that I am malicious, and I believe I would be the loser if I were any other way.

If all those people to whose hands I will lose these pages immediately after they are published only knew how hard and bitter was their preparation, they would pity me rather than hate me. These pages are a true child of pain. They were conceived and born in pain. Their entire contents are the result of much sorrowful experience, some of it even my own. It is not easy for a writer to write a book under more adverse conditions, with less encouragement, with more distrust of his insight, overwhelmed from all sides by a more painful sense of his own weakness overwhelming from all sides, with more consideration for the inevitable disapproval, the world's censure, new enemies and persecutions, and even with more physical and domestic suffering, amidst the ruins of his happiness and his family, with more frequent interruptions, and thus writing, so to speak, with the medicine bottle in hand. My contemporaries have done everything possible to destroy my self-confidence from the ground up and to render me as ineffective as possible, me, who in a more effective position could without a doubt have accomplished so much more; they have misjudged me in a way that is not easy to misjudge someone.

I shall be lov'd, when I am lack'd.

The Idiot's Guide to the Cryptocracy

by Craig Heimbichner

If you are outside enough of the mainstream current, you may know something of the Cryptocracy. Nevertheless for many the term remains mysterious, if only because it is not commonplace, although the reality is as immediate as the water in which a fish swims — and for similar reasons remains unnoticed. The term provokes responses which range from knee-jerk dismissals in the halls of academia, to wide-eyed fascination from those who have transferred credibility from Yale professors to Internet blogs. Either group serves the Cryptocracy well enough; what the Cryptocracy fears is persistent, intelligent activism born of reflection.

To this writer's knowledge, the term *cryptocracy* was first used in 1960 by Louis Pauwels and Jacques Bergier in their reckless but creative work *Le Matin des Magiciens (The Morning of the Magicians)* where they write, "The language of knowledge and power is incomprehensible to the outside world. Physico-mathematical research presupposes a different king of mental structure. At the highest level, those who, in Einstein's phrase, have 'the power to make far-reaching decisions on good and evil,' constitute a real 'cryptocracy' (or secret autocracy)." The term was later picked up by Walter Bowart, who described the operation of CIA "Manchurian Candidates" in *Operation Mind Control*. The term has also been used by Michael A. Hoffman II in his study *Secret Societies and Psychological Warfare*.

Introducing the Cryptocracy

One could introduce the Cryptocracy in a number of ways. A famous description of the reality which predates the term itself occurs in Benjamin Disraeli's 1844 classic *Coningsby*: "... the world is governed by very different personages from what is imagined by those who are not behind the scenes." As a member of the British Parliament, thrice chancellor of the exchequer, first earl of Beaconsfield, and twice prime minister of England, Disraeli was in a position to know both the scenes and what — and who — stood behind them. In other words, Disraeli observed and described the Cryptocracy, or at least part of it. Nor was he alone.

Passing from example to definition, cryptocracy as a concept is relatively easy to understand: it refers to a secret rulership, a hidden, elite network of power brokers or puppet masters who covertly pull the strings behind the show which passes for government or similarly observable societal structures. In principle the term can cover a miniature body effecting a small-scale change, or can also refer to an umbrella organization under which any number of plots and bodies could be objectives and targets of influence and control.

In a sense, cryptocracy is a corollary to corruption, and hence implies conspiracy. But the Cryptocracy is not reducible to any particular conspiracy theory, and is incompatible with several simplified theories. Nonetheless the Cryptocracy is an assumption behind sound conspiracy analysis, behind accusations or suspicions which resonate with contemporary skepticism about governmental integrity. In this sense, positing a Cryptocracy, whether local or large, multiform or conceptually overarching is tantamount to declaring that one is not incredibly naïve.

Academia and Media Gatekeepers

In spite of a show of independence on display in the halls of academia, many educational institutions serve as information gatekeepers and thought police. Classrooms often become props for the Establishment while feigning inquiry about limited aspects of some governmental activities.

An example of such control is the consistent denunciation in universities and media regarding "conspiracy theories," when in fact these same gatekeepers promote Establishment-sanctioned conspiracy theory, often as fact. For example, after the vaunted, alleged "terror plot" to down ten airliners proclaimed by U.S. and British intelligence agencies on August 10, 2006, the media parroted the story for days even though no independent corroboration was given to a story whose source was the same "intelligence agencies" that led us into a war in Iraq based on the deception regarding "weapons of mass destruction." The following day, the Los Angeles Times stated that "This is the latest in a series of conspiracies apparently rooted in the disaffection of young British-born Muslims, many of Pakistani descent, who cast themselves as part of a jihadist struggle against Britain, which they see as an outrider of the United States in Iraq, Afghanistan and now Lebanon."

When conspiracy theory serves the purposes of the Cryptocracy, it is proclaimed as fact from the rooftops in a relentless media blitz of Big Lie repetition. Retailing conspiracy theory serves the Establishment by demonizing others and taking the focus off the average couch potato's current complicity by inaction in U.S.-Israeli joint governmental extermination operations in the Middle East. The percipient is thus distracted and can't see the evil that this government is pulling off literally beneath his nose.

Sorcery Under Your Nose

Dismissal of the Cryptocracy indicates a staggering state of denial. To expose the intellectual bankruptcy of *a priori* denials of cryptocracy requires but a short list. One can turn to the memos, now unearthed (see Stinett, *Day of Deceit*) proving FDR's foreknowledge, deliberate inaction and cover-up in order to secure war. Or fast-forward to a *déjà vu* replay on 9/11 by Dubya, whose lies, cover-ups, and complicity in the Twin Tower ritual demolition are undeniable (see David Ray Griffen, *The 9/11 Commission Report: Omissions and Distortions*).

No Neo-Con propagandist like Michael Weiner (a.k.a."Michael Savage") has been able to explain the most obvious proof of government complicity — the coordinated failure of the mandated military response of jet interception during the 9/11 assault. Such a staggering coordinated non-response could only have happened if an override stand-down order had been issued from the highest levels of our government.

This "inside job" aspect of 9/11 did not escape notice in Europe. In July, 2003, Michael Meacher, longtime cabinet minister, noted that the massive coordinated vacuum of military interception pointed to the obvious fact that "U.S. air security operations had been deliberately stood down on September 11."

Meacher cited an advance plan of the event posted by the Neo-Con think tank, the Project for the New American Century (a group which included Bush Team leaders Cheney, Rumsfeld and Wolfowitz). This plan specifically called for a "new Pearl Harbor" prior to 9/11 in order to make America "tomorrow's dominant force." In Germany, high-ranking cabinet minister Andreas von Buelow published a book claiming that the U.S. government directed the attacks on 9/11. Europe looked at 9/11 and saw the Cryptocracy: only in America is the obvious routinely ignored like the proverbial elephant in the room with the help of a few Newspeak terms.

These are only two interrelated instances of the Cryptocracy in action, both of which simultaneously reveal and conceal via misdirection (the "moving hand" of the stage magic show). The Cryptocracy has in fact entered the phase in which it is revealing its own plans to its enslaved servitors. As James Shelby Downard pointed out, the Cryptocracy wants more than power: its aims are sorcerous, evoking mass manipulation of psychic processes through occult-Masonic rituals enacted on the trestle board of history. *In Blood on the Altar: The Secret History of the World's Most Dangerous Secret Society*, this writer explained: "The Cryptocracy is not a myth; it seeks to transform humanity through an alchemical processing of the mass consciousness or Group Mind which involves various tests and corresponding responses through channels linked to secret societies. The result is both psychological and cultural control; but more importantly, transformation. The Cryptocracy has essentially kept the mind of the masses cooking in a cauldron like a Renaissance alchemist, and occasionally tastes, adds ingredients, and stirs."

A Landscape of Corpses Courtesy the Lodge

The Cryptocracy essentially functions through networks, through secret societies based on the Masonic model, ranging from the elite Skull and Bones Order of Bush and Kerry to the serpentine Ordo Templi Orientis or Order of Oriental Templars (OTO), which is more a phenomenon than an organization, rising and disappearing with a trail of effects via high-level operatives which is completely out of proportion to its size and history. The occult dimensions and convictions of the Cryptocracy are a defining element, and a lack of understanding such matters at a deep level accounts for the plethora of shallow analyses which, for example, reduce the linguistically misnamed "War on Terror" to an oil grab. The Cryptocracy may seize oil, but it wants much more, for its egomaniacal network of would-be Wizards in urbane business suits meets in backrooms for considerably more than money. These puppet masters seek to implement a perverse kabbalistic Utopia built on a magically and orgasmically-charged landscape of corpses.

The power of secret societies, whose exposure was once the domain of shunned researchers, has now been thrust into national prominence since the presidential election carried opposing candidates Bush and Kerry both from the same fringe-Masonic cult, the Order of Skull & Bones. The good-old-boy nature and catalytic power of such networks is an open secret, captured by the comment of Goethe, himself a one-time member of the Lodge: "Freemasonry creates a state within a state... I consider it dangerous..."

Testing and Deepening the Trance

The alchemical closure phase of the Cryptocracy involves the Revelation of the Method, explicated by Michael A. Hoffman II in *Secret Societies and Psychological Warfare*. Hoffman points out the increasing obligation which such revelations place upon the percipients — an important element of the process. These revelations also function as standard hypnotic "tests." A veteran hypnotist knows that such successive tests involve a risk of awakening the patient, but if passed successfully, yield two critical results: First, the tests reveal the depth of trance; second, they sink the receiver down to a deeper level. Revelation of the Method functions exactly in this manner, and the fact that the "leaks" and cues regarding 9/11 have not yet widely enraged and mobilized the populace into revolution indicates the trance level to be somewhere around "deep somnambulism," and the Cryptocracy for the moment to be in the driver's seat of the Hummer of the American Group Mind.

A key epic historical instance of these transformative psychomechanics was the Kennedy assassination which ushered the modern world into the maelstrom of subconscious transformation. The direct revelation of the presence of a dark, hidden power that could remove the popular King of Camelot left its indelible mark, and the Sixties felt the Shadow even as the nervous populace reveled in its Woodstocks, orgies and trips. The official story of the Kennedy assassination was so tangibly thin that Oswald attorney Mark Lane was able to rip it quickly into shreds in *Rush to Judgment* (1966), recognized as unanswerable by historian Hugh Trevor-Roper. But it took the genius of James Shelby Downard to decode the alchemical game in his slender classic *King Kill 33°*, an unequaled collage of deconstruction of not only the Kennedy assassination, but also of the Cryptocracy behind it.

The stark nature of the Cryptocracy and its modern machinations, from 9/11 to the current U.S.-Israeli wars, smacks so strongly of fraud that some academics are beginning to break ranks and rehabilitate the anathematized word Conspiracy (will Cryptocracy soon follow?). Predictably, careers are suffering as a result. Academia has its own Inquisition, and professors who deviate must recant their "heresies" or suffer the proverbial Black Ball.

Professor Norman G. Finkelstein's opposition to Zionist aggression has been libeled as everything from an "anti-Semite" to a "Holocaust denier" — two of the strongest current heresy stigmas of the Cryptocracy for slating victims for the academic ghetto or, in a growing number of countries, a prison cell. Standing against his colleagues' dogmatism, Finkelstein comments, "In *The Wealth of Nations*, Adam Smith observes that capitalists 'seldom meet together, even for merriment and diversion, but the conversation ends in a conspiracy against the public, or in some contrivance to raise prices.' Does this make Smith's classic a 'conspiracy theory'? Indeed, 'conspiracy theory' has become scarcely more than a term of abuse to discredit a politically incorrect sequencing of facts..." Similarly, a growing number of scholars have taken a stand against the official lies covering up the Cryptocracy's role in 9/11, following the initial work and example of Dr. Griffin noted above.

Charles Fort intuited the psychic mechanism driving toward systems of certainty which conveniently redefined new orthodoxies (usually under the guise of modern learning and science) and swept aside unwelcome facts. Fort pulled no punches in his disdain for those who followed redefined dogmatism: "A hypnotized host of imbeciles of us: told to look up at the sky: we did — like a lot of pointers hypnotized by a partridge." The marginalizing of dissent through new, state-defined orthodoxies is an important control mechanism of the Cryptocracy, buttressing its hypnotic and alchemical games and simultaneously enabling the prosecution and persecution of the new heretics.

VNRs, PR and Media Whores

Severely weakened is the old jibe against critics of the Cryptocracy's media whores ("are you really suggesting that newspapers coordinate what story they are going to tell?"), thanks to disclosures regarding VNRs or "video news releases," a major mechanism for pre-packaging "news" segments. According to the Center for Media and Democracy (CMD)'s report, Fake TV News: Widespread and Undisclosed (see www.prwatch.org/fakenews/execsummary), government and corporate publicists and PR firms create "information" in the form of VNRs which are provided free to stations and are designed to be seamlessly integrated into newscasts. The source of these VNRs is not given in the broadcast material, so that viewers have no idea that they are actually watching in many cases "reports" bought and paid for by the subjects of the story.

According to journalist Sharon Frederick, "TV stations disguise VNRs as their own reporting. In every VNR broadcast that CMD documented, the TV station added station-branded graphics and overlays to make VNRs indistinguishable from reports that genuinely originated from their station. A station reporter or anchor re-voiced the VNR in more than 60% of the VNR broadcasts, sometimes repeating the publicist's original narrative word-for-word." ("Fake News: Are you watching news or someone's PR hype?" Because People Matter, July/August 2006) Noam Chomsky writes, "Public relations is a huge industry. They're spending by now something on the order of a billion dollars a year. All along its commitment was to controlling the public mind. The bewildered herd never gets properly tamed, so this is a constant battle."

Nevertheless the Cryptocracy does not orchestrate events via simple, definable routes as imagined by most conspiracy researchers. The alchemical transformation of the Group Mind involves an interaction between mechanism and Zeitgeist or the "spirit of the age," part plot and part cipher. Missing this point can lead dupes within the local lodge to mistake their narrow experience for the apprehension of something essentially beyond organization, which exists at the level of a phenomenon. A secret society's transformative power is better indicated by its historical cast of characters who have played key roles in critical moments of cultural alchemy. These events and players need not be analyzed independent of the evolving Zeitgeist, but interact with it as guides who are also a symbiotic part of the process.

The Kabbalah of Psychodrama

The Cryptocracy manipulates the waves of Groupthink most effectively through imposing the kabbalistic paradigm. Different from the New Age version popularized by Madonna, the real Kabbalah contains black magick. Rabbi Aryeh Kaplan writes, "Many techniques of the magical schools of

Kabbalah involved incantations and amulets, and these were often used for trivial and even questionable purposes... We also find formulas for protection against one's enemies, or even some for doing away with them." Kaplan shows the Kabbalah fall within the domain of black magic and include the hallmark of occult "black brothers," namely the intention of harm.

Kaplan does not explicate the larger framework of the Kabbalah, for while the average superstitious Judaic practitioner may dabble with amulets and curses, advanced rabbis view it as a comprehensive framework. Masonic lodges inherited this perspective and have played with the symbolism of the Kabbalah in a panoply of ceremonial psychodramas. The Cryptocracy thus grounds itself in the "red thread" of the Kabbalah while offering the masses two false, partial choices of opinion, the Left and Right, based on Rabbi Luria's formulation of Kabbalah with its twin Pillars of Mercy (Left) and Severity (Right).

The entire basis of political ping-pong and the games of opinion molders stand revealed as one grasps the importance of this charade of false dilemmas, a game which was updated into modern philosophical language by Hegel (his kabbalistic "thesis-antithesis" is still the model framework for education). The Hegelian-Lurianic paradigm is the tube of the Cryptocracy's transmission plugged into the back of the zombie's head: disconnecting it immediately brings him to a state of cognitive dissonance, which if pursued leads ultimately out of the illusory matrix.

Disinformation and the Two 9/11s

Another staple of psychological warfare in the arsenal of the Cryptocracy is the managing of group opinion via disinformation. In this age of information overkill such a tactic is not only effective in maintaining a requisite level of confusion, but also disturbs and numbs the Group Mind, keeping percipients unsure and unwilling to confront clues to their own subjection. This tactic has been so successful that rarely are researchers of the Cryptocracy eliminated outright as they once were in the days of Captain William Morgan, the famous whistleblower on the Masonic Lodge who was murdered on 9/11 in 1826, touching off the temporarily successful Anti-Mason movement in the United States.

The Cryptocracy thus wages psychological warfare and revels in the superstitions of symbol, number and ritual as weapons against the mind, grounded in Masonic lore and the dark "Nightside of Eden" concepts of the Kabbalah. The unfolding of events on the trestle board of modern history can be analyzed as played-out Lodge dramas, rituals of initiation — ceremonial psychodrama (Downard) with a correlated component of psychological warfare (Hoffman). From this standpoint one should note that the timing of 9/11 corresponds well as a Kabbalah Pillar counterbalance to the 9/11 of the

Nineteenth Century in which William Morgan was murdered for revealing considerably less than the Cryptocracy made clear about itself in the stand-down of the U.S. planes. In essence the contemporary 9/11 was a Twin Tower (Pillar) ritual unfolded with the ceremonial staging of a 3rd Degree Lodge drama, akin to the Lodge-enacted "murder of Hiram Abiff" (carried out on the blindfolded or "hoodwinked" initiate with a moderate blow to the head).

Morgan revealed what happens in every Lodge to Hiram Abiff and was murdered on 9/11: the Cryptocracy initiated the Group Mind on a new, parallel 9/11, the mallet to the forehead of the hypnotized, consisting of repeated images flashed on the mass consciousness from every TV screen for weeks. The second or "twin" 9/11 was a masterpiece of diablé psychodrama and psychological warfare, and the Hoodwinked populace largely succumbed.

Terminating Hypnosis

Such dynamics of Masonic sorcery illustrate the tactics and nature of the Cryptocracy, a quilt whose sections can be seen (i.e., the OTO, the Lodge, Skull & Bones, intelligence agencies, financial institutions) but whose dimensions are elusive, since they are partly hidden and partly revealed. In analyzing the Cryptocracy, the important point is not a grasp of the totality (i.e., "getting the complete list of names"), but rather dehypnotization. To emerge from the trance is immediately to see the fabric and seams — and that is sufficient for standing against the stream even as one continues to study the meaning of events.

Initial emergence from hypnosis is itself a bracing satori which rejuvenates and energizes; it can make of one a true revisionist: one who is determined not only, in the credo of the late Professor Harry Elmer Barnes, to "bring history into accord with the facts," but also to bring one's mind into accord with the depths of reality, shedding the temptation to acquiesce in the kabbalistic paradigm of false duality. To the proportion that individuals of such dynamic awareness are present at this moment in the Masonic endgame, to such a degree the Cryptocracy trembles, its illusions fade, its grip is broken, and the hidden, kabbalistic guardians of its Masonic Matrix are derided and dethroned.

References and Related Reading

Barnes, Harry Elmer, ed., *Perpetual War for Perpetual Peace: A Critical Examination of the Foreign Policy of Franklin Delano Roosevelt and its Aftermath.*
Bowart, Walter, *Operation Mind Control.*
Chomsky, Noam, *Open Media Collection: 9-11, Media Control, Acts of Aggression.*
Disraeli, Benjamin, *Coningsby or the New Generation.*
Downard, James Shelby and Hoffman, Michael A., *King Kill 33° (from Apocalypse Culture* edited by Adam Parfrey).

Hoffman II, Michael A., *Secret Societies and Psychological Warfare*.

Finkelstein, Norman G., *The Holocaust Industry*.

Fort, Charles, *The Complete Books of Charles Fort*.

Frederick, Sharon, "Fake News: Are you watching news or someone's PR hype?" in *Because People Matter: Progressive News and Views*, July/August 2006.

Griffin, David Ray, *The 9/11 Commission Report: Omissions and Distortions*.

Kaplan, Aryeh, *Meditation and Kabbalah*.

Lane, Mark, *Rush to Judgment: A Critique of the Warren Commission's inquiry into the murders of President John F. Kennedy, Officer J.D. Tippit and Lee Harvey Oswald*.

Morgan, Capt. William, *Illustrations of Masonry by One of the Fraternity Who has devoted Thirty Years to the Subject*.

Pauwels, Louis and Bergier, Jacques, *The Morning of the Magicians*.

Stinnett, Robert B., *Day of Deceit: The Truth About FDR and Pearl Harbor*.

Brotherhood of the Gun: The Masonic World of the Police and Military

by Craig Heimbichner

Judging by the list of books and articles published in the past several years, Freemasonry appears to be enjoying a literary renaissance. Following the successful secret society-themed movies *National Treasure* (2004) and *The DaVinci Code* (2006) — including the 2007 sequel *National Treasure 2: Book of Secrets* — public interest seems to have been stimulated, and that interest was met with a plethora of "dummies guide" publications on the topic, as well as more serious, if slanted, works on Masonic history.

The dominant image of Freemasonry (the "Craft") as a powerful institution appears to have been studiously relegated, in most of these writings, largely to the past — to the founding of the United States republic, reaching a lodge power peak in the 1960s. Currently, we are told, Freemasonry is dying out, populated by old men: nothing to form the stuff of conspiracy theories. *The Book of Hiram: Freemasonry, Venus and the Secret Key to the Life of Jesus* (2004) by Freemasons Christopher Knight and Robert Lomas begins with three words: "Freemasonry is dying." Similarly, the *U.S. News & World Report 2007 Special Edition on Secret Societies* states that "the [Masonic] order has slowly lost more than half its members."[1]

Suppressed in these analyses, however, is the immense power of lodges among the police and military, an unspoken fact of Masonic history. The image of a Brotherhood armed and ready to arrest — or kill — belies the popular image of the Lodge as a decaying Elks Club, and just might factor in, as we shall see, to our current military misadventure in Iraq, which carries strange overtones of mystical toponomy and associations in Masonic lore.

To grasp the intersection of Freemasonry with bedrock institutions such as the police or the military, one must understand that Freemasonry exists in both a narrow and a larger sense. In the narrow sense — usually invoked by Freemasons when pressed about such matters — Freemasonry is properly restricted to the activities of the Grand Lodge and official Masonic lodges which have received a warrant or charter from the Grand Lodge in their jurisdiction. Freemasons are technically correct in stating that they have no jurisdiction over related orders such as those which form, in part, the subject of this article.

However, this answer is less than forthcoming, and seems in the eyes of critics to provide a bit of cover (something Crypto-sleuth James Shelby Downard termed the "Masonic Hoodwink," a term derived from the blindfold administered to a candidate in the Lodge during initiation).[2] It is easy to document the intersection of the Grand Lodge with police and military lodges, both in terms of overlapping membership and direct support. These relationships are complex but resolvable if we take Freemasonry, as we do here, to involve a larger fraternal sphere of institutions modeled upon its structure, purposes, and core attitudes, derived from the original Masonic Constitutions and Landmarks.[3] Many of these Masonic facets are imitated and adapted in the sprawling world of Fraternal Orders derived from Freemasonry proper, including Orders for police and military personnel. In this defensible wider sense, Freemasonry is hardly the domain of shriveled old men, nor is it dying or powerless, as we shall see.

"Keystone" Cops and the FOP

Let us begin with the police. Movie buffs will immediately recall the rollicking, good-natured slapstick fun of the Keystone Kops, but they might easily miss the Masonic reference, for the Keystone is the topmost stone of an arch — and "an important symbolic element in Royal Arch Masonry."[4] It might also come as a surprise to many readers to learn that the lodges of the Fraternal Order of the Police (FOP) carry a membership, according to their most recent official count, of "more than 324,000 members in more than 2,100 lodges."[5] Since the retirement age for police typically begins at 55, this fact should somewhat modify the image of Masons as "powerless old men" — if we include fraternal police brothers in the picture.

The Fraternal Order of the Police has a long history, nearly a century long. Begun in 1915 by two Pittsburgh patrol officers, Martin Toole and Delbert Nagle, 21 other cops met on May 14, 1915 and held the first meeting of the Fraternal Order of the Police, forming Fort Pitt Lodge #1. Interestingly, the FOP not only mimicked the Masonic structure, but also adopted a five-pointed star as their emblem, containing twin Masonic images of the All-Seeing Eye and a typical Masonic-style grip (handshake).

The adoption of the five-pointed star carries significance. The five-pointed star or pentagram is a key esoteric symbol in Freemasonry called the Blazing Star, with ancient roots in the occult veneration of the binary Dog Star Sirius. As Grand Commander Albert Pike writes in his defining Masonic work *Morals and Dogma of the Ancient and Accepted Scottish Rite of Freemasonry,* "Sirius still glitters in our Lodges as the Blazing Star, (*l'Etoile Flamboyante*)."[6] These symbolic ties illustrate an intimate connection between the Fraternal Order of the Police and the Masonic Lodge, from whence the former is derived by imitation and inspiration.

It is not uncommon to see mutual association between the FOP and a local Masonic lodge. For example, the website of the FOP, Oregon Pioneer Lodge #4, expresses gratitude to the Masonic Lodge for hosting and supporting their members:

"We would also like to thank the Officers and Brethren of Beaverton Lodge #100 Ancient Free and Accepted Masons of Oregon for their support. When we started this F.O.P. Lodge in January, 1996 we were given a place in the Beaverton Masonic Temple to hold our meetings and receive our mail. The Masons did this without charging us a nickel."[7]

Similarly, we find a direct acknowledgement of Masonic roots of the FOP on the website of the Political Action Committee for the Tulsa (Oklahoma) Fraternal Order of Police: "The traditions found in the Lions Clubs, the Elks Clubs, or Masonic Lodges were the foundations of the FOP traditions and ceremonies."[8]

Bobbies for the Lodge

In addition to the FOP, police membership in the Grand Lodge itself became a source of controversy in England in the 1980s following the publication of Stephen Knight's *The Brotherhood: The Secret World of The Freemasons* (1984). Knight spent several chapters detailing the extensive membership and effect of Freemasonry among police in England, including Scotland Yard. Typical of Knight's successful interviewing technique is this statement, obtained from a Scotland Yard Deputy Assistant Commissioner: "Nearly all of my colleagues and seniors are Masons... A lot of people at the Yard have got into positions they shouldn't be in purely and simply because they've got Masonry behind them. But if you think anything can be done about it, you're wasting your time."[9]

Knight's book touched off a sensation in England. Knight died a year later at the age of 33 (coincidentally the top degree in the Masonic Scottish Rite); his work was carried on in Martin Short's *Inside the Brotherhood* (1989). Short spends several chapters covering the police-Masonic connection, beginning with revelations about the British police lodge, the Manor of St. James's, number 9179, which was founded by brethren, "all of whom had served as Police Officers in 'C' or St James's District of the Metropolitan Police."[10] The founder members included some of the highest-ranking officers in Scotland Yard (listed by Short).[11] Short also recounts an exchange which he witnessed in the Palace of Westminster, in which a non-Masonic Tory MP heard from one of his constituents, a businessman claiming to have been victim of a Masonic conspiracy. The businessman thought the police investigating the affair were "dragging their feet in order to protect Masons inside and outside the force." Hence he met the MP and asked him to mention Freemasonry in a letter of complaint to the chief constable. The MP's reply?

> I don't think you should mention the Freemasons. If you want these people to do their job properly, it's best not to upset them.[12]

Both Knight's and Short's books touched off a furor with the British general public, leading to a March 1997 report in the House of Commons (Home Affairs Committee) on *Freemasonry in the Police and Judiciary* recommending that "police officers, magistrates, judges and crown prosecutors should be required to register membership of any secret society and that the record should be publicly available."

A follow-up second report of May 25, 1999 on *Freemasonry in Public Life* noted the acceptance and extension of these recommendations by the Home Office. The report cites the concerns of a "Mr Rourke," stating that "if it is possible for a freemason of Mr Rourke's experience to believe that masonic influence can sometimes be used improperly, then it is not unreasonable for those who are not freemasons to reach the same conclusion."

Allowing for some public paranoia about Freemasonry, the report finishes: "It is clear, however, from some of the examples cited in this Report, and the previous Report, that there are cases where allegations of improper Masonic influence may well be justified."[13] This "improper Masonic influence," let us keep in mind, was documented to have operated within the sphere of the police and the English system of justice, and was due to Lodge membership by elements of both ranks.

Some citizens of the UK reacted. A vivid example was the formation by one James Todd of VOMIT, or Victims of Masonic Ill-Treatment. The VOMIT website was shut down in February, 1999, ostensibly for defamatory remarks made about government officials in the United Kingdom — whom Todd had criticized as corrupt members of a Masonic good-ol'-boy network.[14] A modern Mark Twain might observe that there is nothing like the exercise of heavy-handed power to convincingly refute accusations of heavy-handed power.

J. Edgar Hoover: Cross-dresser and Mason's Mason

Thus far we have only explored some examples of Masonic and fraternal interplay within the "ordinary" world of the police. But our examination would be cursory if we neglected to turn a spotlight on the intersection of the Lodge and the world of special intelligence, including the Federal Bureau of Investigation (FBI) and the Central Intelligence Agency (CIA). Indeed, Masonic and fringe-Masonic involvement in espionage and back-scene power-brokering in various countries is part of an unseen tapestry of history which has been left out of public school textbooks and prime-time, corporate network discussions.

J. Edgar Hoover's membership in Freemasonry, for example, is seldom mentioned, although his hidden laundry as a homosexual and transvestite has been aired by Anthony Summers in *Official and Confidential: The Secret Life of J. Edgar Hoover.*[15] Hoover was an icon of Freemasonry in the world of Intelligence and stood at the pinnacle of Masonic honor and membership. According to a Grand Lodge website, Brother Hoover was "raised" (made a Master Mason) November 9, 1920 at Federal Lodge No. 1, Washington, D.C.[16] The website of the Library and Museum of the Supreme Council, 33º, Southern Jurisdiction [of the Scottish Rite] gives much more detail in the online "J. Edgar Hoover Collection:" "During his 52 years with the Craft, he received innumerable medals, awards and decorations. In 1955, for instance, he was coroneted a Thirty-third Degree Inspector General Honorary and awarded the Scottish Rite's highest recognition, the Grand Cross of Honour, in 1965."[17]

Masons Bury the Truth about a Dead Kennedy

Hoover's dubious role in the aftermath of the John F. Kennedy assassination included supplying strong testimony and information to the Warren Commission, which in turn issued a report which has been ventilated for its omissions and distortions.[18] Hoover, for example, stated that there was no "scintilla of evidence" of any conspiracy, and that "Oswald shot the President."[19] Hoover's testimony provided the Warren Commission with an appearance of solidity which stood like a wall for decades against evidence to the contrary — including direct evidence from Charles A. Crenshaw, the surgeon who tried to save JFK and who testified that the bullet wounds came from the front, not the back, in contrast to the Hoover-Warren company line.[20]

Other authors have explored in detail an alleged symbolic Masonic staging to the entire assassination of President Kennedy. James Shelby Downard dissected the specific numerological and occult associations of the JFK assassination as part and parcel of Masonic lore. One of the most famous of his observations correlates the mysterious "three hoboes" at the scene with the "three unworthy craftsmen" who play the role of assassins in the Master Mason Degree ritual.[21] Downard considers their mysterious appearance in an anomalous photograph to be a Masonic calling card. In addition, Hoover's role in the Masonically-dominated Warren Commission is noted by Downard: "Mason Lyndon Johnson appointed Mason Earl Warren to investigate the death of Catholic Kennedy. Mason and member of the 33rd degree Gerald R. Ford, was instrumental in suppressing what little evidence of a conspiratorial nature reached the commission. Responsible for supplying information to the commission was Mason and member of the 33rd degree, J. Edgar Hoover. Former CIA director and Mason Allen Dulles was responsible for most of his agency's data to the panel."

Downard concludes: "Is it paranoid to be suspicious of the findings of the panel on these grounds? Would it be paranoid to suspect a panel of Nazis appointed to investigate the death of a Jew…?"[22]

The CIA and the Blackfriars

Downard's observations of the Masonic membership of CIA director Allen Dulles (1893–1969) bring us directly to the topic of Freemasonry within the CIA. Dulles, co-founder and first civilian Director of Central Intelligence, was fired by JFK, only to sit ironically on the Warren Commission, as Downard notes. But Allen Dulles also crops up on lists of famous Freemasons — also observed by Downard — along with former CIA director William Casey.[23]

One of the greater scandals connecting the Masonic world and the CIA in the past few decades is the notorious "P2" case in Italy, which broke the spring and summer of 1981 and created a national press sensation. "P2" is a popular abbreviation for the Masonic Lodge *Propaganda Due*. The P2 lodge was a Grand Orient lodge, and the Grand Lodge immediately used this fact to distance itself from the scandal, citing the historical divergence of the two lodges. But what was the scandal, and how did the CIA enter the picture?

Briefly, P2 was formed in 1966 with support from Giordano Gamberini, the Grand Master of the Grand Orient of Italy. Placed in charge was Freemason Licio Gelli, who created the reputation of this lodge as an elite and powerful secret society, using blackmail and extracting "dues" in the form of official secrets which he used to consolidate and extend the lodge's power and his own. Gelli was an honored guest at Ronald Reagan's inauguration as President in January, 1981, even as rumors spread of the P2 connections to the Mafia and the underworld. Nor were these the only shadowy connections: according to researcher David A. Yallop, "from the very early days of P2, he [Gelli] had the active support and encouragement of the CIA operating in Italy."[24]

A police raid on the lodge blew the scandalous lid to the ceiling, resulting in a list of members which included Italy's most powerful men — ranging from Prime Ministers to members of Parliament, judges, bankers, newspaper editors and journalists, police chiefs and 30 generals and eight admirals. 953 in all. The scandal culminated on June 18, 1982 when Roberto Calvi, president of Italy's Banco Ambrosiano and P2 member — known as "God's banker" for his close ties to the Vatican Bank — was found hanging by the neck from a rope (a "cable tow" in Masonic ritual) suspended from scaffolding beneath Blackfriar's Bridge in London, his pockets weighted with chunks of masonry. One day prior, Calvi's secretary plunged to her death from a fourth floor window at the bank leaving behind a questionable suicide note. Interestingly, in Italy the logo of the Masonic Brotherhood is the figure of a Blackfriar.

Fringe-Masonic Spooks and Spies

P2's support by the CIA is not an isolated example of the intersection of the Masonic realm and the galaxy of spooks and spies. (Short includes an entire chapter dubbed "Spooks in Aprons," scouring this topic with the P2 scandal as a washboard.) The frequent association between secret societies and the world of special intelligence has been noted by researcher and author John Carter (pseudonym), who writes that it "is interesting to note how many famous occultists are said to have had connections with intelligence organizations, the military, and the police, such as Reuss, Crowley, Parsons, John Dee, Grady McMurtry, Anton LaVey, Michael Aquino, to name a few."[25] While the list of individuals cited by Carter contains members of fringe-Masonic groups such as the esoterically-Masonic *Ordo Templi Orientis* (Order of Oriental Templars or OTO), these associations are within the wider spectrum of the Masonic landscape.

The role of Freemason and OTO leader Aleister Crowley in British Intelligence has been freshly excavated by historian Richard B. Spence, consultant for Washington D.C.'s International Spy Museum.[26] According to Spence, Crowley played a large role in the sinking of the *Lusitania*, a plot to overthrow the government of Spain, and even the 1941 flight of Rudolf Hess. Years after Crowley's death, the struggle for leadership of the OTO wound up in the U.S. courts, and the Brazilian OTO leader Marcelos Motta, who came out on the losing end, accused the OTO branch in the U.S. of having engineered this "courtroom coup" with the help of the CIA.[27] Finally, OTO leader and famed rocket scientist John Whiteside Parsons transferred secret documents relating to U.S. rocket and defense technology to the Israelis from October 1948 until June 1950. He appears to have been rescued from prosecution by none other than brother J. Edgar Hoover.[28]

To those who fear the creeping advance of a Police State, the image of an internal "good ol' boy" structure within the police, giving assistance and possibly cover, is hardly comforting. The tie-in to the leadership of the FBI and the CIA (or to the British equivalents of MI5 and MI6) raises even more questions about the role of Masonic and Masonic-style structures. But the police-Masonic intersection is not the end of the Lodge power tie, and almost pales compared to the pronounced compenetration of the Masonic and the military.

Mobile Masons and Field Fraternizing

The interrelationship of Freemasonry and the military is old and complex. Anti-Masonic writers tend to accuse Masonry of fomenting, plotting, and executing numerous revolutions in Europe, South America and the United States, including (famously) the French Revolution and, according to some writers, both world wars.[29]

While an in-depth examination of these claims is beyond the scope of this essay, the relationship of Freemasonry and military units, small to large, is beyond question. One of the oldest models, noted by Masonic historian Albert Mackey, is the "Field Lodge, or Army Lodge," which Mackey defines:

> A lodge duly instituted under proper authority from a grand body of competent jurisdiction, and authorized to exercise during its peripatetic existence all the powers and privileges that it might possess if permanently located.[30]

On the British side, the Lodge was already a given fact of English life, and this pattern carried over to the New World. As Martin Short writes, "No British institution, not even the police, is more steeped in Freemasonry than the army. England's first recorded initiate, Elias Ashmole, was a captain in Lord Ashley's Royalist regiment when he joined a Warrington lodge in 1646."[31] Records of the colonial period illustrate the British debt to Freemasonry in a "St. Johns Day" festival celebrated by the Master and brethren of Lodge No. 210 on June 25, 1781, while the British Army occupied New York:

> To the King and the craft,
> The Queen...with masons' wives
> Sir Henry Clinton and all loyal Masons
> Admiral Arbuthnot...and all distressed Masons
> Generals Knyphausen and Reidesel...and visiting Brethren
> Lords Cornwallis and Rawdon...with Ancient Fraternity.[32]

The British Army assisted in the spread of Freemasonry from 1732 forward in the form of regimental field lodges. The first lodge was created in the 1st Foot, and later the Royal Scots. These mobile lodges were ready for travel; frequently, the colonel was the lodge's original master. Field lodges served as a channel of communication, an opportunity for young soldiers to advance themselves, and also as a means of redressing grievances. By 1755 29 field lodges existed, including the Royal Northumberland Fusiliers, the Royal Scots Fusiliers, the Royal Innskilling Fusiliers, the Gloucestershire Regiment, the Dorset Regiment, the Border Regiment and the Duke of Wellington's (West Riding).[33]

While these early field lodges were not chartered by the Grand Lodge of England, they carried in their ranks some of the most prominent figures of the day, including the Duke of Cumberland, General Sir John Ligonier (one of the most important British military commanders) and Lord Jeffrey Amherst. But perhaps the most notorious member was George Sackville, later Lord Germain, who became the Colonial Secretary and played a significant role during the American Revolution.[34]

In a Janus-faced split, field lodges also popped up on the colonial side, with assistance from George Washington. Field lodges dotted the Connecticut,

North Carolina, Massachusetts, Maryland, Pennsylvania, and New Jersey lines, and the Pennsylvania Artillery Regiment.

The most illustrious military lodge, however, was the American Union Lodge Number One, in which Washington celebrated the Feast of Saint John the Baptist in 1779, 1780 and 1782, and the Feast of Saint John the Evangelist in 1779.[35] While Washington indicated some distance from Freemasonry in a letter in 1798, it had not always been so. On December 27, 1778, following the colonial victory in Philadelphia, Washington marched in full Masonic attire, including the jewels, sword and insignia of the Brotherhood, at the head of a solemn procession of 300 Freemasons into Christ Church, where a Masonic service was held.[36]

Washington's popularity was such that the field lodges of the Army supported a movement which culminated in a request from prominent Masons in the army to the Grand Lodge of Boston, petitioning the creation of a National Grand Lodge — Washington himself being the hoped-for National Grand Master. However, the Grand Lodge of Boston killed the scheme, apparently in the larger interests of Masonic peace.[37]

Masonic Troops: Licensed to Kill, Brethren Excepted

The fraternal (or treasonous, depending on one's perspective) role of Freemasonry during this intriguing period deserves attention. Lodge affinities on both sides influenced behavior on the battlefield and treatment of the enemy, if that enemy was a lodge brother. To give one example: Mohawk Chief Joseph Brant, whose sister had married the Provincial Grand Master of New York, was initiated as a Freemason himself on a visit to London in 1776. Brant's tribe later bagged a Captain McKinstry, an unfortunate man who was within a hair's breadth of being burned alive tied to a tree, but due to a last-ditch "Masonic appeal" — which was recognized by Brant — he was ordered released and received further British assistance.[38]

Or take the story of a Freemason named Joseph Burnham, a colonial prisoner-of-war escapee who climbed onto the top of a local lodge, fell through into the hands of the British, then thought quickly and gave the proper Masonic signs. The result? The British officers "made a generous contribution for Brother Burnham, who was afterwards transported with secrecy and expedition to the Jersey shore."[39]

While some details of these stories have been questioned, so many of these tales of Masonic indulgence during wartime have been recorded that they indicate a pattern which further points to a fact. Nor was such behavior a mere aberration of the time, a strange episode in a strained war for independence: for we find similar events during the Civil War. For example, during the Battle of Douglass' Church on April 13, 1863, the Confederate Captain Gray was ordered to counterattack and take no Northern prisoners. As he charged up the hill toward what had been Freeman's Battery, he found a trooper and pointed his pistol at him. The soldier quickly made a Masonic sign: the pistol dropped and the Federal trooper was sent to the rear.[40]

Much later, the SS in Third Reich Germany complained of the "shameful behavior" of German Freemason members of field lodges during the first World War, who "had the colossal tastelessness and lack of dignity to enter a foreign lodge in the uniform of a German office, and there to fraternize with Belgian, that is, hostile, lodge members."[41]

Objections to SS reports notwithstanding, research supports this complaint. British military Masons in World War I could apply for a special Masonic pass or "Service Certificate," which entitled the Freemason to special protection and treatment. The pass, intriguingly, was printed in five languages: English, French, Italian — languages of the Allies — but also German and Turkish, languages of the enemy.[42]

A Masonic scandal from the same era involved the French military, known as the *affaire des fiches* or episode of the index-slips. As reported in the May 1912 *Oxford and Cambridge Review,* French Masonic lodges had organized a vast network of espionage so that the War Office, staffed by Freemasons, made all promotions in the army dependent on one's attitude toward Masonic principles and practice. These reports included information regarding whether the candidate sent his children to a Catholic school, or if his wife attended Mass — both black marks. The slips were collected into a register codenamed "Carthage," and any officer whose name made it to "Carthage" had his career advancement cut short.[43]

Similarly, the senior-most sergeant-major in the United States Army (upon his retirement from active service) told me personally that it had long been an old rule that advancement as an officer more or less required Masonic membership. We will return to some facets of this man's story later.

While Masons might downplay or dismiss reports of lodge-based career favoritism, they tend, in their books of Masonic lore, to boast of wartime preferential treatment for the brethren as an example of Masonic benevolence. Such treatment might impress outsiders or "cowans" differently. The examples cited above suggest that one of the effects of Masonic military or field lodges has been the creation of a supranational loyalty which can trump national concerns and obligations, even during war. If Goethe, himself a Freemason, later criticized the Lodge for creating a "state within a state," then perhaps we can similarly ask if military lodges do not by their very nature lead to the interesting phenomenon of an army within an army, determined by "higher" loyalties and recognized by secret signs.

An Officer, a Gentleman, a Master Mason

One of the most interesting and important chapters in Masonry's intersection with the United States military begins in the Philippines, where a field lodge in Manila was established on August 21, 1898. According to reports of the Worshipful Master, "nearly every organization of the 8th Army Corps was represented" at Lodge meetings, and "brothers from the Navy were in frequent attendance."[44]

By early 1900, a "Sojourners Club" developed in Manila and was granted a charter by the Most Worshipful Grand Lodge of California on October 10, 1901. This club later became the Masonic Sojourners Association in 1907. In 1917 returning military Masons formed a national Masonic organization, and by February 28, 1918, the Sojourners were reborn on U.S. soil, "composed of officers and former officers of the various uniformed services of the United States."[45] By 1921 the Sojourners in Chicago had grown, and the National Sojourners arrived on the scene — the Masonic core of the United States military, from that day to ours.

The Masonic provenance of the term *sojourner* is old, rooted in the rituals of the Craft. As Albert Mackey explains:

> The Hebrew word...which we translate "a sojourner," signifies a man living out of his own country....In the English Royal Arch system there are three officers called Sojourners. But in the American system the three Historical Sojourners are represented by the candidates, while only the supposed chief of them is represented by an officer called the Principal Sojourner. His duties are those of a conductor, and resemble, in some respects, those of a Senior Deacon in a Symbolic Lodge; which office, indeed, he occupies when the Chapter is open on any of the preliminary degrees.[46]

As the former National President, John D. Billingsley, Brigadier General, U.S. Army, Rtd., writes: "National Sojourners has provided a means for Master Masons who share another bond, that of being Commissioned Officers of Warrant Officers of the Uniformed Forces of the United States, to meet together in practically all parts of the world... By being provided this opportunity, Master Masons from widely separated Grand Lodge jurisdictions are permitted to continue their associations in Masonry no matter where their duties may take them."[47]

In other words, Master Masons who are military officers join the National Sojourners, which makes that organization a unique facet of Freemasonry — a commanding Masonic presence within the "Uniformed Forces of the United States."

The Committee of 33

In Freemasonry, the number 33 possesses a long history, based on kabbalistic numerology. Fortean scholar William N. Grimstad notes that alchemy is "said to be based upon the symbolism of the number 33: 3 x 3

= 9, the number of 'esoteric man,' and the number of emanations from the kabbalistic 'tree,' one of the key symbol conglomerates."[48]

Grimstad continues: "The most powerful branch of Freemasonry in the world today, the Scottish Rite, has always been American-based, despite its name. It was founded in Charleston, South Carolina, apparently because this city is located approximately on the 33rd degree of north latitude, and offers its members 33 degrees of initiation... The Southern Jurisdiction includes the 33 other contiguous states.... the most conspicuous Masonic edifice in the Washington area today is the George Washington Masonic national Memorial, a replica of the ancient Lighthouse of Alexandria. It is 333 feet high....

"The official version of the U.S. Great Seal has 33 feathers on the eagle's sinister wing..."[49]

The Committee of 33 was formed on June 10, 1925 during the Fifth Annual Convention of National Sojourners in Washington, D.C., to "include the National Officers, to draw up definite plans, specifying definitely the object of the Sojourners and its war time and peace time policies... empowered to act and carry out the plans approved."[50]

How wide is the scope of these "definite plans" for both "war time and peace time policies"? It is difficult to say, but one suspects the influence of the Sojourners is considerable. The roster of military officers is enormous, encompassing a "who's who" of the military. Lavon Parker Linn, National Historian of the National Sojourners, compiled lists, photographs, and celebrations of military Masons which filled a book — including, significantly, astronauts. While this essay cannot detail the NASA-Freemasonic connections or the links between Spacecraft and Craft, it is worth noting that the 1997 NASA probe of Mars included a rover named *Sojourner* which was carried in a tetrahedral-shaped lander to 19.5° x 33°.[51]

Military Mystical Toponomy

In the light of the overwhelming presence of Freemasonry among military officers, it is fair to ask: could Masonic perspectives or agendas influence war plans? While Freemasons are quick to claim that Freemasonry has no covert agenda, it is difficult to ignore two prominent factors within the world of Freemasonry: 1) the obsession with numbers, place, symbol and ritual, and 2) the ritualized focus on Middle Eastern symbolism in general and to construct the Temple of Solomon in particular.

James Shelby Downard defines *mystical toponomy* as pertaining "to the magic and mystery of words intersecting with the Masonic science of symbolism... My study of place names imbued with sorcerous significance necessarily include lines of latitude and longitude and the divisions of degrees in geography and cartography (minutes and seconds)."[52]

We have already observed a focus on the number 33 as a locus of mystical toponomy. As Robert Macoy writes in his *Dictionary of Freemasonry,*

"Freemasonry is a complete system of symbolic teaching, and cannot be known, understood or appreciated only by those who study its symbolism, and make themselves thoroughly acquainted with its occult meaning."[53]

Albert Mackey writes of the "respect paid by Freemasons to certain numbers" which is founded on the assumption that they are "types or representatives of certain ideas."[54]

One notable instance of military Masonic symbolism is the very shape of the Pentagon, which, as Downard points out, is the "third figure from the exterior in the camp of the Sublime Princes of the Royal Secret, or 32nd degree of the Scottish Rite."[55]

In addition to looking for mystical toponomy at work in military staging, we should also keep in mind the Masonic focus on the Middle East. Mackey explains that:

> With Palestine, or the Holy Land, the mythical, if not the authentic, history of Freemasonry has been closely connected. There stood, at one time, the Temple of Solomon, to which some writers have traced the origin of the Masonic Order; there fought the Crusaders, among whom other writers have sought, with equal boldness, to find the cradle of the Fraternity; there certainly the Order of the Templars was instituted, whose subsequent history has been closely mingled with that of Freemasonry; and there occurred nearly all the events of sacred history that, with the places where they were enacted, have been adopted as important Masonic symbols.[56]

These "important Masonic symbols" fill the ritual of the Masonic degrees of initiation, none of which are more important than the ritual enactment of the construction of the Temple of Solomon in the Third or Master Mason Degree — a work interrupted, left to be completed.

Alexander Horne, 33°, Ancient and Accepted Scottish Rite, Southern Jurisdiction, USA, penned a detailed study entitled *King Solomon's Temple in the Masonic Tradition*. Horne is a leading Masonic scholar and a member of Quatuor Coronati Lodge No. 2076, the premier lodge of Masonic research in England. Horne attempts to untangle fact from myth in determining how the Temple became a central motif in Freemasonry, and ends his book giving due consideration to the theory that Hiram Abiff, the builder of the Temple in the Master Mason ritual, was a makeover of Noah derived from an old Jewish necromantic legend, if not from witchcraft.[57]

A Zionist bias, although denied by official Grand Lodge statements affirming the neutrality of politics within the Lodge, seems clearly implied in one of the most important degrees, the Royal Arch, deemed a "completion" of the Master Mason rite. The Royal Arch contains the dramatic line, "For the good of Masonry, generally, but the Jewish nation in particular."[58]

Dig That Temple

Mackey notes that the "desire to obtain an accurate knowledge of Palestine" gave rise in 1866 to a London association under the patronage of the Queen called the "Palestine Exploration Fund," including a long list of the nobility "added to which followed the Grand Lodge of England and forty-two subordinate and provincial Grand Lodges and Chapters." What did this "exploration" entail? According to Mackey, "mining in and about the various points which had been determined upon by a former survey as essential to a proper understanding of the ancient city..."[59]

These excavations continued under Lieutenant-General Sir Charles Warren (1840–1927), who dug around from 1867 through 1871. Warren later became a founding member of the premier Masonic research lodge, Quatuor Coronati Lodge no. 2076, warranted on November 28, 1884, and was elected its first Master, 1886–87. Given the high patronage and Lodge sponsorship of these very physical "Palestine exploration" activities, it would appear that Masonic interest in the Temple of Solomon has a history of passing beyond the abstract, and is arguably more than an exercise in armchair symbolism and philosophy.

Historian John J. Robinson studied the origins of Freemasonry afresh in *Born in Blood: The Lost Secrets of Freemasonry,* reaffirming a Templar origin of the Craft. Robinson ends his work with a chapter entitled "The Unfinished Temple of Solomon" in which he writes:

> The other problem in Israel brings us right back to Freemasonry, because it is squarely centered on the original site of the Temple of Solomon on Mount Moriah, the Temple Mount in Jerusalem, the birthplace of the Knights Templar. Perhaps no spot on earth cries out for the brotherhood of men of different religions more than the site of the original Temple of Solomon, in a situation so tense that some writers have speculated that it could well trigger World War III. And for the first time in this book, we are not discussing allegories based on the temple, but the real temple, on the Temple Mount in Jerusalem.... What I am suggesting is that about 5 million Freemasons in the world, who do accept brotherhood with men of all faiths, in that spirit might take the lead in solving the problem of the Temple Mount by combining their religious attitudes with their veneration of the Temple of Solomon, to the benefit of the whole world... It would be a wonderful way to complete the unfinished Temple of Solomon and to complete a full-circle circumambulation back to the very first purpose of their predecessor Knights of the Temple, the safe passage of all pilgrims to the holy place.[60]

Robinson's book was highly praised by numerous Masonic reviewers. Robinson went on to pen an apologetic for Freemasonry *(A Pilgrim's Path)* and then joined the Lodge himself.

Bagging Baghdad

Between 1858-1874, Brother Sylvanus Cobb, Jr., produced a number of Masonic stories, but none surpassed *The Caliph of Bagdad*. Originally published in serial form in the New York Ledger in 1868 under the title *The Mystic Tie of the Temple,* demand soon dictated a book length version. Albert Mackey includes an entry for the book in his encyclopedia, describing it as the most widely read of Masonic novels. Cobb, a Navy man, was Worshipful Master of his lodge five times, and reached the 32nd degree in 1874.

Published by *Masonic News*, Lafayette at First Street, Detroit, Michigan, Cobb's Masonic novel sensation was smothered with praise from Masonic leaders. "It is far from the usual Masonic book, and so close to the real Masonic heart that I enjoyed every word of it," writes Roe Fulkerson 33°, Grand Master of the Grand Lodge, District of Columbia. Silas H. Shepherd, Chairman, Committee on Masonic Research, Grand Lodge of Wisconsin, comments that the book is "so imbued with the spirit of Freemasonry as to make it one of the foremost works of Masonic fiction."[61]

The story involves Dagon, the hero, initiated into the Brotherhood of the Mystic Tie in Jerusalem, who returns to his native Baghdad to relieve the stress caused by a Caliph tyrant. The story is full of staple Masonic symbolism such as a secret vault, all of which is instantly recognizable to Masons who have been exalted to the Royal Arch Degree.

Interestingly, we find a modern tale written in history within our time, involving a tyrant in Baghdad — Saddam Hussein — and military Freemasons "relieving the stress" of his reign. Is there a Mystic Tie to all of it?

From the perspective of mystical toponomy, it is worth noting that *Baghdad is on the 33rd parallel.* In the first Gulf War, my military friend mentioned earlier led his Rangers into Baghdad. He found that his team met with little resistance, most Iraqis at that time appearing quite willing to surrender. As he stared at Baghdad, he felt confident that the city would surrender without much trouble. Then came the cryptic order to refrain, to leave Saddam Hussein in power. Completely baffled, he left the modern "Caliph tyrant" in place — for the time being.

Years later, in the second Gulf War, he was once more contacted by the Pentagon, promoted, and sent off to the Middle East. I lost all track of my friend, but evidently this time, the game plan included the removal of Saddam Hussein.

One facet of this strange tale seems almost cut from Cobb's Masonic classic: for where did our military "Dagons" find the new "Caliph tyrant," Saddam Hussein? In a "spider hole" — that is, in a *type of secret vault*, which is both the name of a chapter in Cobbs' book, and a basic element of Royal Arch Masonic ritual.

If much of our warfare seems staged, perhaps we should consult the Masonic scripts to make heads or tails out of the confusion and bring order, as the Masons say, out of the chaos.

Beyond the bizarre elements of mystical toponomy and hints of ritualized references to Masonic lore in the Iraq War, we also should note that some of the actual reasons for the war appear to be grounded in long-range Zionist ambitions, bringing us back once again to Masonic pipe dreams regarding the Temple Mount.

Professor James Petras, Bartle Professor Emeritus of Sociology at Binghamton University, New York, writes that the "only major beneficiary of the war has been the State of Israel, which has succeeded in having the US destroy its most consistent Arab adversary in the Middle East — the regime that extended the greatest political support to the Palestinian resistance... Iraq, together with Iran and Syria, had formed the core resistance to Israeli expansionist plans to expel the Palestinians and conquer and occupy all of Palestine."[62] Such a conquest would make it finally possible to solve the problems of the Temple Mount — if it could all be done without World War III, which seems unlikely.

Ideologically-driven fanatics never seem to mind another World War.

Team Freedom and the Iraq Lodge

According to the neo-con, Moonie-funded *Washington Times*, Saddam Hussein had prescribed the death penalty for "those who promote or acclaim Zionist principles, including freemasonry."[63] Originally a number of Iraqi Lodges dotted the landscape under the British Mandate following the first World War, but apparently that changed dramatically under Saddam Hussein, if we can believe the report.

With the "liberation" of Iraq, Land Sea and Air Lodge No. 1 was soon up and running in Iraq.[64] Freemasonry had returned, even if running water had not. First things first.

Although the rhetoric of "liberation" and "freedom building" as excuses for the military operation in Iraq has been deconstructed and exposed as a tissue of ludicrous lies,[65] Freemasons still use this cheap propaganda to shore up support for military ventures. A webpage for "Team Freedom"[66] details the programs available for *supporting Masonic troops* (their expression). These include the Masonic Troop Support Program (MTSP) and the Masonic Military Support Fund (MMSF). The website is topped by a photo of several white people in white shirts standing in front of an American flag — the "good guys," apparently. No link is provided to an Iraqi civilian body count.

Quo Vadis, Brethren?

We end this brief historical survey by asking where this conglomeration of Masonic cops and military men is headed. Many observers have commented on the disturbing tendency of police to ramp up their armory and weaponry, mobilizing into a virtual army themselves, distinct from the old, Mayberry-style friendly cop-on-the-beat. Similarly, the United States military seems hell-bent on swarming to the Middle East for wars based on lies and secret agendas. Signs are currently pointing to a joint U.S.-Israeli attack on Iran. Is all of this empire-building a prelude to a Mystic Tie operation in Jerusalem, to be centered on Temple Mount? Are the Sojourners hoping for the day when another "Palestine Excavation" project can finish where Sir Charles Warren left off — or, for that matter, where Hiram Abiff left off in the Master Mason ritual, slain before he could finish the Temple? Will an obsessive Masonic focus on the Middle East lead us to the brink of national disaster, and will our freedoms be increasingly stomped into a Gitmo sewer by fraternal police?

Perhaps only time will tell — if we still have the time, and if we peel back the layers of propaganda to discern hidden intentions and ask uncomfortable questions.

Endnotes

1   Jay Tolson, "How the Freemasons Made Their Mark," *Secret Societies: Masons, Mormons, Scientology, Opus Dei, The Mafia, Skull & Bones, & more*, Washington, D.C.: *U.S. News & World Report*, p. 39.

2   See, for example, James Shelby Downard's *The Carnivals of Life and Death* (Los Angeles: Feral House, 2006) for an extended autobiographical drama illustrating the interplay of the "Masonic hoodwink" and various ties between Lodges and other fraternal Orders, including the Ku Klux Klan.

3   Landmarks are "A set of beliefs and practices that have traditionally set Freemasonry apart from other organizations" — C. Bruce Hunter, *Masonic Dictionary*, Richmond, Virginia: Macoy, 1996, p. 54.

4   *Ibid.*, p. 51.

5   http://www.grandlodgefop.org/

6   Albert Pike, *Morals and Dogma of the Ancient and Accepted Scottish Rite of Freemasonry*, Washington, D.C.: House of the Temple, 1966, p. 486.

7   Website of Fraternal Order of Police, Oregon Pioneer Lodge #4: http://www.geocities.com/Heartland/Pointe/2954/oregonlodge4/index.html

8   "Back the Badge — Tulsa Political Action Committee," http://www.backthebadge.com/fop.asp

9   Stephen Knight, *The Brotherhood: The Secret World of the Freemasons*, n.p., Dorset Press, 1984, p. 80.

10   Martin Short, *Inside the Brotherhood: Explosive Secrets of the Freemasons*, London: HarperCollins, 1989, p. 197.

11   *Ibid.*, p. 197.

12   *Ibid.*, pp. 364–65.

13   http://www.publications.parliament.uk/pa/cm199899/cmselect/cmhaff/467/46703.htm

14   http://www.masonicinfo.com/vomit.htm

15   Anthony Summers, *Official and Confidential: The Secret Life of J. Edgar Hoover*, New York: G.P. Putnam's Sons, 1993, pp. 240–45, 254–58.

16   http://freemasonry.bcy.ca/biography/hoover_j/hoover_j.html

17   http://www.srmason-sj.org/library/hoover/j-e-hoover2.htm

18   The work of Lee Harvey Oswald's attorney Mark Lane in *Rush to Judgment* (New York: Holt, Rinehart and Winston, 1966) was introduced by historian Hugh Trevor-Roper and praised by Bertrand Russell, who wrote, "I believe this exhaustive and unchallengeable book to be a great historical document."

19   *Ibid.,* from introduction by Hugh Trevor-Roper, p. 8.

20   Charles A. Crenshaw, M.D., Jens Hansen, and J. Gary Shaw, *JFK: Conspiracy of Silence,* New York: Penguin, 1992. Also see James DiEugenio and Lisa Pease, editors, *The Assassinations: Probe Magazine on JFK, MLK, RFK and Malcolm X,* Los Angeles: Feral House, 2003.

21   A fleshed-out version of Downard's thesis appeared in the first volume of *Secret and Suppressed:* "Sorcery, Sex, Assassination and the Science of Symbolism." See note following.

22   James Shelby Downard, "Sorcery, Sex, Assassination and the Science of Symbolism," *Secret and Suppressed: Banned Ideas and Hidden History,* Venice, California: Feral House, 1993, p. 88.

23   Cited in Devon Jackson, *Conspiranoia! The Mother of All Conspiracy Theories,* New York: Penguin, 1999, p, 11.

24   David A. Yallop, *In God's Name: An Investigation into the Murder of Pope John Paul I,* New York: Bantam, 1984, p. 116.

25   John Carter (pseudonym), *Sex and Rockets: The Occult World of Jack Parsons,* Los Angeles: Feral House, 2004, p. 37.

26   See Richard B. Spence, *Secret Agent 666: Aleister Crowley, British Intelligence and the Occult,* Los Angeles: Feral House, 2008.

27   For Motta's suspicions, see Craig Heimbichner, *Blood on the Altar: The Secret History of the World's Most Dangerous Secret Society,* Coeur d'Alene, Idaho: Independent History & Research, 2005, p. 91.

28   Carter, *op. cit.,* pp. 169–172.

29   Representative writers in this vein would include Nesta Webster (*The French Revolution, World Revolution, Secret Societies and Subversive Movements*) and Bernard Faÿ. The latter author, director of France's Bibliothèque nationale, not only wrote extensively on Freemasonry, but also assisted in the production of the 1943 Vichy-era production *Forces Occultes,* which portrayed Freemasons as the culprits behind war and secret plots for world domination.

30   Albert G. Mackey, *An Encyclopedia of Freemasonry and Its Kindred Sciences,* Masonic History Company: Chicago, 1921, Vol. 1, p. 265.

31   *Ibid.,* p. 502.

32   Michael Baigent and Richard Leigh, *The Temple and the Lodge,* New York: Arcade Publishing, 1989, p. 218.

33   *Ibid.,* pp. 203–04.

34   *Ibid.,* p. 205.

35   Bernard Faÿ, *Revolution and Freemasonry,* Boston: Little, Brown and Company, 1935, p. 245.

36   *Ibid.,* pp. 245–46.

37   *Ibid.,* pp. 246–47.

38   Baigent and Leigh, *op. cit.,* p. 253. For more on the fascinating career of the Mohawk Mason Chief Joseph Brant, see William M. Stuart, *Masonic Soldiers of Fortune,* New York: Macoy Publishing and Masonic Supply, 1928, pp. 105–22.

39   R.F. Gould, "Military Masonry," *Ars Quatuor Coronatorum,* vol. xiv, 1901, pp. 47–8, cited in Baigent and Leigh, *op. cit.,* p. 253.

40   Allen E. Roberts, *House Undivided: The Story of Freemasonry and the Civil War,* Richmond, Virginia: Macoy Publishing and Masonic Supply, 1961, p. 151.

41   Dieter Schwarz, *Freemasonry: Ideology, Organization and Policy,* Berlin: Central Publishing House of the NSDAP, 1944, pp. 33–4.

42   Short, *op. cit.,* pp. 514–15.

43   From Flavien Brenier, *Oxford and Cambridge Review,* May, 1912, pp. 168–69, cited in Rev. E. Cahill, *Freemasonry and the Anti-Christian Movement,* Dublin, Ireland: M.H. Gill and Son, 1952, p. 20.

44   Lavon Parker Linn, *Fifty Years of National Sojourners,* Washington, D.C.: National Sojourners, 1970, p. 13.

45   *Ibid.,* pp. 19–27.

46   Mackey, *op cit.,* Vol. 2, p. 588.

47   *Ibid.,* p. 5.

48   Jim Brandon (William N. Grimstad), *The Rebirth of Pan,* Dunlap, Illinois: Firebird Press, 1983, p. 175.

49   *Ibid.,* p. 176–77.

50   Lavon Parker Linn, *op cit.*, p. 140.
51   See Mike Bara, *The Secret History of NASA,* in this volume.
52   Downard, *op. cit.*, pp. 69–70.
53   Robert Macoy, *A Dictionary of Freemasonry,* reprint, New York: Random House, 1989, p. 367.
54   Mackey, *op. cit.*, vol. 2, p. 521.
55   James Shelby Downard, "The Call to Chaos," in Adam Parfrey, editor, *Apocalypse Culture,* expanded and revised edition, Los Angeles: Feral House, 1990, p. 322.
56   *Ibid.*, p. 541.
57   Alexander Horne, *King Solomon's Temple in the Masonic Tradition,* Wellingborough, Northamptonshire: Aquarian Press, 1972, pp. 336–345.
58   Malcolm C. Duncan, *Duncan's Masonic Ritual and Monitor,* New York: David Mackay, n.d., p. 249.
59   Mackey, *op. cit.*, vol. 2, p. 541.
60   John J. Robinson, *Born in Blood: The Lost Secrets of Freemasonry,* New York: M. Evans & Company, 1989, pp. 340–341, 344.
61   Comments from book sleeve.
62   James Petras, *The Power of Israel in the United States,* Atlanta, Georgia: Clarity Press, 2006, p. 28.
63   "Saddam to be formally charged," *Washington Times,* July 1, 2004.
64   http://www.dcmetronet.com/landseaandairlodge1iraq/
65   By numerous authors, including James Petras (see above citation), who also goes one step further and argues provocatively that oil was not a significant reason for the war, but rather Zionism.
66   http://www.masonictroops.com/

Holy War, Ground Zero

by Adam Parfrey

As the navel is set in the centre of the human body,
so is the land of Israel the navel of the world...
situated in the centre of the world,
and Jerusalem in the centre of the land of Israel,
and the sanctuary in the centre of Jerusalem,
and the holy place in the centre of the sanctuary,
and the ark in the centre of the holy place,
and the foundation stone before the holy place,
because from it the world was founded."
Midrash Tanchuma, Qedoshim.
— from *TempleMount.org,*
an Apocalyptic Christian Pro-Zionist Website

The Prophet Muhammad flew off to visit heaven from the Sacred Rock atop Jerusalem's Mount Moriah within the mosque Al-Aqsa, the same place that Messianic Jews and Zionist Christians say the ancient Jewish Temples existed, the first one destroyed by the Babylonians in 586 BCE and the second one destroyed by the Romans in 70 CE.

Here at what Temple Mount is Ground Zero of the monotheistic holy wars: Christian, Jewish, Islamic.

Messianic Orthodox Jews believe that the messiah will come once the mosque is destroyed, the area purified by the sacrifice of animals, and the temple rebuilt.

Fundamentalist Christians view the Jewish conquest of Temple Mount as the fuse lighting Armageddon, the end time scenario to which Jesus Christ will return to impose his thousand-year dominion. The "left behind" genre of Tim LaHaye sells millions of copies of dispensational premillennialist beliefs through novelized sermons, promoting the idea of Temple Mount as ground zero for the apocalypse.

"Zionist Christians," who have raised hundreds of millions of dollars for the most warlike elements of Israel, actually share an apocalyptic belief with Muslims. The devil coming these impending end days is a Jew. The late Jerry

Falwell, a "close friend" of Israel, particularly financially, said in January 1999 that the antichrist was probably alive and "must be male and Jewish."

Muslims also believe that a historical figure named Jesus Christ existed, but didn't actually die, and was transported to heaven in wait of the nasty final days in which he will touch down to earth once again to destroy Jews for Islam, after which he will die a natural death. In his bestselling Arabic book, *Al-Masih al-Dajjal*, Sa'id Ayyub writes that the antichrist will come in the form of the Jewish Prophet who will live at "the Temple in Jerusalem. For this reason they sometimes try to burn Al-Aqsa, and try to conduct archeological excavations, and even try to buy the ground through the Masons of America."

Ayyub's strange accusation that American Masons attempted to purchase Temple Mount is not without historical credibility. Freemasonry, the seemingly decaying fraternal society linked to American, British, French and Italian power structures, and to which most American presidents have belonged — including Harry Truman, who pressured allies to support the United Nations' creation of the Jewish state — is "blended indestructibly with the rites, ceremonies and traditions of Hebrew worship," as writes Robert W. Bowers in his Masonically sanctioned 1899 book, *Freemasonry and the Tabernacle and Temple of the Jews*. And Gavin Lambert, the Zionist Christian, claims on his site that on July 15, 1968, "The President of the Moslem Court of Appeals turned down a request by an American Masonic Temple Order who asked permission to build a $100 million 'Solomon's' temple on Temple Mount." Masonic theology and ritualism is intimately constructed around the rebuilding of the Temple of Solomon.

The monotheistic fundamentalists pray that their struggle for the possession of Temple Mount will bring on the final war that will at last sort out whose apocalyptic belief rises to the top.

Messianic Jews, with support from the state of Israel, are already laying the cornerstone for the new temple, predicated on the destruction of Islam's holy spot.

Says the Christian Zionist website templemountfaithful.org: "The cornerstone of 4.5 tons in weight is very similar to the stones of the First and Second Temples...It will be transported on a big truck painted with Israeli flags and the Star of David, and the stone will be covered with a [prayer shawl]...We are doing and shall continue to do everything that the Third Temple will soon be built in our lifetime for the honor of the G-d of Israel and to fulfill His prophetic wishes. For this goal we have completely dedicated our lives, we left everything and we are acting full-time for this godly prophetic purpose. We shall do everything to save the Temple Mount from the terrible abomination which is done today by foreigners and enemies and to purify the Temple Mount for the G-d of Israel and the universe exactly as our forefathers did when they liberated Temple Mount from foreign occupation and abomination.

"We trust in G-d that this godly end-time vision will soon be a reality in our lifetime and our activities will be accomplished."

It was Ariel Sharon's tour of Temple Mount that instigated the radical escalation of Palestinian protest and terror with "Al-Aqsa Intifada." Sharon was known by Palestinians as a "pig" and "butcher," responsible for the first of Israel's invasions of Lebanon, both designed to remove Arabs from within bombing distance of Northern Israel. Sharon's 1982 Lebanese invasion helped bring on the "Beirut massacre," in which 800 Palestinian civilians were murdered in the Sabra and Shatilla refugee camps. It wasn't Sharon's troops who carried out the killings, but the Christian Phalangist allies. The Kahan Commission, formed by the Israeli government to investigate the massacre, found Sharon to be "personally responsible" and recommended his removal from the government. Sharon now exists (as of July 2008) in a permanent vegetative state in an Israeli hospital.

In the meantime, the Rabbi Chaim Richman claims to be close to breeding the "miraculous" red heifer, whose sacrifice and ashes would provide the appropriate groundwork for the destruction of the Islamic Dome of the Rock and the rebuilding of the Temple of Solomon. According to Gershom Gorenberg in *The End of Days*, the biblical verse that moved a Mississippi cattleman named Clyde Lott to assist Rabbi Richman's apocalyptic and sacrificial obsession is simply misunderstood. "In Hebrew, the [Genesis] verse says nothing of cows. It refers, unmistakably, to the offspring of sheep and goats, as any Orthodox Israeli schoolchild who was awake in second grade class knows. In the English of King James' time, 'cattle' meant any livestock, not specifically bovines." In December 1998, Rabbi Richman broke off his friendship with the red heifer-breeding cattleman over a financial dispute.

OCCULT NASHVILLE

The mysteries inside "The Athens of the South"

by Jim Marrs

Nashville, Tennessee, "Music City, USA," has long been home to rock and roll, blues, the Country Music Hall of Fame and the Grand Ole Opry.

Nashville also is known as "The Athens of the South," due to the city's emphasis on education, culture and religion. It is even home to a full-scale replica of the Greek Parthenon, built in 1897 for Tennessee's Centennial Exposition.

Being a major center for Bible publishing, the city has come to be known as "the buckle of the Bible Belt," that southern rim of the United States filled with Christian fundamentalists. This center of Christian conservatism makes it all the more puzzling that within Nashville can be found traces of ancient mysteries and theologies.

Nashville has a hidden and esoteric, even occult, side with mysteries that range from ancient Greece and Egypt to an abiding curiosity regarding Nashville by President Franklin D. Roosevelt.

Foremost among those who have discovered the hidden, or occulted, side of Nashville is William Henry, an "investigative mythologist" who has lived in the city since 1981. Henry is the author of several self-published books, including one describing the Nashville mysteries entitled *City of Peace*.

The metaphysical side of Nashville may extend back many centuries long before the coming of white settlers. Legend has it that the area was once a huge sacred burial ground for Native Americans. In the 19th century, archeologist Dr. Joseph Jones discovered the skeletal remains of a seven-foot-tall man. Henry noted that in 1998 the Tennessee National Football League team, the Tennessee Oilers, changed the name to the Tennessee Titans, that mythological race of giants of Greek legend. He compared the Titans to the Bible's giant Nefilim, who, according to the Book of Genesis, came to the Earth from the stars and took human women (the "daughters of man") for wives.

This venerable site may have also had connections to other sacred themes.

Thirty miles north of Nashville, a Confederate general named Gates

Thurston discovered an engraved tablet which he attributed to a group of "Tennessee Mound builders."

This "Thurston Tablet" depicted an Indian warrior holding a shield and a club. On his chest were several circles within circles. According to Henry, this was the Hopi sign for "Massau," translated as the "True White Brother."

"*Massau* is a word that is strikingly similar to the Aramaic *meshiha*, the Hebrew *mahsiah* and the Greek *messias*. These words mean 'anointed.' To the Hebrews, the Messiah is the expected king and deliverer. To the Christians, the Messiah is Jesus, the Christ. And to the Hopis, Massau is the deliverer and purifier who came before and who will return from the east as 'the true white brother' of all the Hopis, the peaceful ones."

Working from this premise, Henry compared the Hopis to the Essenes of Palestine which have been connected to Jesus and his preaching of love and freedom for the individual. "The Hopis say Massau gave the Hopi commandments or laws written on Sacred Stone Tablets and taught them to live in a true democracy in which every individual has absolute freedom, but is responsible to the whole," said Henry.

There is evidence that this "white brother" may have been a member of the legendary Knights Templar who escaped arrest in Europe in the early 1300s. At least one segment of the Templar fleet may have made its way to America 185 years before Christopher Columbus set sail.

Columbus found his way to the New World using maps by the 16th-century Turkish cartographer Admiral Piri Reis, who wrote that he had obtained ancient maps from the Library at Alexandria based on even older sources.

The claim of a Templar presence in North America begins with a group called the Mandaean sect, those who believed that John the Baptist was the true Messiah. In medieval time, the "heresy" of this belief was coded into some church artwork by depicting a human skull which represented the severed head of John.

Furthermore, the Mandaeans have been connected to Nazoreans, thought to be part of the Qumran Essene community where Jesus studied and whose scrolls were found in 1945. Muslims forced the Mandaeans from the banks of the Jordan River into Persia where remnants of the sect still exist.

The Mandaeans, like the Essenes, believed that the souls of good people would go to a wonderful and peaceful land across the sea when they died, a land they believed was marked by a star called "Merica." Since it is likely the documents discovered by the Templars in Jerusalem were duplicates of those found at the Qumran community, the Templars may have found a reference to the new lands as well as the name "Merica" and set sail for there following the outlawing of their order in 1307.

These intrepid sailors, flying their well-known skull-and-crossbones battle flag, reportedly arrived in New England in the year 1308.

Compelling evidence of such a landing can be found in Westford, Massachusetts, where today a punched-holes engraving of a knight can be found on a rock. This figure, dressed in the style of a 14th-century knight, carries a shield containing a picture of a sailing ship following a single star. Historian and radio host Dr. Robert Hieronimus in his book, *Founding Father, Secret Societies*, made a compelling argument that the founders of the United States received much of their ideas on freedom and individual liberty from the Templars, who became part of Freemasonry, as well as North American natives, notably the League of the Iroquois.

Henry wondered if the knowledge of the Mandeans, Essenes and Templars had been handed down to the Native Americans. He noted that the Great Seal of Nashville and Davidson County depicted an Indian gazing at a human skull in his left hand.

The archeologist Jones offered the possibility that the creators of the stone burial grounds in Nashville might have been a tribe of Mandan Indians, a name amazingly similar to the Mandeans. Reportedly, the Mandans were "white Indians" who could speak English. Pottery, other artifacts and burial mounds all seemed to connect the Mandans with other tribes in central North America and even to the pyramid-building Olmecs in Mexico.

Henry pointed out that Mandan means a "man of Dan" and noted that Dan was an older brother to the Biblical Joseph with his coat of many colors. "The Viking explorers of America, like Bjarni Herjulfon, Eric the Red and his son Leif Ericsson who landed in America long before Christopher Columbus, were Danes (Dan-ish), descended from their Israelite father Dan," he explained.

He also noticed that "Mandan tradition included several stories embodying a more or less confused and garbled memory of Christian beliefs, i.e.: the virgin birth of a child who later performed miracles [and] feeding a multitude with a small amount of food leaving fragments as great as when the feeding began."

Legend has it that buffalo hunters moving westward hundreds of years after the Templars found a spring of clear, sparkling but salty water and called it "The Salt Lick." It was here that the Tennessee state capitol now stands. Nearby was a large strange mound. Asked about the origins of this mound, tribal leaders said it had always been there. Digging into the mound in later years, ancient stone graves were found which explained the religious significance of the area in the minds of the natives.

In 1779, a group led by James Robertson settled in the area which came to be known as Sulfur Spring Bottom. The settlement was named Nashborough after a Gen. Francis Nash, who had served with Robertson in George Washington's revolutionary army. In 1784, an act of the Tennessee Legislature changed the name to Nashville. Four years later, future president Andrew Jackson arrived and became the state's first lawyer.

A new administrative district was formed in central Tennessee and named the Mero District in honor of a Louisiana governor called Mero. Henry said the name Mero is so close to Meru that he saw a synchronicity at work.

In Egyptian mythology the Saba or "love gods" dwelled on a Mount Meru, located near a mountain called Ida. Henry said the word Ida may be the root for Iuda or Juda. This mount was reportedly made entirely of crystal and was the repository of knowledge from gods who came from the sky. Of great interest to Henry is the fact that the only mountain of pure quartz crystal found on Earth is Mt. Ida, located near the Oklahoma border in western Arkansas, due west from Little Rock and Memphis, Tennessee.

Albert Ross Parsons in 1893 published a book entitled *New Light from the Great Pyramid*. Parsons expressed the belief that the legendary Mt. Meru was located in the United States and noted the customs of the Hopi were strikingly similar to those in Mongolia.

"Did the myth of Mt. Ida originate in America?" wondered Henry. "Did the gods originally dwell in Arkansas?

"To the average person, I'm way out on a limb with that question," conceded Henry, but added, "The average person has probably not looked into the matter."

Henry said that narratives from Tibet to Central America told of a string of "Cities of Peace" which dotted the planet. These cities — variously called Tula, Sabala or Shambhala — were the home to Mystery Schools where people gathered to learn the secrets of the sky gods and to learn the way to unify heaven and earth.

Dr. J.J. Hurtak, Founder and President of The Academy for Future Science, is a social scientist and scholar who has written, translated, and published more than fifteen books, including ones on the ancient Coptic texts illustrating Jesus' work and especially involving the "Lost Scriptures" being found in the Middle East. An anthropologist and archeologist, Dr. Hurtak published a map of the likely locations of these "Cities of Peace." They included the Pyramids of Giza, Lourdes and Rennes le Chateau in France, Hawaii, Sinkiang near Mongolia, Vancouver, B.C., the Four Corners area of the U.S. Southwest and a southeastern area that encompassed Nashville, Tennessee.

In ancient Egypt, worshipers in the cults of Osiris and Isis were headquartered on the Island of Meroe (Meru?). Here they constructed a huge pillar in which it was claimed the head of Osiris was kept. In Egyptian mythology, Osiris was slain by his half-brother Set and his body cut into 14 pieces.

Called the Pillar of Meru, or the Pillar of Love, this casket containing the head was reportedly 20 stories tall, the same height as the front of the Biblical Temple of Solomon. Also called the "ladder to Heaven," the pillar was said to have linked the earth to heaven. Henry linked this pillar to a similar tower depicted in a Mesopotamian carving of 800 B.C. The goddess depicted in this carving was called Mari and was an earlier version of the Greek goddess Athena.

In fact, the legends of the Egyptians and the Greek blend together in such a remarkable fashion that it appears they are talking about the same people and events. Only names are changed to reflect the different languages.

According to Greek mythology, Athena was born from the head of Zeus, chief of all the gods. Both Athena and Isis were considered an Earth Mother, the goddess of love, arts and wisdom.

Henry wondered if it was sheer coincidence that placed a 42-foot-high gilded statue of Athena in the recreated Parthenon in Nashville's Centennial Park. It is the tallest indoor statue in the Western world. He also pondered the Tennessee state flag which depicts three star outlines within a circle.

"When most people look at the Tennessee flag they see the three stars in a circle. This is the exoteric or foreground interpretation," he explained. "Within the circle (the symbol of wholeness), however, the three stars of the Tennessee flag converge to form a triceps. This may be the true inner meaning of the Tennessee flag."

He explained that the triceps, a Nordic design of three Earth diamonds linked together at the ends, is an ancient symbol invoking power as well as a symbol of feminine power, usually seen as three stylized fishes swimming away from each other. This again evokes the female power as seen in Athena and the earlier Isis.

Addressing skeptics who might write all this off as speculative nonsense, Henry pointed out that none other than President Franklin D. Roosevelt and his secretary of agriculture turned vice president Henry Wallace both had an abiding interest in the occultism surrounding Nashville.

Roosevelt and Wallace joined with Nicholas Roerich, a Russian painter and spiritual leader born Nikolai Konstantinovich Rerikh. Roerich and his wife Helena were co-founders of the theosophical Agni Yoga Society. The three men met in 1929 and their search for esoteric knowledge began. Wallace wrote more than 117 letters to Roerich which became known as "the Guru letters" due to their opening salutation of "Dear Guru."

In a 1933 letter, Wallace wrote, "Yes, the search, whether it be for the Lost Word of Masonry or the Holy Chalice or the personalities of the age to come, is the one supremely worthwhile in objective. All else is karmic duty."

Researcher Henry said a 1933 letter from Wallace to Roerich contained words which led him to believe that the three men were actively interested in Nashville. Wallace's letter began:

> Dear Guru,
> I have been thinking of you holding the casket — the sacred most precious casket. And I have thought of the New Country going forth to meet the seven stars under the sign of the three stars. And I have thought of the admonition "Await the Stone."

According to William Henry, this opening paragraph indicates that Roerich, Wallace and Roosevelt were seeking — if not had already procured — the "Stone of God," also referred to as the "Philosopher's Stone" or the Holy Grail. It is a fact that in 1935, Roosevelt ordered printed on the reverse side of the one-dollar bill the image of the "All-Seeing Eye," also called the "Stone of God." This is considered Masonic symbolism and alludes to the Second Coming of Christ. Jesus, in Matthew 21:42, compared himself to, "The stone rejected by the builders has been made the honored cornerstone. How remarkable, what an amazing thing the Lord has done."

In addition to the "Stone of God," Roerich, Wallace and Roosevelt also sought a casket, which Henry equates to the Meru pillar said to contain the head of Osiris.

Henry wondered if the three stars mentioned in Wallace's letter might refer to the three stars in the Tennessee flag. This idea took on more substance when Henry saw the overall plan for the Tennessee Bicentennial Capitol Mall, located just across from the state capitol in Nashville. He believes he has found just such a pillar embedded in the mall's design.

The diagram of the pillar from Mount Meru was found in the Tun-huang manuscript, an collection of ancient texts in Chinese, Tibetan and other Asian languages, which now resides in the National Library of China.

Many theories have been advanced as to the exact meaning of the "Pillar of Meru," thought to have inspired the name of the mountain. The most common, and mystical, meaning is that the pillar closely resembles the human spinal column, which then brings in the subject of chakras or the seven energy centers of the body.

According to Henry, early students of the Hebrew mystical work, the Cabala, regarded Mount Moriah or Meru "as an axis which reached its highest point in the brain."

One scientist who had worked on government particle-beam weapons said the base of the pillar appears similar to a particle accelerator used for energy weapons.

"The massive $55 million public works/temple building project in Nashville is a museum of science and history. Though constructed to commemorate the Tennessee State Bicentennial in 1997, the Capitol Mall temple transcends time," wrote Henry in *City of Peace*. "Its long, green lawn is lined on both sides by oak trees and other vegetation indigenous to Tennessee. The temple stretches over 2,200 feet in length and covers 19 acres. At the apex of the walkway is the fantastic Court of Three Stars, a plaza surrounded by two concentric rings of limestone columns. Each column is four feet in diameter and approximately 25 feet tall. Ninety-five chimes or bells — one for each county in the state — are mounted within the tops of the columns. The bells and columns create a C-shaped (the image of the crescent moon) acoustic chamber or musical instrument called a carillon."

In the center of the Court of Three Stars is an embedded iron nail at the conjunction of three giant stars. When visitors place one foot on the nail and call out, an eerie acoustical effect amplifies the sound as it reverberates off the tall columns.

Of special interest in the mall is a huge 16,861-pound black reflective black granite globe floating on 1/8th inch of water which serves as a memorial to those who worked and served in World War II. When the sun is high and bright, the granite globe — granite's composition includes tiny quartz crystals — gleams with the brightness of the sun. Researchers of the esoteric know that a "Black Sun" was the primary symbol of the Vril Society, an occult group at the center of the black-clad Nazi SS. Even more uncanny is the fact the Nashville's WWII black globe was manufactured in Germany.

On one side of the mall is a black granite wall inscribed with a timeline of Tennessee's history going back ten billion years. Curiously, the timeline, which begins with 1996, moves backward in ten-year increments until the year 1766 after which it leaps to 1600 A.D. In the early 1600s, Sir Francis Bacon, believed by some to be the real author of Shakespeare's work, published *The New Atlantis*, a book which impelled many early colonists to the new lands of America.

The Nashville timeline then amazingly skips back to 10,000 B.C. a time that many people believed encompassed the sinking of fabled Atlantis.

Considering that the design of the Tennessee Capitol Mall compares so favorably to Mount Meru, Henry said this may mean that it is a Holy Grail temple, the temple of King Solomon rebuilt in America on the powerful energy lines perceived by the Native Americans even before the arrival of the settlers.

"Lending credence to this speculation is the fact that the Tennessee Capitol Mall complex is a detailed model of the complete chakra system in plan and elevation on the Earth," he said, explaining, "In the Orient, the seven levels of the caduceus (could this be the seven stars under the three stars mentioned in Wallace's letter?) and psychophysical transformation are known as chakras which are "plexuses," knots or zones of energy that must be "united" or "untied" to achieve enlightenment."

Could the goal of this enlightenment be found in the design of an erstwhile public park in "Music City, U.S.A."?

William Henry also asked, "Is Nashville the new city of the enlightenment rivaling Athens, Rome, Jerusalem and even Luxor or Heliopolis, Egypt, in importance?"

Since 2000, Henry has been taking groups on a tour of the Bicentennial Capitol Mall in the hope that people from all across the world will not only appreciate its beauty but will continue to research its hidden meanings.

"Whether we choose to bring the potential energy of this temple energy into our world or not is our choice," he said. "If we do, a brand new world will emerge."

Tiffany Overtakes Tuesday Weld

Occult Secret Societies in Santa Cruz

by Adam Gorightly

with Douglas Hawes

Santa Cruz, California was the venue for one of my latest adventures in the realms of conspiracy sleuthing. My tour guide for this paradigm-shattering experience was Douglas Hawes, a former Santa Cruzan and part of the city's punk music scene in the late 1980s. Doug and I specifically planned this outing to discuss certain theories revealed to him over the last decade by a certain mysterious "source" he'd mentioned to me numerous times over the course of a yearlong email correspondence.

Doug and I met up at the town's famous eatery, Zachary's, and over breakfast swapped tales of mind control conspiracies and UFO high weirdness. After a couple hours of spirited conversation Doug suggested that we visit his aforementioned "source," to whom he had made many a reference throughout the course of our correspondence, which included stunning revelations regarding a worldwide Illuminati conspiracy engineered by none other than '60s screen starlet Tuesday Weld.

The source of these mind-cracking revelations was 49-year-old Jeffrey Turner, and that being in the presence of this individual, he said half-jokingly, was what he termed "The Jeff Turner Experience." The phenomenon was akin to, Doug went on to say, witnessing The Jimi Hendrix Experience circa '67 behind a hit of Owsley Blue: you leave with a mind fully blown, reeling in the aftermath of said encounter.

Doug first met Jeff Turner in 1987, and soon became privy to Turner's conspiratorial cosmology, which revolves in part around sex kitten Tuesday Weld, who, Turner contends, descended from a royal bloodline of Druid witches. During her childhood, Weld exhibited amazing clairvoyant gifts that quickly brought her to the attention of a concealed Druidic network of families, which Turner claims forms the current Illuminati leadership. In this arena of behind-the-scenes world politics and ritual magic, Weld became a fast-rising prodigy in the Illuminati, and at the youthful age of 15 was chosen as the new Queen and high priestess of the Druids. The initiation rite that signaled her ascension into leadership was the plane crash that carried Buddy Holly, Ritchie Valens, and the Big Bopper to their deaths in February of 1959. According to Turner, the plane had been sabotaged by backers of Weld as part of this ritual which signified her inauguration as Illuminati Queen and High Priestess. Two decades later, this "sacrificial rite" was memorialized in the 1972 #1 hit "American Pie," Don McLean's musical memoir of "the day the music died."

And as the flames climbed high into the night,
To light the sacrificial rite,
I saw Satan laughing with delight,
The day the music died.

These Weldian revelations were just the tip of a weighty iceberg Douglas Hawes laid on me as we walked the two blocks of Pacific Avenue to his car. Along the way, Doug bumped into a young man named Jordy, and the two talked briefly about a certain "project." After parting, Doug stated that Jordy was among a group of filmmakers currently producing a documentary film on none other than Jeff Turner.

During our drive over to Jeff Turner's place, Doug described Turner as someone who is "well connected" and "in the know"; an insider into the shadowy doings of an occult world to which most of us are totally unaware. For whatever reasons, Jeff has become finely tuned into this shadow world, able to read between the lines and make those conspiratorial connections that elude the common man.

Yet, on the other hand, this man of mystery and perpetual conspiracies is a societal outcast, inhabiting a low-rent hovel and subsisting on SSI disability, mainly due to the difficulty he finds functioning in the workaday world. Considered by some an unemployable mooch, Turner isn't overly concerned with clean clothes, tidy living quarters or people's opinions. A certifiable slob, Jeff is unimpressed with social status or what you might have to say about those stains on his shirtsleeve; he is in many ways a man "not of this world." And if even a small percentage of what he says is true, then you sure can't blame the guy for not wanting to play the game of getting ahead or climbing some corporate ladder. Perhaps Jeff sees the limitations of "playing the game" and "getting ahead" as shortsighted in terms of the big picture of what's really going on behind the scenes of world events. I guess washing your clothes or removing that unsightly ring from your toilet bowl is ultimately irrelevant when it comes to exposing satanic cults involved in ritual human sacrifice.

Slob though he may be, Jeff isn't a sloppy thinker. He has a cohesive worldview — however far out it may seem to mainstream America. Jeff possesses an eidetic memory, and a wealth of conspiratorial knowledge that never fails to tie things together in some meaningful fashion. Like his friend

Douglas Hawes insists, there's a consistency to the strange universe Jeff Turner presents in his rapid-fire discourses that could conceivably go on forever, as one subject leads to another and ties back into a convoluted conspiratorial framework, inevitably inspiring the cornered listener to eventually make use of a window of opportunity to ensure a quick getaway.

As we drove over to the Capitola Book Café, Jeff — aware that I had written a tome on the Manson Family — informed me that he had actually known Charles Manson! Jeff went on to say that he and Manson had met a number of times, it turns out, after Charlie was released from prison in 1967, during the Tuesday Weld/Illuminati-inspired conspiracy called "The Summer of Love." When I asked Jeff how he came to meet Manson (was it mere coincidence or something more?) Jeff attributed it all to synchronicity, that perplexing phenomenon widely known to conspiracy buffs and Discordians alike, which attempts to explain those unexplainable coincidences, such as how Jeff's path had been interwoven with the likes of Charles Manson and Tuesday Weld, for strange and unfathomable reasons.

At first exposure to such extraordinary claims, one's natural reaction is to dismiss them as the ravings of the drug-addled or brain-damaged. But the fact of the matter is Jeff doesn't drink or use drugs, and is a regular churchgoer. And while his theories might seem outlandish, there was nothing that came out of our conversations that led me to suspect he'd made this stuff up, which is not to suggest that many of Jeff's central theories aren't simply colorful extrapolations on known facts, or outright confabulations. As Douglas Hawes explains, "(Jeff's) stories have remained consistent over many years. I have asked him repeated questions, using different angles, about the same subjects, time and time again. And his stories remain consistent."

Midway through our Capitola Book Café scone repast, Doug got a cell-phone call from Sean Donnelly of Double Chin Productions, who was on his way over to document our meeting of the minds, which by now was beginning to raise the collective eyebrows of the store's staff. Meanwhile, Jeff — oblivious to the curious reactions of those within earshot — continued to hold court amid the comings and goings of the store's puzzled patrons.

A few minutes later, Donnelly started interviewing Jeff about Tuesday Weld and her Illuminati stranglehold on the '60s counterculture. According to Turner, throughout the late '50s and early '60s, Weld established herself as the "Darling of the Beats," a wild child romantically linked to many leading Hollywood actors of the time, including men twice her age, privately boasting that she was Hollywood's "Lolita." Weld was ahead of her time in terms of her flippant attitude and sense of irreverence, anticipating a social stance that became widely adopted in the heady days of the '60s countercultural explosion.

Behind the scenes, Hollywood insiders heard a different story; that of a divinely ordained priestess with remarkable paranormal powers. Stories circulated among a small group of confidantes about these spiritual gifts, and how Tuesday Weld represented an ancient lineage dating back far into Celtic prehistory. According to these inside sources, Weld was apparently able to levitate, demonstrating her aerial abilities at the Towers of the Flying Men in Rhodesia (now Zimbabwe), flying upward out of those ancient pyramids constructed of basaltic boulders.

Hollywood has always been a focal point for the intrigues of secret societies. Tuesday Weld's Druidic network played a central role, and films that allude to this Weldian influence include the 1962 classic *The Manchurian Candidate*, a film depicting a mind-controlled war hero who has been programmed to assassinate a major political figure. Among the cast of characters, there is a strange figure played by Janet Leigh, who seems like a deliberate invoking of the behind-the-scenes role played by Tuesday Weld in the shadow establishment of the early '60s. This figure seemingly is cognizant of the full dimensions of the plot, is there at all critical points of the story, and appears to be some "guiding hand," or "control," keeping an eye on the whole operation. She speaks in enigmatic, impenetrable phrases, and is a mystery in the context of the film. The character Frank Sinatra plays begins to work with her in an unspecified fashion, and she is there at the end in the final climactic scene. This 1962 film, kept under tight seal for years by Sinatra after the assassination of John Kennedy in 1963, is one of the most important documents of the early '60s.

Screenwriter George Axelrod, *The Manchurian Candidate* scriptwriter, would later direct the 1966 film *Lord Love A Duck,* starring Tuesday Weld. *Lord Love A Duck* was seemingly crafted to propel Weld to a cult-like status, while furthering a countercultural agenda by bringing the beatnik worldview to the masses, thus ushering in the forthcoming rock and roll revolution. Tuesday Weld was right there at the beginnings of the rock and roll scene, appearing as a teenager in the 1956 movie, *Rock! Rock! Rock!* with Chuck Berry, Johnny Burnette, and Frankie Lymon and the Teenagers. She was romantically linked with Dion DeMucci of the famous '50s doo-wop band "Dion and the Belmonts," and was also involved with Elvis Presley, Fabian and Sal Mineo.

Later, according to Turner, Tuesday Weld would intervene to help the Beatles secure their visas for their first American tour in 1964, and she also played a behind-the-scenes role in landing the Beach Boys their Capitol Records contract — as well as singing backup in the studio on their rendition of "Barbara Ann" — at the same time that she was filming *Lord Love a Duck*, playing the character Barbara Ann Greene. But it was really the emergence of the full-blown '60s countercultural revolution that paved the way for Weld's ascendance into popular culture. Here through rock and roll, a vehicle was found through which the concealed Druidic establishment could bring their worldview to the masses, and change the cultural landscape.

Weld's influence on the Beatles was most noticeable during the group's psychedelic phase, and is alluded to in such songs as the dark, foreboding classic "I Am the Walrus" in which the lyrics refer to "stupid bloody Tuesday." The song cryptically mentions a "pornographic priestess" amidst a haunting melody that suggests occult secrets. "I Am the Walrus" appears on *Magical Mystery Tour,* an album littered with bizarre symbolism, such as the white-clad men lining the wall of some strange temple, or the curious walrus costume worn by Paul McCartney, which at the time was seen as embodying the Druidic symbol of death. Other Beatles songs with highly evocative Weldian lyrics include "Lady Madonna," as well as "She Came In Through the Bathroom Window," from the *Abbey Road* album with its chorus, "Tuesday's on the phone to me."

The 1967 Rolling Stones album *Between the Buttons* featured "Ruby Tuesday," a song purportedly about a famous rock groupie. Turner asserts that a long out-of-print biography states that the song was really about Tuesday Weld. The 1968 album *Their Satanic Majesty's Request* was claimed by the band to be a play off of a request made by the Queen of England, but one wonders if it might actually reflect the hidden influence of the concealed satanic majesty that was Tuesday Weld's Illuminati birthright.

Also during this period, Anton LaVey established the Church of Satan in San Francisco. LaVey would soon dedicate his *Satanic Bible* to Marilyn Monroe and Tuesday Weld. In the 1972 book, *Popular Witchcraft,* published by Bowling Green University Press, LaVey described his *Satanic Bible* dedication to Tuesday Weld as "part of the magical ritual." In his explanation of this dedication, LaVey revealed a deep and intimate acquaintanceship with Weld's character.

As previously mentioned, Tuesday Weld had a close relationship with the Beach Boys and, as is now generally known, members of the group became closely involved with the dark personality of Charlie Manson. Interestingly enough, in the months preceding Sharon Tate's murder, and the related LaBianca murders of August 1969, Charlie Manson was named "man of the year" by a street publication distributed in Hollywood titled *Tuesday's Child*. In the wake of the Tate-LaBianca murders, Tuesday Weld — along with quite a few other Hollywood personalities — was called in by the Los Angeles County Sheriff's Department for questioning.

These were just some of the stunning revelations that Jeff Turner shared with us that day over coffee and scones.

As it turns out, Jeff Turner's seemingly bizarre conspiratorial cosmology involves a former Santa Cruz resident, whose name shall go unwritten for obvious legal reasons. We'll simply refer to her as the abbreviated "K.M."

According to Turner, K.M., as an adolescent in the late 1960s, got involved in satanic circles in the South Bay, and soon became a protégé of Tuesday Weld. Over time, K.M. built an occult crime club around herself and, in 1974, assumed control of the notorious Process Church of the Final Judgment, a satanic organization linked by conspiracy literature to the Manson Family and the Son of Sam killings.

In time, the Weld/K.M. alliance soured and they became bitter enemies. Up until 1991, the two engaged in an ongoing war carried out by K.M.'s supporters and the opposing Weldian faction. Concurrently, K.M. cultivated a powerful satanic cult — with ties to the World Nazi Network — conducting a virtual reign of terror throughout Santa Cruz and Santa Clara counties.

As Douglas Hawes explained, "Back in 1986–88 Santa Cruz was a whirlpool of weird psychic energies. Anton LaVey was rumored to be living in a house on Wharf Road in Capitola. Tuesday Weld and her archrival K.M. were waging a behind-the-scenes occult war for supremacy in the city...

"There is no public knowledge of K.M.'s involvement in the Process Church." A four-and-a-half-year-long investigation by the Santa Clara County District Attorney into her activities was never made public because an indictment was never issued. So she has "received absolutely no publicity of any kind ... The Federal government has some kind of ongoing investigation into K.M.'s activities. My hunch is that the Feds realize that she knows too much, has compromised too many powerful people, and so could not be taken down without exacting a terrible toll."

Meanwhile, according to Doug, K.M. has promoted the public image of a concerned community activist with important connections and influence in political circles, who remain unaware of her occult and criminal activities.

As synchronicity would have it, Turner was a contemporary of K.M., attending the same high school as this wicked high priestess, who, he asserts, has been involved in child sacrifice rituals. Due to this dangerous knowledge, and his opposition to K.M., Turner was subsequently persecuted by her satanic henchmen. Several years after graduating from high school, Turner claims he was approached by the CIA and recruited into their network directed against K.M. More recently, Turner claims to have provided a sizeable body of materials to former governor George Deukmejian's Special Select Task Force on Satanic Abatement.

In December, 1991 (Turner went on to inform me), Tuesday Weld stepped down from her lofty perch as the "all-seeing eye" of the Illuminati at the request of someone by the name of Tiffany. I didn't have a clue who this Tiffany person was that Turner was going on about, until he explained that she was the famous pop singer by the same name. When Turner mentioned the song "I Think We're Alone Now" that triggered dim recollections of the short-lived Tiffany phenomenon, which hit its peak in the late 1980s.

Tiffany Renee Darwish began performing at an early age on the country and western circuit. In the early '80s, according to Turner, Tiffany became an MK-ULTRA mind-control victim at the diabolical hands of certain well-known country music stars that were later exposed in the controversial tome, *Trance Formation In America* by Cathy O'Brien and Mark Phillips. Eventually, Tiffany was able to break free of her programming and by the late 1980s became an MTV sensation. During this period, Tiffany's mother filed a missing person's report, and in return, Tiffany, then 17, filed for legal emancipation status as a minor. This made-for-TV production played itself out in a Los Angeles court trial in 1988, with Tiffany eventually winning the case. This is where our story takes another bizarre twist...

As I later discovered, Jeff Turner — the unconventional hero of our story — appeared at the courthouse after the trial and presented Tiffany with a samurai sword and bouquet of flowers to congratulate her on the victory. When sheriffs saw the sword, they became alarmed and placed Turner under arrest, which in Turner's estimation was a gross overreaction; he claimed it was a simple and loving gesture. Jeff later testified that he chose the sword and flowers because Tiffany likes Japan and receiving these items was considered a high honor in that country. Charges were later dropped against Turner when he repeatedly stressed to the authorities that the sword was dulled, and had been declared a ceremonial art object.

At a subsequent hearing, Turner was charged with falsifying DMV documents to obtain Tiffany's home address and, as a result, was slapped with a restraining order. However, Turner claims that the restraining order was not Tiffany's actual doing, but that of her aunt, who had developed an irrational hatred of him. According to the Sept. 27, 1989 edition of *Santa Cruz Register*, Turner was quoted as saying that Tiffany intended to marry him and, against her wishes, had been forced by family members to request the restraining order. Turner further claimed he was a distant relative to Tiffany, and that her mother and father had betrothed the two before their births per Lebanese tradition. In the aforementioned article, Turner stated that he was born to a "Lebanese mother, who was part of this arranged marriage." Turner further claimed that his mother's maiden name was Darwish, the same as Tiffany's, and he was unaware of his lineage until informed of it by Tiffany's family, who purportedly kept tabs on him over the years.

The 1989 *Register* article states that the petition for the restraining order alleged that "(Jeff) Turner wrote love letters to Tiffany. Turner said he wrote about 10 letters, but that Tiffany also wrote him love letters. Turner said she sent a cousin to stay in his rooming house and read the letters to him, in accordance, Turner said, with Middle Eastern tradition..." As it so happens, Douglas Hawes met this particular individual, Khalid Mansour, alleged to be Tiffany's cousin. Mansour lived with Turner in a boarding house in Santa Cruz in 1988, which is where Turner claims he viewed the letters in question. Hawes suspects that under heavy family pressures, and Tiffany's own gut instinct, she bailed out on the arranged marriage, as she didn't really know who Jeff Turner was until she encountered him over a period of time, and had a chance to reassess the arranged marriage proposal.

As previously noted, Turner claims that Tiffany was responsible for breaking up Tuesday Weld's purported occult organization and is currently attempting to dismantle K.M.'s satanic network as well. In this regard, Tiffany is the leader of the "All Nations Movement," a super-secret society attempting to bring order to the world. Furthermore, Tiffany — whose Lebanese family initiated her into the Sufi tradition — is now recognized as a master in international Sufi circles, and has used this influence to weed out negative elements that exist in certain secret societies and occult orders, such as those affiliated with K.M. and, formerly, Tuesday Weld.

Whatever the case, by the time we departed the Book Café my brain was suffering from severe sensory overload, saturated to the point where any further conspiratorial information was sure just to lap over my brainpan and form a lunatic puddle at my feet for me to ooze away in.

As Douglas Hawes readily admits, "You might be scratching your head about Jeff Turner, and I acknowledge he is an oddball, but he is indeed "inside the loop"... I have learned an immense amount of stuff through my association with him, over a 17-year period."

Afterwards, we returned to Turner's apartment. As we made our way to his front door, we were discussing a couple different topics: 1) the unkempt nature of Jeff's living quarters, and in particular his bathroom, and 2) a certain radionics/psychotronics device in his house that allowed Jeff to quantum mechanically travel through time and space. I made the tongue-in-cheek quip that maybe Jeff could adjust the waves from his radionics machine to psychotronically clean his bathroom.

Once inside, we were barely able to navigate through Jeff's living room, scattered as it was with overflowing clothes piles amid bedding, books and magazines stacked to the rafters. As we entered Turner's bedroom and beheld his legendary psychotronic machine I felt like I'd stumbled into a scene from Richard Linklater's *Slacker*. The machine itself consisted of a half dozen or so small transformer boxes with antennas poking out resembling items you could purchase at a Radio Shack. Situated around the antenna boxes were a potpourri of curiosities, which included a dozen or so small vials, one that said something like "Cosmic Energy Elixir"; assorted medallions that bore some seemingly mystical relation to "All Nations Movement" leader Tiffany; and several film developing envelopes with "Tiffany" scribbled on them. Next to this strange contraption — which I will henceforth refer to as the "Psychotronic Tiffany Shrine" — rested a chair with an old-school-looking football helmet on it that was hard-wired (you guessed it) into the Psychotronic Tiffany Shrine. Turner apparently places this retro space-age helmet on his head, then fires up the psychotroni whatchamacallit, ostensibly beaming his cerebral cortex to Tiffany across time and infinite space.

Reverently, Turner removed the photo envelopes marked "Tiffany" from his psychotronic shrine. Then, holding them up for us to see, thumbed through a half-dozen or so photos that featured him and Tiffany posing happily together in a series of typical fan-type shots taken at a Santa Cruz Boardwalk concert last summer, as well as the GlamourCon event in Los Angeles. Tiffany, now in her thirties, interacts with Turner at events such as these in a chummy fashion, which is surprising given their checkered history. According to Douglas Hawes, there's a lot that will be revealed about the Jeff Turner/Tiffany connection in the forthcoming documentary.

From a chest of drawers, Turner pulled out some photos of a display he'd put together a couple years earlier for the Santa Cruz Public Library. Presented under a glass case, it featured a Tiffany photo arranged in the center of the display surrounded by an array of books dedicated to time travel, quantum physics and the paranormal. Apparently, Turner believes that Tiffany is not only the leader of a feel-good secret society and high Sufi master, but is also a multi-dimensional time traveler.

As late afternoon rolled around, I bid Jeff and Doug farewell, having a three-hour drive back home. Next time I see him, I'll have to ask if Tiffany can do something about the traffic.

A great deal has transpired since these interviews took place in Santa Cruz in early December 2004. The documentary *I Think We're Alone Now* (www.ithinkwerealonenow.com) premiered at the Slamdance Film Festival in Park City, Utah in January 2008, and is now being shown to audiences at film festivals throughout North America. Turner's assertions about the unique behind-the-scenes role of Tuesday Weld were the basis of the cover story "Tuesday Weld: High Priestess of the Illuminati?" which appeared in the Spring 2008 issue of *Paranoia* magazine.

PARASCIENCE

Are Aliens and Their Technology Underground and Undersea?

by Richard Sauder

I don't see any way around this issue: repeatedly in my underground and underwater bases and tunnels research I have encountered the theme of purported aliens. I will be frank with you from the outset: I positively do not know the truth behind these stories.

Having said that, this highly strange issue of purported *aliens* underground and/or underwater is exceedingly persistent. I can conceive of a whole wide gamut of possibilities, of lies within lies, conspiracies within conspiracies, insidious agendas of cover-up, concealment and deception — as well as the very real possibility that there is a substantial kernel of truth to at least some, and perhaps most of the accounts. If the realm of clandestine underground and underwater bases and tunnels is a strange and highly secretive place (and it is!), well then, adding purported aliens to the mix and stirring up the whole caboodle to boot, makes the whole affair even stranger.

My intention is not to draw firm conclusions on the matter, because I cannot. I simply do not know for certain what is going on and I am telling you that now as plainly as I can. But what I can do is to present for you representative information that I have encountered in the course of my research. What I will set out for you here is not exhaustive. I have not read everything there is to read; I have not talked to everyone there is to talk to; I do not know all the stories there are to know.

I have read a lot of mind-bending literature over the years, including my own, but little can top the first few pages of *The Ultimate Alien Agenda*, by James Walden. I picked up this intriguing little book in a used bookstore and have read and reread the first several pages multiple times — that's how puzzling I find the author's story.

To make a long story short, James Walden alleges that he was abducted by alien beings and taken to a secret, deep underground facility where he was subjected to an involuntary, intimate and intrusive examination procedure that was observed by upwards of 100 others who were in attendance. Moreover, he alleges that not all of the beings present were aliens — some of the other beings present were human beings, much like himself. It appeared to him that the ostensible aliens who purportedly abducted him were in cahoots with other human beings who were in on the game — whatever this highly strange game may involve.

At the conclusion of the intrusive and humiliating medical examination to which he was subjected, he was informed telepathically:[1]

> You are in an underground facility located beneath southeast Kansas.

As the alien voice spoke he saw a vision of the rural Kansas countryside far above. The telepathic voice went on to say that he was "participating in a peaceful, cooperative experiment" and added that he would not be harmed. As he pondered the other humans he saw gathered around him, the telepathic voice spoke again and said:[2]

> These human workers are volunteers who are learning to control human disease.

Walden's strange story continues on from this juncture at some length. If you want to know the rest of the details you will have to read his book. But for the purposes of this chapter the bare bones of his story as presented above are quite fascinating enough, in and of themselves.

But can it be true? Are there really secret underground bases under the American Midwest in which aliens and human researchers work in great secrecy, cheek by jowl, and to which unsuspecting humans such as James Walden are abducted, there to be poked and prodded — as if they were nothing more than laboratory subjects in a medical school amphitheater?

I reiterate that I don't know the answer to this question. However, more and more people seem to be coming forward to report this sort of experience as the years pass. It certainly appears possible that highly covert and uncommonly strange goings-on might be transpiring underground.

Joint Military and Alien Abductions to Underground Bases?

In an important book, *MILABS*[3], that examines the many arcane aspects of the American military's research into mind control technology and experimentation, Helmut and Marion Lammer point out that a number of people who have reported being abducted and taken to underground bases have reported seeing both human military personnel and aliens present together in clandestine subterranean facilities, or, alternatively, of being taken underground by means of technology that seems alien, where they may encounter yet more alien-seeming technology. The reasons for these experiences and the possible reality behind these unusual reports remain perfectly obscure. Whatever is going on, it is largely kept hidden from public view; many of the stories only filter out at the periphery of consensual reality, in books such as *MILABS* and *The Ultimate Alien Agenda*, that are issued by small, unconventional publishers who are willing to take a chance on subject matter that the huge publishing houses in New York and London won't touch.

Here is just one of the thought-provoking stories that the Lammers include in *MILABS*. The account stems from the experiences of a pseudonymous woman named Evelyn.[4]

> I can remember flying in a beautiful, golden ship and it went into a mountainside and flew under the ground, into a huge cavernous room, where to my surprise, were human beings, dressed in military uniforms, with machine guns slung behind their backs. I walked in a line with some other people and we passed through an "energized" gate that somehow does something to your atoms. I remarked to myself: "The military have some alien technology."

This is certainly a most unusual story. At first blush it seems like such a radical departure from consensual reality that it is not credible, and is more likely a fantasy or a surreal dream of some sort. But what if it is true? What if this brief account as told by "Evelyn" faithfully reflects an experience that really happened to her? I pose this question because in recent years I have heard and read more unusual stories like this than I would have formerly dared think possible. I can see two possibilities: either an awful lot of people are telling wonderfully entertaining and confabulated fibs, or something highly strange involving *aliens* (whoever and whatever they may ultimately prove to be) and covert elements of the United States military, working together underground, and possibly undersea, as well, is taking place.

Alien Bodies Kept Underground in California?

In the fascinating book *Glimpses of Other Realities, Volume II: High Strangeness*,[5] journalist Linda Moulton Howe cites the puzzling experiences of an abductee named Linda Porter. I want to mention two aspects of Linda Porter's story that are directly germane to the underground and underwater bases theme of this article. I also want to say that Linda Porter's reported experiences resonate to a certain degree with certain aspects of my own research, such that I am inclined to listen to what she has to say with a little more care than I otherwise might. Ms. Porter's experiences have to do in part with an alleged secret underground base in the San Diego, California area and another alleged base underwater, beneath the seabed off the California coast. It would be my educated guess that the United States Navy, as well as other agencies and organizations, whether publicly known or completely unknown to the public at large, have secretly constructed and operate underwater bases in California coastal waters. I have been told that there are underground bases onshore, not only in the San Diego area, but elsewhere in California, as, for example, at the massive U.S. Navy installation at China Lake, near the town of Ridgecrest.

With regard to the underground base near San Diego, Linda Porter alleges that her alien abductors told her that there was an underground facility called "Sycamore Remote Facility run by General Dynamics." And in this alleged, highly secure underground facility, the United States government is said to hold alien beings in suspended animation, in transparent, computer-monitored containers. One specific human-like being held in this facility was of particular interest to the aliens who wanted him back. Adding further to the air of mystery surrounding this story, Linda Porter says that there are "underground tram systems that lead from the naval base in San Diego to this facility and to another place."[6]

Porter goes on to say that the "other place" is a normal-looking house with an attached garage that is the actual entrance to the underground facility where the bodies of the alien beings were being held. If her story is true then this would be very clever concealment indeed.

Linda Porter also describes an undersea facility. Her description fascinates me:[7]

> I was supposedly taken to an underground base off the coast of California. For some reason I was led to believe it was in the Santa Barbara area. If you were standing on sand at the bottom of the ocean (where this place is), all you could see is what looks like a silver submarine conning tower rising up out of the sand. And it would probably be the height of a two or three story building. I was told this tower thing was camouflaged by an electronic net of some kind that renders it invisible. And they also have something around it that seems to repel people and fish for some reason.
>
> Inside the building the floors and the walls and the ceiling were all a silver-grey color. There was a lot of light. But the doors — and there seemed to be doors all over the place — were brightly colored. They were either bright red or bright blue or bright yellow. And over each door was some kind of writing that looked like hieroglyphic or Arabic writing or something like that.

No doubt there will be those who will read Linda Porter's stories about her reported experiences and dismiss them as too fantastic to be credible. But I believe that Linda Porter's stories may very possibly contain a substantial kernel of truth. Here is why I find it easy to believe that the U.S. Navy might have a clandestine underground facility in the vicinity of its important base at San Diego, and why there may even be multiple underground bases in that region of California. Simply put, my research reveals unambiguously, via the U.S. Navy's own documentation, that the Navy has an interest in constructing underground facilities, and that the interest goes back many years into the past. Given the Navy's longtime presence in the San Diego area, and its technical capabilities, it should be veritable child's play to construct such facilities in and around San Diego.

When I read Ms. Porter's account of the alleged undersea base off the coast of California, I instantly recognized that what she describes is perfectly consonant with the technology for constructing a manned undersea base that is put forth in an official U.S. Navy document from 1966[8] — a document that I cited in my 2001 book, *Underwater and Underground Bases*. In this eye-opening, U.S. Navy "Rock-Site" document, the Navy proposes building undersea bases by cementing a huge metal cylinder, or pipe, in the ocean floor, and then using that huge, metal pipe as an entrance to the sea bed, from which a large, manned, undersea base can be constructed.

In other words, Ms. Porter describes an underwater facility off the coast of California that corresponds almost precisely to the planned entrance to a United States military "Rock-Site" underwater base, as described decades earlier in an official, U.S. Navy document.

What if the U.S. Navy has secret underwater and underground bases where highly strange activities transpire? Activities that may strain the boundaries of what the "dumbed-down" mass mind of popular American culture considers to be possible? I am willing to entertain the idea that the world just may be a far stranger place than the majority of people who read this book are prepared to believe.

Underground Alien Communication Training?

Other possible evidence for covert dealings between the United States military and purported alien beings (whoever or whatever they may finally prove to be, and from wherever or whenever they may hail) appears in an enigmatic little book by Dan Sherman titled *Above Black: Project Preserve Destiny*,[9] purporting to be a true-life account of Mr. Sherman's experiences. In a nutshell, Dan Sherman is an ex-Air Force sergeant who maintains that he was covertly trained in a clandestine underground facility in Maryland as an intuitive communicator between the National Security Agency and ostensibly alien beings. He served in the Air Force as an electronic intelligence specialist and says that he performed duties for the NSA on the side as an alien communicator, using his regular Air Force duties as a cover.

His saga began when he was ordered to Ft. Meade, Maryland, where the NSA is headquartered, to attend an electronic intelligence course. As it turned out, he attended the assigned course and much more. In the evenings, after his regular classes had finished, he was driven to an unknown underground facility which he entered via an elevator ride straight down, where he was trained to mentally communicate with aliens. After a three-year period as an alien communicator, he began to receive communications that appeared to him to have something to do with the abduction of humans by aliens. Ultimately, he decided to abandon his participation in the alien communication project and to leave the Air Force.

Dan Sherman's is yet another strange story, in a slightly different permutation of the increasingly familiar elements of extreme military secrecy, alien beings and clandestine underground (or undersea) facilities. Story after story, book after book, the personal experiences keep coming.

What on Earth is going on? Or, should I say, what *under* Earth is going on?

What About Area 51?

Unsubstantiated stories about alleged aliens at Area 51 have been making the rounds of the UFOlogical rumor mill for years. I have heard and read stories that purport to tell of aliens held captive there, or of exotic flying saucers stored there, undergoing back engineering and flight testing. The truth of these sorts of stories remains very much in question. And still they keep coming.

One of the most interesting of these accounts that I have seen appeared in an interview in *Nexus* magazine.[10] David Adair, a former teenage engineering prodigy, alleges that he designed a type of fusion rocket prototype that came to the U.S. Air Force's attention back in early 1971. The Air Force was so interested in what he had done that they bundled him off to Area 51 for a personal consultation. Once at Area 51 they took him underground to examine what he surmised was a real fusion rocket engine, albeit one that he believes must have been alien technology, owing to its large size and sophisticated, exotic engineering.

The elevator that took him and his escorts underground was the size of a football field, clearly designed to raise and lower very large and heavy equipment. According to Adair, the elevator platform was supported by a dozen or more giant worm screws, the physical dimensions of which he compared to sequoia trees. These enormous worm screws could bear an extremely heavy load and slowly dropped the entire platform straight down about 200 feet to a vast underground work area. The subterranean region was so stupendously big that it seemed to him that it could accommodate one hundred Boeing 747 jumbo jets with plenty of room to spare. The underground room had a huge ceiling and stretched completely out of sight into the distance. On the way to examine the alien fusion engine he was escorted past a series of exotic aircraft, some of which he recognized, others of which he did not.

Adair alleges that once he examined the novel fusion engine, which was the size of a bus, he came to the following conclusions: 1) it was of extraterrestrial manufacture; 2) it had to have been built in deep, intergalactic space; 3) it was a self-aware, living machine that seemed to be an amalgam of organic and inorganic components; 4) its manufacture was seamless, as though it had been grown, not built; and 5) the U.S. Air Force appeared to not understand the engine.

And to top it all off, at the time he was only 17 years old, and therefore not of legal age. This mattered, because as a legal minor he could not legally be held to a National Security Oath and thereby prevented from talking about what he saw and experienced underground at Area 51 in 1971.

If Adair's story is true, and if the other stories of aliens or alien technology underground are equally true, then one very powerful motive for the high degree of secrecy that conceals clandestine underground and undersea activities becomes clear: to cover up extraterrestrial and/or alien realities. The prime impetus to secrecy then becomes social control, and not national security. It's hard to control people's minds and thoughts (and hence their bodies and actions) once they firmly grasp that not only are we not alone in the universe, we are not even alone on *this* planet. And perhaps never have been.

Unearthly Disclosure

The bestselling British author and researcher Timothy Good has written a series of fascinating books dealing with the question of a possible alien presence on Earth. I won't take the trouble of summarizing the entire body of his work, but Good has traveled the world in pursuit of answers to this intriguing question. He has spoken to myriad, knowledgeable individuals, in and out of government, and come to a carefully considered conclusion.

Good has come down in support of a probable alien presence on Earth, albeit a rather crafty presence. At the end of his book *Unearthly Disclosure*, he states:[11]

I, for one, would welcome an official disclosure to the effect that we share this planet with denizens of other planets.

Earlier in *Unearthly Disclosure* Good devotes several passages to information about purported alien bases said to be located both underground and undersea. He discusses a variety of locations around the world for these alleged undersea and underground alien bases, including Puerto Rico and adjoining waters of the Caribbean Sea, various locations beneath the Pacific Ocean, as well as a number of states in the USA, including New Mexico, West Virginia and Alaska, and also at Pine Gap, Australia.

Timothy Good is a careful researcher; his writing style is deliberate and measured. In mentioning the vicinity of the American military intelligence base at Pine Gap, Australia as a possible alien underground base site,[12] we see once again the idea of American military knowledge of an alien presence, if not outright interaction between the American military and certain alien factions.

This is a theme that I have encountered repeatedly in my research. It may be a disinformation ploy intended to deflect serious scrutiny of clandestine activities that various agencies and organizations wish to conceal from public view. Alternatively, maybe there truly are aliens on Earth and maybe the American military really does have knowledge of them and really does secretly interact with them. A growing body of evidence suggests that may be the case.

Is This The Real Flying Saucer?

What are the great secrets that the covert underground and underwater bases are hiding? Have huge advances and discoveries really been made and kept hidden in enormous bases beneath the surface of the land and sea, away from the open gaze of the public who have been fooled into silence and ignorance?

This question must be asked because of the information presented in *Look* magazine in 1955. Beginning in the immediate post-WWII years with the Kenneth Arnold UFO sighting and the rumors of a crashed flying saucer near Roswell, New Mexico, there has been a continuous stream of unexplained UFO sightings and encounters in the United States and around the world. The 1950s were certainly no exception. As a young child I can remember very well that UFOs were seen in tidewater Virginia near my boyhood home.

So it was not out of the ordinary to have a popular, mass-circulation magazine ask, "Is This The Real Flying Saucer?"[13] To read it a half-century later is to ponder what might have been made public — but perhaps has been hushed up instead.

The original *Look* magazine article supplied the following caption for an illustration: "Future airports built for vertically rising saucers would have no need of the long, vulnerable runways today's fighters require. The complete operation could go underground. Tunnels with take-off shafts set into the ground, complete with maintenance bays, fuel and crew quarters, would be bombproof shelters for a saucer squadron. The shafts would be sealed after take-off for camouflage and protection." (Source: *Look*, 14 June 1955.)

Where in the world did this idea for a huge, camouflaged, underground, flying saucer base beneath a rugged mountain chain come from? The idea of secret underground bases did not have popular currency in 1955, not the way it does now. Flying saucers were a great mystery in those days, as they still are.

In its second paragraph, the *Look* article lets fly with this broadside: "Persistent and fairly credible rumors recur that a Canadian aircraft manufacturer, A.V. Roe, Canada, Ltd., has had a saucer design under development for two years."[14] And the article continues: "The A.V. Roe people maintain a confusing silence about the whole thing."[15]

In 1958 A.V. Roe purchased the Dominion Steel Company,[16] which just happened to own, through a subsidiary, the undersea Wabana iron mines at Bell Island, Newfoundland, where undersea mining production was carried out up until 1966.[17] These seemingly trivial facts have caught my attention, because just three years after iron mining ceased, the abandoned Wabana mine was mentioned in a 1969 report as a potential candidate site for development into a prototype, manned, United States Navy sub-sea-floor base.[18] Is this just a coincidence or is there a connection? Is it possible that A.V. Roe developed a working flying saucer technology and based such machines in clandestine underground or undersea bases, perhaps working through a subsidiary in concert with the United States Navy? Though the Wabana Mine is now officially out of production, and the A.V. Roe Canada company no longer exists,[19] the documentary evidence trail is curious enough that the question begs to be asked.

The *Look* article continues by observing that a military fighter plane that could fly very fast and maneuver easily and vertically, as well as attain very high altitudes, would be a desirable component of the United States military's arsenal. It even provides a large and detailed sketch of what such a saucer might look like and closes with these enigmatic words: "(B)ased on the current requirements of our defense effort and the demonstrated abilities of our engineers, an educated guess is that a flying saucer much like this one may well be flying within the next few years."[20]

Such a flying saucer, if actually built, has never been publicly displayed. And A.V. Roe made a very splashy, public display of its *failure* to produce a working flying saucer and the whole A.V. Roe flying saucer story quickly dried up and, for the most part, went quietly away.[21]

Interestingly, people the world over have continued to see flying saucers, through the years to the present day. Moreover, my research has conclusively demonstrated the existence of covert underground bases, and the probable existence of clandestine, manned, sub-sea-floor bases, as well.

As my research continues, and the stories and evidence accumulate, I am left with the feeling that quite a lot is going on in clandestine facilities, programs and projects located deep underground and undersea — *and we are not being told about it*. My abiding suspicion is that my research but scratches the surface of what there is to know and discover on this topic.

Endnotes

1   James L. Walden, *The Ultimate Alien Agenda: The Re-engineering of Humankind* (St. Paul, Minnesota: Llewellyn Publications, 1998), 6.

2   Ibid., 7.

3   Helmut and Marion Lammer, *MILABS!: Military Mind Control and Alien Abduction* (Lilburn, Georgia:

IllumiNet Press, 1999.)

4   Ibid., 88–89.

5   Linda Moulton Howe, *Glimpses of Other Realities, Volume II: High Strangeness* (New Orleans, Louisiana: Paper Chase Press, 1998). Although another edition of *Glimpses of Other Realities* was subsequently published in 2001 by LMH Productions as ISBN 0-9620570-3-7, I cite only the Paper Chase Press edition here.

6   Ibid., 249–250.

7   Ibid., 244.

8   C.F. Austin, *Manned Undersea Structures- The Rock-Site Concept*, NOTS TP 4162, U.S. Naval Ordnance Test Station, China Lake, California, October 1966.

9   Dan Sherman, *Above Black: Project Preserve Destiny* (Wilsonville, Oregon: OneTeam Publishing, 2001).

10   Robert M. Stanley, "Electromagnetic Fusion and ET Space Technology," *Nexus New Times Magazine* USA/Canadian Edition, Vol. 9, No. 5 (September-October 2002): 53–57, 74–75.

11   Timothy Good, *Unearthly Disclosure* (London, UK: Arrow Books, 2001), 323.

12   Ibid., 315–316.

13   Ben Kocivar, "Is This The Real Flying Saucer?", *Look* Vol. 19, No. 12 (14 June 1955): 44–46.

14   Ibid., 44.

15   Ibid., 44–45.

16   Bill Zuk, *Avrocar: Canada's Flying Saucer: The Story of Avro Canada's Secret Projects* (Erin, Ontario: Boston Mills Press, 2001).

17   Call For Proposals On Exempt Mineral Land, Bell Island, Avalon Peninsula, Newfoundland and Labrador, Canada, Department of Natural Resources, Mines Branch, St. Johns, Newfoundland and Labrador, August 2004, at http://www.gov.nl.ca/mines&en/cfp/bellisland.pdf, 2004.

18   Carl F. Austin and William A. Wundrack, *The Potential For Converting An Existing Undersea Mine To A Rock-Site-I Installation,* unpublished manuscript, circa 1969.

19   *Avro Canada,* at http://www.brainyencyclopedia.com/encyclopedia/a/av/avro_canada.html, 2004.

20   Ben Kocivar, *Look*, 46.

21   See Bill Zuk, Avrocar.

The Secret History of NASA

by Mike Bara

> *All government agencies lie part of the time, but NASA is the only one I've ever encountered that does so routinely.*
> — George A. Keyworth, Science Advisor to President Reagan, in testimony before Congress, March 14, 1985

For many Americans, the name NASA brings back a rush of patriotic memories of the 1960s space race with the Soviet Union. It was a time of clean-cut heroes, rock-jawed Mission Control technicians, can-do engineers and visionary politicians. Astronauts were hurtled into the void in primitive capsules mounted on rickety missiles that were barely more than contained bombs. We watched in wonder as our boys achieved one space-related miracle after another. When a major catastrophe befell the men of Apollo 13, all these titanic forces joined together and brought them home against impossible odds. Not to be deterred, we resumed our explorations of the Moon and sent probes to Mars and the outer planets. It would be hard to imagine a more optimistic era, a time when we believed as a nation in our ability to do anything and the righteousness of our causes.

The public façade presented by the NASA was in every way congruent with this perception. But the truth was that the Agency had been literally born in a lie and had purposefully concealed many unpleasant truths about the men who walked its hallowed halls.

Some of their names are synonymous with America's achievements, men like Dr. Wernher von Braun and astronauts like Alan Shepard and Buzz Aldrin. Unfortunately, in many cases these were also men with dark pasts and secret allegiances. And there are equally as many names that you have most likely never heard associated with our space program, but who had just as much influence over where we went and why we went there. They are German, Egyptian, English and American, but they are hardly representative of the best each of these nations has to offer.

What they are, in fact, are men at the very fringes of rational thought and conventional wisdom.

These fringe elements were divided into three main groups inside the space agency. For purposes of clarity we (myself and Richard C. Hoagland, my co-author on *Dark Mission)* call them the "Magicians," the "Masons," and the "Nazis." Each of these groups has stamped their own agenda on our space program in indelible ways. And each is dominated by a secret or "occult" doctrine that is far more closely aligned with ancient religion and mysticism than it is with the logical science and cool empiricism they promote to the general public.

Boosted by the science of archaeo-astronomy — the practice of using computer-generated star maps to literally look back in time — we discovered that NASA and these secret societies that quietly dominated the Agency appeared to be very interested in the possibility that someone had inhabited vast tracts of real estate throughout the Solar System in a far-distant epoch. They sought to discover (and then hide) not merely the existence of these ruins, but apparently also the secret of what happened to the builders of them.

Using these computer programs we were also able to establish a pattern of behavior on NASA's part that points to an internal obsession by the Agency with three gods and goddesses of ancient Egypt; Isis, Osiris, and Horus. It is these same three Egyptian gods that are also the key to understanding the history of not only the Masonic Order, but those we call Magicians and the Nazis as well.

The true and secret history of NASA cannot be understood without appreciating not just the influence that these gods of ancient Egypt had on Freemasonry, but also the corresponding influence that the Freemasons and the other groups had on NASA itself. For that, we must go back to the beginning.

* * *

The National Aeronautics and Space Administration was created by an act of Congress on July 29th, 1958. Its ostensible purpose was to act as a civilian science agency for the betterment of mankind and to enhance the defense of the United States of America. We have always been taught that NASA was a civilian agency, beholden only to the will of the people through their representatives in Congress. The Act itself however, paints a far different picture. From the beginning, NASA was subservient to the Department of Defense, subject to the whims of the Pentagon on any issue judged to be "necessary to make effective provision for the defense of the United States." It was required under the Act to make available "to agencies directly concerned with national defense ... discoveries that have military value or significance." The upshot of this is that the agency was compromised almost from its inception.

Shortly after its birth, the newly-formed government agency commissioned a study by the Brookings Institute, then the most influential think tank in North America, to determine the future course of its explorations into space and to study the implications on American society of any discoveries it might make. The report, formally titled *Proposed Studies on the Implications of Peaceful Space Activities for Human Affairs,* was a wide-ranging document that included what would later be viewed as extremely significant passages. These passages dealt with the potential consequences to our culture in the event that NASA discovered *"artifacts left at some point in time... on the Moon, Mars, or Venus..."* It went on to recommend that if such a discovery was made, NASA should give serious consideration to the possibility of withholding disclosure of it, on the grounds that such a revelation, if made prematurely and without a sufficient period of "cultural preparation," could result in the literal *disintegration* (it actually used that word) of American society.

Such is how a cover-up is born.

It is our position that these recommendations made to NASA at the very dawn of the space age became the occult, official policy of the Agency behind the scenes. In this light, NASA's otherwise inexplicable behavior when confronted with evidence of exactly the kind of discovery that Bookings warned of — evidence of extraterrestrial artifacts on Mars a generation later — suddenly seems to make sense.

On July 25, 1976, a project scientist at NASA's Jet Propulsion Laboratory in Pasadena named Tobias Owen put a magnifying glass over Viking 1 Orbiter frame 35A72 and exclaimed "Hey, look at this!" What he saw was a mile-wide, 1,500-foot-tall edifice that would come to be popularly known as "The Face on Mars."

The next day, NASA held a daily press briefing in which the Face was the unquestioned highlight. Dr. Gerald Soffen, a Viking project scientist, addressed the assembled press, including at the time my *Dark Mission* co-author. Soffen introduced the Face image with the statement "Isn't it peculiar what tricks of light and shadow can do? When we took another picture a few hours later, it all went away; it was just a trick, just the way the light fell on it."[1]

That last statement was later proven to be an outright falsehood, and it eventually became the first chink in the armor of the previously unassailed integrity of the space agency. Although the Face made newspaper headlines all over the world the next day, no journalist, including Hoagland, took it seriously. They all accepted NASA's explanation that there were disconfirming photos taken later that same Martian day.

A few years later, a pair of imaging specialists at NASA's Goddard Space Flight Center, Vince Dipietro and Gregory Molenaar, decided to look up the Face image. They quickly found 35A72 (labeled simply "Head" in the Viking image files) and their early enhancements seemed to argue against the "trick of light and shadow" explanation. They then searched for other possible images of the Face taken on later orbits. They were surprised to find both that potentially interesting images of the Face taken on subsequent orbits seemed to have disappeared from the archive, and there seemed to be no trace of the "disconfirming photographs" that Dr. Soffen had alluded to five years earlier. After an exhaustive search of the Viking images library, they discovered a second misfiled Face image, 70A13, taken 35 orbits later at a 17° higher sun angle. They never did find the supposed "disconfirming" image and subsequently established that since the next Viking orbit took it nowhere near Cydonia and was at Martian nighttime, no such image could have conceivably existed.

After this, Richard C. Hoagland became involved and formed two separate independent Mars investigations into the possibility that the Face was exactly what it appeared to be — a sculpture of a humanoid face. He found a collection of anomalous pyramidal mountains nearby, which he promptly dubbed The City, and eventually brought in curious professionals like Dr. Mark Carlotto and NASA astronaut Dr. Brian O'Leary. In 1988, Hoagland was approached by Erol Torun, a satellite imaging specialist who worked for the then Defense Mapping Agency (now NIMA). Torun was fascinated by a massive pentagonal mountain south of the Face which had been nicknamed the D&M Pyramid in honor of Dipietro and Molenaar. Torun held that not only was there no conventional geologic explanation for its formation, he also asserted that it had a consistent and redundant internal geometry. Hoagland later found that these same angular measurements repeated again when they were checked against the City, the Face and other potential monuments at Cydonia.

The key to unlocking the mathematical mystery of these Martian monuments were the angles 19.47° (rounded to 19.5) and 33°. Both of these numbers related to not only each other (the sine 19.47 is .3333), but also to the characteristics of circumscribed tetrahedra (a four-sided pyramid with identical triangular faces encircled in a sphere).

Eventually, Hoagland and Torun wrote a paper in which they hypothesized that the message of Cydonia was to inculcate knowledge of this specific geometry, and observed that most planetary bodies (including Earth) had at least one "upwelling," or energy release point, at or very near the 19.47° latitude. Later, they developed a physics hypothesis which explained these observations based on James Clerk Maxwell's early electro-magnetic equations (which used this same tetrahedral geometry as a starting point) which Hoagland called "Hyperdimensional Physics."

It was only after Hoagland presented these findings to scientists at a series of briefings at NASA facilities in the late 1980s that things began to unravel. JPL in particular raised objections to allowing Hoagland to continue the briefings, and a PBS television special based on the research, which was being supported by NASA headquarters, was suddenly cancelled. Soon after, NASA/JPL announced plans to return to Mars and map the planet with a much higher-resolution camera, to be carried on the *Mars Observer* spacecraft.

By 1992, NASA had gone from openly courting Hoagland and the independent researchers to vilifying and attacking them. NASA even took to revisiting the long-discredited "disconfirming photos" argument on the Face in official correspondence to congressional inquiries and public requests. Beyond that, Dr. Michael Malin, a private contractor who was given unprecedented control over the Mars Observer camera and all of the images it obtained, had dismissed the Face and Cydonia in general as a possible target for his new camera on the grounds that it would be "pure luck" to get a good picture of the Face.

Later, Hoagland would recollect this period in the investigation this way: "It was almost as if they were using us to figure out certain things for them, and then when we did, they disposed of us. They didn't need us anymore."

Watching this controversy from a distance was Dr. Stanley McDaniel, an epistemologist and Professor Emeritus at Sonoma State University in California. He decided that a study of the Cydonia debate and how it was being portrayed in the media might be a good subject for his post-graduate epistemology students. Using various political and academic contacts, he began to put pressure on NASA and JPL from several directions, forcing them to address, on the record, just why they were not able to target Cydonia or the Face specifically. NASA responded with various contradictory if not disingenuous (McDaniel's words) arguments, including those by Dr. Malin. At each and every turn, McDaniel and Hoagland shot down the arguments, even finally getting the NASA Headquarters Public Affairs Office to officially admit (in a Headquarters letter) that the infamous "disconfirming photos" of the Face never existed.[2]

McDaniel's final Report, a voluminous document which lambasted NASA for its unscientific approach to the Cydonia issue (and conversely praised the independent researchers for their work) concluded, among other things, that actually getting a picture of the Face on Mars was "about as difficult as hitting a door with a baseball from a distance of about one foot." The McDaniel Report also went on to declare that not only was NASA's public stance on the Face and Cydonia unethical and unscientific, it questioned whether NASA could be relied upon to share unfiltered scientific data from *Mars Observer*.

By the time *Mars Observer* was nearing orbital insertion, the political pressure on NASA had become enormous. Hoagland and McDaniel had engaged a number of congressional allies and the press was covering the controversy on a regular basis. Four days before *Mars Observer* was scheduled to make its orbital burn and commence operations, McDaniel delivered his final report simultaneously to NASA, Congress, the White House and the media. The following Sunday, August 22, 1993, Dr. Bevan French, the Mars Observer Chief Program Scientist, was scheduled to debate Hoagland on ABC's *Good Morning America* over the issue of whether any Observer images of Cydonia would be taken at all.

Hoagland destroyed French in the open forum, using the opportunity to bludgeon French's weak and sometimes contradictory arguments. Forced to defend an indefensible position — that NASA should willfully allow Dr. Malin to have godlike powers over data paid for by the American taxpayers — French wilted under the pressure. The final insult came at the end, when the exasperated host, Bill Ritter, finally confronted French point-blank: "Dr.

French, why don't you just take the pictures, immediately release them and *then prove these guys wrong?*" French, unsurprisingly, had no real answer. Then, at exactly 11 a.m. Eastern time, just moments after Hoagland had humiliated French on national television, NASA announced that *Mars Observer* had simply disappeared some fourteen hours earlier.

The timing of this announcement, just a few minutes after the Mars Observer Program Scientist had badly lost a nationally televised debate, seemed a bit too coincidental. Why hadn't French simply admitted that the *Mars Observer* was lost at the top of the segment? Is it conceivable that he, the Chief Program Scientist, didn't know for over 14 hours that "his" spacecraft had been lost?

In hindsight, it isn't difficult to figure out what actually happened. After other high NASA officials (and their bosses) watched French's lame Cydonia spin control fail miserably on live television, NASA simply went to Plan B. They either pulled the plug on the mission outright out of fear of what uncensored images of Cydonia might reveal, or NASA (remember, an official "Defense Agency of the United States") simply took the entire Mission "black."

With no new images of Cydonia coming for at least the next half-decade, the investigation then turned to other areas of potential interest, specifically the Moon. Working on the assumption that an advanced spacefaring civilization had flourished on Mars in the distant past, it seemed logical that they would also have visited other planets or moons in the solar system. With much of our only satellite already photographed at medium and high resolution by NASA in the 1960s, it offered a potentially vast catalog of research material. The search was immediately fruitful.

Starting in a region of the Moon called Sinus Medii (literally "The Sea in the Middle") Hoagland quickly found evidence of a completely different kind of artifact on the Moon; miles-high, crystalline towers of semi-transparent glass. The more images he obtained, the more the evidence mounted that these were real structures towering over some of the Apollo landing sites.

Taking these newfound images on a lecture tour around the country, including places like Ohio State University, Hoagland eventually met Ken Johnston, a NASA veteran who had trained the Apollo astronauts to fly the Lunar Module and then went on to work at the Lunar Receiving Laboratory. Johnston told Hoagland a disturbing tale of his days at the LRL. While there, he was put in charge of four duplicate sets of all the hand-held photographs taken by the Apollo astronauts on the surface of the Moon. Near the end of his time at the LRL, he was ordered by his bosses to destroy all four sets of this priceless first-generation photographic data. He protested and begged to be allowed to donate the images to universities or other academic institutions, but he was told that NASA headquarters had dictated the policy and to destroy the photos as he'd been ordered to do. Fortunately, he disobeyed these direct orders and kept one set, some of which he still had in his possession. These images completely confirmed the earlier findings from the orbital data that Hoagland had obtained.

Johnston's images were put through a series of tests to verify the reality of the structures that appeared to be spanning the horizon behind the astronauts. Computer artifacts, emulsion scratches and simple age degradation of the prints were quickly ruled out by independent photographic experts. The geometry of the lighting was also completely consistent with the scattering of sunlight through an intervening transparent medium, like glass. More research revealed that in the hard lunar vacuum, glass would actually be stronger than steel, making it the perfect material for protective lunar dome construction.

Later, architect Robert Fiertek did a painstaking reconstruction of the original 3D structure of the lunar domes by inserting tens of thousands of point source lights from the images into a CAD program. The resulting 3D model matched the predicted results precisely.

Fortunately, Ken was a packrat and he had kept numerous other awards, certificates and patches from the period. It was in going through Ken's storehouse of this Apollo data that they made the discovery that would turn the investigation in a completely different direction.

They had come across an official Apollo logo patch from the early days of the program. The entire motif was built around the constellation of Orion. This was incongruently bizarre because NASA had based their program mythology around the Greek pantheon of gods, like Apollo himself. Orion was worshiped not by the Greeks, but by the *Egyptians*, as the stellar representation of their god of resurrection, Osiris. In fact, the story of Orion/ Osiris, his murder at the hands of his evil brother Set/Taurus, his magical resurrection by his wife and sister Isis (represented by the star Sirius and sometimes associated with the Moon) and his vengeance against Set through the hands of his son and heir Horus/Leo, is the most ancient and sacred of the Egyptian origin myths. So what was it doing on a project patch named for the Greek god Apollo?

Knowing that the ancient Egyptian religion was a stellar one, on a hunch Hoagland bought an astronomy program for his computer and started looking at the sky over the landing sites for various Apollo missions. Johnston had tipped him that Buzz Aldrin, the second man to walk on the Moon after Neil Armstrong on Apollo 11, was a 32nd degree (now 33rd) Scottish Rite Freemason, as was Johnston himself. In reading through Aldrin's own account of the Apollo 11 mission, *Men from Earth*, they found this curious entry:

> During the first idle moment in the LM before eating our snack, I reached into my personal preference kit and pulled out two small packages which had been specially prepared at my request. One contained a small amount of wine, the other a small wafer. With them and a small chalice from the kit, I took communion on the Moon, reading to myself from a small card I carried on which I had written the portion of the Book of John used in the traditional communion ceremony.

We next discovered that Aldrin's "communion ceremony" actually had its real roots in ancient Egypt as an offering not to Christ, obviously, but to Osiris. Further, we discovered that the date of the Apollo 11 landing and this mysterious ceremony honoring Osiris was a sacred one in ancient Egypt. July 20th was the date of the annual inundation of the Nile Valley, marked by the so-called "helical rising" of Sirius around 2500 B.C. This sacred ceremonial date marked the start of the Egyptian New Year, ushered in by Isis' stellar equivalent, Sirius.

In going over the transcripts of the Apollo 11 mission, we found that the first real break in the astronauts' work schedule was exactly 33 minutes after they had landed and established Tranquility Base. That was interesting enough. But when we looked at the sky over the landing site with the astronomy software, we found Sirius was hovering over the Apollo 11 landing site at 19.5° above the lunar horizon.

There was no question that Aldrin's Masonic offering to Osiris was carefully planned for this precise moment and location on the Moon, with Osiris' wife, Isis (as Sirius) looking down from her exact 19.5° elevation in observation of the sacred moment. And it all took place on a date (July 20th, 1969) that was also a sacred "Isis date" in the ancient Egyptian calendar. After further checking, it was determined that the landing site of Apollo 11, "Tranquility Base" as it will be forever known, was the only location on the lunar surface where this precise set of stellar alignments could take place at that specific time and on that specific date. Perhaps this explains why Armstrong found it necessary to land some five miles downrange from the original planned landing site.

The fact that Sirius was at 19.5°, not on the horizon or meridian as a truly pure interpretation of the ancient stellar religion of Egypt would call for, had far deeper implications. It suggested that as far back as 1969, NASA was fully aware of the significance of the Cydonia tetrahedral geometry, and perhaps the physics behind it, even though this was more than half a decade before the first images of that Martian region would be taken. A further clue was found in the hieroglyphic symbol for Sirius: an equilateral triangle, the 2D representation of the 3D tetrahedron.

We later discovered that Aldrin had carried a Masonic apron adorned with the equilateral triangle symbol with the number 33 inside it to the Moon with him. When he returned, he presented this Masonic flag to the head of the Scottish Rite at a ceremony in the House of the Temple in Washington, D.C. It is this same Masonic flag (in place of Old Glory) which symbolically graces the cover of *Dark Mission*.

We then began to check for similar stellar alignments on other historically significant NASA missions and events. The landing of *Apollo 12* a few months later, the Trans Lunar Injection of Apollo 8 (the first manned mission to leave Earth orbit), and even the landing site of *Apollo 17* (19.5°) all had significant stellar alignments associated with them (Orion's belt at 19.5° or 33°, for instance). Most if not all of NASA's major historical events seemed to be built around following this Egyptian/Masonic tetrahedral alignment model.

A rudimentary check of the spacecraft names found a similar pattern. The Apollo 15 Lunar Module had been named *Falcon*, seemingly a reference to the mascot of the Air Force Academy. But the falcon is also associated with Horus, the avenging son of Osiris. The Apollo 16 LM had been openly named *Orion*, an obvious reference to Osiris. And the Apollo 11 Command Module *Columbia* drew its name from St. Columba, a sixth-century monk who in Masonic lore brought a sacred stone to Scotland from Egypt. Even the Apollo 13 LM, *Aquarius*, was named after the water-bearing goddess of Egypt who was a later stand-in for Isis.

Even today, NASA's new "Apollo on steroids" moon program is named — you guessed it — Orion. And the International Space Station has an unofficial nickname as well: ISS or "Isis."

In looking at the people who had directed and manned these missions, we soon discovered that everybody who was anybody at NASA in the 1960s was associated with either the Nazis, the Masons, or the JPL Magicians.

The man who selected the landing sites and times was Dr. Fahrouk El-Baz, an Egyptian geologist who also just happened to be the son of a professor who was an expert in the ancient Egyptian stellar religion. James Webb, the director of NASA at the time, was a 33rd degree Scottish Rite Freemason. Dr. Wernher von Braun, the father of the American rocketry programs, was a Major in Hitler's SS (a secret society within Nazi Germany that worshipped Isis, Osiris and Horus as their gods). Reichsführer-SS Heinrich Himmler even attended his induction ceremony personally. At least four of the 12 astronauts who walked on the Moon (Aldrin, Thomas P. Stafford, Edgar D. Mitchell, James Irwin and possibly Alan B. Shepard) were Scottish Rite Freemasons, as was Kenneth S. Kleinknecht, director of the Mercury, Gemini and Apollo programs and whose brother, C. Fred Kleinknecht would later become the titular head of the Scottish Rite in the United States. John Whiteside Parsons, one of the founders of JPL, was a follower of Aleister Crowley and consorted with L. Ron Hubbard in his Pasadena mansion during a series of magical workings designed to bring on the apocalypse.

As we went even deeper, we also discovered the fingerprints of von Braun and his Nazi cohorts on "our" space program. On April 20th, 1967, NASA landed *Surveyor 3*, an unmanned probe, on the Moon. The date was significant because it also happened to be Adolf Hitler's birthday. Later, the Apollo 16 Lunar Module *Orion* (Osiris) landed on the Moon on this same date in 1972, with Sirius precisely 33° below the visible horizon. So a spacecraft launched by a rocket designed by a member of Hitler's SS, named for the god of the SS, lands on the Moon on Adolf Hitler's birthday with Sirius, the stellar stand-in for another of the gods of the SS, at 33°, a sacred Masonic number.

All this is just a coincidence, say our critics.

We amassed so many of these ritual Egyptian/Masonic/tetrahedral alignments and references (the sole runway at Cape Canaveral is Runway 33, the only launch pad at the White Sands Missile Range where von Braun conducted his postwar tests is Launch Pad 33, the only two active launch pads as Cape Canaveral are pads 39a and 39b [39 divided by two is — you guessed it — 19.5]) that we stopped even bothering to check for them. A probabilities expert did an independent study and calculated that the odds of all these alignments being coincidental were 19 billion to 1 against. Even our critics had to concede we were on to something when NASA sent the *Mars Pathfinder* probe to the Red Planet in 1997. The little rover *Sojourner* (a Masonic term for a Mason who is traveling from his home lodge) was carried in a tetrahedral-shaped lander which bounced to a halt in a very significant location on the Martian surface — 19.5° x 33°. Even author Graham Hancock, who had been reluctant to endorse our Ritual Alignment Model, had to admit that this one was too much to swallow. In his 1999 book *The Mars Mystery*, he wrote:

> Still, we cannot deny that the act of placing a tetrahedral object on Mars at latitude 19.5 contains all the necessary numbers and symbolism to qualify as a "message received" signal in response to the geometry of Cydonia. Moreover, such a game of mathematics and symbolism is precisely what we would expect if NASA were being influenced by the type of occult conspiracy that Hoagland, for one, is always trying to espouse.

But if the missions like Pathfinder and Apollo 11 were purely symbolic ones, consecrating these sites as temples for the Masonic order, other missions had more practical aims. The next two missions to successfully explore the Moon after Apollo 11, Apollo 12 and 14, landed just 112 miles apart (Apollo 13 never made it after an in-flight accident nearly left its crew stranded in interplanetary space). This makes absolutely no sense if the real purpose of the Apollo Program was to conduct a diverse geological study of the lunar surface. Fortunately, Johnston's salvaged first generation prints (when compared with other photographic data from 16mm film sources and TV transmissions) allowed us to pinpoint specific structural objects over the horizon from both landing sites, effectively proving the presence of the megalithic Crystal Towers of the Moon.

Later missions, like Apollo 17 (which as I mentioned landed at the ubiquitous 19.5° latitude) appeared to be out-and-out salvage missions to bring back whatever remaining technology they could obtain from these epic ruins. The second EVA on that mission made a beeline for a feature called Nansen at the base of hexagonal "mountain" named the South Massif. Nansen, from aerial images taken from the Apollo 17 command module, actually appears to be a depression leading *under* the massive hexagonal ruin that is the South Massif. In fact, EVA maps used by the astronauts to locate Nansen point to the area with the caption "access region." As they approached it on the Lunar Rover, Astronaut Harrison Schmitt is heard exclaiming "Look at Nansen! My goodness gracious!" His commander, Eugene Cernan, is heard to say, "Man, you talk about a mysterious-looking place." The astronauts subsequently explored Nansen mostly off-camera for over 64 minutes, without once positioning the TV camera to actually look *into* the crevasse they were so excited about. They also indicated that they took multiple photographs of Nansen, but no pictures of the inside of the feature (looking straight in) have ever been found in the photographic archives. "Well, I have some good pictures of Nansen, anyway," Cernan says, in complete contrast to the actual photographic record. "And you know, I look out there, I'm not sure I really believe it all."

Next, they went straight to Shorty Crater where they made an even more astonishing discovery — orange soil. As it turned out, the orange soil near Shorty had been heavily oxidized, resulting in the odd color. But there was something even more bizarre laying in the bottom of the shallow crater.

There, resting amongst a collection of what appeared to technological devices and broken machinery, was an object that seemed to be a severed head. The object had two symmetrical eye sockets, a protruding nose, a skull structure, everything you would expect a real head to have. But we knew instantly it couldn't be biological. Although it was the right size and shape to be a human head, no fossil could have survived even a few decades in the harsh lunar environment. Color enhancements revealed a bright red anodized stripe around the mouth area, apparently painted in a neat horizontal manner across the "skull." The only logical explanation was that this head, like all of the other bits of metal around it, was mechanical.

We shared the image with one of the astronauts who walked on the Moon to get his opinion. Instead of laughing it off or simply dismissing it, he asked us to get back to him "when you get higher-resolution images of it." This implied two things: First, that there *were* higher-resolution images of it, and second, that he took the possibility that it was an artifact seriously. Dr. Robert Schoch, a geologist from Boston University who was shown the image at the 2006 CPAK conference, described himself as "freaked out" by it and stated categorically that it was not a rock.

What we don't know for certain is if they brought it, or some sample of technology like it, back from the Moon.

After Pathfinder, NASA sent the replacement for *Mars Observer* to the Red Planet. *Mars Global Surveyor* entered orbit in the fall of 1997 and in April of 1998, after months of public pressure, Dr. Michael Malin (who once again had total autonomy over the data) was forced to take an image of the Face on Mars. JPL released the image on the morning of April 4th, 1998.

It was, to say the least, a disappointment. The image looked nothing like the Face we or anyone else had expected, and it was quickly dubbed the "Catbox" image by radio host Art Bell, who compared it to a pattern his cat might make in her litter box. All of the major networks reported on it that evening on their primary broadcasts, and uniformly dismissed the Face as "just a pile of rocks." One JPL official was quoted as saying "I hope we've scotched this thing for good."

Three minutes after the major networks signed off their broadcasts for the evening, JPL released a second, dramatically better version of the image. It still looked odd, because the Face was imaged from below and in poor lighting conditions, but one scientist, Dr. Tom Van Flandern, a

Yale-educated astronomer who spent more than 21 years at the U.S. Naval Observatory and was chief of the Celestial Mechanics Branch of the Nautical Almanac Office, declared that based on the image "there is no longer room for reasonable doubt of the artificial origin of the face mesa, and I've never concluded 'no room for reasonable doubt' about anything in my 35-year scientific career."

Within a few days, we discovered that the new image of the Face only contained about 50% of the data it was supposed to have, making improvements in the quality of the low-resolution, high-contrast Catbox image impossible. Later, a NASA contractor named Lan Fleming reconstructed the Catbox image and duplicated it almost exactly. In order to do this, he had to use a high pass filter (which removes high-frequency data) and a low pass filter (which removes low-frequency data) as well as an embossing filter (which creates false visual cues and throws false shadows). It was no wonder it looked like just a pile of rocks.

In May 2001, under more public pressure to take a true overhead image, NASA released a new MGS image of the Face. It was certainly better, but still distorted because JPL and Malin had done an improper orthographic rectification on it, enhancing the appearance of asymmetry. The image release appeared with a highly political article published on the NASA website which derided the Face. Unfortunately, in order to accomplish this they turned the image upside down and flipped it horizontally, swapping the western half for the eastern half. They also included a 3D model of the Face which NASA claimed was generated from the MGS' Mars Orbiter Laser Altimeter (MOLA). The article stated that the MOLA had a resolution of "a few centimeters," and that the 3D view proved the Face had "no eyes, no nose, and no mouth." What they failed to tell their readers was that the *vertical* resolution of the MOLA is a few centimeters, meaning it knows how high above the Martian surface it is to within a few centimeters accuracy. What they also didn't tell their readers was that the horizontal resolution of the instrument was 150 *meters*, or about 527 feet. In other words, one pixel, or "picture element" of data from the MOLA was as big around as a baseball stadium. At that resolution, it could take a measurement of New York City and completely miss such landmarks as Yankee Stadium, the Empire State building and Ground Zero. Even the crude Viking 1 camera that took the first Face image was made up of tens of thousands of such pixels.

* * *

The one objection we regularly confront in bringing these issues to the public's attention is relevance. Many readers, even if they are convinced by the evidence that NASA has not only conspired to withhold proof of extraterrestrial archeology from the general public, but may also have engaged in a series of bizarre astrological machinations, still argue that it is meaningless, that it has had no real impact on the realpolitik of the day. We don't agree.

On April 12, 1961, Yuri Gagarin had become the first human in space aboard a Soviet spacecraft. Six days later, NASA finally delivered the report they had commissioned on the proposed plan for space exploration — the aforementioned Brookings Report — to Congress. Just about two weeks later, as if he was responding directly to the calls in the Report for NASA to consider suppression of the discovery of ET artifacts, Kennedy made a speech in which he signaled that he intended his administration to be an open one. He took the opportunity of a speech before the American Newspaper Publishers Association at the Waldorf-Astoria hotel in New York City to openly bash what he called "secret societies."

> The very word "secrecy" is repugnant in a free and open society; and we are as a people inherently and historically opposed to secret societies, to secret oaths and to secret proceedings. We decided long ago that the dangers of excessive and unwarranted concealment of pertinent facts far outweighed the dangers which are cited to justify it. — President John F. Kennedy, April 27, 1961

Kennedy's opening comments, speaking of secret societies and the dangers of excessive and unwarranted concealment of things he felt the American people had a right to know, was an unmistakable shot across the bow of these fraternal organizations and a direct reference to the recommendations contained in the Brookings Report. Within a little over a month of drawing this important line in the sand, Kennedy addressed a Joint Session of Congress and issued his ringing call for landing an American on the Moon before 1970.

Soviet premier Nikita Khrushchev's son, Sergei (now a senior fellow at the Watson Institute at Brown University) has stated that less than ten days after his public call to go to the Moon, Kennedy then did an extraordinary thing: he secretly proposed to Khrushchev at their Vienna summit that the United States and the Soviet Union merge their space programs to get to the Moon together. Khrushchev turned Kennedy down, in part because he didn't trust the young President after the Bay of Pigs fiasco, and also because he feared that America might learn too many useful technological secrets from the Russians.

The situation was surely made worse in 1962 by the Cuban Missile Crisis, in which both nations stared down the barrel of nuclear annihilation and carefully stepped back from the brink. In August 1963, Kennedy met with Soviet Ambassador Dobrinyin in the Oval Office and once again secretly extended the offer. This time, Khrushchev considered it more seriously, but ultimately rejected it.

Kennedy then surprised the entire world when only two days later he went before the United Nations General Assembly and startlingly repeated his offer of cooperation, this time in public.

It is unclear what NASA thought of the President's idea, but the Western press was very cautious and powerful congressmen openly opposed the proposal. Within a couple of weeks, the lack of support within the US Congress seemed to have scuttled the idea permanently, and Kennedy began to publicly back away from his own proposal. Then, strangely, the notion abruptly resurfaced.

On November 12, 1963, Kennedy issued National Security Action Memorandum #271. The memo, titled "Cooperation with the USSR on Outer Space Matters," directed NASA Director Webb to personally (and immediately) take the initiative to develop a program of "substantive cooperation" with his Soviet counterparts in accordance with Kennedy's U.N. proposal.

A second, even stranger memo later surfaced, dated the same day. The document is titled "Classification Review of All UFO Intelligence Files Affecting National Security" and is considered by researchers to have a "medium-high" probability of being authentic. The memo directs the director of the CIA to provide files on "the high threat cases" with an eye toward identifying the differences between "bona fide" UFOs and any classified United States craft. He informs the CIA director that he has instructed Webb to begin the cooperative program with the Soviets (confirming the other, authenticated memo) and that he would then like NASA to be fully briefed on the "unknowns" so that they can presumably help with sharing this information with the Russians.

Whether this second memo is genuine or not — and it certainly is consistent with Kennedy's stated plans — what is quite clear is that something dramatic happened between late September 1963, when Kennedy's proposal seemed all but dead, and mid-November, when it suddenly sprang back to life. Sergei Khrushchev, in an interview given in 1997, confirmed that while initially ignoring Kennedy's U.N. offer, his father Nikita changed his mind and decided in early November 1963 to accept it.[3] He recalled walking with his father as they discussed the matter, and went on to place the timing of his father's decision as about a week before Kennedy's assassination in Dallas, which would date it right around November 12–15. Later, in a 1999 PBS interview, he repeated the claim.

So what logically happened is that sometime in early to mid-November, 1963, Nikita Khrushchev communicated in some way that he was willing to accept Kennedy's proposal. Kennedy responded by ramping up the bureaucracies at his end, as reflected in the two November 12th memoranda. Unfortunately, there are no declassified documents to this point which confirm that the two men had any specific communication during this period. Still it seems quite unlikely that Kennedy would suddenly resurrect a dead policy without some hint from Khrushchev that it would be positively received.

All we can say for certain is that as of November 12, 1963, John Kennedy's grand plan to use NASA and the space program to melt the ice of the Cold War — and to share whatever Apollo discovered on the lunar surface with the Russians — was alive, vibrant and finally on its way to actual inception.

And ten days later, Kennedy was dead.

And that might be highly relevant to the real world that we all live in. As Sergei Khrushchev put it in the 1997 interview: "I think if Kennedy had lived, we would be living in a completely different world."

* * *

There is a great deal that could not be covered in this essay, simply because of space and time considerations. For these extensive details, you'll have to go to *Dark Mission* itself. But after a combined 35 years researching this arcane subject, we have reached a few preliminary conclusions. We have shown that NASA's original assertions about the Face and Cydonia — that it was just a trick of light and shadow — are fallacious and its attacks on the Cydonia investigation duplicitous. Even today, while still professing no interest whatsoever in Cydonia or the Face, NASA and Michael Malin continue to gather data on it. In early 2001, word got around that Dr. Malin was taking so many pictures of Cydonia and the Face on Mars that other scientists were complaining they couldn't get time on the MGS to get images of regions of interest to them. By last count, there are more than a dozen full or partial images of the Face publically released since 1998. It is, hands down, the single most imaged piece of Martian real estate.

We take it as an axiom that the Brookings Report, with its terse and chilling recommendations, has been adopted as policy within NASA. We have further shown that there is an undeniable, symbolic "Orion-Osiris" Egyptian connection to both the Apollo program and our current space initiative. We have shown that all of the major power brokers inside NASA at the time of the Apollo program had connections to one of three secretive societies. And each of these societies has as its core faith a reverence for the same three ancient Egyptian gods: Isis, Osiris, and Horus.

We have shown, over and over again, that key moments in NASA's exploration of the solar system have been planned around esoteric stellar rituals that pay homage to these long forgotten gods of ancient Egypt.

What we recognize we have yet to prove is the "why" of this eccentric behavior. The Brookings report alone seems insufficient to explain the artifacts cover-up and even less adequate to explain the occult naming rituals and curious affinity for stellar alignments. After 40 years of *Star Trek* and *Star Wars*, we would seem to have a populace that is not simply conditioned, but eager to find extraterrestrial life, or its remnants. Yet still, NASA prevaricates, ignoring the obvious evidence and cloaking their true objectives in misdirection and deception, in double entendre spacecraft names and in odd rituals. We believe this is because there is one question that NASA fears the most, that it must never allow to be asked:

"If there are ruins on Mars and ruins on the Moon, what happened to the builders of them?"

If this was Apollo's true objective — to discover what happened to a vast and far-reaching civilization that once flourished throughout this solar system — then perhaps the answer, that it was destroyed in some unimaginably sudden and cataclysmic event eons ago, was the real reason for John F. Kennedy's murder. Was his discovery of NASA's secret motivation for Apollo the unspoken reason he quietly decided to share our lunar program with our archenemies?

We may never know. After all, as one of our inside sources declared about NASA some years ago:

"The lie is different at every level."

Endnotes

1   Hoagland, Richard C. *The Monuments of Mars — A City on the Edge of Forever.* Fourth edition. p. 5.
2   *The Monuments of Mars.* p. 405.
3   *www.spacer.com/news/russia-97h.html*

The Darwin Wars

by Joan D'Arc

An unpopular opinion is almost never given a fair hearing.
— George Orwell

The Darwin wars began in October 2004, when the town of Dover, PA, became the first school district to mandate the teaching of Intelligent Design (ID theory). However, to be clear on this, the school board had adopted a policy that simply required 9th graders to hear a prepared statement about ID theory in the Biology classroom. In no way was equal time being given to the new theory. Nonetheless, two dissenting board members resigned on October 18, 2004.

In May 2005, the Kansas School Board voted to teach Intelligent Design in public schools alongside the theory of Darwinian evolution. The fight that ensued was billed by the media as the anti-Darwinists against the scientific establishment, which considers the evidence of the origins of life to be "beyond dispute." It was clear the fight had gotten real down and dirty when, at a hearing, William Harris (co-founder of Intelligent Design Network Inc.) projected a "strategy letter" from a Kansas Citizens for Science member onto a screen. The letter stated that the way to defeat the "anti-evolution forces" was to portray them as "political opportunists, evangelical activists, unprincipled bullies and ignoramuses."

Darwinists indeed see the I.D. movement as driven by a bunch of hicks in a junk wagon. If anyone is interested in applying rationality to the issue, they could start by reading the 117-page Kansas Science Education Standards (www.ksde.org, which at this revision in 2008 is no longer posted). The curriculum is nothing short of the sentinel of science. Approved on November 8, 2005, the curriculum states, "All scientific theories should be approached with an open mind, studied carefully, and critically considered." It asserts: "Compelling student belief is inconsistent with the goal of education. Nothing in science ... should be taught dogmatically."

The Kansas Standards "defines good science, how science moves forward, what holds science back, and how to critically analyze the conclusions scientists make." It calls for students to "learn about the best evidence for modern evolutionary theory, but also to learn about areas where scientists are raising scientific criticisms of the theory." The curriculum's objectives are to help students understand the "full range of scientific views" on evolutionary theory, to develop understanding of the scientific method by studying "opposing scientific evidence," and to ensure that science education in Kansas is "secular, neutral and non-ideological."

In September 2005, the National Academy of Sciences responded to the Kansas Standards deeming anything contrary to Darwin is simply not science: "There really is no "range of scientific views" on this issue — those views that are being touted today are not scientific (despite statements to the contrary by their proponents), but they are ideological." By November 2006, Dorothy had returned safely from Oz and the conservative board of education in Kansas had shifted to a more moderate majority, and promised to restore a science curriculum "that does not subject evolution to critical attack." The moral is, don't buck the System, Dorothy.

There is no "range of scientific views" because Darwinism is the state religion of America. In her book *Evolution as a Religion*, philosopher Mary Midgley argues that evolution functions dually as a creation myth and a scientific theory, and that its sociobiological "escalator model" (of Herbert Spencer) is not only non-Darwinian, but distorts the theory's scientific standing toward that of ideology and myth. Midgley asserts, "The theory of evolution is not just an inert piece of theoretical science," but is also "a powerful folk tale about human origins." She warns against applying the confidence due to well-established scientific findings to a "vast area which has only an imaginative affinity with them," and where only the "trappings of a detached and highly venerated science are present."

My approach to this subject is not religious in any way. As for my papers, I have a B.A. in Anthropology and I was a card-carrying atheist for many years, including my time studying in college. I now consider myself to be an atheist creationist, if there can be such a crypto-animal. My Darwinian dissent began shortly after college, and in 1997 I began writing *Space Travelers and the Genesis of the Human Form*, published in 2000 by The Book Tree. A second book called *Phenomenal World* followed.

In 2003, I founded a secular-based website, BIPED: Beings for Intelligent Purpose in Evolutionary Design (biped.info) to highlight valid scientific alternatives to Darwinian evolution other than "creation," although I'm not particularly opposed to that term (if it walks like a duck). Among those alternatives are: Gaia Theory, Vitalism, Morphic Resonance (a.k.a. Formative Causation), Intelligent Design, Panspermia and Directed Panspermia. This article provides an overview of these theories for those who do not realize there are valid scientific hypotheses that are contrary to Darwinian theory — they just aren't part of the naturalist paradigm. As such they have a right to exist and students have a right to learn about them, if not in school then at least on their own on the Internet.

Gaia Theory

Microbiologist Lynn Margulis and chemist James Lovelock formulated the Gaia Hypothesis in the 1970s (now upgraded to a theory). They proposed that life creates the conditions for its own existence, challenging the reigning theory that the forces of geology set the conditions for life, while plants and animals, accidentally along for the ride, evolved by chance under the right conditions.

The Darwinian concept of adaptation to the environment has been seriously questioned by Margulis, Lovelock and others working from a systems point of view. Evolution cannot be explained by the adaptation of organisms to local environments, they argue, because a network of living systems is also shaping the environment. The evolution of life, according to the Gaia Theory, depends on a cyclical, self-regulating feedback relationship. Margulis has stated that one day neo-Darwinism will be judged as "a minor 20th-century religious sect within the sprawling religious persuasion of Anglo-Saxon biology." She has also asserted that Darwinism is based on outdated reductionist concepts, asserting that "It's wrong like infectious medicine was wrong before Pasteur. It's wrong like phrenology is wrong. Every major tenet of it is wrong."

Lovelock popularized his Gaia theory in 1972 in a paper titled, "Gaia as seen through the atmosphere," and in his 1979 book, *Gaia: A New Look At Life on Earth*. His initial hypothesis proposed that the whole Earth behaves like one self-regulating organism wherein all of the geologic, hydrologic, and biologic cycles of the planet mutually self-regulate the conditions on the surface of the Earth so as to perpetuate life. When the mainstream scientific body got hold of the theory it changed significantly and we can guess why. It didn't conform to the Darwinian paradigm, which holds that evolution has no overarching purpose or goal. Lovelock's theory was *teleological*: some force *outside of nature* was possibly controlling the evolution of forms. According to Darwin himself, if any outside force (super- or supra-natural) was found to be at work, we were instructed to throw out his baby with the bath water.

Lynn Margulis still insists that consciousness evolved, but where did the consciousness come from? Answer: It had to come from inside the system (Earth-based) in the "naturalist" framework. According to evolutionists, consciousness has to evolve; it can't have been there in the first place. This conjecture is based on the anthropic principle: the minimum time required for the evolution of "intelligent observers." In this scheme, a billion years is required for the evolution of intelligence. The anthropic timescale argument posits that the types of processes allowed in the Universe must be of such an age that "slow evolutionary processes will have had time to produce intelligent beings from non-living matter." (Barrow)

Pondering how consciousness "arose in the Universe," this peculiar Western viewpoint refuses the primacy of consciousness, and instead assumes a chain of linear metamorphoses, accidental and directionless, from nonsentience to sentience. As I have written in *Space Travelers and the*

Genesis of the Human Form, the evolution story dramatizes the "natural" transfiguration of mankind through a linear procession of metamorphoses that eventually separate him from the animals of his ancestry — evolution is Western man's totem.

Vitalism vs. Natural Selection

Many people I talk to are under the assumption that Darwinism is playfully malleable and open to their mishmash of supernatural ideas. I try to inform them that Darwinian evolution is an all-or-nothing theory; it will not allow inclusion of any vitalist or supra-natural process — or, goddess forbid, any anthropomorphism. It is very exacting on that rule. If you are espousing any form of supernaturalism, you are clearly not a Darwinian. Perhaps you are a vitalist.

Vitalism is the doctrine which espouses that life processes arise from a nonmaterial essential principle that cannot be explained by physics and chemistry alone. One of its adherents was Swedish chemist Jöns Jackob Berzelius (1799–1848), who hypothesized that only living tissue, by possessing a "life-force," can produce organic compounds. French philosopher Henri Bergson (1859–1941) proposed the idea of an *élan vital*, or creative force, at the heart of evolution. Bergson advocated a return to neo-vitalism, which maintains that the phenomena of life are unpredictable, chaotic, and beyond the range of science. Wilhelm Reich was a vitalist and Darwin's peer Jean Baptiste de Lamark utilized vitalism in his theory of acquired characteristics.

Yet, the notion of a life-force (perhaps involving the "ether" which Einstein wrongly abandoned) is flatly contrary to Darwinian theory, which emphasizes no purpose, goal or outside force at work in the development of new species.[1] To be sure, the principle of natural selection is the only suspicious force allowed in through the back door of Darwinism.[2] What force in nature does the *selecting* of the *fit* characteristics and how does it produce new and (at the same time) useful structures by random chance? Indeed, Darwin later regretted his use of the term because it suggested a mysterious guiding force was at work.

Natural selection is a supposedly blind "natural" process which somehow ensures (let's not say "chooses") that the most *fit individuals survive to produce the most offspring*. Darwin's concept of natural selection simply defines the *fittest* as the individuals that survive — the fittest organisms are, plain and simple, the ones that produce the most offspring. Hence, natural selection is a meaningless tautology which essentially states, "those organisms which leave the most offspring, leave the most offspring."

There is no evidence that would confirm the hypothesis, argues zoologist Pierre Grasse, that the concept of natural selection is "an evolutionary process capable of producing innovative designs" (i.e. new species). He explains that supposed proofs of evolution in action are simply "observations of demographic facts, local fluctuations of genotypes and geographical distributions" — not new and distinct forms.

The Fields of Morphe

A modern example of vitalist theory is Rupert Sheldrake's theory of Morphic Resonance ("formative causation"), described in detail in his book *A New Science of Life*. Sheldrake believes morphogenetic fields are non-physical carriers of information (intelligence) which guide the development of an organism in the form of its species. He believes DNA is not the source of structure, but is a "receiver" that translates information into physical form. In this sense, genes are grossly overrated, he states.

Morphic fields (from the Greek *morphe*, which means *form*), he explains, are the organizing fields of nature. Morphic fields organize in living organisms as well as in the forms of crystals and molecules. Each kind of molecule has its own type of morphic field, and even our own mental lives depend on this field. In his book *The Presence of the Past*, Sheldrake explains that morphogenetic fields contain an inherent memory, and he believes the structure of the fields "depends on what has happened before." Inheritance depends on cumulative memory built up through "a pool of species experience" in a process he calls morphic resonance. Sheldrake believes vitalism has come back to life as a scientific theory and is being embraced in many corners.

Intelligent Design

Intelligent Design is the science that detects "signs of intelligence." In his book *The Design Inference*, its leading proponent, mathematician William Dembski, employs statistical testing of the natural world to see if it shows evidence of intelligent design. He explains:

> To say intelligent causes are empirically detectable is to say there exist well-defined methods that, based on observable features of the world, can reliably distinguish intelligent causes from undirected natural causes. Many special sciences have already developed such methods for drawing this distinction — notably forensic science, cryptography, archaeology, and the search for extraterrestrial intelligence (SETI). Essential to all these methods is the ability to eliminate chance and necessity.

For instance, scientists such as Dr. Mark Carlotto and Professor Stanley

McDaniel explore the artificiality of formations on Mars. They argue that natural features do not exhibit a high degree of parallelism, symmetry or geometrical straight-edged patterns. Statistically, a feature on another planetary body such as the moon or Mars which was found to exhibit a high degree of parallelism or geometry, such as large-scale patterns that look like walls or streets, could perhaps be artificial constructions. Likewise, according to Richard Hoagland, such geometries might be construed as a mathematical "signal" from an intelligent race.

Although the late SETI pioneer Carl Sagan believed that such investigations are scientifically legitimate, many scientists disagree that Intelligent Design is comparable to SETI. In his essay entitled "Design Yes, Intelligent No," Massimo Pigliucci asserts:

> Dembski is absolutely correct that plenty of human activities, such as SETI, investigations into plagiarism, or encryption, depend on the ability to detect intelligent agency. Where he is wrong is in assuming only one kind of design: for him design equals intelligence and, even though he admitted that such an intelligence may be an advanced extraterrestrial civilization, his preference is for a god, possibly of the Christian variety. The problem is that natural selection, a natural process, also fulfills the complexity-specification criterion, thereby demonstrating that it is possible to have unintelligent design in nature.

According to this argument, the comparison of ID theory with SETI is flawed because the highest design in the court of naturalistic science, in fact the *only* design allowed, is unintelligent design. Stripped of any meaning or explanatory power outside of Darwinian scientism, this phrase only reiterates Phillip Johnson's assertion that natural selection is simply an algorithmic theory of non-random death.

Try as it will, Dembski argues, Darwinian evolution cannot explain human consciousness. The concept of natural selection, he explains, "places a premium on survival and reproduction and has no stake in truth or conscious thought. Indeed, meat-puppet robots are just fine as the output of a Darwinian evolutionary process."

When the Darwinian establishment charges that ID theory is not science, they are really saying it is not based on scientific naturalism. The heart of the reigning paradigm of naturalism is that intelligence is an accidental byproduct of evolution. In contrast, Intelligent Design tells us that we live in an intelligent universe. In ID theory, intelligence trickles down from the cosmos, if you will, and in naturalism it builds up incrementally from prebiotic chemical soup. As William Dembski has charged, "For the naturalist, the world is intelligible only if it starts off without intelligence and then evolves intelligence."

Ballistic Panspermia

Panspermia is the ultimate trickle-down theory that life on earth was seeded by microbial life from space. This theory was advocated by many, among them the Greek philosopher, Anaxagoras (500–428 BCE), Hermann von Helmholtz (1821–1894), and William Thomson Kelvin (1824–1897). Swedish physicist Svante Arrhenius later promulgated the theory of Radio Panspermia, wherein microbes from space are transported by light pressure.

The proponents of modern-day Panspermia are British astronomer Sir Fred Hoyle and Sri Lankan mathematician-astronomer Chandra Wickramasinghe, who theorize that DNA arrived on earth via meteorites (Ballistic Panspermia) or by comets (Modern Panspermia). In fact, Hoyle mathematically dismissed the chance of evolution having actually occurred the way Darwinists propose, arguing, "even if the whole universe consisted of organic soup ... the chance of producing merely the basic enzymes of life by random processes without intelligent direction would be . . . a probability too small to imagine."

Hoyle concluded that "Darwinian evolution is most unlikely to get even one polypeptide sequence right, let alone the thousands on which living cells depend for survival." Given that there are trillions of different kinds of cells in delicate balance, he argues, each of these varied cellular structures would also have to develop by chance. This mathematical impossibility is well known to scientists, he said; yet most of them "cling to Darwinism because of its grip on the educational system." They do not want to be branded as "heretics."

Directed Panspermia

As molecular biologist Michael Denton articulates in *Evolution: A Theory in Crisis*, "Nothing illustrates as clearly just how intractable a problem the origin of life has become than the fact that world authorities can seriously toy with the idea of Panspermia." Such describes the dilemma of British molecular biologist Francis Crick, who received the 1962 Nobel Prize for the discovery of the double helix structure of DNA.

After discovering the astonishingly huge and complex information storage capacity of the DNA molecule (humans have three billion coding letters in each nucleus), Crick could not imagine any conditions under which this information vehicle could have evolved from non-living chemicals. He argued that since the earth has too short a history for life to have developed here, it must have developed on another planet in a solar system several billion years older than ours.

Crick's aversion to religion led him and Leslie Orgel, in 1973, to put forth the theory of Directed Panspermia. To get around the idea of God, Crick proposed that the primordial seeds of life were shipped to earth in spaceships billions of years ago by intelligent beings. After proposing this idea, Crick was left in the predicament of explaining the origin of the ET beings, and finally had to acknowledge the paucity of the idea, saying, "Every time I write a paper on the origin of life, I swear I will never write another one, because there is too much speculation running after too few facts." (*Life Itself*, 1981)

Although an atheist, Crick was quoted as saying, "An honest man, armed with the knowledge available to us now, could only state that in some sense the origin of life appears to be almost a miracle."

Writing in his essay "Astrogenesis," William Hamilton explains, "The real paradigm shift is to consider that the Universe is a life-producing nursery and that the genesis and evolution of life is not earth-centered but rather is distributed among the stars of the galaxies." Let's not forget, however, that the theory of Panspermia still leaves us with the question of the origin of those stars and those galaxies, which of course was never addressed by Charles Darwin; nor was the actual origin of any species.

A Scientific Revolution

In his book *The Structure of Scientific Revolutions*, Thomas Kuhn defines a scientific revolution as a "non-cumulative developmental episode" whereby an older paradigm is replaced in whole or in part by an "incompatible new one." Such scientific revolutions begin with a growing sense that "an existing paradigm has ceased to function adequately in the exploration of an aspect of nature." The emergence of new theories is usually preceded by a period of "pronounced professional insecurity," since it involves large-scale paradigm destruction.

The essential problem is, scientists cannot do research in the absence of a controlling paradigm. They cannot pull the floor out from under themselves, and when it goes this structure will fall hard. Kuhn explains, a scientific theory "is declared invalid only if an alternative candidate is available to take its place." The normal response to crisis, he explains, will be to loosen the rules of normal problem solving in ways that will permit the new paradigm to emerge. This essentially describes the action taken by the Kansas School Board in its Science Education Standards. The new paradigm will emerge when the youth of tomorrow are not so emotionally and financially committed to the old one. Reading alternative science on the internet is a place to start.

Intelligent Design is a mathematically-based theory, not a religious theory. Paranoid tirades about Christians taking over the world have nothing to do with the facts of the matter. Those who react this way are reacting emotionally to the messenger rather than opening the message with the minimum decorum expected of adult human beings. By dogmatically rejecting Intelligent Design without fully comprehending it, we allow the reigning naturalist, materialist scientific paradigm to become a fascist element in society. We do a great disservice to democratic scientific debate and to the way our children learn. And as for the separation of church and state, shouldn't we also be concerned about the separation of science and state?

The question we should ask is, Do we want our children and grandchildren to be *taught* or do we want them to be *indoctrinated*? Indeed, America's educational system is in dire trouble when a Chinese paleontologist notices that, "In China it's OK to criticize Darwin but not the government, in the U.S. it's OK to criticize the government but not Darwin."

Footnotes

1. Darwin never quite defined the term *species*. He wrote in *Origin of Species*, "it will be seen that I look at the term species as one arbitrarily given for the sake of convenience to a set of individuals closely resembling each other, and that it does not essentially differ from the term variety, which is given to less distinct and more fluctuating forms." He wrote that "varieties" are simply "incipient species." Forever teetering on the edge of potentiality, species are always in a hapless phase of *becoming*.

2. Some evolutionists argue that Darwin never claimed natural selection to be the exclusive mechanism of evolution. Selection merely preserves or destroys something that already exists. Mutation must provide the innovative changes in design which natural selection then tests out in the field. Problematically, mutations that are large enough to cause visible and immediate changes are deadly.

References and Further Reading

Barrow, John, and Frank Tipler, *The Anthropic Cosmological Principle.*

Behe, Michael, *Darwin's Black Box: The Biochemical Challenge To Evolution.*

Collins, Phillip, "Illuminating the Occult Origin of Darwinism," biped.info

Cremo, Michael, *Forbidden Archeology.* (and interview at biped.info)

d'Arc, "Darwin and the Origin of the Humanoid Form," biped.info

d'Arc, "Darwinism and the Anthropic Principle," biped.info

d'Arc, *Space Travelers and the Genesis of the Human Form,* (thebooktree.com)

Dembski, William, *The Design Revolution.*

Denton, Michael, *Evolution: A Theory in Crisis.*

Johnson, Phillip, *Darwin on Trial.*

Kuhn, Thomas S., *The Structure of Scientific Revolutions.*

Lovelock, James, *Gaia: A New Look at Life on Earth.*

Margulis, Lynn, *Symbiotic Planet.*

Midgley, Mary, *Evolution as a Religion.*

National Academy of Science, www.nationalacademies.org/morenews/includes/20051027c.pdf

New York Times, Aug. 2006, "Evolution Fight Shifts Direction in Kansas Vote," www.nytimes.com/2006/08/03/us/03evolution.htm

Overman, Dean, *A Case Against Accident and Self-Organization.*

Pigliucci, Massimo, "Design Yes, Intelligent No," www.infidels.org/library/modern/features/2000/pigliucci1.html

Polanyi, Michael, Google: "Life's Irreducible Structure," 1968.

Sheldrake, Rupert, *The Presence of the Past* and *A New Science of Life.*

Adam Weishaupt

Robert Anton Wilson

President Dwight Eisenhower and fellow military Masonic Sojourners

Masonic trench art from
World War I

Sojourners logo

Masonic Police Forces

On February 19, 1973, President Richard Nixon pleases good friend and fellow UFO-obsessed Jackie Gleason with his putt shot at Florida's Inverrary Golf Club. According to Gleason's wife Beverly McKittrick, Nixon had taken Jackie to nearby Homestead Air Force Base to view the remains of small aliens. Photo by Dirck Halstead.

Wilhelm Reich led away in handcuffs to his final weeks in prison.

Wilhelm Reich and fellow researchers in Arizona with a cloudbuster spacegun. From Reich's banned book, *Contact With Space*.

ARCHIVES
of the
ORGONE
INSTITUTE

January 29th, 1954

To
U.S. Airforce Intelligence

III 92 Ɛ⊂.

Gentlemen:

I have been asked to forward to you the following report on observations made by Dr. Wilhelm Reich and myself on the evening and during the night of January 28th to January 29th,1954.

At about 22 hours, the following was clearly visible with unaided eyes as well as with binoculars from the North window of the lower house at Orgonon, Rangeley, Maine: A brightly shining light was seen moving in the direction of Badger's Camps to the North, moving in the direction West to East among the trees, and disappearing as it passed behind the trees and appearing again as it reached spaces between the trees. When the light was behind the trees, and not directly visible, a bright shine illuminated clearly the surrounding atmosphere. If there was ever any doubt about whether such moving lights were stars, mistaken for moving objects, this time any such doubt was removed in the following way: The bright, white-yellowish light was moving in the valley in front of Spotted Mountain, or, in other words, with Spotted Mountain as its background. The object seemed headed toward Round Pond, and later on this shining glimmer was to be seen further to the right, or to the East respectively. Within a few minutes, a second, similar, lighted object was seen again coming into the same region from the left or the West, moving toward the right or the East among the trees in the valley with Spotted Mountain as background. It was the same appearance and disappearance and the same shining glimmer. Only the second time, the shining object was moving slightly lower than the first one. There was no doubt whatsoever, to judge from these appearances, of the reality of this observation. This time "mistaken stars" could be eliminated with certainty, since the object was not moving as usual among stars,"out of formation" as it were, but it was found in a region where no stars could possibly ever be.

Miss Ilse Ollendorff reported in the morning of January 29th, 1954, that about 12 Midnight (she did not look at the clock), she observed a similar, but brighter and bigger because closer object to the East of Dodge Pond, hovering in front of Saddleback Mountain

somewhere near Dallas Hill or closer. It was seen rising once vertically upward, settling down again and disappearing.

There was no fear or excitement connected with these observations which seem to confirm somewhat subjectively doubtful similar observations reported to you as observed in January 13th, 1954.

Sincerely yours,

Ilse Ollendorff

ORGONE INSTITUTE
Secretary

(handwritten addition in original) :

These details were dictated by me this morning. Factual observations as well as theoretical considerations are removing any doubt as to the reality of "visitors", no matter whether from outer space or from elsewhere.

There is much more to be said about this in a different connection.

January 29th, 1954

signed: Wilhelm Reich M.D.

Will. Reich

Correspondence from Wilhelm Reich to U.S. Military Intelligence regarding UFOs.

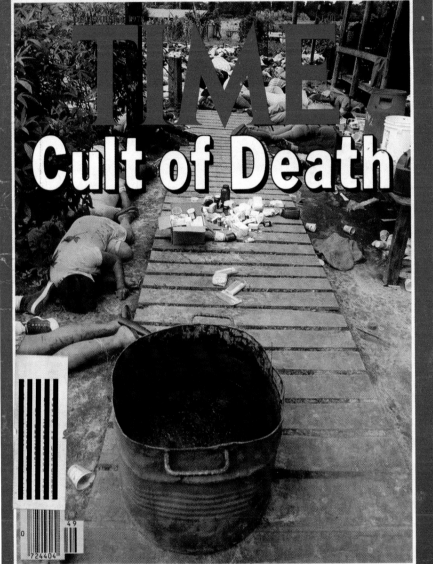

TIME
Cult of Death

Druid Goddess Tuesday Weld

Himmler

Von Braun in SS
Uniform
Behind
Himmler

Heinrich Himmler attends Wernher von Braun's initiation into the SS.

Apollo 11 astronaut Buzz Aldrin presents the Scottish Rite flag he took to the Moon to Sovereign Grand Commander Luther A. Smith (*New Age Magazine*)

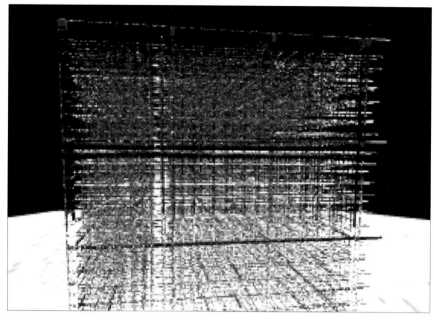

Three dimensional reconstruction of box-like "dome" over Sinus Medii by architect Robert Fiertek.

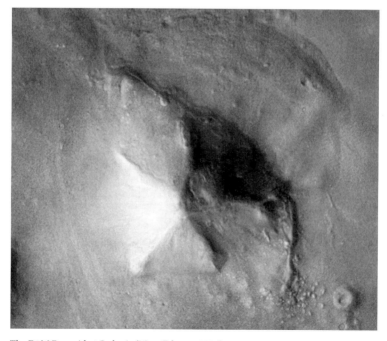

The D&M Pyramid at Cydonia (Mars Odyssey 2001)

Wilhelm Reich, Eisenhower and the Aliens

by Kenn Thomas

In one version of events, President Dwight Eisenhower was flown to Wright Patterson Air Force Base on February 20, 1954 to see the debris and dead bodies from the Roswell crash. Some versions weave a far more elaborate tale, that Ike met with Nordic-looking creatures and began intergalactic peace talks with them, the greys and several other alien races. He struggled to deal with those alien presences in the remaining years of his presidency by secret negotiations and by building up the military way out of proportion to peacetime needs. He retired in frustration with it all in 1961, giving a gravely foreboding warning that the military industrial complex he helped create would get out of control.

Although it remains a well-known legend in the UFO lore, like all such legends little actual proof exists. Unlike many other legends, however, what corroborative historical trail does exist provides some provocatively concrete details. Strangely enough, archival documentation and secondary historical sources come together in remarkable ways regarding Eisenhower's UFO involvements. If aliens do not exist, an objective observer is left to wonder why the historic trail makes it seem so much like they do and that they visited 1950s America.

Stranger still, those crossroads occur primarily in the biography and career of one of Sigmund Freud's most renowned protégés, the psychologist Wilhelm Reich. Reich spent the last of his years in the U.S. chasing flying saucers. He did this with weapons he created based on an energy source he called orgone, and ostensibly with Dwight Eisenhower's blessing. As the consummate documentary historian of his own life, Reich left behind an unusual paper trail that intertwined with the Eisenhower alien legend.

Reich's story begins in Vienna in the 1920s. Recognized as a maverick in Freud's inner circle whose ideas included a Marxist strain, Freud eventually dismissed him. As a member of the Communist Party, Reich's ideas were deemed too psychoanalytic, and he was dismissed from that as well. With the ascendancy of the Nazis in Germany, Reich fled first to Norway and then to America, moving away from both psychoanalysis and Marxism into equally controversial ideas on biophysics. Reich discovered what he termed "orgone," a biological energy found in living organisms and in the atmosphere. In Eisenhower's America, Reich not only used this energy to combat UFOs, history suggests, too, that he met with the president at around the time Eisenhower supposedly met with the aliens.

Dwight Eisenhower's contact with aliens happened in February 1954, according to the legend. The president's cover story — that he was on vacation in Palm Springs — was belied by the fact that he had just returned from a vacation in Georgia. Even newspapers of the day reported the alarming news of a total disappearance by Ike on the night of February 20 during the Palm Springs stay. The official explanation, offered after the fact, was that the president lost a tooth cap in some chicken he was eating and had to make a late-night visit to a local dentist. Evidence of this does not appear in the existing, extensive medical record on Dwight Eisenhower from his time as president, however. The widow of the dentist had only vague memories of the event, which by any measure should have made a detailed and lasting impression, and a photograph exists of Ike on Sunday morning, February 21, shaking hands with a pastor Blackstone, smiling, none the worse for wear after the dental work.

Was Ike actually flown to Wright Patterson Air Force Base that night to view the recovered saucer from the crash at Roswell and the alien bodies, as the persistent rumors go? Enter Wilhelm Reich. In the course of his UFO adventure, Reich traveled through Roswell, New Mexico the following year. He was on his way to Tucson, Arizona with his orgone equipment, to both study its capacity to alleviate desert conditions, and to do battle with UFOs. He recorded these experiences in his last book, *Contact With Space*, now an extremely hard-to-find underground classic. Although his immediate destination was Ruidoso Downs, New Mexico for an overnight stay on his way to Tucson, there seems little doubt that Reich had aliens on his mind as he passed through Roswell.

From *Contact With Space*:

> Although it was very hot as we neared Roswell, New Mexico, no OR flow [OR was Reich's abbreviation for orgone] was visible on the road, which should have been shimmering with 'heatwaves'. Instead, DOR [Reich's abbreviation for "deadly orgone radiation," which he believed came from the exhaust of UFOs] was well-marked to the west against purplish, black, barren mountains, in the sky as a blinding grayness, and over the horizon as a grayish layer. The caking of formerly good soil was progressively characteristic and eventually caked soil prevailed over the vegetation, which now consisted only of scattered low brushes, while grass disappeared.

Reich's concern about the environmental impact of UFOs stemmed from experiences he had at his lab in Rangeley, Maine, called Orgonon. It was there, in 1951, that he first discovered DOR, the noxious reaction of the natural energy he called orgone with nuclear material. He put a milligram of radium into one of his orgone boxes, an invention he created to accumulate and harness the orgone energy. It resulted in highly polluted air around the facility, with a great deleterious effect on fauna and animals. The DOR clouds formed and an odd black substance fell on the area. Strange, red pulsating lights, UFO, appeared in the sky over Rangeley. In response to all of this, Reich came up with a second invention, the cloudbuster gun, which intensified and redirected the healthy orgone, causing the pulsating lights to twinkle out and diminishing the DOR effect on the environment.

The Roswell episode in *Contact With Space* concludes, "After the desert valley it was a relief to spend a night in Ruidoso, New Mexico, in the Sierra Blanca Mountains (near 7000 feet). Here a strong, reactive secondary vegetation had sprung up, again more marked on the western slope..."

Skeptics of the Roswell story often claim that interest in the event dropped off immediately after its initial media flash, only to be revived in the late 1980s by unreliable UFO researchers seeking to profiteer from a myth of their own creation. Reich's visit to Roswell, with its clear references to aliens, contradicts that assumption. So does remarkably strong archival documentation from several disparate sources that show the interlocking connection between Reich and Dwight Eisenhower.

First in this line of documentation is the Cutler-Twining memo. The National Archives in Washington, D.C. still contains this onion-skinned carbon of a memo calling for the postponement of a special studies section of the group MJ-12. Ufologists recognize MJ-12 as the group ostensibly started by Harry Truman in response to the Roswell crash, established to secretly deal with the alien presence. Skeptics claim that the documents reflecting this possibility, the infamous MJ12 documents, have all been faked. Nevertheless, the National Archives retains this one letter, unwilling or unable to establish that it is not authentic. Its date: July 14, 1954, five months from Eisenhower's supposed meeting with the aliens. Since no proof is absolute, even the government's retention of the document (authenticated by paper-lot and typewriter style dating) for a half-century, skeptics suggest that the Cutler-Twining memo was smuggled into the archives.

The author of the C-T memo, Robert Cutler, served in the CIA under Eisenhower in its division of psychological operations and as the first National Security Adviser, a post most recently held by Condoleezza Rice. Cutler had virtually written Ike's famous "Atoms for Peace" speech, which took as its title a phrase used by Reich long before to describe his orgone work. The recipient of the C-T memo, Nathan Twining, is well-known among students of ufology as the general to whom Air Force investigators regularly reported UFO sightings and retrievals. One such retrieval, involving flying saucers in the Maury Island area in the Pacific Northwest, also involved the kind of black substance that Reich had described at his lab in Maine.

But the second curious document in this research line was recovered only recently by the researcher Jim Martin, as part of his comprehensive look at Wilhelm Reich's life in the 1950s called *Wilhelm Reich and the Cold War.* Entitled the Moise-Douglas memo, Martin discovered it in the archives of Lew Douglas, a member of Eisenhower's "kitchen cabinet" who was assigned to a presidential committee on weather control. In *Contact With Space,* Reich claimed that he had corresponded with Douglas, and Martin discovered this memo as proof. It's from Douglas describing the latest of several failed attempts by Reich's assistant, William Moise, to make contact with this high-ranking official in the Eisenhower administration. Although the memo itself is not dated, a handwritten note at its bottom indicates a great change of heart by Douglas, who ultimately did telegraph Moise on July 27, 1954.

This timeline is the best indication in the historic record that MJ-12 existed and, by inference, that Eisenhower met with aliens. Douglas' about-face with regard to Reich, coming at any point in July 1954, indicates that he had been briefed at the MJ-12 meeting described in the Cutler-Twining memo. The object of the "Special Studies Project" mentioned in the C-T, then, would be Reich's counterattack on UFOs, and at it Douglas was directed to take a greater interest. In the end, Douglas wound up bankrolling in part some of Reich's environmental work in Tucson. As some measure of how seriously the military took Reich's technology, the U.S. Air Force actually did develop a weather modification in the early '60s and named it the "Cloudbuster."

Finally, there's Reich's own meeting with Eisenhower. One witness claimed that during a hunting and fishing trip to Rangeley, Maine, where Reich's Orgonon lab was located, Eisenhower met face to face with the inventor of the anti-UFO technology. The Eisenhower Library even records a visit to Rangeley during that UFO-laden period of the mid-1950s, from June to July, 1955. In the end, however, the memory of the witness to the meeting became as vague as that of the dentist's widow from Ike's alien visit of the year before.

The historic trail vaporizes after that, to re-emerge obliquely only once. According to the biography of his second wife, the screen comedian Jackie Gleason caught a glimpse of alien bodies in 1973 at the behest of then president Richard Nixon. Nixon, of course, had been Eisenhower's vice president. He took his friend Gleason to a secret facility in Palm Springs, where Ike had disappeared for one night for his visitation with aliens all those years ago.

Does any of this amount to proof that such creatures exist and that Eisenhower met with them? Such questions always contain relative judgments, and in the end no absolute proof can be offered for anything. However, more historic evidence exists for this bizarre proposition, for instance, than for Lyndon Johnson's claim of an attack on U.S. ships in the Gulf of Tonkin or George Bush's claims for the existence of WMDs in Iraq. Those two bits of mythologizing started major wars. Whatever high-level contacts Reich had within the Eisenhower government, however, they did not save him for getting in trouble with the authorities.

Reich was eventually prosecuted for his orgone devices. They had been unfairly characterized as quack cancer cure machines and a technical violation of an FDA injunction led to Reich's imprisonment. Federal authorities destroyed much of his scientific equipment and even had his books burned. Many believe that the prosecution resulted from big-money medical and pharmaceutical interests threatened by Reich's work. The FDA, of course, never truly followed Reich's scientific protocols on either orgone technology or cloudbuster guns, and convicted Reich on a technical violation of its injunction to stop distributing orgone boxes.

Authorities threw Reich in a prison cell in Lewisburg, PA from which he did not emerge alive. In memos to the prison chaplain before his death, however, Reich continued to write passionately about the social situation in the 1950s Eisenhower cultural era. His note from September 1957 even includes reference to the famous racial disturbance at Little Rock Central High School. He emphasized the psychological and emotional undercurrents he felt were being ignored in the broader social arena of that paranoid time, something that also prevented many from seeing the spaceships he saw in abundance:

I am merely fulfilling my public duties as a U.S. citizen and worker in planetary affairs if I continue to point out where the true danger to our social and personal existence is placed — Emotional Poisoning: disruption through sowing distrust throughout our society, doping and drugging of our population, espec. our YOUTH; draining us financially through areas [...] race, a camouflage of the true menace, the Emotional Poisoning a la Little Rock racial upheavals; keeping our high placed officials at bay through fear of sexual scandals, railroading efficient men and women into prisons or lunatic asylums through [?] up there environments; subverting justice by whispered little lies & frightening or using judges. Doing all this destruction unnoticed as it were by all those responsible... now lyrics were subverted by such use of stupidities & evasions on our part, especially by the staid reluctance to talk bluntly and take the bull by the horns. The bull is really no more than a few slimy tape worms eating away at our emotional guts. It is high time to start giving social power to the established functions of Love, Work & Learning as bastions against the tapeworms.

The prison memo form also includes this banal and perhaps prescient statement: "Your failure to specifically state your problem may result in no action being taken." Reich's imprisonment was in part the end result of misreporting on him that appeared in the *New Republic* under the editorial leadership of a now-confessed communist spy named Michael Straight in a book entitled *After Long Silence*. *New Republic* made its own pronouncement about Little Rock in its July 7, 1958 edition, complaining about the Supreme Court's failure to stop legal challenges that were slowing down the integration process. The Supreme Court, opined *New Republic*, "must stand the ground they themselves have assumed, or the grand experiment they inaugurated will end in bitter farce, with consequences for the state of the union that stagger the mind."

Clearly the magazine had a better view of the possible consequences of Supreme Court actions than the Court itself. The consequences of Reich's work with UFOs, and the implications of the study of psychological character structure on the understanding of race issues has continued over the years. Writing in a chapter called "Racism and Slavery" in *The American Slave: A Composite Autobiography* (1972), historian George Rawick notes the impact of Reich's classic book, still taught in college curricula on psychology, entitled *Character Analysis*, first published in German in 1933, and its less well-known but significant companion, *The Mass Psychology of Fascism*: "While I cannot subscribe to all of Reich's system, this chapter could not have been written without his monumental attempt to relate Marx and Freud which loosened the ideological armouring of Western rationalism for me and many others."

Although Reich never stated it explicitly, clearly he saw that same "armoring" as the block that keeps so many from accepting the realities of the UFO issue.

Reich died in the Lewisburg prison in 1957.

Some of the language in Dwight Eisenhower's retirement speech, the one that coined the phrase "military-industrial complex," conjures up an image of Wilhelm Reich, Ike's possible secret ally in the war against extraterrestrials. "Today," Eisenhower notes, "the solitary inventor, tinkering in his shop, has been overshadowed by task forces of scientists in laboratories and testing fields...a government contract becomes virtually a substitute for intellectual curiosity. The prospect of domination of the nation's scholars by Federal employment, project allocations, and the power of money is ever present ..."

Although the record suggests that Reich had the interest and support from the Eisenhower administration in his desert battles against UFOs, he never required it. Although he believed in nuts-and-bolts spaceships piloted by extra-terrestrials, he regarded contact with them as characterological events, not simply sightings of craft. But he needed no stamp of approval from government authority to make this claim.

"There is no proof," wrote Reich in *Contact With Space*, "There are no authorities whatever. No president, Academy, Court of Law, Congress or Senate on this earth has the knowledge or power to decide what will be the knowledge of tomorrow. There is no use in trying to prove something that is unknown to somebody who is ignorant of the unknown, or fearful of its threatening power. Only the good old rules of learning will eventually bring about understanding of what has invaded our earthly existence."

That seems to have been Reich's last word on the subject.

Secret Weather Wars:

Mind Control, HAARP and Chinese Take-Out

by Jerry E. Smith

"If man can modify the weather, he will obviously modify it for military purposes. It is no coincidence that the U.S. Army, Navy, Air Force and Signal Corps have been deeply involved in weather modification research and development. Weather is a weapon, and the general who has control over the weather is in control of an opponent less well armed... The idea of clobbering an enemy with a blizzard, or starving him with an artificial drought still sounds like science fiction. But so did talk of atom bombs before 1945."

So wrote author Daniel S. Halacy Jr. in his book *The Weather Changers*, published in 1968.

Modern scientific attempts to control the weather began with Dr. Bernard Vonnegut's discovery in 1946 that microscopic crystals of silver iodide (AgI) nucleate water vapor to form ice crystals. His breakthrough invention of a practical way of generating tiny AgI particles to serve as nuclei for ice crystals led to the modern practice of cloud-seeding. More than 50 years later his method continues to be the most common. Control of the weather, at least to some degree, is today an established and expanding field of scientific and commercial endeavor across North America and around the world.

Uncle Sam's Disappearing Federal Budget Trick

Mankind has always had a keen interest in the weather. Throughout human history we have seen the effects of weather on crops, and the loss of life and property through the violence of storms. In ancient times people made sacrifices to the gods in a crude attempt at influencing the weather. In many parts of the world today people still conduct elaborate rituals for rain and fertility.

The modern interest in making rain for profit and/or the public good began, surprisingly enough, following the American Civil War. A large volume of literature on the subject was generated between 1890 and 1894 alone. Martha B. Caldwell in her article "Some Kansas Rain Makers," published in the *Kansas Historical Quarterly* in August of 1938, summed up much of this material. She wrote:

> These writers had various theories as to the methods of producing rain. A French author suggested using a kite to obtain electrical connections with the clouds. James P. Espy, a meteorologist from Pennsylvania, proposed the method of making rain by means of fires. This idea is prevalent on the Western Plains where the saying, "A very large prairie fire will cause rain," has almost become a proverb. The Indians on the plains of South America were accustomed to setting fire to the prairies when they wanted rain. A third method patented by Louis Gathman in 1891 was based on the supposition that sudden chilling of the upper atmosphere by releasing compressed gases would cause rapid evaporation and thus produce rain. One of the oldest theories of producing artificial rain is known as the concussion theory, or that of generating moisture by great explosions. The idea originated from the supposition that heavy rains follow great battles. Gen. Daniel Ruggles of Fredericksburg, Va., obtained a patent on the concussion theory in 1880, and urged Congress to appropriate funds for testing it.
>
> By 1890 the subject of artificial rain making had attained considerable dignity; two patents had been issued and through the efforts of Sen. C.B. Farwell, Congress had made appropriations, $2,000 first, and then $7,000 to carry on experiments. In 1892 an additional appropriation of $10,000 was made to continue the work. The carrying out of these experiments naturally fell to the Department of Agriculture, and the Secretary selected R. G. Dryenforth to conduct them. In 1891 Mr. Dryenforth with his assistants proceeded to the "Staked Plains of Texas" to begin work. Included in the equipment which he took with him were sixty-eight explosive balloons, three large balloons for making ascensions, and material for making one hundred cloth covered kites, besides the necessary explosives, etc. He used the explosives both on the ground and in the air. An observer stated that "it was a beautiful imitation of a battle." The balloons filled with gas were exploded high in the atmosphere. After a series of experiments carried on in different parts of Texas over a period of two years, his conclusions were to the effect that under favorable conditions precipitation may be caused by concussion, and that under unfavorable conditions "storm conditions may be generated and rain be induced, there being, however, a wasteful expenditure of both time and material in overcoming unfavorable conditions."

Twenty thousand dollars in 1890 would have the purchasing power of about a quarter million today. Over the next 80 years Congress maintained an on-again, off-again interest in funding this research. One notable expenditure occurred in 1967 when the U.S. Senate passed the Magnusson Bill authorizing the Secretary of Commerce to accelerate programs of applied research, development and experimentation in weather and climate modification. That bill allocated $12 million, $30 million and $40 million over the next three years, respectively. They projected expenditures of some $149 million annually by 1970.

It can be argued that by the beginning of the 1970s portions of the U.S. government and/or military viewed weather and climate modification research as having transitioned from the "basic research" stage to the "operational" stage. Experiments were occurring — or had occurred — in 22 countries, including Argentina, Australia, Canada, Iran, Israel, Kenya, Italy, France, South Africa, Congo and the U.S.S.R. Airborne seeding programs were undertaken to combat drought in the Philippines, Okinawa, Africa and Texas. Fog clearing had become a standard operation at airports, as had hailstorm abatement, which had been proven successful in several parts of the world. Forest fire control had been carried out in Alaska and watershed seeding was widely practiced, while lake storm snow redistribution was under extensive investigation. By 1973 there were over 700 degreed scientists and engineers in the U.S. whose major occupation was environmental modification (EnMod).

And then it all changed. In 1978 the United States became a signatory to the United Nations Convention on the Prohibition of Military or Any Other Hostile Use of Environmental Modification Techniques (EnMod Convention or ENMOD for short). The EnMod Convention prohibits the use of techniques that would have widespread, long-lasting or severe effects through deliberate manipulation of natural processes and cause such phenomena as earthquakes, tidal waves and changes in climate and weather patterns.

Independent journalist Keith Harmon Snow wrote a massive report entitled: "Out of the Blue: Black Programs, Space Drones & The Unveiling of U.S. Military Offensives in Weather as a Weapon." In it he tells us:

> In 1976, U.S. government officials outlined 50 experimental projects and 20 actual pilot programs costing upwards of $100 million over the next eight years.
>
> It was an explosive subject, up [through] the 1970s but, after 1977, EnMod interest seemed to disappear almost overnight. In other words, after decades of intense research and development, after billions of dollars of investment, after major institutions and governmental bodies were created and charged with oversight of EnMod and its many peripheral issues, and after the entire reorganization of the U.S. Government to channel and guide and map out the future of this new and promising military and civilian "technology" — said to be more important than the atom bomb — everything stopped.
>
> Or did it?

It was as if a huge curtain fell over the subject as all research, all institutional interests, huge salaries and thousands of jobs — vanished. And the mass media stopped reporting anything and everything as if struck by plague. That — sudden and total silence — is perhaps the most telling and suspicious indication of the secrecy and denial that the EnMod arena was shackled with. Today it is almost as if it never happened.

Could it be that the U.S. government said, "Oh gee, we can't do that any more" and just gave up on military EnMod — or did the whole program go "black"?

Project Popeye

The American military-industrial-academic complex early on recognized the importance of weather as a weapon. After the great battles of the Civil War it was noted that rains seems to follow. A General patented an idea for making rain from this observation, but it would take nearly 80 years for a technology to be developed that was GI-friendly. The Battle for Britain was partially won because Allied forces successfully used a fog-dispersal system known as FIDO to enable aircraft takeoff and landing under otherwise debilitating fog conditions. Cold fogs were similarly dissipated during the Korean War. cloud-seeding became a weapon in Vietnam under Project Popeye.

Project Popeye is a now exposed and proven conspiracy on the part of the military to circumvent the laws of humanity in time of war using environmental modification as a weapon — and to keep this secret, the Secretary of Defense was forced to lie to Congress!

Project Popeye was originally conducted as a pilot program in 1966. It was an attempt to extend the monsoon season in Southeast Asia with the goal of slowing traffic on the Ho Chi Minh Trail by seeding clouds above it in hopes of producing impassable mud. Over the course of the program silver iodide was dispersed from C-130s, F4 Phantoms and the Douglas A-1E Skyraider (a single engine propeller driven fighter-bomber), into clouds over portions of the trail winding from North Vietnam through Laos and Cambodia into South Vietnam. Positive results from the initial test led to continued operations from 1967 through 1972.

Some scientists believe that it did hamper North Vietnamese operations, even though the effectiveness of this program is still in dispute. In 1978, after the efforts at cloud-seeding in Vietnam produced mixed results, the U.S. Air Force declared its position to be that "weather modification has little utility as a weapon of war." Recent military publications indeed have stated quite the opposite. For example the U.S. Air Force's own Air University's "SPACECAST 2020" contained a section on Counterforce Weather Control for force enhancement, which pointed out that:

Atmospheric scientists have pursued terrestrial weather modification in earnest since the 1940s, but have made little progress because of scientific, legal, and social concerns, as well as certain controls at various government levels. Using environmental modification techniques to destroy, damage, or injure another state are prohibited. However, space presents us with a new arena, technology provides new opportunities, and our conception of future capabilities compels a reexamination of this sensitive and potentially risky topic.

"SPACECAST 2020" has been superseded by the now infamous "Air Force 2025" series of White Papers, which made this same point saying:

The influence of the weather on military operations has long been recognized. During World War II, Eisenhower said, "In Europe bad weather is the worst enemy of the air [operations]. Some soldier once said, 'The weather is always neutral.' Nothing could be more untrue. Bad weather is obviously the enemy of the side that seeks to launch projects requiring good weather, or of the side possessing great assets, such as strong air forces, which depend upon good weather for effective operations. If really bad weather should endure permanently, the Nazi would need nothing else to defend the Normandy coast!"

Clearly, weather control could have a marked effect on the outcome of military operations. The problem the military has is not whether weather control should be affected, but how it could be done, meaning technically, legally and politically. Many researchers, myself included, believe that the DoD never truly gave up trying to find out.

Project Popeye reached broad public consciousness when syndicated columnist Jack Anderson revealed it under the code name "Intermediary-Compatriot" in his *Washington Post* column of 18 March 1971.

U.S. Defense Secretary Melvin Laird was forced to testify before Congress about it in 1972. He told the U.S. Senate that Anderson's wild tales were untrue and that the United States never tried to seed clouds in Southeast Asia. But on 28 January 1974 a private letter from Laird was leaked to the press. By 1974 he had left Defense and was counsel to President Nixon, who was fighting for his political life following the break-in at the Democratic Party's National Committee offices in the Watergate Hotel on 17 June 1972. In the letter he privately admitted that his 1972 testimony had been false and that the U.S. did in fact use weather modification in North Vietnam in 1967–68.

On 20 March 1974 the United States Senate held a top-secret hearing in which representatives of the military finally admitted to the existence of Operation Popeye. They conceded that the cloud-seeding program had been conducted over neutral Cambodia and Laos (in violation of international law), as well as both North and South Vietnam. The testifying Pentagon officials stated that Popeye had been ongoing from 1966 through 1972 and that at least 2,600 flights had released over 47,000 units of cloud-seeding materials during the program, at a total cost for the operation of around $21.6 million.

These hearings also revealed that the U.S. military had attempted other environmental modifications as well. The U.S. had used massive spraying of chemical herbicides in the hopes of depriving its foes of both food supplies and shelter. According to analyst L. Juda (from "Negotiating A Treaty On Environmental Modification Warfare: The Convention On Environmental Warfare And Its Impact On The Arms Control Negotiations," published in *International Organization*) the idea was simple:

> If, as has been suggested, the guerrilla is to his base area as fish are to the sea, the destruction of the sea would kill the fish and the elimination of the base area with its supports would destroy the guerrilla.

The implications of this operation staggered Senator Claiborne Pell, a Democrat from Rhode Island. In 1976 he said:

> The U.S. and other world Powers should sign a treaty to outlaw the tampering with weather as an instrument of war. It may seem farfetched to think of using weather as a weapon — but I am convinced that the U.S. did in fact use rainmaking techniques as a weapon of war in Southeast Asia. We need a treaty now to prevent such actions — before military leaders of the world start directing storms, manipulating climates and inducing earthquakes against their enemies. It may seem a great leap of imagination to move from an apparent effort by the United States to muddy the Ho Chi Minh trail in Laos by weather modification to such science fiction ideas as unleashing earthquakes, melting the polar ice cap, changing the course of warm ocean currents, or modifying the weather of an adversary's farm belt. But in military technology, today's science fiction is tomorrow's strategic reality.

Senator Pell had conducted the Senate hearing in 1972 in which he was lied to by Defense Secretary Laird and the secret one in 1974 that learned the horrible truth. After these he became a leading advocate for what became the EnMod Convention. A subcommittee chaired by Minnesota Congressman Donald Fraser did the same in the House of Representatives in 1974 and 1975. Senator Pell did a lot of stumping and article writing to force the world to act. In one article he wrote:

> Apart from the sheer horror of the prospect of unbridled environmental warfare, there is, I believe, another compelling reason

to ban such action. We know, or should know, by now, that no nation can maintain for long a monopoly on new warfare technology. If we can develop weather warfare techniques, so can and will other major powers. Experience has taught us that the weapons that make us feel secure today, will make us feel very insecure indeed when our adversaries possess the same capabilities.

In *The Cooling*, Lowell Ponte describes the events that led to the ENMOD Convention:

> During a summit meeting between President Nixon and Soviet Premier Leonid Brezhnev on July 3, 1974, the nations agreed to conduct discussions toward a ban on environmental warfare. Before the first of these discussions, set for Moscow in November, got underway, the Soviet Union introduced a resolution before the United Nations General Assembly to ban environmental warfare. When revised, the resolution was passed by the body 102 votes to none. The United States and half a dozen other nations abstained from the vote. Senator Pell suspected that the president felt miffed by the surprise Soviet action, a move that made it appear that the Soviet Union and not the United States had taken the lead in trying to ban environmental modification. In fact, the Soviet resolution was similar to one passed by the North Atlantic Assembly in November 1972 and to another authored by Senator Pell and passed by an 82 to 10 vote by the United States Senate in July 1973.
>
> Discussion between U.S. and Soviet negotiators resumed in Washington, D.C., on February 24, 1975. On August 21, 1975, the two nations presented their jointly produced draft treaty banning environmental modification as a weapon of war to the thirty-one-nation Geneva Disarmament Conference.

The EnMod Convention (ENMOD) was later passed by the United Nations General Assembly and opened for signature in 1977. It came into effect 5 October 1978, when it was certified by the required total of 20 nations. It prohibits the use of techniques that would have widespread, long-lasting or severe effects through deliberate manipulation of natural processes and causing such phenomena as earthquakes, tidal waves and changes in climate and in weather patterns. The treaty was warmly received by most of the international community — the exception being a coalition of American environmental groups who thought that its threshold level of a violation needing to be widespread, long-lasting or severe was too high. Another complaint was that it does not ban the development of this technology, leaving it open for beneficial techniques to be discovered and employed in the service of mankind. The environmentalists (correctly) believed that the failure to ban research in this field would allow the military to develop technologies that adhered to the letter of the law while violating its spirit, as blatantly detailed in the Air Force 2025 White Paper "Weather as a Force Multiplier: Owning the Weather in 2025." Unfortunately for us, the EnMod Convention is a total failure with only 70 nations thus far signatory to it, and it is unenforceable in any realistic sense.

Secret Weather Wars?

Zbigniew Kazimierz Brzezinski, a Polish-American political scientist, geostrategist, and statesman who served as United States National Security Advisor to President Jimmy Carter from 1977 to 1981, wrote in his 1970 book *Between Two Ages*:

> It is ironic to recall that in 1878 Friedrich Engels, commenting on the Franco-Prussian War, proclaimed that "weapons used have reached such a stage of perfection that further progress which would have any revolutionizing influence is no longer possible." Not only have new weapons been developed but some of the basic concepts of geography and strategy have been fundamentally altered; space and weather control have replaced Suez or Gibraltar as key elements of strategy.

After events like the Christmas 2004 Asian tsunami and 2005's record-shattering Atlantic hurricane season many people have wondered just how "natural" those natural disasters were. Has "weather control" really become a key element of national strategy?

In the post-EnMod U.S. of the 21st century, weather control is an activity mainly confined to local governments and privately owned commercial enterprises ("civilian contractors") like Weather Modification, Inc. (WMI) of Fargo, North Dakota. WMI provides services to universities, governmental agencies, and private sector entities across the country and around the world. These services include hail suppression in Argentina, snowpack augmentation in Idaho, and cloud-seeding in Nevada. Interestingly, one of the senior scientists at WMI went on Art Bell's *Coast To Coast AM* radio show in 2005 to "out" himself as having been one of the scientists involved in Operation Popeye!

Intentional hostile control of the weather and other environmental processes is collectively called geophysical warfare. Dr. Gordon J. F. MacDonald wrote: "The key to geophysical warfare is the identification of environmental instabilities to which the addition of a small amount of energy would release vastly greater amounts of energy." This was in "Geophysical Warfare: How to Wreck the Environment," a chapter he contributed to Nigel Calder's 1968 book *Unless Peace Comes: A Scientific Forecast of New Weapons*.

In the 1960s Dr. Gordon J. F. MacDonald was a distinguished geophysicist and climatologist. He was Associate Director of the Institute of Geophysics and Planetary Physics at the University of California, Los Angeles (UCLA).

Dr. MacDonald was also a member of the President's Science Advisory Committee and the President's Council on Environmental Quality, as well as being a senior member of NASA's first Physics Committee. He was also a member of the Council on Foreign Relations and one of the JASONs, a military think tank at the top of the Military-Industrial-Academic pyramid. Dr. MacDonald wrote many articles on future weapons. In "Space," an article for the book *Toward the Year 2018*, released in 1968, Dr. MacDonald elaborated on the possibilities of geophysical warfare writing: "... technology will make available to the leaders of the major nations a variety of techniques for conducting secret warfare ... techniques of weather modification could be employed to produce prolonged periods of drought or storm, thereby weakening a nation's capacity and forcing it to accept the demands of the competitor." Elsewhere he wrote: "Such a secret war need never be declared or even known by the affected population. It would go on for years with only the security forces involved being aware of it. The years of drought and storm would be attributed to unkindly nature and only after a nation was thoroughly drained would an armed takeover be attempted." He warned that these geophysical weapons systems, should they in fact be developed, would produce long-term upsets in the climate.

Business Week magazine reported on 24 October 2005: "China has 35,000 people engaged in weather management, and it spends $40 million a year on alleviating droughts or stemming hail that would damage crops." North Korea, downwind of China, has been ravaged by droughts for a decade. It is entirely possible that China has been intentionally stealing North Korea's rain so as to force North Korea to follow China's political dictates and buy Chinese food (I wonder if it comes in those little white cartons — with six million you get egg rolls?). Reports from North Korea make not just the nation's dictator, Kim Jong-Il, but the whole country sound crazy. Could their seeming mass insanity be induced?

HAARP

One much discussed project that embodies both civilian and military geophysical applications is the High-frequency Active Auroral Research Program (HAARP). Although HAARP proponents claim it is nothing more than a simple civilian research station designed to investigate the properties of the upper atmosphere, few investigators buy that explanation.

HAARP does have the appearance of a civilian project with open access and the work being done by civilian scientists. However, the project is managed by a joint U.S. Air Force and Navy committee and is funded out of the Department of Defense (DoD) budget. Most recently the heart of the program, the Ionospheric Research Instrument (IRI), was completed by one of the world's largest defense contractors working under the direction of the Defense Advanced Research Projects Agency (DARPA), a top research and development (R&D) organization for the DoD. DARPA manages and directs selected basic and applied R&D projects for the DoD pursuing research and technology "where risk and payoff are both very high and where success may provide dramatic advances for traditional military roles and missions."

Under construction since 1990, the HAARP IRI is a field of antennas on the ground in Southeastern Alaska. The facility was probably completed late in 2005 with the announcement of same added to the DARPA website in March of 2006. It is now the world's largest radio frequency (RF) broadcaster, with an effective radiated power of 3.6 million watts — over 72,000 times more powerful than the largest single AM radio station in the United States (50,000 watts). The IRI uses a unique patented ability to focus the RF energy generated by the field, injecting it into a spot at the very top of the atmosphere in a region called the ionosphere. This heats the thin atmosphere of the ionospheric region by several thousand degrees. HAARP, then, is a type of device called an ionospheric heater. This heating allows scientists to do a number of things with the ionosphere. Controlling and directing the processes and forces of the ionosphere is called "ionospheric enhancement." An early HAARP document stated:

> The heart of the program will be the development of a unique ionospheric heating capability to conduct the pioneering experiments required to adequately assess the potential for exploiting ionospheric enhancement technology for DoD purposes.

What might those DoD purposes be? Something about winning wars? How might those purposes be achieved? What technologies will be needed to win the wars of the future? Researchers trying to answer those questions have come up with a vast number of possibilities, most bordering on science fiction. But then again, good science fiction is about recognizing the problems of the future, and suggesting solutions to them before they happen.

On 23 March 1983 President Ronald Reagan called upon "... the scientific community in our country, those who gave us nuclear weapons, to turn their great talents now to the cause of mankind and world peace, to give us the means of rendering these nuclear weapons impotent and obsolete." This quest for the creation of a technology, of a weapon or weapons system that would make atomic war impossible was officially named the Strategic Defense Initiative (SDI). The press lost no time in dubbing it *Star Wars* after the George Lucas movie.

That Initiative sent the United States military-industrial-academic complex on the greatest and costliest weapons hunt in human history. Thousands of ideas were floated, hundreds of those were funded. While SDI research has since been officially abandoned, some ideas are still being actively pursued to this day.

Not all of these ongoing developmental programs are taking place in laboratories of the military and its contractors. Some of these ideas involve technologies or applications that, as weapons, violate international treaties;

others, the use of which would be repugnant to the ethical and moral values of the majority of Americans. In an effort to avoid public outcry (and international condemnation) some of these programs have been disguised as civilian science. One of those may be HAARP.

As Dr. Bernard Eastlund, the putative inventor of HAARP, put it: "The boundary between science fiction and science comes with can you actually make the thing that you're proposing." Bernard J. Eastlund is a physicist who received his B.S. in physics from MIT and his Ph.D. in physics from Columbia University. He led a team of scientists and engineers working for Advanced Power Technologies, Inc. (APTI), a wholly owned subsidiary of ARCO. Eastlund's team developed the concept of a massive antenna array that could produce the kind of shield called for by President Reagan.

The APTI patents that HAARP is probably based on openly discuss manipulating the weather by moving the jet stream and using other techniques to create floods and droughts at will. These patents also describe a way to raise the ionosphere, sending it out into space as an electrically-charged plasma capable of destroying anything electronic (like an incoming ICBM or a spy satellite) passing through it. HAARP certainly looks like a ground-based Star Wars weapons system, a "relic" of the Cold War. But unlike most such relics this one is up and running and now fully funded.

In August of 2002 the Russian State Duma (their version of Congress or Parliament) expressed concern about HAARP, calling it a program to develop "a qualitatively new type of weapon." A joint commission of the State Duma's International Affairs and Defense Committees issued a report that said:

> Under the High Frequency Active Auroral Research Program (HAARP) the USA is creating new integral geophysical weapons that may influence the near-Earth medium with high-frequency radio waves. The significance of this qualitative leap could be compared to the transition from cold steel to firearms, or from conventional weapons to nuclear weapons. This new type of weapon differs from previous types in that the near-Earth medium becomes at once an object of direct influence and its component.

The report further claimed that the USA's plan to carry out large-scale scientific experiments under the HAARP program, and not controlled by the global community, would create weapons capable of jamming radio communications, disrupting equipment installed on spaceships and rockets, provoke serious accidents in electricity networks and in oil and gas pipelines and have a negative impact on the mental health of people populating entire regions.

An appeal, signed by 90 deputies, demanding that an international ban be put on such large-scale geophysical experiments was sent to President Vladimir Putin, to the United Nations (U.N.) and other international organizations, to the parliaments and leaders of the U.N. member countries, to the scientific public and to mass media outlets.

Getting back to Dr. MacDonald... Among the coming "advances" he wrote about were manipulation or control over the weather and climate, including destructive use of ocean waves and melting or destabilizing of the polar ice caps; intentional ozone depletion; triggering earthquakes; and control of the human brain by utilizing the earth's energy fields. Today the polar ice caps are indeed melting and holes in the ozone layer are growing. Could these be the handiwork of advanced weapons? What about earthquakes and mind control? Are we, the private citizens of the world, in the crosshairs of bizarre, unthinkable weapons?

What about the Russian Duma's claim that HAARP could have a negative impact on the mental health of people populating entire regions of the globe? In "Vandalism In The Sky?," their seminal article on HAARP in *Nexus Magazine*, Dr. Nick Begich and Jeane Manning describe how HAARP could be used to induce mental dysfunction, quoting from Brzezinski on a proposal from Dr. MacDonald saying:

Political strategists are tempted to exploit research on the brain and human behavior. Geophysicist Gordon J. F. MacDonald — specialist in problems of warfare — says [an] accurately-timed, artificially-excited electronic stroke "...could lead to a pattern of oscillations that produce relatively high power levels over certain regions of the Earth... In this way, one could develop a system that would seriously impair the brain performance of very large populations in selected regions over an extended period..."

Studies of the effects of natural electromagnetic fields on animal and human biology date to as far back as 1935, and possibly even earlier. One such study successfully correlated the occurrences of solar-generated magnetic storms with increases in the incidence of such things as deaths from myocardial infarction, mental hospital admission, and automobile accidents. Russian studies of animals and humans experimentally exposed to electromagnetic fields found that such exposures induce hypermotility (excessive movement; especially excessive motility of the gastrointestinal tract) and impairment of conditioned reflexes. These would therefore be of keen interest to the behavioral scientist (mind controllers) as well as to the climatologist.

Dr. MacDonald commented on the possible use of the destructive effects of electromagnetic fields in the environment on human health and performance. He said that weapons systems could be developed that would increase the intensity of the electromagnetic field oscillating in the spherical-shaped cavity between the Earth and the ionosphere, and that these weapons could be used to "seriously impair brain performance in very large populations in selected regions over an extended period" just as the Duma feared HAARP might do. Could HAARP, or another similar antenna elsewhere, be the source of North Korea's madness? Could Kim Jong-Il be a true Manchurian Candidate? And if so, whose?

In 1969 Dr. MacDonald wrote: "Our understanding of basic environmental science and technology is primitive, but still more primitive are our notions of the proper political forms and procedures to deal with the consequences of modification."

It would appear that the gap between our understanding of environmental science and technology and our ability to grapple with this knowledge as a body politic has changed little in the intervening decades. You, my friend, must take action to create the necessary "forms and procedures to deal with the consequences of modification." It is, after all, your planet.

The Bussard Fusion Reactor and Its Detractors

The Bureaucratic Plot Against Cheap Energy

by William W. Flint

November 10, 2005. Doc Bussard was 77 years old. He was already in pain, but this latest setback had intensified it. For such an elegant, promising machine to come to such an ignominious end was nauseatingly painful to him. The WB-6 had represented his highest hopes for the future of humankind; and it was quite literally sitting there — cooked — in its own vacuum chamber. Its owner, Doc's company, was near bankruptcy. The annual lease on the Santa Fe lab had expired on November 1st, and there was no money to renew it. Doc explained, "The Iraq war budgets had been consuming everything in sight in Washington, and when it came time for the budget process for fiscal 2006, the total Navy R & D budget was cut by 26% across the board. We were a victim of that."

Doc called the WB-6 a polywell — short for polyhedral potential well. Later, people started calling it a BFR, for Bussard Fusion Reactor. Others called it an IEC device, or a nuclear fusion reactor. The polywell used a positively charged, magnetically shielded grid to pull electrons into a dense ball of negative charge at the center of the grid. In turn, that "electron ball" of negative charge (the potential well) pulled positive ions of heavy hydrogen (deuterium) together, accelerating the ions to such a high speed that when they collided, they fused to make helium atoms and neutrons. This was nuclear fusion, and the polywell had done it very well, producing 2.5 billion fusion reactions per second, more than 100,000 times the previous record for ion acceleration devices.

The total mass of the reacting heavy hydrogen was greater than the total mass of the helium and neutron products. Mass was most definitely not conserved in the polywell. The lost mass was released as energy in accordance with E = mc^2, Einstein's relativity equation. The symbol c^2 represented a very large number: the speed of light squared — 90 quadrillion meters squared per second squared $(3 \times 10^8 \text{ m/sec})^2$. When a very small loss in mass was multiplied by this enormous number, the resulting product was correspondingly enormous.

Four milligrams (1 milligram = the wing of a housefly) of deuterium would have lost about 0.0024 milligrams in fusing to make Helium 3 and a neutron. But that 24/10,000ths of a milligram could have produced enough energy to run a 5000-watt electric generator for 12 hours — or enough energy to have driven his Honda Civic the 300 miles from Santa Fe to El Paso — these were dramatic ways of looking at the polywell's ability to change extremely small amounts of matter into vast amounts of energy.

Doc knew that with proper funding the polywell could have been scaled-up to become a 100 megawatt commercially viable nuclear fusion power plant. (A 100-megawatt plant could easily have provided all the electrical needs for a city of 20,000.) He also knew that the polywell could be made to use boron instead of heavy hydrogen. Boron is a harmless element found in Boraxo™. This nuclear reaction would have produced no neutrons, and no ionizing radiation such as beta or gamma. (Neutrons are one of the reasons that most nuclear reactions today are considered dirty. The neutrons spray objects surrounding the nuclear reaction, and can sometimes make those objects radioactive. They can penetrate many feet of shielding, and are a hazard to living things.) The only product of the boron reaction would have been helium, which is completely harmless. He knew that the boron reaction would have produced no sulfate or nitrate air pollutants and no greenhouse gases (carbon compounds) such as carbon dioxide or methane. From the standpoint of environmental pollution, the boron-fueled polywell power plant would have been vastly superior to traditional coal-fired or nuclear fission power plants.

But after almost 20 years, struggling to research and develop the polywell on little more than a shoestring — with occasional small hand-outs from the U.S. Navy — Doc's attempt to produce a vastly superior energy source with near-zero environmental impact had clearly come to an end.

* * *

Nearly a year after shutting down the lab, Doctor Robert F. Bussard presented his work — for the first time in more than a decade — to the International Astronautical Congress. He later discussed his results with Google, the online search engine company, in a talk entitled "Should Google Go Nuclear?" which is widely available on the Internet. In a letter to an Internet forum on his 2005 results, Doc wrote that he believed "the survival of our high-tech civilization depends on getting off of fossil fuels ASAP, and — if we do not — we will descend into a growing series of 'oil wars' and energy confrontations that can lead only to a huge cataclysm. Which *can* be circumvented if only we build the clean fusion machines in time … the political reality is that oil companies have no interest in supporting fusion research… There is only one thing the oil companies want, and that is to sell oil, and more oil … and keep raising the price, until finally foolish solar and windmills become competitive."

Robert F. Bussard graduated in 1950 from UCLA with a degree in engineering. In 1953, he wrote a paper on nuclear rocket propulsion while he was at Oak Ridge National Laboratory. It got the attention of the Air Force, and the result was the start of a national nuclear rocket program in the spring of 1955. Doc described the work of his team: "We ended up with a 250,000-ton thrust engine that could be cycled 40 times on and off. It ran hydrogen through graphite cores at very high temperatures, and produced a specific impulse 2.5 to 3 times higher than anything obtainable from chemical propulsion. The program ended up being controlled by NASA who intended to use it for a 1978 manned Mars mission; but it fell flat due to wars between the chemical and nuclear rocket communities and the budget office. Then along came the Vietnam war, and that killed everything." Then, in frustration, he exclaimed, "Fifty years ago, we had nuclear rockets that could take people to Mars!"

Doc was recognized in 1960 for his design of the Bussard ramscoop interstellar space drive, made famous by Carl Sagan in his *Cosmos* series and used by such science fiction authors as Larry Niven and Poul Anderson. He received his doctorate in plasma physics from Princeton University in 1963. In the early 1970s, when he was an assistant director of the Atomic Energy Commission (AEC), he helped start the U.S. tokamak fusion program. (A tokamak is a large donut-shaped magnetic confinement intended to produce fusion by heating a plasma cloud containing deuterium and tritium, two isotopes of heavy hydrogen.) Robert also designed a small variation of the tokamak, called the Riggatron, in the late 1970s.

These efforts led him to think seriously about how to work around the problems that plague tokamak reactors. He thought it was a shame that the heavy hydrogen ions were so much more massive than electrons, because a tokamak would be able to magnetically confine electrons at high density far more easily than it was able to confine the tritium and deuterium ions. He knew that a spherical positive grid could be used to pull electrons into a ball (or well) of negative charge inside the grid, but he also knew that too many electrons got lost when they ran into that grid. (He knew then that such a device, called an IEC machine, could be used to attract positive ions and make fusion.) Then he had an inspiration: he began to wonder if the grid could be magnetically insulated from the electrons, to keep them from striking the grid and getting lost. He thought that if he placed a circular magnetic coil on each face of a cube, with each coil pointing the same magnetic pole inward, it might form a working magnetic bottle for the electrons. This was the birth of a new idea — what he called the Whiffleball™ concept — a "quasi-spherical" magnetic field with holes, inside of the positive grid, into which one could inject electrons. By 1987 he had become so confident in the concept, that he formed a new company, Energy Mass Conversion Corporation — EMC² — to research it. He tested the first polywell, the WB-1, seven years later. (The WB stands for Whiffleball™.)

We took our polywell concept to the Strategic Defense Office where Jim Eisenstein was the technical director. He immediately understood what we were proposing, thought it was a great idea, and agreed to fund it through the Defense Nuclear Agency, which became DARPA. It was initially funded for $30 million, but a new technical director killed the funding after four months. The new director said, "We don't do fusion in DARPA."

In 1994 Dr. Bussard gave a talk about his program to the Westinghouse Nuclear Society on Advanced Technology for the 21st century. That talk was evidently successful, because the American Nuclear Society asked him to repeat it at their annual meeting in May. Doc said, "When I turned to our contract monitor and asked should we accept this invitation, he said, 'No. Now that you got this thing working, no more talks, don't go to any more physics conferences, don't write any papers, just lay quiet. Do your work and don't publish.'"

So from that day in 1994 until November of 2005, Robert Bussard was embargoed from publishing anything about his polywell research. One consequence of the embargo was that during this time period he was not allowed to rebut his critics. The most articulate critic of the polywell was recent MIT graduate Todd Rider, whose doctoral dissertation purportedly demonstrated that devices such as the polywell could not possibly produce net fusion. Almost certainly, this was one of the reasons that Bussard received such limited funding. Tom Ligon was an employee of EMC^2 who worked for Dr. Bussard during this same time period. He has a lot to say on the subject:

> You want to know why Dr. Bussard was embargoed by the Navy against publishing? The answer is a major pissing contest between the group funding him and somebody in the Office of Naval Research (ONR). You want to know who was funding Todd Rider as he pursued his thesis? Look at the acknowledgements in it, which state, and I quote, "The author is partially owned and operated by a graduate fellowship from the Office of Naval Research."
>
> Ask yourself how a recent EE grad, new to plasma physics, comes up with the idea to tackle an entire field of fusion physics? Does he do this entirely on his own, or does a sponsor suggest it, and provide some guidance? I'm not criticizing this practice ... I would guess this is the way most dissertations go ... you find a sponsor and work on something that interests them, that they will know (about), can assist on, and can judge.
>
> Now realize that 1994 is the year Dr. Bussard gave some extremely damning testimony to Congress regarding the fusion research programs in the Department of Energy (DOE), earning himself some highly motivated opponents, at least one of whom was causing trouble from ONR.
>
> If you ask Dr. Bussard directly about what he thinks of Dr. Rider, he will very probably tell you EXACTLY what he thinks. I'm not going to repeat it here.

The polite version is that Rider selects his conditions to support his conclusions. And he doesn't listen when you try to explain how IEF machines actually work.

The embargo was, at least in part, to prevent Dr. Bussard from responding to Rider, due to the infighting going on within the Navy. I don't know the exact circumstances or motivations ... probably would make good political intrigue.

In fact, while he apparently does not like to refer to him by name, Dr. Bussard has basically addressed all of Rider's objections. He has not ignored them. He tries to point out the way he believes the machines operate. I was witness, in fact, in 1995–96, to Dr. Bussard thinking Rider had actually found a fatal flaw in the idea. He disappeared into his office for a couple of days of furious analysis and calculation, and emerged about the most jubilant I'd ever seen him. He'd discovered that not only was Rider wrong, but the machine itself had held the built-in cure all along, and would work better than the original model had predicted.

Frankly, I wish Dr. Bussard and Dr. Krall would take off the gloves and rebut the critics for all they're worth.

Later, the U.S. Navy funded the EMC^2 polywell research and development program with $12.7 million from 1999 to 2004.

But $12.7 million was just not enough: four to five years and $200 million would be required to build a full-scale boron fusion plant that could produce net energy (also called "break-even" — the point at which the energy produced begins to exceed the energy required to start the reaction). Doc continued:

> Since 1989, in report after report, we've told the Navy and the Department of Defense that the cost of this program is $200 million. They've known this from the beginning. But they say, "We can't do that because if we do that, it becomes visible to the staffers on Capitol Hill. Then everyone becomes aware that this is what the Navy is doing. The Department of Energy will see it [and they] will say, 'No you can't do that – We [DOE] have the charter to make fusion (not the Navy).' And that [will be] the end of the program, because they will co-opt it and shut the Navy down."
>
> So we [would] get funded [again] at a level below the radar level and the politics. The funding has always been way too small. We had a staff of five to ten people working for 12 years. The result was that we learned the physics slowly and we learned it all. But [solutions to a lot of] engineering problems were way beyond such limited budgets. We couldn't run the machine steady state and we had to use small coils and capacitor banks. That made things very difficult. You don't have time, you have problems with the cooling, you can't control the gas flow.

To really make this work, we need expertise and assistance from companies like Westinghouse, GE, and Raytheon. For example, if you need 200 kV standoffs, you need someone like Westinghouse to design and build them. The major impediments have always been money.

The problem is that most of the fusion research money has gone to various tokamaks and the NIF project in Livermore, California. As of 2008, the United States Department of Energy (DOE) and other U.S. federal agencies have spent a total of approximately $18 billion dollars on such programs. Creators of these devices intend to produce fusion by compressing and heating a plasma of deuterium and tritium. The tokamak uses a magnetic field to do this. Dr. Bussard comments, "... magnetic fields do not contain neutral plasma worth a darn, which is the tokamak problem." Then, talking about the polywell, he says, "In contrast, in an electron acceleration device, all of the ions falling into the well acquire the same amount of energy, causing them all to have sufficient energy to make fusion. If you have a 500 kV well, you can do [boron] fusion, something essentially impossible for a tokamak design."

In his earlier Valencia paper, he said, "...it is always possible to reach a condition of break-even power in [a polywell] with any fusion fuel combination. This is *not* the case in [tokamaks] as these are severely limited by ion collisional losses to their wall." Dr. Nicholas Krall, a top fusion researcher, is much more blunt, "We [the United States] have spent $15 billion studying tokamaks, and all we know about them is that they're no damn good!"

The polywell — much simpler and cheaper than NIF or the tokamak — can do boron fusion, which involves no neutrons and no radiation. In contrast, NIF and the tokamak can only do heavy hydrogen fusion which produces neutrons and requires tritium, a fuel that is both radioactive and expensive. Of the billions of dollars that have been spent on fusion research over the past 50 years, only a few million (about one *ten-thousandth* as much!) has been spent on the polywell. One has to wonder how such a state of affairs can be possible.

Ironically, part of the answer goes to Bussard himself. He helped start the U.S. tokamak fusion program in the early 1970s. Much later, in a June 6, 1995 letter to the U.S. Congress, Bussard tried to put an end to the tokamak boondoggle he had helped to create. He explained:

> DOE is almost certainly not ever going to give the nation any safe, technically viable, or economically useful fusion power plants or systems. ... DOE commitment to... [the giant magnetic tokamak] ensures only the need for very large budgets; and that is what the program has been about for the past 15 years — a defense-of-budget program, not a fusion achievement program. As one of the three people who created this program in the early 1970s (when I was

assistant director of the AEC's Controlled Thermonuclear Reaction Division) I know this to be true; we raised the budget in order to take 20% off the top of the larger funding, to try all of the things that the mainline labs would not try. Each of us left soon thereafter, and the second generation management thought the big program was real: it was not.

One has to wonder why tokamak research continues. Doc thinks:

> After we left, nobody understood we were doing it to raise enough money to scrape some money off the top to try and do some real things, and it became a budget program. Harry Lidsky, an MIT professor, wrote an article in the *MIT Technology Review,* "The Trouble with Fusion." The subject of his article was that when the program became large and budgeted, it ceased to [be] a fusion research program. Instead everyone focused on continuing the large budgets ... year after year, so they could maintain their large-scale laboratories. It's a human failing: people want things to stay the way they are.

* * *

In August 2007 Dr. Bussard got another $1.8 million in government funds, with the help of Alan Roberts, EMC²'s longtime Navy contract monitor. Bussard's wife, Dolly Gray, who co-founded EMC² with him in 1987 and served as its president and CEO, has helped to assemble another small team of scientists headed by Dr. Richard Nebel on leave from Los Alamos National Laboratory (LANL). Besides Nebel, 54, this new group includes Jaeyoung Park, a 37-year-old physicist who is also on leave from LANL; Mike Wray, the physicist who ran the key 2005 tests, and Wray's brother, Kevin, who is the computer guru for the operation.

Doc died in October of 2007. He had been dreadfully ill since shortly after the old lab had closed in 2005. That was a really sad time, but the new team is working hard to see his dream through. Their goal is to reproduce the WB-6, improve on it, and have it hold together for peer review — probably in early fall of 2008. They achieved "first plasma" on the new WB-7 in early January 2008, and more recently, in June 2008, they have seen "very encouraging" results.

Speaking about Robert Bussard, Richard Nebel said, "I've met and worked with a lot of really smart people. Not many were real innovators, and that's what he was. He would try to do things other people said you couldn't."

"He was a first-class guy, a super person, extremely innovative, a wonderful engineer," confirmed Robert Hirsch, Bussard's boss from the time they both served in the Atomic Energy Commission's Controlled Thermonuclear Reaction Division. About the polywell, Hirsch said Bussard was, "… swimming upstream as far as the fusion community was concerned. Unless somebody can repeat and show other people that it's operating, it's really not scientifically acceptable. But if the idea works the way he thinks it could, and there's a good chance he's right, it will not take a very big machine to show net energy."

"If this works, it's going to be a big deal. It could take the entire energy market," Nebel said. "And drag the oil companies into the 21st century," Gray added.

THE CONTROLLERS

The Next Vietnam

by Colonel L. Fletcher Prouty

Critics of the Iraq War look back in vain for another foreign policy tack that better served U.S. interests. Boycotts against Iraq of food and medicine immediately preceding the war led to the deaths of hundreds of thousands of Iraqi children. The first Persian Gulf War preceded that; precipitated by the green light U.S. diplomat April Glaspie originally gave to Saddam Hussein to invade Kuwait. Prior to that, the U.S. sold weapons to both sides of the Iran-Iraq War. Of course, the Kurdish holocaust in Iraq was brought on by expected U.S. military support that never happened. Indeed, the war critics can go all the way back to 1968, when the Baathists, and Saddam Hussein in particular, came to power with American help. That went little noticed at the time because the U.S. found itself much more wrapped up in the quagmire to which the current conflict is most often compared: Vietnam.

The late Colonel Fletcher Prouty understood pre-emptive action perhaps better than most conspiracy researchers. Stationed in Christchurch, New Zealand at the time of the JFK assassination, he was alarmed to discover that a full profile with photo of Lee Harvey Oswald appeared in the local paper before the accused assassin was even charged with the crime. This led him to conclude that Kennedy had died as the result of a well-coordinated conspiracy and that, indeed, much U.S. foreign policy resulted from similar types of conspiratorial manipulation. Prouty's most known book, The Secret Team, linked the assassination to the earlier shootdown of Gary Powers' U2 plane, which Prouty characterized as a deliberate move to derail peace talks between Dwight Eisenhower and Nikita Khrushchev. Prouty claimed that JFK was killed because of his ambition to remove U.S. troops from Vietnam. . He spent his later life as a citizen critic of his country, tirelessly working to expose secrets that he felt corrupted its ideals. He worked as a consultant to Oliver Stone's movie JFK, and his character appeared in it as "Mr. X," the Pentagon back-channel played by Donald Sutherland to Kevin Costner's portrayal of prosecutor Jim Garrison.

The fall of the shah of Iran stymied the covert op described by Prouty in the following essay, which first appeared three years before the Iranian hostage crisis. Since then, a deal was struck with the shah's emergent opposition cleric and ultimate successor as Iran's ruler, the Ayatollah Khomeini, to hold on to 52 American embassy hostages until Ronald Reagan won the U.S. presidential election over Jimmy Carter. That set up a pattern of trading-with-the enemy that eventually led to the Iran-contra scandal, where illegal U.S. weapons sales to Iran funded an equally illegal war in Nicaragua. Prouty helped chronicle the long, sad ordeal of Iran's transformation from the situation described in the following into America's biggest enemy, poised now also as its next battlefront, and still perhaps its next Vietnam. — Kenn Thomas

In what must have been the greatest gathering of royalty and near-royalty in the history of the world, hundreds of guests from Princess Grace of Monaco to Madame Onassis traveled to the ancient city of Persepolis in Iran to celebrate the crowning of the shah as the true descendent and heir to the throne of Cyprus in October 1971, when the Empire of Cyprus celebrated its 2,500th year.

Reza Shah Pahlevi, the son of a one-time army General, not only wears this crown ceremoniously but, already surfeited with newly earned oil billions, he sees the new Iran as the fourth greatest nation on earth.

At the same time the former director of the U.S. Central Intelligence Agency sees Iran as the new Thailand, just as his predecessor, Gen. William "Wild Bill" Donovan made Thailand the base of clandestine American operations in Asia. Both men served nominally as ambassadors after having led the clandestine services of the U.S.

In the fragile balance that has become part of life in the Middle East, Reza Shah Pahlevi, who openly despises his Arab neighbors, is now the man of destiny.

Shortly after his royal guests left Persepolis, the proud shah flexed his newfound oil muscles, and "with London's prior agreement," took over three islands in the lower Persian Gulf — Abu Musa, Greater Tunbs and Lesser Tunbs. The islands are strategically situated for the shipment of oil. Arabs from Libya to Iraq rose in protest over this rash act. Libya nationalized British oil interests and withdrew all its funds from British banks.

This was but a beginning. More recently, while Henry Kissinger was jetting from one capital to another in the Middle East, the shah landed 1,500 of his U.S.-styled and U.S.-trained "special forces" in the sheikdom of Dhofar. The shah claims that his troops were delivered in the U.S.-made C-130 transport aircraft and that they landed at the "invitation" of the Sultan of Oman. Although the Assistant Secretary of State for Middle Eastern Affairs, Joseph Sisco, has said recently that the government of neighboring Yemen is under a leadership that is "basically indigenous," the shah believes that the "rebels" are supported by the U.S.S.R. and Communist China.

Few places in the world could be more remote and desolate than Salalah, the capital city of Dhofar. I have stopped there, and have been amazed to find it a large, man-made oasis of luxurious vegetation, including plums, grapes, and bananas — all nurtured by an ancient irrigation system powered by blinded camels that drive a massive waterwheel device that brings water from a deep well. Salalah is where the British purchased aircraft landing rights with Maria Teresa silver dollars minted every year by the British with the same date, "1780," because that was the date of the originals the then sheikh possessed. Today this strange bit of green has become another outpost of the aggressive new Iran.

To the east and across the Gulf of Oman, the shah is rushing to completion of a huge new airport at the old landing ground of Jask, once the pioneering stop for BOAC and Air France. The old gravel field where we used to land the faithful DC3 and C-47 transports of World War II is now being readied for the hottest jet fighters in the world, and for the very heavy C-135 Boeing, in-flight refueling tankers that will be added to the shah's air force in the summer of 1974.

On another front, the shah has placed his elite forces on the border of Iraq, barely 100 miles east of Baghdad. Serious fighting has broken out in the area and neither side seem ready to give an inch. The passing years have seen other disputes between Arabs and Persians on the borders of the gulf at oil-rich Kuwait and on the strategic island of Bahrain just across the shallow waters from the greatest oil deposits in the entire Middle East — the ARAMCO concessions in the eastern territories of Saudi Arabia.

Only recently the age-old conflict between the Kurds and Iraq has broken out again into active fighting, and although the shah would not want to be brought into any fight on his own long borders with the Kurds, whose lands lie between Iraq and Iran, some insiders believe that the shah, with strong American assistance, may have made overtures to the wily old Eagle of the Mountains, the Kurdish General Mustaf al Barzani. It is known that the United States has made available to the Kurds a number of old but still combat-effective F-105 fighter bomber aircraft. Barzani's pilots are being trained in Iran and the F-105s will most likely operate and be maintained from Iranian airfields. In the heightening pressures of the coming Middle East war, this type of open "covert peacetime operation" says more about the nature of the Iranian-American relationship than anything else."

All of this would appear to be more of the same old "Arab problem" if it were not for several ominous incidents that signal the beginning of what seems destined to become another "Vietnam." In the Feb. 16, 1974 issue of *The Nation*, Senator Aborezk said, "At the moment when peace seems possible in the Middle East, the United States appears to be helping to sow the seeds for future conflict." Commenting on developments in southern Arabia west of Oman, the *Christian Science Monitor* has called that action "a brewing mini-Vietnam." Already things have gone past the "brewing" stage, and past the point when, in a similar situation John Kennedy became President and inherited 15 years of clandestine developments in Indochina.

In what must be one of the most unusual and ominous bits of big industry advertisements seen in many years, the Boeing Company inserted the following in the January 1977 issue of *Air Force* magazine, the official voice of the Air Force Association and the unofficial but weighty voice of the U.S. Air Force:

> MAINTAIN BOEING TANKERS IN IRAN
> "The Logistics Support Corporation (LSC), an affiliate of Boeing, is seeking qualified veterans or persons who are now separating from the military to service and maintain new 707 (C-135 added) tankers in Iran. LAC is under contract to the Iranian Air Force to provide training for aerial tanker operations beginning in mid-1974. Assignment is for three or more years."

This advertisement means a lot more than it says. Years ago it was my job to provide cover for CIA units around the world. In many cases we used the name "Logistics Support Group," "Logistics Support Activity" etc. and, as in the well-known Cuban Bay of Pigs affair, the agency established many of these covert units as commercial arrangements even when they were going to use "sheep-dipped" military personnel. This would not be unusual in Iran, and there may well be such a clandestine arrangement with this Boeing "Logistics Support Corporation."

The CIA played the major role of overthrowing the government of Premier Mossadegh in 1953 and has been very powerful and influential in Iran ever since [article was published in 1977]. Note that the former Director of Central Intelligence, Richard Helms, served as Ambassador to Iran from 1973 to 1977. The CIA's not-so-secret private cover airline, Air America, was instrumental in helping the shah set up the Iranian National airline, Air Iran, and for many years the CIA, through an affiliate of Air America, took care of maintenance for Air Iran.

Now that the shah has 300 fighter bombers — 80 of them U.S.-built F-4s of an early type and 100 more on order of the most advanced model, he can use aerial refueling tankers to make it possible for him to deploy those first-line aircraft against any target in the Middle East.

Not only has the shah built up a large air force, but he now has a fleet of 700 helicopters that includes 200 gun-ships, 18 giant Chinooks, and 18 antisubmarine warfare models.

700 helicopters require not less than 7,000 highly skilled maintenance personnel if they are to be used effectively in any kind of operational activity — training or combat. According to the testimony of an army expert extracted from the Congressional Record, it takes about 24 man-hours of maintenance for each hour of helicopter operations.

The point is that the shah has an American Military Assistance Group of about 1,000 men, most of whom, it must be assumed, are performing administrative and training functions. This means that he must rely on outside covert help for his logistics and operational support. And this type of support is usually provided by the CIA.

It is exactly this sort of morass that got the United States involved so heavily in Vietnam before the Congress and the general public discovered what was going on. The movement of helicopters to South Vietnam from Laos by the CIA was the first step that led to the massive American involvement in Vietnam.

It is not the usual game of jockeying for position that we are witnessing in the Middle East. It is not Iraq, or the Kurds, or the Sultan of Oman, or the Sheikh of Yemen whom we are watching. Inevitably, in the words of Simon Head, in the March 21, 1977 issue of the *New York Review of Books*, the "fragile balance is not going to survive; it has been upset ... by the rising strength of two regional powers — Iran and Saudi Arabia. For both, the source of this new strength is oil." As in Southeast Asia, the new Thailand, the new base of American involvement, is Iran. The new "Vietnam" will be that national that breaks first and becomes threatened by subversive insurgency." With the shah tightening the noose around both Iraq and Saudi Arabia, it will be either one of them. Then Iran, with American aid, will dash in to save them from dreaded "Communism" and they will suffer the fate of a Vietnamese "liberation." And because all of this preparation is going ahead covertly, in secrecy and by deception, we may never know how we became involved until it is too late.

Jim Jones and the Peoples Temple

by Jim Hougan

Introduction

What follows is a work in progress about Jim Jones and the Peoples Temple. Insofar as it has a central thesis, it is that Jones initiated the 1978 massacre at Jonestown, Guyana because he feared that Congressman Leo Ryan's investigation would disgrace him. Specifically, Jones was afraid that Ryan and the press would uncover evidence that the leftist founder of the Peoples Temple was for many years an asset of the FBI and the CIA. This fear was, I believe, mirrored in various precincts of the U.S. intelligence community, which worried that Ryan's investigation would embarrass the CIA by linking Jones to some of the Agency's most volatile programs — including "mind-control studies" and operations such as MK-ULTRA.

This is, I believe, why Jones' 201-file was purged by the CIA immediately after Jones' case officer, Dan Mitrione, was murdered in Montevideo, Uruguay.[1]

What I believe and what I can prove are, in some instances, two different things. There is no smoking gun in the pages that follow. But I think the reader will agree that there are certainly a great many empty cartridges lying about — enough, perhaps, to stimulate further investigation by others.

That said, it should be added that I am hardly the first to suggest that the Jonestown massacre was the outcome of someone's secret machinations. The affair is inherently mysterious, and conspiracy theories abound, the most prominent among them that "Jonestown" was a CIA mind-control experiment.

This is a view that's been put forward in a number of venues. Congressman Ryan's close friend and chief-of-staff, Joe Holsinger, is persuaded of it. The respectable Edwin Mellen Press has published a book on the subject.[2] And professional conspiracists such as John Judge have embraced the thesis wholeheartedly.

I suspect they're mistaken. In some ways, the truth is even darker.

I.1 Ryan and the Numbers

In the fall of 1978, with Thanksgiving less than two weeks away, Congressman Leo Ryan (D-CALIF.) flew to Georgetown, Guyana accompanied by a contingent of "concerned relatives" and members of the press. The purpose of the trip was at once simple and difficult: to determine whether or not American citizens were being abused or held against their will at the Peoples Temple agricultural settlement in Jonestown.

Reports to that effect had been received from a number of sources, including former members of the Temple, their relatives and the press. Whether those reports should be believed was a separate matter. An American-based political organization that used the trappings of religion to attract members and avoid taxes, the Temple was a controversial institution — a personality cult that put itself forward as a vehicle of "apostolic socialism." Though its membership was predominantly black, the group was run by a white matriarchy that was, in turn, under the spell of a Bible-hating, charismatic sadist named Jim Jones.[3]

Escorted by Richard Dwyer, Deputy Chief of Mission at the U.S. Embassy, Congressman Ryan and a part of his contingent visited the remote commune on the afternoon of November 17, a Friday.

Though the visit was an unwelcome one, and filled with tension, Temple attorneys Charles Garry and Mark Lane arranged for the delegation to be given a tour of the settlement, food and a place to sleep. Accordingly, members of the Ryan party met with the Temple's leader, Jim Jones, and spoke with many of the organization's rank and file. Speeches and entertainment went on until late at night.

By Saturday afternoon, November 18, though Ryan himself had spoken favorably about several aspects of the settlement, a number of "defectors" had declared themselves, saying that they wanted to leave. It was then, as the congressman and his company were preparing to depart, that Ryan was suddenly, freakishly, attacked by a knife-wielding man. Though the scuffle was quickly broken up, and Ryan uninjured, the provocation put an end to the uneasy truce that both sides had cultivated.[4]

Driven to the airstrip at Port Kaituma, where two small planes waited for them, Ryan and his party were ambushed as they prepared to embark. When the shooting ended, five people, including the congressman, lay dead on the tarmac. Nearby, and in the surrounding jungle, survivors of the delegation, having fled from the shooting, hid from sight, tending each other's wounds. Meanwhile, as the death squad returned to Jonestown, one of the small planes, its engine damaged, took off for Georgetown, transporting both flight crews and all the bad news it could carry.

As night fell, both the wounded and the well concealed themselves in a rum shop at Port Kaituma, awaiting evacuation in the morning. Meanwhile, some five miles away, and unknown to anyone in Port Kaituma, a holocaust was unfolding in Jonestown.

Guyanese defense forces arrived at the airstrip shortly after dawn that

Sunday morning. Securing the runway, the troops turned toward Jonestown, marching down the long, rough road to the commune. Arriving there at mid-morning, they were horrified to find a field of cadavers: men, women and children lying in an arc around the settlement's central pavilion.

Some 200 bodies were quickly counted, but the numbers of dead continued to climb throughout the days that followed. Revisions to the toll were continual, and sickening: 363, 405, 775, 800, 869, 910, 912, 913... To newspaper readers and watchers of the evening news, it seemed almost as if the slaughter was ongoing, rather than a fait accompli.

Amid the confusion and horror, the escalating body count provoked suspicions, though explanations abounded. It was said, for example, that the count was consistently low because the bodies of children lay unseen beneath the corpses of adults. Skeptics, however, pointed out that some of the earliest reports listed 82 children among 363 dead.[5] It seemed fair to say, therefore, that the children's presence was known from the beginning, and ought to have been taken into account. Moreover, even if the dead had been counted from the air, and even if one assumed that all of the children had been hidden from sight — which, as photos attest, was not the case — the body count ought to have been more than 600 from the very first day.

But it wasn't. Of course, conditions were primitive, and the circumstances ghastly. Mistakes were inevitable. Nevertheless, 789 American passports had been found at Jonestown within a few hours of the troops' arrival.[6] This discovery, coupled with the low body count, had somehow caused those at the scene to believe that hundreds of "cultists" were "missing." Indeed, it was to find these supposedly missing Templars that military search parties were sent by foot, plane and helicopter to comb the surrounding area.

And meanwhile, incredibly, the dead lay in plain sight — more than 500 of them in an area the size of a football field.

It was a nearly a week, then, before the body count stabilized at 913 and, when it did, skeptics wondered how it was possible that 363 bodies had concealed 550 — particularly when 82 of the 363 were said to have been small children.

Even mathematically, and from its inception, "Jonestown" did not make sense. Something was wrong with the reports from the very first day.

I.2 The Cause and Manner of Death

More than 900 men, women and children were suddenly, violently dead under circumstances that, even at this late date, remain mind-boggling. The mounting body count, as well as the subsequent handling of the bodies, threatened to make conspiracy theorists of even the most gullible.

It was alleged, of course, in newspapers and instant books,[7] that upwards of a thousand brainwashed religious fanatics committed suicide in the jungle because their leader, Jim Jones, told them to. One by one, they'd come forward without protest to drink cyanide-laced "Kool-Aid" from a vat.[8] It was as simple as that. Jonestown was proof positive of the effectiveness of brainwashing, and of the dangers inherent in the new religions.

As it happened, however, this was only a theory and, as it turned out, an inaccurate one. Viz.: Seven months after the massacre, the *New England Journal of Medicine* commented on the handling of the bodies at Jonestown.[9] Citing the criticisms of forensic experts and organizations,[10] the *Journal* noted that:

• only one-third of the bodies at Jonestown had been positively identified more than six months after the massacre;

• no death certificates had been obtained on any of those who'd died in Guyana;

• a medicolegal autopsy ought to have been performed on every body to establish the cause and manner of death in each case.

In fact, however, only seven autopsies were carried out among the 913 victims — an appalling figure. (As one forensic expert, Dr. Cyril Wecht, remarked: every American who dies under suspicious circumstances has a *right* to an autopsy.) Even then, the autopsies that *were* carried out were hardly conclusive: all of the bodies had been embalmed in Guyana, using a procedure that "ripped up" the internal organs, almost a month *before* the autopsies were conducted.[11]

This was unfortunate, to say the least.[12] Indeed, six leading medical examiners described the handling of the bodies (by the military and others) as "inept," "incompetent," "embarrassing," and a case of "doing it backwards."[13] Dr. Rudiger Breitenecker, who assisted at the seven autopsies, agreed. There had been "a series of errors," he said. "We shuddered about the degree of ineptness."[14]

Despite the difficulties, "probable cyanide poisoning" was listed as the cause of death in five of the seven autopsy reports — though, as it happened, *only one* of the five bodies, that of Maria Katsaris, showed any traces of cyanide ("although carefully searched for").[15]

Still, the suspicion of cyanide poisoning in the absence of cyanide itself is not as strange as it may at first seem. As one of the examining physicians pointed out, cyanide is unstable in "the postmortem interval." Perhaps, then, it broke down in the victims' tissues. In any case, the "relevant body fluids" may have been contaminated by the embalming process itself or, in the course of that procedure, the fluids may have been diluted or discarded. The fact that Diphenhydramine was found in the stomachs of several victims and in the "poison vat" as well, suggested that the victims had drunk from the vat's contents. That the contents of the vat included cyanide could not, however, be proven from an examination of the vat itself — which, upon study, betrayed no traces of the poison.[16] (The explanation was offered that the vat had an acid pH at which cyanide is unstable. The assumption, then, was that the poison broke down in the days after the massacre.)

"Probable cyanide poisoning" was, therefore, a conclusion based upon circumstantial evidence: i.e., reports, including press reports, from the scene. These accounts noted the presence of cyanide salts in the inventory of Jonestown's medical dispensary; and, also, the discovery of cyanide in syringes and bottles in the area around the pavilion. Finally, there was the account of Dr. Leslie Mootoo, chief medical examiner and senior bacteriologist for Guyana, who examined scores of bodies within a day or two of the disaster. According to Dr. Mootoo, who labored long and hard taking specimens and samples from many of the dead, cyanide was present in the stomachs of most of those whom he examined. Unfortunately, evidence of his findings disappeared soon after it was collected. According to Dr. Mootoo, his specimens and samples were given to "a representative of the American Embassy in Georgetown, expecting that they would be forwarded to American forensic pathologists." They weren't. No one knows what happened to them.

Of the two remaining bodies that were autopsied, Jim Jones was found to have been killed by a gunshot wound to the head. As for Temple member Ann Moore, her death was attributed to *two* causes because it was impossible to say which came first. She had been shot in the head, and, unlike the others, a massive quantity of cyanide was found in her body's tissues. (Why the poison should have broken down in the bodies of the other victims, but not in the body of Ann Moore, is unknown.)

All in all, physicians were able to determine the cause of death in only two of the more than 900 cases — though Dr. Mootoo's field work lent considerable weight to the conclusion that most had died of cyanide poisoning.

As for the *manner* of death, whether suicide or homicide, the best evidence was again Dr. Mootoo's. The Guyanese physician, trained in London and Vienna, concluded that *more than 700 of the victims had been murdered*. This conclusion was based on several observations. In the case of the 260 children, for example, they could hardly be held responsible for their own deaths. They'd been killed by others. As for the adults, Dr. Mootoo reported that 83 of the 100 bodies that he examined had needle punctures on the backs of their shoulders — suggesting that they had been forcibly held down and injected against their will.[17] (A second possiblity is that they may have given *coup de grace* injections, perhaps after feigning death.) Moreover, Dr. Mootoo noted, syringes containing cyanide, but lacking needles, lay everywhere on the ground at Jonestown — a circumstance which led him to conclude that the syringes had been used to squirt poison into the mouths of those (children and others) who'd refused to drink. Still others seem to have duped into thinking that they were taking tranquilizers: bottles containing potassium cyanide, but labeled "Valium," were scattered on the ground around the pavilion.[18] Based upon this evidence, a conservative estimate would be that as many as 700, and possibly more, of Jonestown's victims were murdered.

No other conclusion seems reasonable. Once Dr. Mootoo's findings are accepted with respect to the *cause* of death, cyanide poisoning, we have little choice than to accept his judgment upon the *manner* in which the vast majority of the victims died. As the only physician to gather evidence at the scene and to examine the dead where they lay, Dr. Mootoo based his findings upon the best (and, sometimes, the only) evidence that was available.

An eyewitness account would help to answer many of the lingering questions, but none would appear to be forthcoming. Those who survived the massacre — Charles Garry, Mark Lane, the Carter brothers, Michael Prokes, Odell Rhodes and others — did so because they fled the scene.[19] The only exceptions to this were an elderly woman named Hyacinth Thrush, who slept through the massacre and remembered nothing of it; a man named Johnny Cobb, who hid through the night in a tree;[20] and a third person whose identity will be discussed subsequently.

Just as the cause and manner of death were to be obscured by the decision to embalm the corpses before they could be autopsied, the identities of those who died were also encrypted. Why this was so is a mystery in its own right.

"Lots of people had identification tags on their wrists, usually their right one," said Frank Johnston, an American magazine photographer who toured the commune shortly after the massacre.[21] Some of these tags were hand-made, apparently by the communards themselves, while others were issued by the medical clinic at Jonestown. Still other victims had been identified on the ground by Ms. Thrush and others who'd known them. These bodies had then been tagged by the military. Relatives of the dead, including Johnny Cobb, saw the tags. So did anyone who glanced at the cover of *Newsweek* in which the massacre was reported.

Inexplicably, however, the wrist identification bracelets and tags were removed prior to the bodies' return to the United States.

As Dr. Mootoo's evidence established, most of the people at Jonestown were murdered. How is it, then, that Jonestown has become synonymous with "mass suicide"? An "After Action Report" of the Joint Chiefs of Staff establishes a chronology.

According to the Pentagon, which took responsibility for transporting the dead back to the United States, the National Military Command Center (NMCC) was first notified of a disaster in Guyana at 7:18 p.m. on Saturday, November 18.[22] This information, apparently based upon the reports brought back from Port Kaituma by the escaping small plane, was that Congressman Ryan had been shot at the jungle airstrip.

At 8:15 p.m., a Department of Defense MEDEVAC was requested by the State Department. Its mission: to evacuate the wounded from Port Kaituma, and to return the bodies of those who had been killed at the airstrip.[23]

At 8:49 p.m., the State Department relayed a request from the Prime Minister of Guyana, Forbes Burnham, asking that a pathologist accompany the MEDEVAC.

At 3:04 a.m. on November 19, the C-141 MEDEVAC left Charleston, N.C. for Guyana.

Twenty-five minutes later, at 3:29 a.m., the JCS chronology indicates that "CIA NOIWON reports mass suicides at Jonestown."[24]

All entries in the JCS chronology are Eastern Standard Time. In Guyana, however, it was one hour and fifteen minutes later than it was in Washington, D.C. — which means that the CIA notified the Defense Department of the "mass suicides" at 4:44 a.m. (Guyana time).

This is clearly one of the most important mysteries in the entire affair. How did the CIA know that *anyone* was dead in Jonestown, let alone so many, as to justify the notion of "mass suicides"? And how could it be so mistakenly certain of the manner in which the dead had died: i.e., suicide as opposed to murder?

Obviously, the CIA somehow learned of the massacre in Guyana prior to 4:44 a.m. Which is to say, while it was still dark, and hours before Guyanese Defense Forces arrived at the commune.

So how did they know?

Until very recently, the evidence pointed to Richard Dwyer, Deputy Chief of Mission at the U.S. Embassy in Georgetown. It was Dwyer who accompanied Ryan to Jonestown, and it was Dwyer who was at the congressman's side when bullets began to fly at the Port Kaituma airstrip.

A Princeton graduate and foreign service officer, Dwyer was widely suspected of being the CIA station chief in Guyana. Having joined the State Department's Bureau of Intelligence and Research in 1959, he'd served in the fly-blown capitals of Syria, Egypt, Bulgaria and Chad, before washing up in Guyana. In the course of his travels, he'd been identified as a CIA officer by Dr. Julius Mader, an East German academician with ties to the Stasi intelligence service.[25] In Guyana, the former Guyanese Minister of Information, Kit Nascimento, confirmed the identification, stating flat-out that Dwyer was the CIA's Chief of Station in Georgetown.

Both Mader and Nascimento were mistaken.

In fact, the CIA station chief in Guyana was a colleague of Dwyer's, working under State Department cover at the embassy. This was James Adkins, who would later come a cropper in the Iran-Contra hearings, during which he was criticized for what might be characterized as "over-achievement" on behalf of the Contras in the early 1980s. He eventually resigned from the CIA.

Adkins is important to the story because it was he who first learned of the murders and suicides at Jonestown.

At the Temple's residence in Georgetown, a modest house called "Lamaha Gardens," a woman named Sharon Amos learned of the ambush by radio, and of Jones' decision to pull the plug on more than 900 lives. Taking her children into the bathroom, Mother Amos obediently slit her kids' throats, then took her own life in despair.

News of the horror quickly got out, but nothing was heard from Jonestown. Jonestown was a black hole.

When the embassy learned of the ambush at Port Kaituma, Adkins got on the radio — and stayed on the radio for hours — listening hard. For a long while, nothing could be heard. But in the early morning hours of Nov. 19, the voice of Odell Rhodes was suddenly heard, transmitting almost hysterically. After witnessing so many murders and suicides, Rhodes had used a pretext to get past a cordon sanitaire of Temple guards armed with shotguns and crossbows. Reaching the relative safety of the surrounding jungle, he'd made his way to the little police station in nearby Matthew's Ridge. It was from there that he broadcast the report that stunned Adkins.

As for Dwyer, he appears to have played a courageous role at the airstrip that night, taking care of the wounded and the dead at considerable risk to himself.

Even so, mysteries remain.

One of them concerns the so-called "Last Tape." This was a cassette found in a tape recorder beside Jim Jones' lifeless body. On the tape, we can hear people wailing and screaming, as Jones asks: "And what comes, folks, what comes now?"

UNMAN[26] [in background]: "Everybody ... hold it! Sit down right here..." [loud background noises, agitated]
JONES: "Say peace, say peace, say peace, say peace... what comes, don't let... take Dwyer on down to the middle (?) of the East House. Take Dwyer on down."
UNWOMAN: "Everybody be quiet, please!"
UNMAN: "Show you got some respect for our lives."[27]
UNMAN: "Let me sit down, sit down, sit down."
JONES: "I know... (Jones begins to hum, or keen.) "I tried so very very hard... Get Dwyer *out* of here before something happens to him."
UNMAN: "Jjara?"
JONES: "I'm not talking about Jjara, I said *Dwyer*."

The Last Tape is anything but indistinct, and it would seem to suggest that Richard Dwyer returned to Jonestown after the ambush at Port Kaituma. Jones appears to be ordering his followers to protect "Dwyer" by taking him to East House (a part of the Jonestown encampment from which attorneys Temple Charles Garry and Mark Lane had already escaped). There is no other "Dwyer" associated with the Peoples Temple, so it would seem reasonable to conclude that it was Richard Dwyer whom Jones hoped to protect. Why he should want to do so is a mystery.

According to Dwyer himself, the incident never occurred. He did not leave Port Kaituma that evening, but stayed there to take care of the wounded. If, as some have testified, he seemed to be elsewhere, that can only be because he was moving back and forth between the two locations at which the wounded were being kept.

"What reasons people may have had for saying these things, I don't know," Dwyer has testified. "I was not present in the tavern, obviously, when I was at the tent. I wasn't present in the tent when I was in the tavern. But that's it."[28]

I.3 Dr. Sukhedo and Dr. Hersh

The CIA's relationship to Jim Jones and the Peoples Temple, and therefore to the Jonestown massacre, is an important issue that will be discussed in subsequent pages.

Here, however, we are concerned with the initial reports of the massacre. And, in particular, with those responsible for labeling the disaster a "mass suicide" — contrary to the evidence being gathered by Dr. Mootoo. And while the CIA report was undoubtedly a significant source of misinformation, an even more important source of spin was a psychiatrist named Dr. Hardat Sukhdeo.

Dr. Sukhdeo is, or was then, "an anti-cult activist" whose principal interests (as per an autobiographical note) are "homicide, suicide, and the behavior of animals in electro-magnetic fields." His arrival in Georgetown on November 27, 1978 came only three weeks after he had been named as a defendant in a controversial "deprogramming" case.[29] It is not entirely surprising, then, that within hours of his arrival in the capital, Dr. Sukhdeo began giving interviews to the press, including the New York Times, "explaining" what had happened.

Jim Jones, he said, "was a genius of mind control, a master. He knew exactly what he was doing. I have never seen anything like this, but the jungle, the isolation, gave him absolute control." Just what Dr. Sukhdeo had been able to see in his few minutes in Georgetown is unclear. But his importance in shaping the story is undoubted: he was one of the few civilian professionals at the scene, and his task was, quite simply, to help the press make sense of what had happened and to console those who had survived. He was widely quoted, and what he had to say was immediately echoed by colleagues back in the States.

That Sukhdeo's opinions were preconceived, rather than based upon evidence, seems obvious. Nevertheless, it is clear that he was aware of the work that Dr. Mootoo had done — which, as we have seen, contradicted Sukhdeo's statements about "mass suicides." In an interview with Time, Sukhdeo refers to an "autopsy" that had been performed on Jim Jones in Guyana. This can only have been a reference to Dr. Mootoo's somewhat cursory examination, in which Jones was slit open on the ground. It is difficult to understand how Sukhdeo could have been aware of that procedure's having been conducted without also knowing of Mootoo's finding that most of the victims had been murdered.

Dr. Sukhdeo was himself a native of Guyana, though a resident of the United States. He claimed at the time that he'd come to Georgetown at his own expense to counsel and study those who had survived. But that is in dispute.

According to his own attorney, Robert Bockelman, the psychiatrist retained him to prevent his having to testify at the Larry Layton trial in San Francisco. Dr. Sukhdeo's primary concern, according to Bockelman, was that it should not be revealed that the State Department had paid his way to

Guyana. You see the problem: was Sukhdeo there to help the survivors — or to debrief them on behalf of some other person or agency?[30] Nor was this all. Prior to retaining counsel in San Francisco, Dr. Sukhdeo had himself been retained by Larry Layton's defense attorneys and family. (Indeed, he testified in Layton's trial in Guyana, where "most of his testimony concerned cults in general and observations about conditions at Jonestown.")[31] And, during the time that he was helping Layton's defense, Dr. Sukhdeo was meeting — surreptitiously, according to his own lawyer — with FBI agents. Asked about this, Sukhdeo says that at no time during these meetings did he disclose any confidential communications between himself and Layton.[32]

The suggestion that Dr. Sukhdeo may have secretly "debriefed" Jonestown's survivors on behalf of the State Department (or some other government agency) may seem unduly suspicious. On the other hand, a certain amount of suspicion would seem prudent when discussing the unsolved deaths of more than 900 Americans who, in the weeks before they died, were preparing to defect *en masse* to the Soviet Union. The government's interest in this matter would logically have been intense.[33]

It is true, of course, that not every psychiatrist agreed with Dr. Sukhdeo's analysis. Dr. Stephen P. Hersh, then assistant director of the National Institute of Mental Health (NIMH), commented that "The charges of brainwashing are clearly exaggerated. The concept of 'thought control' by cult leaders is elusive, difficult to define and even more difficult to prove. Because cult converts adopt beliefs that seem bizarre to their families and friends, it does not follow that their choices are being dictated by cult leaders."

The massacre, according to Dr. Hersh, was "an isolated thing" and "not something the public should fear from other" groups. "We have no information that ... (the new religions) ... are vulnerable to this type of extreme behavior," Dr. Hersh said.[34]

That said, there is more at stake here than public perceptions. Investigators of the Guyana tragedy have a responsibility to both the living and the dead: to find out what actually happened, and to make certain that it cannot happen again.

II.1 The Dog That Didn't Bark

To understand the fate of the Peoples Temple, one must first understand why the intelligence community seemed (against all odds) to ignore the organization for so long — appearing to become interested in it only when Congressman Ryan began his investigation. Consider:

The Peoples Temple was created in the political deep-freeze of the 1950s. From its inception, it was a left-wing ally of black activist groups that were, in many cases, under FBI surveillance.[35] During the 1960s, when the Bureau and the CIA mounted Operations COINTELPRO and CHAOS to infiltrate and disrupt black militant organizations and the Left, the Temple went out of its way to forge alliances with leaders of those same organizations: e.g., with the Black Panthers' Huey Newton and with the Communist Party's Angela Davis. And yet, despite these associations, and its ultra-left orientation, we are told that the Temple was not a target of investigation by either intelligence agency.

In the early 1970s, suspicions began to surface in the press, implicating the Peoples Temple in an array of allegations including gunrunning, drug-smuggling, kidnapping, murder, brainwashing, extortion and torture. Under attack at home, and feeling the pressure abroad, Temple officials undertook secret negotiations with the Soviet Embassy in Georgetown, laying the groundwork for the en masse defection of more than a thousand poor Americans. According to the CIA, it took no interest in these discussions.

Nevertheless, when Congressman Ryan began to scrutinize the Temple in 1978, two things happened. First, according to his aides, he was stonewalled by the State Department. Second, upon arriving in Guyana, he was given an escort who had been identified a decade earlier as a ranking CIA officer.[36]

This second fact would seem to explain how it is that the CIA was the first to learn of the deaths at Jonestown, describing them as "mass suicides" — hours before the bodies were discovered by the Guyanese Defense Forces.

Under the circumstances, only the most naïve could fail to be skeptical of the disinterested stance that the FBI and the CIA claim to have taken. But what does it mean? Why would these agencies give a de facto grant of immunity to the Peoples Temple? And why would the CIA maneuver its Chief of Station into position to surveil Congressman Ryan, the co-author of legislation curtailing CIA activities abroad, on his trip to Jonestown?

The answers to those questions are embedded in the contradictions of Jones' past and, in particular, in that most mysterious period in the preacher-man's life: the 1960–64 interregnum that every biographer has preferred to gloss over. As I intend to show, the enigmas of Jones' beginnings do much to explain the bloodshed at the end.

II.2 Jones and Mitrione in Richmnond

Jim Jones was born in Crete, Indiana in 1931. When he was three, he moved with his family to the town of Lynn.

His father was a partially disabled World War I vet. Embittered by the Depression and unable to find work, he is alleged (without much evidence) to have been a member of the Ku Klux Klan. Jones' mother, on the other hand, was well-liked, a hard-working woman who is universally credited with keeping the family together.

Jones' religious upbringing took place outside his own family. Myrtle Kennedy, a friend of his mother's who lived nearby, saw to it that he went to Sunday School, and gave him instruction in the Bible. While not yet a teenager, Jones began to experiment, attending the services of several churches.[37] Before long, he came under the spell of a "fanatical" woman evangelist, the leader of faith-healing revivals at the Gospel Tabernacle Church on the edge of town.[38] (This was a Pentecostal sect of so-called "Holy Rollers," a charismatic group that believed in faith-healing and speaking in tongues.) Whether there was more to their relationship than that of a priestess and her protégé is unknown, but it is a fact that Jones' association with the woman coincided with the onset of nightmares. According to Jones' mother, he was terrorized by dreams in which a snake figured prominently.[39]

Whatever the nature of his relationship to the lady evangelist, Jones soon found himself in the pulpit, dressed in a white sheet, thumping the Bible. The protégé was a prodigy and, by all accounts, he loved the attention.

In 1947, 15 years old and still a resident of Lynn, Jones began preaching in a "sidewalk ministry" on the wrong side of the tracks in Richmond, Indiana — 16 miles from his home. Why he traveled to Richmond to deliver his message, and why he picked a working-class black neighborhood in which to do it, is uncertain.

What is certain, however, is that, while in Richmond, Jones established a relationship with a man named Dan Mitrione. Like the child evangelist, Mitrione would one day become internationally notorious and, like Jones, his violent death in South America would generate headlines around the world. As Jones told his followers in Guyana, "There was one guy that I knew growing up in Richmond, a cruel, cruel person, even as a kid, a vicious racist — Dan Mitrione."[40]

Myrtle Kennedy has confirmed that the two men knew one another, saying that they were friends.[41]

That Jones knew Mitrione is strange coincidence, but not entirely surprising. A Navy veteran who'd joined the Richmond Police Department in 1945, Mitrione worked his way up through the ranks as a patrolman, a juvenile officer and, finally, chief of police. It is unlikely that he would have overlooked the strange white boy from Lynn preaching on the sidewalk to blacks in front of a working-class bar on the industrial side of town.

What is surprising about Jones' statement, however, is his description of Mitrione as a "vicious racist." There is nothing anywhere else to suggest that Mitrione held any particular views on the subject of race. Communism, certainly — but race, no.[42]

Which is to say that either Jones was wrong about the Richmond cop, or else he knew something about Dan Mitrione that other people did not.

If Mitrione were to play no further part in Jones' story, there would be little reason to speculate any further about their relationship. But, as we'll see, Jones and Mitrione cross each other's paths repeatedly, and in the most unlikely places. Neither family friends nor playmates (Mitrione was 11 years older than Jones), their relationship must have been based upon *something*. But what?

Two possibilities suggest themselves: either Mitrione was counseling Jones in the way policemen sometimes counsel children, or their relationship may have been professional. That is to say, Mitrione may have recruited Jones as an informant within the black community. This second possibility is one to which we'll have reason to return.

II.3 Jones in the '50s

Very little research seems to have been carried out by anyone with respect to Jones' early career. It is almost as if his biographers are uninterested in him until he begins to go off the deep end. This is unfortunate — particularly in light of the possibility that Jones may have been a police or FBI informant, gathering "racial intelligence" for the Bureau's files.

What is known about his early career is, therefore, known only in outline.

He graduated from Richmond High School in about January, 1949, and began attending the University of Indiana at Bloomington.[43] He was married to his high school sweetheart, Marceline Baldwin, in June of the same year.

In the summer of 1951, Jones moved to Indianapolis to study law as an undergraduate. While there, he began to attend political meetings of an uncertain kind. Ronnie Baldwin, Marceline's younger cousin, was living with the Joneses at the time. And though he was only 11 years old, Baldwin recalls that Jones sometimes took him to political lectures. On one such outing, Baldwin remembers, he and Jones went to a "churchlike" auditorium where "communism" was under discussion. They didn't stay long, however. Soon after they'd arrived, someone came up to Jones and whispered in his ear — whereupon Jones took his ward by the arm and exited hurriedly. Outside, Jones said "Good evening" to a man whom Baldwin believes was an FBI agent.[44]

It's a peculiar story, and Jones' biographers don't seem to know what to make of it. What sort of meeting could it have been? The assumption is made, in light of Jones' later politics, that it was a leftist soiree of some kind. After all, they were talking about communism. But that makes very little sense. Indianapolis was a very conservative city in 1951. (It still is.) Joe McCarthy was on the horizon, and the Korean War was beginning to take its toll. If "communism" was being discussed in anything other than whispers, or anywhere else than a back room, the debate was almost certainly one-sided and thumbs-down.

It was at about this same time that Jones gave up the study of law and, to everyone's surprise, decided to become a minister. By 1952, he was a student pastor at the Somerset Methodist Church in Indianapolis and, in 1953, made his "evangelical debut" at a ministerial seminar in Detroit, Michigan.

By 1954, Jones had established the "Community Unity" Church in Indianapolis, while preaching also at the Laurel Tabernacle. To raise money, he began selling monkeys door-to-door.[45]

By 1956, Jones had established the "Wings of Deliverance" Church as a successor to Community Unity. Almost immediately, the Church was christened the Peoples Temple. The inspiration for its new name stemmed from the fact that the church was housed in what was formerly a Jewish synagogue — a "temple" that Jones had purchased, with little or no money down, for $50,000.

Ironically, the man who gave the Peoples Temple its start was the Rabbi Maurice Davis. It was he who sold the synagogue to Jones on such remarkably generous terms. Today, Rabbi Davis is a prominent anti-cult activist, a sometime deprogrammer, and an associate of Dr. Hardat Sukhdeo.

II.4 Jones and Father Divine

By the late 1950s, the Peoples Temple was a success, with a congregation of more than 2000 people. Still, Jones had even larger ambitions and, to accommodate them, became the improbable protégé of an extremely improbable man. This was Father Divine, the Philadelphia-based "black messiah" whose Peace Mission movement attracted tens of thousands of black adherents and the close attention of the FBI, while earning its founder an annual income in seven figures.

For whatever reasons, beginning in about 1956, Jones made repeated pilgrimages to the black evangelist's headquarters, where he literally "sat at the feet" (and at the table) of the great man, professing his devotion. With the exception of Father Divine's wife, Jones may well have been the man's only white adherent.

It was not entirely inconvenient. Living in Indianapolis, Jones could easily arrange to transport members of the Peoples Temple by bus to Philadelphia — where they were housed without charge in Father Divine's hotels, feasted at banquets called "Holy Communions," and treated to endless sermons.[46]

That Jones made a study of Father Divine, emulated him and hoped to succeed him, is clear. The possibility should not be ruled out, however, that Jones was also engaged in collecting "racial intelligence" for a third party.

Whatever else Jones may have picked up from his study of Father Divine, there is reason to believe that it was in the context of his visits to Philadelphia that he was introduced to the subject of mass suicide. Among Jones' personal effects in Guyana was a book that had been checked out of the Indianapolis Public Library in the 1950s, and never returned. In the pages of *Father Divine: Holy Husband*, the author quotes one of the black evangelist's followers:

'If Father dies,' she tells you in the calmest kind of a voice, 'I sure 'nuff would never be callin' in myself to be goin' on livin' in this empty ol' world. I'd be findin' some way of gettin' rid of the life I never been wantin' before I found him.' "*If Father Divine were to die, mass suicides among Negroes in his movement could certainly result.* They would be rooted deep, not alone in Father's relationship with his followers, but also in America's relationship with its Negroe citizens. This would be the shame of America." [Emphasis added.][47]

II.5 Jones Goes to Cuba

In January 1959, Fidel Castro overthrew the Batista dictatorship, and seized power in Cuba. Land reforms followed within a few months of the coup, alienating foreign investors and the rich. By summer, therefore, Cuba was in the midst of a low-intensity counter-revolution, with sabotage operations mounted from within and outside the country.

Within a year of Castro's ascension, by January of 1960, mercenary pilots and anti-Castroites were flying bombing missions against the regime. Meanwhile, in Washington, Vice President Richard Nixon was lobbying on behalf of the military invasion that the CIA was plotting.

It was against this background, in February of 1960, that Jim Jones suddenly decided to visit Havana.

The news of Jones' visit to Cuba — one is tempted to write "the cover story for Jones' trip to Cuba" — was first published in the *New York Times* in March 1979 (four months after the massacre in Guyana). The story was based upon an interview with a naturalized American named Carlos Foster. A former Cuban cowboy, Baptist Pentecostal minister and sometime night-club singer, Foster showed up at the *New York Times* four months after the massacre. Without being asked, he volunteered a strange story about meeting Jim Jones in Cuba during the winter of 1960. (Why Foster went to the newspaper with his story is uncertain: news of his friendship with Jones could hardly have helped his career as a children's counselor.)[48]

Nevertheless, according to the *Times* story, the 29-year-old Jones traveled to Cuba to expedite plans to establish a communal organization with settlements in the U.S. and abroad. The immediate goal, Foster said, was to recruit Cuban blacks to live in Indiana.

Foster told the *Times* that he and Jones met by chance at the Havana Hilton. That is to say, Jones gave the Cuban a big hello, and took him by the arm. He then solicited Foster's help in locating 40 families that would be willing to move to the Indianapolis area (at Jones' expense). Tim Reiterman, who repeats the *Times'* story, adds that the two men discussed the plan in Jones' hotel room, from seven in the morning until eight o'clock at night, for a week. More recently, Foster has elaborated by saying that Jones offered to pay him $50,000 per year to help him establish an archipelago of offshore agricultural communes in Central and South America. Foster said that Jones was an extremely well-traveled man, who knew Latin America well. He had already been to Guyana, and wanted to start a collective there.

After a month in Cuba, Jones returned to the United States (alone). Six months later, Foster followed, on his own initiative, but the immigration scheme went nowhere.[49]

The anomalies in this story are many, and one hardly knows what to make of them. Foster's information that Jones was well-traveled in Latin America, and had already been to Guyana, comes as a shock. None of his biographers mentions Jones having taken trips out of the United States prior to this time. Could Foster be mistaken? Or have Jones' biographers overlooked an important part of his life?

An even greater anomaly, however, concerns language. While Reiterman reports that Foster was bilingual, and that he and Jones spoke English together, this isn't true. Foster learned English at Theodore Roosevelt High School in the Bronx — *after* he'd emigrated to the United States.[50] (Reiterman seems to have made an otherwise reasonable, but incorrect, assumption: knowing that Jones did not speak Spanish, he assumed that Foster must have been able to speak English.)

Today, when Foster is asked which language was spoken, he says that he and Jones made do with the latter's broken Spanish.

The issue is an important one because Foster is, in effect, Jones' alibi for whatever it was that Jones was actually doing in Cuba. That the two men did not have a language in common makes the alibi decidedly suspect: how could they converse for 13 hours at a time, day in and day out, for a week — if neither man understood what the other was saying?

As for Jones' own parishioners, those who've survived have only a dim recollection of the trip. According to Reiterman, "Back in the States, Jones revealed little of his plan, depicting his stay more as tourism than church business." This sounds like a polite way of saying that the trip served no obvious purpose. Nevertheless, he did bring back some strange souvenirs. "He showed off photos of Cuba... One picture — a gruesome shot of the mangled body of a pilot in some plane wreckage — indicated that Jones witnessed the pirate bombings of the cane fields. Jones told his friends that he had met with some Cuban leaders, though the bearded man in fatigues standing beside Jones in a snapshot was too short to be Castro."[51]

It would be interesting to know just what Reiterman is talking about here. The presumption must be that there is a photograph in which Jones is seen with a man who might easily be confused with Castro — if it weren't for the latter's diminutive size. In fact, however, it probably *was* Castro. When Jones arrived in Brazil in 1962, he carried a photograph of himself and his wife Marceline, posing with the Cuban premier. Jones said that the picture was taken on a stopover in Cuba on the way to Sao Páulo.[52] That is to say, in late 1961 or early 1962.

How Jones met Fidel Castro — and why — is an interesting question. So, too, we can only wonder at his proclivity for taking photographs of mercenary pilots in their crashed planes. Pictures of that sort could only have been of interest to Castro's enemies and the CIA.

Returning to Carlos Foster, if the tale that he told to the *Times* was a pre-emptive cover story, a "limited hang-out" of some sort, what was Jones actually doing? Why had he gone to Havana? At this late date, and in the absence of interviews with officials of the Cuban government, there is probably no way to know. What may be said, however, is this:

Emigration was an extremely sensitive issue in the first years of the Castro regime. The CIA and the State Department, in their determination to embarrass Castro, did everything possible to encourage would-be immigrants to leave the island. As a part of this policy, U.S. Government agencies and conservative Christian religious organizations collaborated to facilitate departures.[53] Jones' visit may well have been a part of this program.

But there is no way to be certain of that. Cuba was in the midst of a parapolitical meltdown. While the CIA was conspiring to launch an invasion, irate Mafiosi and American businessmen had joined together to finance the bombing runs of mercenary pilots. Meanwhile, the Soviets had sent their Deputy Premier, Anastas I. Mikoyan, to Havana for the opening of the Soviet Exhibition of Science, Technology and Culture.[54] The visit coincided with the Soviets' decision to give Cuba a long-term low-interest loan, while promising to buy a million tons of Cuban sugar per annum. The "Hilton Hotel" at which Jones was staying was the temporary home of a Sputnik satellite that the Soviets had put on display. According to former CIA officer Melvin Beck, the CIA was trying to photograph it, and the lobby was crawling with spies from as many five different services (FBI, CIA, KGB, GRU and DGI).[55]

While one cannot say that Jones' 1960 visit to Cuba was necessarily a spying mission, the circumstantial evidence suggests that it was. That is to say, virtually every element of the trip can be shown to have been of particular interest to the CIA: encouraging Cuban emigration; documenting the destruction of aircraft piloted by mercenaries; the Sputnik at the Hilton; and, it would seem, Castro himself.

II.6 Jim Jones, His Passport and the CIA

Cuba wasn't the only country to which Jones intended to travel in 1960. On June 28 of that year, at about the same time that Foster arrived in Indianapolis from Cuba, the State Department issued a passport (#2288751) to Jones for a 17-day visit to Poland, Finland, the U.S.S.R., and England. The purpose of the trip, according to Jones' visa application, was "sightseeing — culture."

Which presents us with an enigma. According to State Department records, this was Jones' first passport. How, then, did he travel to Cuba in February if he did not receive a passport until the end of June? Did he enter the country "black"? Was he using someone else's documents? And what about Carlos Foster's certainty that Jones had previously traveled throughout Latin America? Was Foster mistaken, or had Jones in fact visited Guyana?

It is almost as if we are dealing with two Jim Joneses. And perhaps we are. It's a subject to which we will need to return.

Here, however, I want to point out certain coincidences of timing in the lives of Jim Jones and Dan Mitrione, and to discuss Jones' own file at the CIA.

Passports typically require about four to six weeks to be mailed out. Since Jones' passport was issued on June 28, 1960, his application would have been filed in early May. As it happens, it was during that same month that Dan Mitrione was in Washington D.C., being interviewed for a new job with a component of the State Department's Agency for International Development (AID), the International Cooperation Administration (ICA). An acknowledged cover for CIA officers and contract-spooks such as Watergate's E. Howard Hunt and the JFK assassination's George de Mohrenschildt, the ICA would become infamous during the 1960s, funding the construction of tiger cages in Vietnam, and training foreign police forces in the theory and practice of torture.

A few years earlier, in 1957, Mitrione had spent three months at the FBI's National Academy.[56] The connections he'd made stood him in good stead. Immediately after his interview with the ICA, he was hired by the State Department as a "public safety adviser." Three months later, in September, 1960 he was in Rio de Janeiro, studying Portuguese; by December, he was living with his family in Belo Horizonte, Brazil.

Whether Mitrione was an undercover CIA officer in South America is disputed. The Soviets say he was.[57] Officially, however, Mitrione was an AID officer attached to the Office of Public Safety (OPS). But OPS was very much a nest of spies: in the Dominican Republic during the mid-1960s, for example, six out of 20 positions were CIA covers.[58] Moreover, Mitrione's partner at the time of his 1970 kidnapping in Uruguay was a public safety officer named Lee Echols — whose previous assignment had been as a CIA officer in the Dominican Republic.[59]

Whether or not Mitrione was an undercover CIA officer, it is a fact that the CIA's Office of Security opened a file on Jones, and conducted a name-check on him, coincident with Mitrione's departure for Rio. Why it did so is a mystery: the Agency won't say.

It is speculated, of course, that the file and name-check were sparked by the Soviet Bloc destinations for which Jones had applied for a visa. But that could hardly have been the case. The visa requests had been made in May, and the passport issued in June. It was not until November, some five months later, that the Office of Security sent agents to the State Department's Passport Office, there to examine Jones' records — an activity that would hardly have been necessary if the passport application had stimulated the name-check in the first place.

Given the CIA's reluctance to clear up the matter, one can only speculate that the Agency may have been "vetting" Jones for employment as an agent.

Two points should be made here. The first is that the CIA claimed, in the aftermath of the Jonestown massacre, that its file on "the Rev. Jimmie Jones" was virtually empty. According to the Agency, it had never collected data — not a single piece of paper — on Jones or the Peoples Temple.

Nevertheless, CIA records indicate that Jones' file remained *open* for ten years. It was finally closed, without explanation, in the wake of Dan Mitrione's assassination by Tupamaro guerrillas in Uruguay.

Which is to say that the lifespan of Jones' file at the CIA coincided precisely with the dates of Dan Mitrione's rather suspect tenure at the State

Department. What I am suggesting, then, is that Richmond Police Chief Dan Mitrione was recruited into the CIA, under State Department cover, in May, 1960; that a CIA file was opened on Jones because Mitrione intended to use him as an agent; and that Jones' file was closed and purged, ten years later, as a direct and logical result of Mitrione's assassination in 1970.

II. 7 Jones in South America

To understand the significance of what next occurred, one has to go back more than one hundred years. It was then, in the Northwest District of Guyana, that a prophet named Smith issued a call to the country's disenfranchised Amerindians, summoning them to a redoubt in the Pakaraima Mountains — the land of El Dorado.

Akawaios, Caribs and Arawaks came from all around to witness what they were told would be the Millennium. "They would see God," Smith promised, "be free from all calamities of life, and possess lands of such boundless fertility, that a (large) crop of cassava would grow from a single stick."

But Smith had lied. And "when the Millennium failed to materialize, the followers were told they had to die in order to be resurrected as white people...

"At a great camp meeting in 1845, some 400 people killed themselves."[60]

One hundred thirty-three years later, in the fall of 1978, at a great camp meeting in the same Northwest District of Guyana, upwards of a thousand expatriate Americans, most of them black, and about as poor and disenfranchised as the Amerindians who'd preceded them, died under circumstances so similar as to be eerie. They, too, had been promised that they would be freed from the calamities of life, and that they would possess lands of boundless fertility. Like Smith, their charismatic leader had a generic sort of name and he, too, had lied.

This time, 913 people died in front of a large, hand-lettered sign that read: "Those who fail to learn from history are condemned to repeat it."

The coincidence here is so dramatic that is impossible not to wonder if Jim Jones knew of Smith's precedent. Because, if he did know, and if his politics were, as seems very likely, a fraud, then the Jonestown massacre is revealed to have been a ghastly practical joke — the ultimate psychopathic prank.

According to Kathleen Adams, the anthropologist who first related the story about Smith and the Amerindians, Jim Jones was in fact familiar with the suicides of 1845. He had learned of them, she said, while working as a missionary in the Northwest District.

Adams does not tell us when this was, but the implication is that it was long before the establishment of Jonestown. The possibilities here are two:

The first is that Jones' Cuban friend, Carlos Foster, is correct when he says that Jones was well-traveled and had been to Guyana prior to 1960. The difficulty with this, of course, is that Jones' biographers are ignorant of any such travels. But if Jones did not go to Guyana prior to 1960, he must have learned about Smith's precedent while doing missionary work in Guyana — *after* his 1960 visit to Cuba. But when could that have been?

The answer would appear to be at about the end of October, 1961. Arriving at that conclusion is by no means an easy matter, however, given the chronological confusion that his most responsible biographer, Tim Reiterman, relates.[61] Because this confusion raises a number of interesting questions about Jones' activities, whereabouts and true loyalties, the matter is worth straightening out.

In the fall of 1961, Jim Jones was becoming paranoid. Under treatment for stress, he was hearing "extraterrestrial voices," and suffering seizures.[62] Hospitalized during most of the first week in October, he resigned his position as Director of the Indianapolis Human Rights Commission.[63] It was then, according to Reiterman, that Jones confided in his ministerial assistant, Ross Case, that he'd had a vision of nuclear holocaust.

"A few weeks later, Jones took off alone in a plane for Hawaii, ostensibly to scout for a new site for Peoples Temple...." (At a loss to explain why Jones should have gone to Hawaii, Reiterman implies that Jones viewed the islands as a potential nuclear refuge — a ludicrous notion in light of their role as stationary aircraft carriers.)

"On what would become a two-year sojourn, Jones made his first stop in Honolulu, where he explored a job as a university chaplain. Though he did not like the job requirements, he decided to stay on the island for a while anyway, and sent for his family. First, his wife, his mother and the children, except for Jimmy, joined him. Then the Baldwins followed with the adopted black child.... During the couple of months in the islands, Jones seemed to decide that his sabbatical would be a long one."[64]

According to Reiterman's chronology, therefore, Jones left Indianapolis for Hawaii near the end of October, 1961. He then sent for his family, which joined him in what we may suppose was November. The family remained in Hawaii for a "couple of months": i.e., until January or February.

"In January, 1962, *Esquire* magazine published an article listing the nine safest places in the world to escape thermonuclear blasts and fallout.... The article's advice was not lost on Jones. Soon he was heading for the southern hemisphere, which was less vulnerable to fallout because of atmospheric and political factors. The family planned to go eventually to Belo Horizonte, an inland Brazilian city of 600,000."

Jones' biographer goes on to say that, after leaving Hawaii, his subject traveled to California, and then to Mexico City, before continuing on to Guyana. There, Jones' visit "made page seven of the *Guiana Graphic*."[65]

That Jones made page seven of the local newspaper is a matter of fact. Unfortunately for Reiterman's chronology, however, he did so on October 25 (1961). Which is to say that the head of the Peoples Temple is alleged to have been in two places at that same time: in Hawaii and Guyana during the last week in October — with intervening stops in California and Mexico City.

Obviously, Reiterman is mistaken, but the issue is not merely one of a confused chronology. There is evidence (including, as we'll see, a photograph) which strongly suggests that two people may have been using Jones' identity during the 1961–63 period. Because of this, rumors that Jones was hospitalized in a "lunatic asylum" during that time should not be dismissed out of hand. The rumors were started by a black minister in Indiana who is said to have been jealous of Jones' success among blacks at the Peoples Temple. While the allegation has yet to be documented, there are many other references to Jones having been under psychiatric care at one time or another.

Ross Case says that Jones sometimes referred to "my psychiatrist." Others have suggested that the real reason Jones went to Hawaii was to receive psychiatric care without publicity.

In later years, Temple member Loretta Cordell reported shock at seeing Jones described as "a sociopath." The description was contained in a psychiatrist's report that Cordell said was in the files of Jones' San Francisco physician (probably Dr. Carleton Goodlett).

In a recent interview with this author, Dr. Sukhdeo confirmed that Jones had been treated at the Langley-Porter Neuropsychiatric Institute in San Francisco during the 1960s and '70s. According to Sukhdeo, he has repeatedly asked to see Jones' medical file from the Institute, and he has been repeatedly refused permission.

"I have asked (Langley-Porter's Dr.) Chris Hatcher to see the file several times," Sukhdeo told this writer. "But, each time, he has refused. I don't know why. He won't say. It's very peculiar. Jones has been dead for more than 20 years."

"The nation's leading center for brain research," Langley-Porter is noted for its hospitality to anti-cult activists such as Dr. Margaret Singer and, also, for experiments that it conducts on behalf of the Defense Department's Advanced Research Projects Agency (ARPA). While much of that research is classified, the Institute has experimented with electromagnetic effects and behavioral modification techniques involving a wide variety of stimuli — including hypnosis from a distance.

Some of the Institute's classified research may be inferred from quotations attributed to its director, Dr. Alan Gevins (see *Mind Wars* by Ron McRae, St. Martin's Press, 1984, p. 136). According to Dr. Gevins, the military potential of Extremely Low Frequency radiation (ELF) is enormous. Used as a medium for secret communications between submarines, ELF waves are a thousand miles long, unobstructed by water, and theoretically "capable of shutting off the brain (and) killing everyone in ten thousand square miles or larger target area."

"No one paid any attention to the biological affects of ELF for years," says Dr. Gevins, "because the power levels are so low. Then we realized that because the power levels are so low, the brain could mistake the outside signal for its own, mimic it (a process known as bioelectric entrainment), and respond when it changes."

The process is one that would no doubt fascinate Jonestown's foremost psychiatric interpreter, Dr. Hardat Sukhdeo. Interestingly, virtually every *survivor* of the Jonestown massacre seems to have been treated at Langley-Porter. This occurred as a result of San Francisco Mayor George Moscone's request that Dr. Hatcher undertake a study of the Peoples Temple while counseling its survivors. (Hatcher's appointment was made with surprising alacrity since Moscone himself was assassinated only nine days after the killings at Jonestown.)

Returning to the *Guiana Graphic* article about Jones' visit to Guyana, it is worth pointing out that the story throws a crimp in much more than Reiterman's chronology. It makes hash as well of Jones' motive for going to South America. The *Esquire* article, published in January, 1962 could hardly have prompted Jones to go anywhere in October, 1961.

So, too, the story in the *Graphic* provides clear evidence of Jones' immersion in political intrigue.

At the time of his visit, the former British colony was wracked by covert operations being mounted by the CIA and MI-6.

By way of background, the most important political group in the country was the Peoples Progressive Party (PPP), established by Dr. Cheddi Jagan during the 1940s. A Marxist organization, the PPP's activities had caused the British to declare "a crisis situation" in 1953. Troops had been landed, the Constitution suspended, and recent elections nullified in order to "prevent communist subversion."

Over the next four years, MI-6 and the CIA established a *de facto* police state in Guyana. Racial tensions were exacerbated between the East Indian and black populations — with the result that the PPP was soon split. While Jagan, himself an East Indian, remained in charge of the party, another of its members — a black named Forbes Burnham — began (with the help of Western intelligence services) to challenge his leadership.

Despite the schism, the PPP was victorious in 1957 and, once again, in 1961 — just prior to Jones' visit. Coming on the heels of Castro's embrace of the Soviets, Jagan's re-election chilled the Kennedy Administration. Accordingly, the CIA intensified its operations against Jagan and the PPP, doing everything in its power to increase its support for Burnham, provoke strikes and exacerbate racial and economic tensions. It accomplished all these goals, secretly underwriting Burnham's political campaigns, while using the American Institute for Free Labor Development (AIFLD) as a cover for operations against local trade unions.

Eventually, these operations would succeed: Jagan would be ousted, and Burnham brought to power. A decade later, that same Burnham regime would facilitate the creation of Jonestown, leasing the land to the Peoples Temple and approving its members' immigration.

It was in this somewhat dangerous context that Jim Jones arrived in the Guyanese capital. Putting on a series of tent shows, replete with faith-healings and speaking in tongues, he warned the local populace against thieving American missionaries and evangelists — who, he said, were largely responsible for the spread of Communism.

Even Reiterman, who accepts almost everything at face value, is puzzled by this: "Entering politically volatile South America," he writes, Jones "seemed to want to put himself on the record as an anticommunist."[66]

Exactly. And how convenient for the CIA, whose activities were being hindered by reform-minded missionaries.

II. 7 Belo Horizonte

After entering Guyana, and making anti-communist speeches, Jones seems to have dropped off the face of the earth. Following the *Guyana Graphic* article of October 27, he disappears from the public record for almost six full months.

It is possible, of course, that he journeyed into the interior of that country to work among the Amerindians — but the evidence for this is so slim as to be invisible. Indeed, it consists solely of a remark by anthropologist Kathleen Adams, who wrote that Jones had at one time worked as a missionary in Guyana. Where and when is left unstated, but it was presumably during that period that Jones learned about his homicidal predecessor, the Reverend "Smith."

The only disturbance in the empty field of Jones' whereabouts from 10/61 until 4/62 is the information that Passport #0111788 was issued in his name at Indianapolis on January 30, 1962.

This is a considerable anomaly. As we have seen, Jones already had a passport — #22898751, issued to him in Chicago on June 28, 1960. This earlier passport, which he had planned to use on a trip to the Soviet Union, was still valid. Why, then, did someone make an application for a new passport, and who picked it up? Moreover, how is it possible that Jones' second passport had a lower number than the one that he'd received more than a year before?

These questions cannot be answered at this time; the evidence reposes in the files of the State Department. What may be said, however, is that there is good reason to suspect that someone was impersonating Jim Jones during this period, and that, in fact, a photograph of the impostor survives. We'll return to this subject shortly.

According to the Brazilian Federal Police, Jim Jones arrived by plane in Sao Paulo on April 11, 1962. There does not seem to be any surviving record of his point of embarkation, but it may well have been Havana. According to Bonnie (Malmin) Thielman, who met Jones at about this time, there was "a picture of him and Marceline standing on either side of Fidel Castro, whom they had met during a Cuban stopover en route to Brazil..."[67]

An American family, making "a Cuban stopover," seven to 11 months *after* the Bay of Pigs? Physically, transportation would not have been difficult to arrange; both Mexico City and Georgetown were transit-points for Havana. But Cuban visas were by no means issued automatically — especially to Americans making well-publicized, *anti*-communist speeches in Guyana. How much harder it must have been for Jones to arrange to have a photo taken of himself with Castro (who was at that time the target of CIA assassination attempts planned by yet another Indianapolis native, William Harvey).

It's a peculiar, even eerie, business. I'm reminded of the man who impersonated Lee Harvey Oswald while applying for a visa at the Cuban Embassy in Mexico City during 1963.[68]

Whatever his reason for visiting Cuba during the winter of 1961–62, and whatever the reasons he was permitted to enter the country, Jones had no trouble entering Brazil that April. Given a visa that was valid for 11 months, he and his family traveled to Belo Horizonte where, as we have seen, Dan Mitrione had settled in as an OPS adviser at the U.S. Consulate.

Jones took rooms in the first-class Hotel Financial until he and his family were able to move to a house at 203 Rua Maraba.[69] This is a pretty street in an attractive neighborhood on a hill in one of the best parts of town. Accordingly, his new neighbors were almost all professionals: doctors, lawyers, teachers, engineers, and journalists. It was not the sort of place from which one could easily minister to the poor.

Not that it mattered. Jones' stay in Belo Horizonte had little or nothing to do with alleviating poverty.

According to his neighbors, Jones would leave his house early each morning, as if going to work, and return very late at night. Sebastiao Carlos Rocha, an engineer who lived nearby, noted that Jones usually left home carrying a big leather briefcase; on a number of occasions, Rocha said, he saw Jones walking in Betim, a neighboring town.[70]

Elza Rocha, a lawyer who lived across the street and who sometimes interpreted for Jones, says that her neighbor told her that he had a job in Belo Horizonte proper, at Eureka Laundries.[71]

This is a huge dry-cleaning and laundry chain, a quasi-monopoly whose central plant is serviced by more than a score of pick-up points (small storefronts) throughout the city. In essence, a customer delivers his laundry to one of the stores, where it is later collected by a delivery truck. The truck takes the dirty clothes to the central plant, where they're cleaned, and then returns them to the store from which they came. It's a big business.

But it's not one in which Jim Jones ever worked. According to Sebastiao Dias de Magalhaes, who was head of Industrial Relations for Eureka during 1962, Jones' claim to have been an employee of the laundry was false.[72] Señor de Magalhaes and two other Eureka workers have told the press that Jones lied in order to conceal what they believe was his work for the CIA.[73]

Still, if you didn't know better, Jones' cover story served three purposes: first, it explained where he went during the day — to work. Second, it offered a theoretically visible means of support: he had a check from Eureka (everyone knows Eureka). And third, it gave Jones an alibi for a mysterious period during which he'd vanished from Belo Horizonte. According to Elza

Rocha, when Jones returned, he told her that he had been sent to the United States for "special training" in connection with the machinery used by Eureka. Where Jones actually went, and why, is a unknown.[74]

Eureka wasn't Jones' only cover, however. He didn't mention Eureka to Sebastiao Rocha. Instead, he claimed to be a retired captain in the U.S. Navy. He said that he had suffered a great deal in the war, and that he received a monthly pension from the armed services. The implication was that he had been wounded in the Korean conflict. According to Señor Rocha, "Jim Jones was always mysterious and would never talk about his work here in Brazil."[75]

Yet another Rocha, Marco Aurelio, was absolutely certain that Jones was a spy. At the time, Marco was dating a young girl who was living in the Jones household.[76] Because of this, and because Rua Maraba is a narrow street on which parked cars are conspicuous, he noticed that a car from the American Consulate was often parked outside Jones' house. According to Marco, the car's driver sometimes brought groceries to the Joneses — which, if true, was definitely not standard consular procedure.

Marco Rocha's interest in Jones was more than idle, however. According to him, he was keeping a loose surveillance on the American preacher at the request of a friend — a detective in the ID-4 section of the local police department. The detective was convinced that Jones was a CIA agent, and was trying to prove it with his young friend's help. Unfortunately, the policeman died before his investigation could be completed, and Jones moved shortly thereafter.[77]

Gleaning the purpose behind Jones' residency in Belo Horizonte is anything but easy. He is reported to have been fascinated by the magical rites of Macumba and Umbanda, and to have studied the practices of Brazilian faith-healers. He was extremely interested in the works of David Miranda, and is said to have conducted a study of extrasensory perception. These were subjects of interest to the CIA in connection with its MK-ULTRA program. So, also, were the "mass conversion techniques" at which Jones' Pentecostal training had made him an expert.

Whether these investigations were idle pastimes or Jones' actual *raison d'etre* in Belo Horizonte is unknown. Neither is there hard evidence that Jones' presence was related to Dan Mitrione's work at the Consulate — though Jones was certainly aware of Mitrione's post. According to an autobiographical fragment that was found at Jonestown, Mitrione "... was known in Belo Horizonte by everybody to be something other than a mere 'traffic advisor.' There were rumors that he participated with the military even then, doing strange things to dissenters... Mitrione's name would come up frequently." Subsequently, according to that same fragment, Jones went out of his way to socialize with the Mitrione family. "I'd heard of his nefarious activities in Belo Horizonte, and I thought 'I'll case this man out.' I wasn't really inclined to do him in, not me personally, but I certainly was inclined to inform on his activities to everybody on the Left. But he wouldn't see me. I saw his family and they were arrogantly anti-Brazilian..."

Because Jim Jones was a sociopath, a suspected agent of the police/

intelligence community, and a man whose historical stature was intimately entwined with his false public identity as an "apostle of socialism," there is good reason to be skeptical of the sincerity of his pronouncements about Dan Mitrione and his family. If Mitrione was, as seems likely, Jones' first "control," then Jones would obviously fear the revelation of that fact. In particular, he would fear the chance discovery of their past association, and the questions such a discovery would raise. To allay such suspicions, Jones may well have acted to co-opt the discovery — explaining it away in advance. Thus, he tells us that he knew Dan Mitrione as a child, and that, in Brazil, he wanted to "inform on his activities to everybody on the Left." So it was, we're told, that he decided to "case this man out," and came to know his family.

This may explain the presence of a consular car outside Jones' house: if Jones was socializing with the Mitrione family, the consular car was probably theirs. But who are the people on the Left to whom Jones refers? Whom was he going to tell about Dan Mitrione? So far as anyone knows, Jones' acquaintances in Brazil were all conservatives. Indeed, like Bonnie Thielman's father, the Rev. Edward Malmin, they should more accurately be described as right-wingers. And, as such, they would undoubtedly have approved of Mitrione's work.

Nevertheless, while there is every reason to be skeptical of Jones' memoir, it is interesting that he characterizes his relationship to the Mitriones as that of an informant, or spy. Given Jones' sociopathic personality (not to mention his right-wing sermons in Guyana and the implications of his CIA file), it is very likely that Jones was working *for* Mitrione rather than against him.

While Jones is said to have gone to the U.S. Consulate often, the only person whom he is *known* to have seen there was Jon Lodeesen.[78]

On October 18, 1962, Vice Consul Lodeesen wrote a peculiar letter to Jones on Foreign Service stationery. The letter reads:

> Dear Mr. Jones:
> We received a communication and we believe its your interest to come at the Consulate at your earliest convenience." [sic]

Signed by Lodeesen, there is a redundant post-script to the letter, requesting that Jones "Please see me."

While the letter itself is entirely opaque, an attachment to it is not. This is a passport-type photograph of a man who, despite his mustache and receding hairline, looks remarkably like Jim Jones — or, more accurately perhaps, like Jim Jones in disguise. While one cannot be certain, it may well be that the photo is related to the peculiar circumstances under which a second passport was issued to Jones — while the first passport was still valid.[79]

That it was Jon Lodeesen who contacted Jones is significant in its own right. This is so because Lodeesen has been a spy for much of his life. According to Soviet intelligence officers, he is a CIA agent who taught at the U.S. intelligence school in Garmisch Partenkirchen, West Germany — a sort of West Point for spooks. Subsequently, he worked at the U.S. Embassy in Moscow — until he was declared *persona non grata* for suspected espionage activities. Kicked out of the Soviet Union, he went to work for Radio Liberty, a CIA-created and financed propaganda network based in Munich. There, he was Deputy Director of the Soviet Analysis and Broadcasting Section.[80] More recently, Lodeesen was recommended for work with a CIA cover in Hawaii.[81] In a letter to the proprietor of the cover, Lodeesen was described as "fluent in the principal Russian tongues" and an expert on "Soviet double agents, dissidents and escapees."

Just the man, in other words, to handle the passport problems of an American psychopath who'd applied for a visa to visit the Soviet Union; who'd made repeated trips to Castro's Cuba; who had two valid passports at the same time; and who seems to have been the victim of, or a party to, an impersonation.

II.8 Jones in Rio

Friends of the Jones family in Belo Horizonte are agreed that he lived in the city for a period of eight months, beginning in the spring of 1962. He then moved to Rio de Janeiro.

Once again, Jones seems to have been following Dan Mitrione's lead. In mid-December, as the Jones family packed for the move to Rio, Mitrione left Belo Horizonte for a two-month "vacation" in the U.S. At the beginning of March, he returned to Brazil — but not to Belo Horizonte. Instead, he found an apartment in the posh Botafogo section of Rio de Janeiro.

There, he was not far from Jim Jones, who was recumbent in equally elegant surroundings, having found an expensive flat in the Flamengo neighborhood.[82]

According to Brazilian immigration authorities, who are said to keep meticulous records, the Jones family left Rio for an unknown country at the end of March. And they did not return.

According to Jones, however, he and his family lived in Rio until December of 1963. The assassination of President John F. Kennedy (in November of that year) was the stimulus for their return to Indiana.

There is, in other words, a nine-month period in which Jones' whereabouts are at least somewhat questionable. One would think, of course, that there would be a great many records and witnesses to the matter. Unfortunately, that isn't the case. Those members of Jones' family, and his associates, who might have seen him in Rio either died at Jonestown — or were too young at the time to be certain where they were in 1963.[83]

The issue should have been settled, of course, by the newspaper articles that appeared in Brazil after the Jonestown massacre. These were stories with local angles, describing Jones' life in Brazil. Curiously, however, none of the articles originating in Rio quote identifiable sources. This is quite unlike counterpart articles written about Jones' stay in Belo Horizonte. In the latter, almost everyone seems delighted to get his name in the paper. In Rio, nobody wants to be identified.

By far the most extensive account of Jones' stay in Rio de Janeiro was published in a newspaper that is thought by many to have been owned, or secretly supported, by the CIA. This was the English-language *Brazil Herald*.[84]

According to the article, it was "through a friend in Belo Horizonte" that Jones "found a job as a salesman of investments" in Rio. The source for this information is unstated, as is the identity of Jones' friend in Belo Horizonte.

The company for which Jones is said to have worked was Invesco, S.A., which had offices in the Edificio Central in downtown Rio.[85] At least it did until the firm went bankrupt, under scandalous circumstances, in 1967. Though this occurred more than ten years before, Invesco's former assistant manager — Jim Jones' boss — was still in Rio at the time of the Jonestown massacre. An American who'd come to Brazil in the late 1940s, and stayed, he was willing to confirm Jones' employment at Invesco — but not much more. And he did not want his name used.

"As a salesman with us," he told the *Herald*, "(Jones) didn't make it. He was too shy and I don't remember him selling anything."

Applied to Jim Jones, this is a remarkable statement. Is it possible that someone who sold monkeys door-to-door in Indianapolis during the '50s could be too timid to sell mutual funds in Rio de Janeiro during the bull markets of the '60s? The mind boggles. Here is a man who is said to have talked 900 people into killing themselves for what he hoped would be his greater glory... and he was "too shy"?!

"We hired him on a strictly commission basis and as far as I know he didn't sell anything in the three months that he worked for us," the former assistant manager said.

This, too, is an interesting remark because it implies that, while Jones worked for Invesco, there would be no record of the fact as a consequence of his failure to record any sales. Without putting too much of a point on it, the reader should know that commission-only sales jobs are favorite covers for CIA agents in foreign countries. This is so because the agent is not required to produce any cover-related work product for his civilian boss (i.e., he doesn't need to sell anything at all) — because he's working strictly "on commission." At the same time, salesmen working on commission are expected to travel, and to cultivate a broad spectrum of acquaintances.

Thus, whether Jones was working for Invesco or not, it served as a good cover for whatever else he might have been doing.

Still, if the sales job which Jones is supposed to have held down produced no income at all, how did he support himself? According to the *Brazil Herald*, he "was receiving donations of checks sent by his followers in the U.S. His ex-boss notes having seen Jones' briefcase filled with checks." This is possible, of course, but extremely unlikely. Membership in the Peoples Temple had plummeted during Jones' absence, dwindling from

2000 members in 1961 to fewer than 100 parishioners at the time of the Kennedy assassination. By the end of 1963, the electric and telephone bills had gone unpaid, and disconnection threatened. The idea that parishioners were supporting Jones in high style, by sending him personal checks, is ludicrous. Not only did they not have money, but Jones would probably have starved had he depended upon cashing small personal checks, written on Indianapolis bank accounts, in Rio de Janeiro.

Elsewhere in the *Brazil Herald* story, the December 4, 1978 article in *Time* magazine is cited. According to *Time*, Jones spent a part of 1963 working at the "American School of Rio." Asked about this, the American School issued the following statement: "Neither the salary records maintained in the business office nor the personnel records maintained in the headmaster's office reflect this name (i.e., Jim Jones) as having been connected with our school as an employee."

Jones' former boss at Invesco was not the only source for the article in the *Herald*. A second source was a Cariocan who claimed to be a Jones' closest friend in Rio. In the article, she is identified only as "Madame X."

After leaving Invesco, Madame X said, Jones went to work at the Escola Sao Fernando, while his son, Stephan, attended the British School. As it happens, however, there is no "Escola Sao Fernando" in Rio, and the British School denies that Stephan Jones was ever one of its students.

Elsewhere, Madame X says that Jones decided to return to the U.S. upon hearing of President John F. Kennedy's assassination (on November 22). The trip to the States was supposed to be a temporary visit. Jones intended to straighten out the problems that the Peoples Temple was experiencing in his absence — and then to return to Brazil. Accordingly, Madame X added, a friend of the family continued paying Jones' rent on the apartment in Rio. Eventually, when it became clear that the Joneses would not return, Madame X sold their furniture and other goods, and donated the money to charitable causes.

The "friend of the family" is, like Madame X and Jones' boss at Invesco, never identified.

So who is Madame X?

The author of the *Brazil Herald* article, Harold Emert, doesn't know. The reason he doesn't know is that he himself never spoke to her. Jim Bruce did. Who, then, is Jim Bruce? According to Emert, Jim Bruce was at that time an American freelancer based in Brazil. It was he who inspired the Jim-Jones-in-Rio story and he who provided the sources: i.e., the Invesco executive and Madame X.

Why Bruce failed to write the story himself is unclear.[86]

II.9 Invesco

There have been persistent rumors that Jim Jones worked for a CIA cover during his stay in Rio. The cover is said to have been an advertising agency, but no one can say why they think so. The *Washington Post's* Charles Krause and then-*New York Times* reporter John Crewdson each pursued the story, but neither was able to track it down.

Clearly, Invesco was at the heart of the matter, though its connection to Jones cannot have been more than a faded memory when Crewdson and Krause were looking into it. The only public reference to Jones' association with the firm was in the weekend edition of a small, almost ephemeral, newspaper. The sources for the story were anonymous, and the newspaper itself no longer existed, having long since been swallowed up by a rival. As for Invesco, its 1967 bankruptcy had taken place under military rule amid strict censorship of the press. Because bankruptcies reflected poorly on the economy, and therefore on the ruling junta, their occurrence — however scandalous — often went unreported.

For these reasons, then, Invesco has remained almost entirely unknown.

Here, it needs to be emphasized that, for whatever reason, Jim Jones felt the need for some sort of cover in Brazil. That's why he lied to his neighbors in Belo Horizonte, telling some that he was employed by the Eureka Laundries and others that he was a retired Navy captain living on a pension. In Rio, which has a small and gossipy expatriate community, the need for a cover would have been even more strongly felt. And for Jones' purposes, Invesco was ideal.

In essence, the company was an offshore analog of Bernie Cornfeld's Investors Overseas Services (IOS). In South America, at least, it pioneered the practice of selling shares in mutual funds.

Created as a venture-capital firm in 1951, its original name was Expansao Tecnico Industrial, S.A. (ETIN). It was a subsidiary of Victorholt, S.A. Industria e Commercio, whose President was Lewis Holt Ruffin. According to an old Rio hand, ETIN was set up by employees of Price, Waterhouse, including a man who was reputed to have been a German spy during World War II.

While ETIN/Invesco has always had Brazilian investors, its affairs have tended to be dominated by the participation of Rio-based Americans, English, Germans and "Swiss." This last contingent includes a number of individuals who arrived in Brazil in the mid-to-late 1940s. While they claimed to be Swiss, they are thought to have been Germans.

Sources in Rio say that several of Invesco's principals are associates of a former owner of the *Brazil Herald*, Gilbert Huber, Jr.[87] Among other business activities, Huber is a part owner of American Light and Power, and publishes the Rio de Janeiro "Yellow Pages."[88] Huber is credited by many Brazilians with helping to pave the way for the reign of terror that followed the 1964 *coup d'etat*. By this is meant that Huber was one of two people credited with founding the Instituto de Pesquiasas e Estudos Sociais (IPES). Known in English as the Institute for Social Research Studies, IPES was established in 1961 by conservatives who were alarmed by the Cuban revolution and the leftward drift of the Brazilian government. Similar in many ways to the John Birch Society, IPES was almost certainly funded by covert American sources.[89]

Initially, IPES was an instrument of propaganda, saturating the country with films, books, pamphlets and lectures attacking communism and "the threat from within," but propaganda was only a part of its strategy. Within a year of its founding, the Institute had begun to organize armed, paramilitary cells. It had also established a clandestine hand-grenade factory, and developed plans for a civil war. At the same time, it had hired a network of retired military officers 'to exert influence on those on active duty.'[90] One of those retired officers was General Golbery do Couto e Silva. His job was to compile 40,000 dossiers on Brazilians whose loyalties were considered suspect. When the coup succeeded, Golbery came out of "retirement" at IPES. Moving to Brazilia with "hundreds of thousands" of files, he established Brazil's first intelligence service, the SNI — a South American fusion of its counterpart services in the United States, the FBI and the CIA. Many of the men and women in Golbery's political dossiers suffered mightily under the junta. Some were placed under house arrest or imprisoned, while others were tortured. Still others fell prey to the *esquadraos da mortes* (death squads).

While Gilbert Huber's connection to Invesco is merely rumored, another Huber's is not. This is Joyce Huber Blumer, who owned 55,000 shares in the firm.[91] British by birth, she has attracted a certain amount of attention in the Brazilian press for what has been characterized as a "baby-selling" enterprise. Two other owners of Invesco were a Swiss or German national named Werner Blumer (24,000 shares), and an American named Scott McAuley Johnson (54,000 shares). Blumer owns an art gallery in Rio, while Johnson is described by various sources as "a mystery man" of independent means.

II.10 The Train Robbers

Which brings us to an interesting story.

In the same year that Jones went to work for Invesco, a British hoodlum named Ronald Biggs participated in what came to be called "the Great Train Robbery," sharing more than $7 million in cash and valuables stolen from a Glasgow-to-London mail train.

Apprehended, and sentenced to 30 years, Biggs escaped from prison in 1965. Fleeing to France, he relied upon an international criminal network to obtain plastic surgery and passage to Australia. Tracked by the police as the "most wanted" man in the world, Biggs subsequently found his way to Rio de Janeiro (where extradition is, at best, a rarity). According to a reporter who was ultimately instrumental in revealing Biggs' whereabouts, the fugitive's patrons in Rio were the same people who owned Invesco: Joyce Huber, Werner Blumer, Scott Johnson and others.

How Biggs, while hiding out in Rio, came to live at Scott Johnson's apartment, where he was patronized and protected by Huber and the others, is an important question.[92] Among other things, it suggests the possibility (indeed, the likelihood) that the firm which provided cover (or an alibi) for

Jim Jones' activities in Rio was part of the so-called ODESSA network.[93]

In this connection, Piers Paul Read's *The Train Robbers* is of interest.[94] Read undertook to write the book more than a decade after the robbery, and long after several other books had already been published on the subject. What made these unpromising circumstances augur well, according to Read, were two things: first, he had the cooperation of most of the men who'd pulled off the robbery. Previously, only Ronald Biggs had given an account, and Biggs was considered an outsider by those who'd conceived and executed the plan. Second, and even more importantly, the gang confided important new information to Read. This was that the train robbery, and several of the subsequent escapes, had been financed and finessed by Gen. Otto Skorzeny. Among other things, this explained why it had never been possible to account for more than half of the money stolen in the robbery.

An unrepentant Nazi, Skorzeny had been Hitler's favorite commando. After the war, he'd re-established himself in Madrid as an arms dealer and, with even greater secrecy, as the mastermind behind *Die Spinne* — the underground railroad that obtained forged documents and plastic surgery for war criminals and others requiring safe havens in South America and the Middle East. As the proprietor of a de facto intelligence agency with connections throughout the world, Skorzeny made millions as a consultant to countries and organizations whose politics were compatible with his own (e.g., Nasser's Egypt and the Secret Army Organization in Algiers).

Train-robber Buster Edwards and his wife gave Read a detailed description — names, dates and places — of how *Die Spinne* had smuggled him from England to Germany to Mexico.[95] A woman named "Hannah Schmid,"[96] whose father had served with Skorzeny in the Second World War, saw to it that he received plastic surgery and the documents necessary to travel. Edwards recuperated for nearly a month in the home of a Prussian aristocrat, "Annaliese von Lutzeberg,"[97] and was then sent on his way to Mexico — but not before he'd purchased shares (under an assumed name) in a business that Skorzeny owned.[98]

While in Mexico, Edwards and two of the other train-robbers reunited with Schmid, who "proposed that they should run guns to the Peronists in Argentina; or train troops for a planned putsch in Panama..."[99] Edwards and his friends declined: it just wasn't their scene.

In checking Edwards' story, and the stories of the other robbers, Read found that every verifiable detail was confirmed. Before finishing his book, however, it was left to him to interview Ronald Biggs in Rio. Accordingly, he got on a plane.

Finding Biggs was not that difficult. He was living at Scott Johnson's apartment. What he had to say, however, was in flat contradiction to the accounts of everyone else. According to Biggs, there were no Germans.

Read was flabbergasted. Had he been hoaxed? Or was Biggs lying on behalf of what Read suspected were his Nazi protectors? Read couldn't be sure.

"At best (Biggs) wished me to disbelieve the Skorzeny connection so that he himself could break it to the world and reap the benefit; at worst he was still in the care of Skorzeny's organisation and had been told to persuade me that it did not exist.

"The more I pondered this last possibility, the more convinced I became that this was the explanation — for it still seemed inconceivable to me that June (Edwards) had invented her meeting with Skorzeny in Madrid, or could have discovered that he was a friend of the *Reader's Digest* editor who spoke 14 Chinese dialects. I suddenly realized how thoughtless and foolhardy I had been to come to a country (Brazil) known to be a nest of ex-Nazis. Clearly Biggs had been saved from extradition not because of his child, but because of neo-Nazi influence in government circles. The woman who had been with him at the airport, Ulla Sopher, a German-Argentinian with blonde hair and blue eyes, was part of their network. All the strands of the story came together to form a noose around my neck."[100]

And yet, despite this cogent explanation for what had happened, and despite the evidence that Edwards and the others had provided, Read demurred. Over drinks in a sidewalk cafe, "I began to believe that Biggs was telling the truth."

A bizarre turn-about that occurs at the very end of the book, Read's conversion to Biggs' account makes no sense at all. Biggs' own fugitivity, which (like Edwards') was facilitated by plastic surgery and forged documents provided by an unnamed criminal syndicate, is the best argument against the story he tells.

One wonders if Read would have ended his book differently if he had known about Jim Jones, Scott Johnson and Invesco.

Not that Read didn't have clues to the fact that Biggs was living in the parapolitical twilight — a world defined by the inter-penetration of criminal syndicates and the intelligence community.

One such clue pertained to Biggs' son, "Mikezinho," who was born while his father was a fugitive in Rio. "Little Mikey" had a very interesting godfather, a man with powerful European connections and who, like Werner Blumer, was in the business of selling art.

This was Fernand Legros, who concerns us here only because his association with Biggs, and Biggs' friends in Rio, adds perspective to what might be called "the Invesco circle."

Legros has been described as a "playboy, millionaire, art dealer and CIA agent..."[101] A native Egyptian, with apartments in Switzerland, France and Spain, he was a homosexual whose lovers included the Secretary-General of the United Nations (Dag Hammerskjold) and members of the French cabinet.[102] A naturalized American, Legros resorted to at least four passports: French, American, Canadian and British.

It is alleged (by author Henrik Kruger and others) that Legros played a lethal role in the mysterious (and still unsolved) kidnapping and murder of the Moroccan dissident, Ben Barka — who disappeared from the streets of Paris (where Legros owned an art gallery) in October, 1965. According to Kruger, Legros had been in contact with Ben Barka in Geneva, where the art dealer had a second gallery and both men had apartments. Lured to France, Ben Barka was kidnapped, tortured and killed. While his disappearance remains unsolved, the operation has often been attributed to French gangsters (including a man named Christian David) acting on Legros' orders. Legros himself is believed to have been working at the time for either the CIA or France's SDECE.

In 1967, Legros fled to Brazil upon being implicated in the authentication and sale of forgeries attributed to modern masters. Sold for millions to gullible investors around the world, the forgeries are believed to have been painted by Elmyr de Hory, Clifford Irving's friend and neighbor on Ibiza.

But Legros' influence seems not to have been much diminished by the notoriety surrounding the forgeries. According to Kruger, the art dealer was "a personal friend of Henry Kissinger's ...(and) the man the CIA assigned to snoop on U.N. secretary-general Dag Hammarskjold. Legros helped the CIA kidnap the African leader Moise Tshombe..." Not finally, Legros became an associate (in France and in Brazil) of the legendary French gangster Christian David.

While in Rio and Sao Paulo, David established a Brazilian-based narcotics syndicate to fill the vacuum created when the so-called "French connection" was broken.[103] In this task, he was abetted by fugitive French collaborators and war criminals living in Argentina, Paraguay, Chile and Brazil.

Arrested by the Brazilian authorities in 1972, David was eventually deported to the United States, and then extradited to France — where he was sentenced to death.[104] Meanwhile, David's pal, Fernand Legros, was himself in a Rio prison — occupying the cell next to Ronald Biggs. The circumstances of Legros' imprisonment are murky, but it has been suggested that he was locked up as an exercise in protective custody, supposedly for having helped the CIA to arrange David's arrest. While that allegation is unproven, it is certainly true that Legros had a rather easy time of it behind bars. "Each day ... he was brought lavish meals including lobster, champagne, cognac and fat Havana cigars."[105]

All of which is to say: what? That Jim Jones was somehow involved in the 1963 Great Train Robbery, or in the 1965 murder of Ben Barka? Hardly. Do I mean, then, to suggest that Jones was a party to the making and breaking of the "Brazilian Connection," or that he was implicated in the wave of forgeries that culminated in Clifford Irving's "autobiography" of Howard Hughes? Of course not.

My intention has only been to demonstrate that the milieu in which Jones found himself in 1963 — the Invesco milieu, revolving around Scott Johnson, et al. — was anything but banal. A suspected CIA conduit, Invesco was owned and operated by men and women whose connections to criminals such as Ronald Biggs and spooks like Fernand Legros — and to gangster-spooks such as Christian David — deserve scrutiny. The coalescence of organized crime and the CIA during the early 1960s was responsible for parapolitical enormities which continued to resonate beneath the surface of American politics and culture for the remainder of the century.

Jones' connections to Dan Mitrione and Jon Lodeesen, his resort to cover stories, his use of multiple passports, and his strange involvement with the Invesco circle, strongly suggests that the 1978 tragedy in Guyana was set in motion in Cuba and Brazil some 15 years earlier.

Endnotes

1 As we'll see, Mitrione was, first, a policeman in Indiana, and then a counter-insurgency expert in South America.

2 "*Was Jonestown a CIA Medical Experiment?*" by Michael Meiers, *Studies in American Religion*, Volume 35, Edwin Mellen Press, 1988. Meiers answers the question affirmatively, relying upon circumstantial evidence that is not entirely convincing.

3 My description of Jones is intended without rancor. That he was charismatic is obvious to any who have ever heard him. That he was a sadist is apparent from the "boxing mis-matches" he staged, and from the homosexual attacks that he so often carried out upon his followers. That Jones was Bible-hating, as well as Bible-thumping, is clear from his instruction that the Good Book should be used as toilet paper. Other evidence of Jones' hatred for the Bible abounds in a journal found at Jonestown. In its pages, the anonymous diarist quotes Jones as saying that "The Bible will be used to put you back into slavery." "...the white man used the Bible to keep blacks in slavery." "That God up there doesn't look after the good people down here.... If Harriet Tubman hadn't torn it up, we'd still be in slavery. We've got to get rid of the Bible or the white man will use it to lead us back into slavery." On the same page, the writer notes that "Jim claimed superiority to Jesus." Elsewhere, we are told that "Jim led the congregation in singing, 'The Old Bullshit Religion Ain't What It Used to Be.'" And, by no means finally, the writer quotes Jones to the effect that "Religion is the opiate of the people.... Jim told of God's creation of Lucifer, who led away one-third of the angels. God fouled up. 'Some of you get nervous when I say that.' He said religion was used by the ruling class to control us. 'They" steal, 'they" lie, but they tell us niggers, 'Nigger, don't lie.' They kill all the time, but 'thou shalt not kill.'"

4 Credit for stopping the attack is usually given to the attorneys. In reality, however, it should probably go to one of the Temple's own members, Tim Carter, who seems to have been the first to intervene. Interestingly, Carter reports that Don Sly's attack on Ryan was at best half-hearted. "It was like he wanted to be stopped," Carter told me.

5 *Baltimore Sun,* November 21, 1978. A subsequent report, by the Associated Press on November 25, listed 180 children among 775 cadavers. The final count, recorded by the *Miami Herald* on December 17, reported that 260 children were among the dead.

6 *Los Angeles Times*, November 24, 1978.

7 It is literally true that, even before the dead could be buried, both the *San Francisco Chronicle* and the *Washington Post* had published books about the massacre.

8 In fact, the sweetener used was Fla-Vor-Aid.

9 *New England Journal of Medicine*, "Law-Medicine Notes: The Guyana Mass Suicides: Medicolegal Re-evaluation" by William J. Curran, J.D., LL.M., S.M. Hyg., June 7, 1979.

10 Among them: the National Association of Medical Examiners and the Reference Organization in Forensic Medicine and Sciences.

11 It was Dr. Rudiger Breitenecker who commented on the procedure used in Guyana (trochar embalming). Dr. Breitenecker was the only civilian who participated in the seven autopsies conducted by the Armed Forces Institute of Pathology team at Dover Air Force Base. Those autopsied were: Laurence Schacht; William Castillo; James Jones; Violatt Dillard; Maria Katsaris; Carolyn (Moore) Layton; and Ann Moore.

12 But it was also understandable. The dead were infested and putrefying in Guyana's heat, which made their handling exceedingly unpleasant, and their identification difficult.

13 "Medical Examiners Find Failings By Government on Cultist Bodies," by Lawrence K. Altman, *New York Times*, Dec. 3, 1978.

14 Op cit., *American Medical News*. See also, "Coroner Says 700 in Cult Who Died Were Slain," by Timothy McNulty and Michael Sneed (Chicago Tribune Service story), *The Miami Herald*, Dec. 17,1978.

15 The quote is taken from the autopsy report on Carolyn Moore, prepared by Dr. Robert L. Thompson.

16 With respect to the absence of cyanide in the vat, see page 4 of the autopsy protocol (AFIP #1680274) for Laurence E. Schacht.

17 *American Medical News*, "Bungled Aftermath of Tragedy," by Lawrence Altman, MD, p. 7.

18 "Some in Cult Received Cyanide by Injection, Guyanese Sources Say," by Nicholas M. Horrock, *New York Times*, Dec. 12, 1978.

19 In an interview with this writer, Rhodes emphasized the presence of armed guards, some with rifles and some with crossbows, who formed a perimeter to prevent people from escaping the encampment.

20 According to Johnny Cobb, he heard screams and gunshots throughout the night, and saw flashing lights.

21 "Army to Identify Bodies of Cultists," *Miami Herald*, 22 Nov. 1978, p. 1.

22 "Guyana Operations," After-Action Report, 18–27 November 1978, prepared by the Special Study Group, Operations Directorate, U.S.MC Directorate, Joint Chiefs of Staff (distributed 31 January, 1979). All times are taken from Appendix B, "Chronology of Events."

23 *Ibid.*

24 *Ibid.* The JCS chronology cites the following reference: "CIA 191138Z Nov 78". NOIWON is the National Operations and Intelligence Watch Officers Network.

25 Mader is the author of *Who's Who in the CIA*. It's in that book that Dwyer is named as a CIA officer.

26 "Unman" = Unidentified Man.

27 On the tape-recording that I have, it appears that this is actually Jones' voice, and that he says, "Keep Dwyer alive!" and then adds, "Sit down, sit down, sit down."

28 Dwyer deposition in Layton trial, Book II, p. 221.

29 Sukhdeo was named with "deprogrammer" Galen Kelly in a suit brought by the Circle of Friends on behalf of Joan E. Stedrak. The suit is believed to have been filed on November 6, 1978.

30 Asked about this in a recent interview, Sukhdeo continued to insist that he paid his own way to Guyana.

31 United States v. Layton, Federal Rules (90 F.R.D. 520/1981), pp. 521–22, in re a "Memorandum and Order Denying Plaintiffs Motion to Compel Production of Sukhdeo Tapes."

32 Ibid.

33 The CIA has stated that, in deference to its Charter, which prohibits the Agency from collecting information on Americans, it took no notice of the Temple's approaches to Communist Bloc organizations in Guyana. The disclaimer is widely disbelieved.

34 Associated Press, story by Chris Connell, November 21, 1978.

35 For many years, the FBI maintained a "Racial Intelligence" file. A 1968 Airtel sent to that file refers to the Bureau's concerns the possible emergence of an American "Mau Mau," the "rise of a (black) messiah," and "the beginning of a true black revolution."

36 *Who's Who In the CIA*, by Dr. Julius Mader, East Berlin, 1968.

37 *Raven: the Untold Story of Rev. Jim Jones and His People*, by Tim Reiterman with John Jacobs, E.P. Dutton (New York, 1982), pp. 9–21.

38 It is Jones' biographer, Tim Reiterman, who characterizes the unidentified woman evangelist as "fanatical." See *Raven*, p. 18.

39 The possibility that Jones was sexually abused as a child should not be ruled out — particularly in light of his own abusive sexual behavior as an adult. Even those who remain loyal to Jones, insisting that he was somehow "misunderstood," lament his enthusiasm for sexually humiliating those who had displeased him — not occasionally by resorting to homosexual rape.

40 The quotation is from typewritten fragments of an autobiography found amid the carnage at

Jonestown.

41 It was independent researcher John Judge who asked Kennedy about Jones' relationship to Mitrione.

42 A book about Mitrione, and his 1970 assassination in Uruguay, is *Hidden Terrors*, by A.J. Langguth, Pantheon Books (New York, 1978).

43 Jones moved from Lynn to Richmond in the fall of 1948.

44 Op cit., *Raven*, p. 40.

45 One hardly knows what to make of this bizarre fund-raising method. There can't have been that much demand for the beasts. Nevertheless, the practice is worth noting, if only because it constitutes, however tenuously, Jones' first known link to South America. Contrary to some reports, the monkeys were not obtained from university research laboratories in Indiana, but from suppliers below the Equator.

46 When Father Divine died in the summer of 1972, years after Jones had moved his own congregation to California, Jones nevertheless arranged for a caravan of buses to cross the country to Philadelphia — where Jones announced that he was Father Divine's white reincarnation. In that capacity, he said, he was quite prepared to take control of the Peace Mission movement (and its considerable assets). Mrs. Divine said no.

47 *Father Divine: Holy Husband*, by Sara Harris, pp. 319–20.

48 *New York Times*, "Jim Jones 1960 Visit to Cuba Recounted," by Joseph B. Treaster. As evidence of his veracity, Foster provided the *Times* with letters and an affidavit that Jones had signed, promising to support Foster if he should emigrate to the United States.

49 Foster came to Indianapolis in August, 1960. He accepted the hospitality of the Peoples Temple for the remainder of that summer, and then decamped for New York (where his fiancée was living).

50 *Ascent*, "Lure of the Cowboy Mystique," by Aubrey E. Zephyr, October, 1983. This is an article about Foster's Urban Western Riding Program (for inner-city youngsters).

51 Op cit., *Raven*, p. 62.

52 The reference to a Cuban stopover on the way to Brazil, and to a photo of Jones, Marceline and Castro, is told in *The Broken God*, by Bonnie Thielmann with Dean Merill, David C. Cook Publishing Co. (Elgin, Ill.), 1979, p. 27.

53 *Religion In Cuba Today*, edited by Alice L. Hageman and Philip E. Wheaton, Association Press, New York, p. 32.

54 Mikoyan was in Havana from February 4–13.

55 In this connection, an interesting coincidence concerns the presence of *New York Times* reporter James Reston at the Hilton. He was there to cover the Mikoyan visit, as well as the Soviet exhibition, and it seems fair to say that, in a literal sense, at least, he must have crossed paths with Jim Jones.

It is ironic, then, that nearly 20 years later, his son should one day write a book (*Our Father Who Art In Hell*) about the decline and fall of the Peoples Temple. And in that book, a peculiar story is told:

"In December, 1978, James Reston, Jr. (met) a journalist friend at the Park Hotel in Georgetown. The journalist announced ominously that he now knew the full story behind Jonestown. But he would not write it. He would not tell his editors he knew it. He would forget it and flee Guyana as soon as possible. He told Reston the name of his informant. 'He will contact you at your hotel. If you want it, you will get the full story. I have just heard it, and I've sent the man away. If I were you, I wouldn't take it either. It will make you the most celebrated writer in America, *and you will die for it.*'

"Reston felt a nervous laugh rising from his belly and controlled it."

Reston seems not to have pursued the matter.

56 Mitrione was then Chief of Police in Richmond.

57 *Who's Who in the CIA*, by Dr. Julius Mader, Berlin (1968).

58 "U.S. A.I.D. In the Dominican Republic — An Inside View," NACLA Newsletter, November 1970. This was according to David Fairchild, the Assistant Program Officer for U.S.AID in Santo Domingo. (NACLA is the North American Conference on Latin America.)

59 "Echols takes dead aim on laugh," *San Diego Union*, June 12, 1986, p. 11.

60 *Guyana Gold*, by Wellesley A. Baird, Three Continents Press (Washington, 1982), pp.

164–181. The quotation is from an Afterword by Kathleen A. Adams. Ms. Adams wrote her doctoral thesis (for Case Western Reserve University) on the impact of the gold-mining industry on Amerindian tribes in the Northwest District of Guyana.

61 Op cit., *Raven*, pp. 75–78.

62 Dr. E. Paul Thomas was Jones' physician.

63 Jones' hospital stay is related in the *Indianapolis Recorder*, October 7, 1961.

64 Ibid., p. 77.

65 Ibid., p. 78.

66 Op cit., *Raven*, p. 78.

67 Op cit., *The Broken God*, p. 27.

68 Despite Oswald's demonstration of pro-Castro sympathies — he was arrested in New Orleans after handing out leaflets for the Fair Play for Cuba Committee (FPCC) — his impostor was not given the requested visa.

69 *Estado do Minas*, "Pastor Jim Jones lived and worked in Belo Horizonte with his children," Nov. 23, 1978, p. 23.

70 "To Brazilians, Jim Jones was a CIA Agent," *O Globo*, Nov. 24, 1978.

71 "Leader of the Peoples Temple Lived in Belo Horizonte," *Estado de Minas*, Nov. 23, 1978, p. 1; and, from the same issue, "Pastor Jim Jones lived and worked in Belo Horizonte with his children," p. 23.

72 Ibid.

73 Besides de Magalhaes, Elineu Pereira Guimaraes and Marcidio Inacio da Silva were interviewed. See *O Globo*, "To Brazilians, Jim Jones was a CIA Agent," Nov. 24, 1978.

74 *Estado do Minas*, "Pastor Jim Jones lived and worked in Belo Horizonte with his children," Nov. 23, 1978, p. 23.

75 "To Brazilians, Jim Jones was a CIA Agent," *O Globo*, Nov. 24, 1978.

76 Brazilians newspapers identify the woman as "Joyce Bian." Since one of Jones' ministerial assistants, Jack Beam, is known to have joined him in Belo Horizonte in October, 1962, and to have brought his family with him, we may suppose that this was Beam's daughter.

77 "To Brazilians, Jim Jones was a CIA Agent," *O Globo*, Nov. 24, 1978.

78 Besides Marco Rocha's remarks about a car from the American Consulate, Bonnie Thielman recalls that Jones often went to the Consulate on unknown business.

79 The letter from Lodeesen, with the photograph attached, was provided by the FBI to attorneys in the Layton case.

80 See *CIA in the Dock*, edited by V. Chernyavsky, Progress Publishers, Moscow (1983): "Saboteurs on the Air: A Close-up View" by Vaim Kassis and Leonid Kolosov, pp. 147–67.

81 The letter (dated January 12, 1983) was from Ned Avary to Ron Rewald, then CEO of the Hawaiian investment firm Bishop, Baldwin, Rewald and Dillingham.

82 Jones' address in Rio was #154 Rua Senador Vigueiro.

83 For example, Jones' natural son, Stephan.

84 "The little-known story: Jim Jones' early days in Rio de Janeiro," *Brazil Herald*, by Harold Emert, December 24–26, 1978, p. 9.

85 There have been persistent rumors that Jones, while in Rio, was employed by a "CIA-owned advertising agency." Invesco, while not an advertising agency, is the only firm to which these rumors could possibly refer. It is certainly the case that any number of Brazilians suspected that its American owners were working for the CIA.

86 Once again, there is an interesting parallel between events surrounding Jim Jones and those involving Lee Harvey Oswald. That is to say, shortly after Oswald's arrest, a story went out on the wires describing in detail Oswald's peculiar background as a defector, the time that he spent in New Orleans, and so forth. The author of the scoop was Seth Kantor. Like Emert, however, Kantor was not the ultimate source of the story he reported — another journalist, "too busy to write it himself" (!), had given it to him over the telephone. This was Hal Hendrix, a CIA operative working under journalistic cover.

87 Huber bought the *Brazil Herald* from William Williamson, and later sold it to the *Latin American Daily News*.

88 This information derives from sources in Rio. See also A.J. Langguth's *Hidden Terrors*, Pantheon Books, 1978, p. 88.

89 *United States Penetration of Brazil,* by Jan Knippers Black, University of Pennsylvania Press, 1977, pages 82–86.
90 Ibid.
91 Ms. Huber is said to be Gilbert Huber's sister-in-law, but that information has yet to be confirmed.
92 An anecdotal account of Biggs' life in Rio, which discusses his friendship with Johnson and Huber, can be found in *Biggs: The World's Most Wanted Man,* by Colin Mackenzie, William Morrow & Co., New York, 1975.
93 ODESSA is an acronym for *Organization der Entlassene SS Angehorige* (Organization for the Release of Former SS Members). *Die Spinne* (The Spider), which was also known as the "Swastika Syndicate," was the clandestine operations arm of ODESSA. See *Skorzeny: Hitler's Commando,* by Glenn B. Infield, St. Martin's Press, 1981 (New York).
94 *The Train Robbers,* by Piers Paul Read, W.H. Allen, London (1978).
95 Since this was written, I was able to interview Buster Edwards at his flower-stall outside Waterloo Station in London. In that interview, Edwards confirmed what he'd told Read, and elaborated upon it with further details.
96 The name is a pseudonym that Read used in his book.
97 This name is also a pseudonym, according to Read.
98 Edwards invested 10,000 pounds in a real estate firm that Skorzeny was using to develop land near Alicante.
99 Ibid., p. 195. Besides Edwards, Bruce Reynolds and Charlie Wilson met with Schmid in Mexico City.
100 Ibid., pp. 257–58.
101 *The Great Heroin Coup,* by Henrik Kruger.
102 Hammerskjold died in a plane crash in the Congo on September 17, 1961. The suspicion that the plane was sabotaged is widespread, but to date unproven. See *The Last Days of Dag Hammerskjold,* by Arthur L. Gavshon, Barrie & Rockliff with Pall Mall Press, London, 1963.
103 Following the arrest and extradition of Paraguya's Auguste Ricard, heroin refined in Marseilles was shipped to David in Brazil for transport to the United States.
104 The sentence appears never to have been carried out, and there are unconfirmed reports that David was freed some time ago.
105 Kruger tells us that, in 1974, French intelligence agents kidnapped Legros from Brazil, and brought him back to France. Imprisoned there, he was released upon the demands of Henry Kissinger, who protested the mistreatment of an American citizen.

Exposing the Nazi International: An Analysis

by Joseph P. Farrell

Many years before I had begun my own researches into the postwar wheeling and dealing of Nazis, and of course years before my own books on the subject were published, I ran across the initial edition of the book which you now have in your hands, *Secret and Suppressed II.* As World War II was a subject of fascination with me since my youth, I was naturally intrigued by the article "Exposing the Nazi International." I read the piece with some interest, since, of course, I was by then familiar with the work of Ladislas Farago and Paul Manning on Martin Bormann's postwar survival in South America,[1] and the article did not disappoint.

The problem, however, like all such articles, was that it was purely anecdotal. While it made a number of intriguing observations about the nature of postwar Nazi business "practices," little of it could be corroborated by other sources, or by reasoned argument and extrapolation from its own internal logic and allegations.

All that has changed in the 15 or so years that have passed since Feral House first published *Secret and Suppressed.* When the article first appeared in that book, Germany had just had its *Wiedervereinigung* (reunification), and was once more just beginning to flex its economic and military muscle on the European and world stage, so little of the archival material that became available as a result of that reunification had yet been plumbed by researchers. Prior to the book's first printing we had, of course, been made dimly aware by various researchers that "something" was afoot in the postwar Nazi International. Christopher Simpson's *Blowback* and similar books pulled the veil back on the secret deal between future CIA chief Allen Dulles and German military intelligence, headed by Wehrmacht general Reinhard Gehlen. The deal effectively turned over Gehlen's spy network — lock, stock, and Nazi — in Eastern Europe over to the nominal control of the Americans while leaving Gehlen in de facto day-to-day operational control, thus severely compromising the CIA's civilian charter long before the ink was dry on President Truman's signature of the National Security

Act of 1947, which brought the CIA and NSA into existence. According to Simpson and others, Gehlen's deliberate misinformation and exaggeration of Soviet military strength and intentions contributed greatly to the formation of American foreign, military, and economic policy and contributed no small amount to the Cold War stalemate that followed.

Within a few short years, Russ Bellant, Linda Hunt and others followed up with an examination of how Eastern European émigré organizations, many of them fronts for Gehlen's spy organization — which had since become West Germany's version of the CIA, the BND or *Bundesnachrichtendienst* — had infiltrated the right wing of the Republican Party and were prominent financial contributors to Presidents Ronald Reagan's and George H.W. Bush's election campaigns in 1980, 1984, and 1988. And for those old enough to remember, early conspiracy theorist and Warren Commission critic Mae Brussell minced no words that there was a Nazi connection to the JFK assassination. She was followed in this assertion by an obscure book called *The Assassination Chain* by Bert Sugar and Sybil Leek — with a Foreword by famous columnist Jack Anderson — that exposed the little-known fact that Lee Harvey Oswald's notebook contained the address of none other than American Nazi Party leader George Lincoln Rockwell. And most of us were dimly aware of the fact that NASA's moon rockets and indeed the whole American nuclear missile arsenal simply would not have existed without the participation and collusion of Nazi rocket scientists Von Braun, Rudolf, Dornberger, et al.

But all this was a far cry from there actually *being* a "Nazi International," i.e., a covert independent organization of Nazis infiltrating corporations and governments and manipulating them for its own sinister purposes. With the passage of time, however, we are now in a position to verify — at least in a general fashion — some of the article's astonishing allegations.

The Article's Allegations: An Analysis

But what *are* those allegations? Let us look closely at what "K" actually states at the very beginning of the article:

My name is K., and for the past ten years I have served with the international Nazi Party organization as Inspector General or Liaison between central headquarters and operatives in the field. I would report on actions under way, supply data, information for possible actions in the future, and financial and personal data on individuals in different parts of the world. The Nazi Party organization is composed in two basic parts: the working organization, made up of former SS military officers, former members of the Nazi party, and the second section of German industrialists and businessmen who financially support and provide the logistics support for operations of this organization. They have been involved with and responsible for a number of operations in the past years, among them the DC-10, the problems it has had; recent fires and calamities in Nevada. They have set up and provided logistic and financial support for organizations such as the Irish Republican Army and the Palestine Liberation Organization; they have and currently are involved with top-level individuals in the Reagan administration...

This requires careful unpacking, for there are a number of specific implications that emerge from this short paragraph:

1) The postwar Nazi Party is *international in extent;*
2) It has a definite *organization* implying *a hierarchy and normalized chain of command,* as evident in K's reference to himself as an "Inspector General;" this organization is moreover split into two components, the operational component composed of former SS and military officers, and the financial component who support the organization logistically and financially;
3) It has a *central headquarters*, which, as is evident throughout the rest of the article, "K" connects to Skorzeny's home in Madrid, though he also implies a remoter, more high-ranking headquarters, somewhere in South America;
4) It conducts active *operations* directly, as in the case of the DC-10 disasters, which forms a central component in the article; these operations include but are not limited to:
   a) sponsoring "natural calamities" such as wildfires in Nevada and other "calamties";
   b) sponsorship, support, and use of front terrorist organizations to further its own agenda;
5) It actively gathers *intelligence* on:
   a) personal data of individuals, presumably for blackmailed coercion and other purposes; and,
   b) financial data on persons and corporations, again, presumably for blackmailed coercion and corporate and organizational infiltration and penetration.
By implication, one may assume that this organization also conducts more hardcore intelligence gathering on the military organization of various countries in which it operates.

Let us briefly analyze each of these general points seriatim, before exploring in more depth "K's" assertions regarding the DC-10 and Nazi corporate and investment practices.

Regarding the *international extension* of the Nazi International, this is entirely consistent with known facts. As already mentioned, the Nazis were successful in penetrating and exercising significant influence in postwar America's space program and intelligence gathering and analysis via the Gehlen organization. Additionally, German technicians aided the Soviet space program, and NKVD-KGB double agents acted inside Gehlen's organization, raising the possibility that they could also have been "triple" agents, working at one level for the Americans, at a deeper level for the Soviets, but at the deepest level for the Organization itself.

We need look no farther than the Internet to learn of the wartime Nazi association with radical Islam in the form of the Grand Mufti of Jerusalem[2] and Nazi sponsorship of the notorious radical Egyptian Muslin, Banna,[3] as well as of the postwar efforts of Dr. Wilhelm Voss — civilian head of the Skoda munitions works' engineering division and an intimate of SS Obergruppenführer Hans Kammler's super-secret black projects think tank, the Kammlerstab — of Hitler's Reichsbank President Hjalmar Schacht, and of Skorzeny himself, in behalf of supplying advanced rocket technology to Gamel Abdul Nasser's regime in Egypt. Skorzeny was instrumental in helping Nasser's junta establish and organize their intelligence services and training the Egyptian army in modern weapons and combat tactics.[4] As for Nazi connections to the PLO and the IRA, these too are now a matter beyond dispute.[5] Additionally, actual Nazi liaison with postwar Neo-Nazi organizations in America, France, the former eastern and western zones of Germany, eastern Europe, and Russia is also no longer in dispute.[6] "K's" allegations of the international extent of the organization, in other words, are entirely consistent with known facts and data.

That said, it is another matter entirely if this international extent is backed up by an actual *organization with one or more headquarters.* Once again, however, recent research permits a rational speculation on where this was (or is), and how it relates to Otto Skorzeny's headquarters in Madrid. As the recent and meticulous research of Carter P. Hydrick indicates, one may reasonably and safely assume that Martin Bormann and his close friend and associate, Heinrich "Gestapo" Müller — the actual head of Hitler's notorious Gestapo — escaped to South America.[7] Hydrick's thesis is stunningly simple even though the scenario he paints is extraordinarily complex, but the bottom line is that Bormann and most likely Müller negotiated the covert surrender of highly enriched U235 to the U.S.A. in return for America turning a blind eye to their escape and existence in South America. In this, Hydrick corroborates from yet another quarter, and with meticulous documentation and argument, the thesis of Ladislas Farago and Paul Manning that Martin Bormann was alive and well, and *functioning,* as the de facto Führer of a postwar Nazi International in South America. And with Heinrich "Gestapo" Müller's probable survival as well, an interesting picture begins to emerge.

As I mentioned in my own books *Reich of the Black Sun: Nazi Secret Weapons and the Cold War Allied Legend, The SS Brotherhood of the Bell: NASA's Nazis, JFK, and* MAJIC-*12* and *Secrets of the Unified Field: The Philadelphia Experiment, the Nazi Bell, and the Discarded Theory,[8]* there is a third high-ranking Nazi who also most likely escaped Europe, along with the super-secret technology and science represented by the Nazi Bell device, and this is SS Obergruppenführer (4-star general) Hans Kammler. Kammler was by the war's end the absolute head of *all* of Nazi Germany's many exotic secret weapons projects, and an administrative genius thoroughly familiar with the management and coordination of advanced research projects.[9] With the escape of these three we have the clear outlines of the emerging Nazi international. As I put it in my most recent book:

> Bormann, Müller, and Kammler: It is an interesting and unholy trinity to contemplate, for in it, one discerns the outlines of a very sinister shadow, the shadow of a postwar "Nazi International," beginning to emerge. Consider: if there was to be a postwar Nazi International continuing to develop its own secret projects, it would need lots of money and someone who knew how to handle it: Bormann; it would need lots of security and someone who knew how to run it: Müller; and lots of engineering expertise and management experience in coordinating large projects and keeping them secret: Kammler. And they would need a suitably advanced project to work on within the limits imposed by post-war circumstances. Large uranium enrichment plants for a-bombs were out, as were large, and very visible rocket gantries. Something truly sensational, which would not require large physical plants (other than large power supplies), and which could pay much larger dividends than any other of the above alternatives, was needed: the Bell.[10]

If this be true, then the clear lineaments of Skorzeny's headquarters, as outlined by "K," are discerned, for any such headquarters in Madrid would be answerable to a higher authority in South America, which Bormann, Müller, and Kammler would certainly constitute, either together or separately. Skorzeny was but the European "branch office" of something much larger. But again, the allegations of "K" insofar as they go fit the overall pattern of known facts. Skorzeny, as an SS colonel, would certainly be answerable to any of these three men, all of whom held rank in the SS as general officers.

As far as this Organization's ability to conduct active operations, either directly or through proxies, we have already pointed out the known involvement of Skorzeny and former Kammlerstab member Dr. Wilhelm Voss in training and equipping Nasser's Egyptian armed forces and intelligence services. And as we have also noted, Nazi penetration and liaison of terrorist organizations such as the IRA and PLO is now a matter of record. So once again, "K's" allegations fit the overall pattern of known facts consistently.

What is interesting to note here is "K's" allegation that there is a Nazi connection to wildfires and other "natural calamities" in the American southwest. It is worth recalling that in the post-9/11 environment, the American media has pointed to the possibility of the involvement of radical Muslim terrorist cells in setting some of these fires. Again, "K's" allegations fit a wider pattern of speculative possibilities, and point the finger to an even deeper and more covert layer of responsibility for such "operations," and given the now well-known and documented connection of Nazism to radical Muslims before and during the war, it is again not beyond the bounds of possibility. As "K's" interviewer puts it, "Then you're saying that Arab control, where it shows up, is German control? That Otto (Skorzeny) and his people are behind that?" "K's" answer is succinct, and points to this wartime connection: "Yes, and it has been German control since before the war, even."

With point 5) above, however, we are in the realm of the specifics of "K's" allegations, and to his specific assertions of Nazi involvement in the problems associated with the McDonnell-Douglas DC-10 jumbo jet we must now turn.

The DC-10 and the Nazi International

With respect to conducting active intelligence gathering and covert operations, "K" is unusually clear and precise for someone offering merely anecdotal information. For example, one unique operation that "K" indicates the Nazi international was involved in was "extracting files from the National Archives, and most of what the National Archives had was not even catalogued, so virtually anything could be missing and no one would know it was missing."[11] I cannot help but let my mind run with this one a bit, for as someone interested in almost all aspects of "alternative research," I cannot resist the idea that of all the missing files UFOlogists, researchers of alternative technologies and experiments like Tesla's Colorado Springs experiments or the Philadelphia Experiment and so on have encountered over the years, how ironic it would be if some postwar Nazi International was not only removing incriminating files about the Nazi regime and its own postwar activities from American archives, but anything else of technical, historical, or financial interest to it as well. The activity and the *target* — in this case the National Archives — are consistent with the presumed agenda of such an organization. Just imagine the goldmine of potential blackmailing opportunities this would give such an organization if, say, some of these files concerned the degree and detailed financial dealings of major American corporations, families, or political figures with the Nazi Reich. What sort of leverage would, say, the *complete* file on the financial dealings of Prescott Bush with the Nazi regime give to such an organization: after all, he was father to U.S. President G.H.W. Bush and grandfather to President G.W. Bush?[12]

Whatever one makes of the almost endless implications of postwar Nazis pilfering files from the American (and therefore presumably *other* nations' archives), "K" does not consider them. Rather, he presses on to the most specific and central of his allegations: the deliberate Nazi sabotage of the DC-10 jumbo jet and its extortion of McDonnell-Douglas, a major American aerospace and defense contractor of the 1960s and 1970s.

"K" begins by mentioning that the source of his information comes from Skorzeny himself,[13] and that behind the Organization, the economic interests of "Messerschmidt-Volkau-Blum" was involved, since it was the German firm represented in the European consortium developing the A-300 airbus, Europe's only competitor to the emerging jumbo-jet market dominated by the three main American contenders, the Boeing 747, the McDonnell-Douglas DC-10, and the graceful Lockheed-Martin L1011 "Tristar."[14]

As "K's" allegations are here quite specific, it is best to recall what exactly they are. The interviewer begins by asking the obvious question:

> *Could you elaborate on the specifics of the extortion of McDonnell-Douglas prior to this event (the induced crashes of DC-10 aircraft) and, specifically, how it was done, for how long and payments and amounts? You had mentioned that there was an Airbus which was competing, could you explain the whole groundwork on that?*
>
> The Airbus was developed and sold through a consortium of French and German manufacturers. They perceived the new generation of aircraft to be middle-range and still large-bodied aircraft, an improvement on the Boeing. They were aware that Lockheed and also Boeing and McDonnell-Douglas were also developing that; however, the costs were deemed too heavy for a single European interest to go it alone and consequently this association was developed. I use this word "developed" and it certainly was encouraged by the German side, who because of the DC-10, which will be explained, wished to profit from this and did not with to tie up a great deal of their own capital in it.[15]

At this juncture it is important to recall the historical fact that of the three main American jumbo contenders, McDonnell-Douglas' DC-10 was the first out of the gate, and thus for a period of time, until its numerous "accidents" began to happen, was the earliest contender for the market. Continuing:

> *When you say "German side," who are you referring to?*
> Messerschmidt-Volkau-Blum [*sic*].
>
> *At what point was the decision made and how was it made, to extort or coerce McDonnell-Douglas?*
> In the embryonic stages of this, in '71, the German interests did see that the DC-10, the L-1011, the other possible competitors were far advanced, would be direct competition, and they could not go it alone, could not be the first of the new generation of aircraft, and it was decided there were two options. Either through extortion or, if necessary, through the accidents that took place. The (methods) of the accidents as they developed were not known in '71, but they

were developing some ideas. The biggest problem in developing an accident is the accident must not appear to be the work of a terrorist because that would not show on the integrity of the aircraft.

The accidents were to discredit...
The aircraft itself, yes.

So the crash in Paris in '74 was a test to see if they had the ability to bring the plane down (Note: 3/3/1974/Turkish/346 dead.) Yes.[16]

In other words, the Nazi International basically *threatened* McDonnell-Douglas with the deliberate and targeted destruction of DC-10s in commercial use — at great loss of life — in such a way that it would reflect poorly on the aircraft, people would refuse to fly on it (as this author has numerous times!), and airlines would refuse to buy it as a result. McDonnell-Douglas, which had invested millions in its development, would take a financial beating. The alternative was for McDonnell-Douglas to pay a considerable percentage on each DC-10 sold to the Organization, via arranged money-drops in Switzerland and elsewhere, money which in turn was used to fund the development of the Airbus![17]

Then, because of American government investigation of kickbacks in the aerospace industry, McDonnell-Douglas' payments suddenly ceased, and this is where the Organization got serious, and brutal, and where "K's" allegations become even more sensational, and paradoxically, provide the one clue that can indeed corroborate his allegations by connecting them to a piece of little-known Nazi secret weapons research and technology:

The Organization couldn't care less why it happened. The payments had stopped and they wouldn't resume. After that, the accidents were in earnest, the arranged accidents. **S. had corrected some problems that had developed in the ultrasonics system and could be very reliable in arranging that structural failures or cracks could be arranged at any point.** They could have it where a crack could be found, reflecting on the aircraft itself, or in the extreme example of the case of the DC-10 in Chicago, they could raise the ultrasonic to such a level that they knew that the natural vibration of the aircraft would complete the work.

Whether it be the DC-10 out of Paris with the problem regarding the cargo door, whether it was the Air New Zealand DC-10, whether it was the Western Airlines DC-10 that crashed on landing in Mexico City, whether it was the DC-10 that crashed at O-Hara Field [*sic*] in Chicago, **the one constant that was used in all cases was ultrasonics, leaving no trace. It would be attributed to structural failure of one type or another.**

On board the DC-10 out of Chicago, it was learned at the airport that two couriers, members of the Organization were to be on that flight and were to meet with a member of MI5, British intelligence, in Los Angeles, by the name of T. whose front is as a representative of a London newspaper. When they were noticed, immediate action was taken to develop the structural crack to such an extent that at certain sound and vibration levels consistent with take-off of the aircraft vibrations necessary to complete structural failure of the aircraft would take place. The two men on the aircraft, part of the Organization, one K. of Austria and S., were subsequently killed in the crash.[18]

In other words, the Nazi International had access to some sophisticated ultrasonics equipment, which was "fixed" by "S," to the point structural failures could be induced in aircraft at will. In the case of the American Airlines DC-10 that crashed in Chicago, the public was subsequently told that the engine mounting had been improperly serviced on the aircraft when it was last in Tulsa, Oklahoma, which, at that time, coincidentally, was home to a large McDonnell-Douglas facility on the east edge of Tulsa International Airport. In the light of "K's" revelations, whether this story was in fact true, or spin control to prevent further damage to the aircraft's reputation, will never be known.

That being said, however, this is precisely where we find the one piece of data that might serve to corroborate "K's" extraordinary allegations!

The ultrasonics equipment, could you explain what this is, a possible description of the equipment, how it was used?

I have never seen the equipment, but from the conversations that I have developed, the equipment sounds a bit like — it's compact, it could be in the seat of a pickup truck or service truck, which indeed it was in the Chicago example, and the actual device that delivered these highly directed waves is through an arrangement where you can direct it, point it, like a... they have these 'guns' you can direct for sound.

Now for the Siemens company...

Their main work is more than just fortunate. A principal facility of Siemens, a facility dealing in the ultrasonics is located very close to the O'Hara [*sic*] Airport.[19]

With this, we have the connection and the lone existing piece of data that tenuously corroborates K's assertions: 1) ultrasonic equipment capable of inducing metal fatigue or fracture in specific areas of a target, and 2) a famous and quite large German firm — Siemens — dealing in sophisticated electronic technology.[20]

German interest in the ultra-technological use of sound waves for a variety of purposes does indeed spring from World War II. For example, according to one postwar source interrogated by the British, the Germans had adapted sonic technology for the distillation of oil![21] In my book *Reich of the Black Sun: Nazi Secret Weapons and the Cold War Allied Legend*, however, I reported on a little-known German secret weapon project called the *Kraftstrahlkanone* or "Strong Ray Gun," an L-shaped gun-like weapon employing a crystal as an energy source and a long projection consisting of various hollow tubes of varying length, like a pipe organ, arranged in circular fashion around the central, and longest, tube. Crystals when subjected to stress are known not only to emit electricity and light, but "bundles of sound" called "phonons," a play on the packets of light called "photons."[22] Research into directed-energy weapons and sonic weapons was, indeed, carried out in Nazi Germany by the Siemens und Halske and other German electrical combines. And one of the purposes of such research was, precisely, to bring down Allied aircraft! It would seem, then, that if "K's" allegations are indeed true, that such research was quietly continued and perfected long after the war was over, and by some of the same firms involved!

While a tenuous corroboration at best, it is nonetheless *corroboration*, for such precise, detailed knowledge of Nazi secret weapons was not known on a widespread basis prior to the appearance of "K's" extraordinary allegations when they first came out in *Secret and Suppressed*. In all likelihood, "K's" knowledge came from where he said it did: by actually seeing the device, and learning about it through his contacts in the Nazi International.

Contemplate that, the next time you step on to an airplane, not knowing if any of the other passengers might be special targets of that or any other such Organization with access to such technology...

Endnotes

1   Ladislas Farago: *Aftermath: Martin Bormann and the Fourth Reich;* Paul Manning, *Martin Bormann: Nazi in Exile.*

2   See for example www.jewishvirtuallibrary.org/jsource/History/muftihit.html. The Grand Mufti's close relative was none other than Yasser Arafat, founder and leader of the PLO. See Martin A. Lee, *The Beast Reawakens: Fascism's Resurgence from Hitler's Spymasters to Today's Neo-Nazi Groups and Right-Wing Extremists* (Routledge, 2000), p. 128.

3   www.warriorsfortruth.com/al-queda-terrorists-nazi-connection.html

4   Martin A. Lee, *The Beast Reawakens: Fascism's Resurgence from Hitler's Spymasters to Today's Neo-Nazi Groups and Right-Wing Extremists* (Routledge, 2000), p. 134.

5   Ibid., pp. 182–3, 292, 216.

6   Ibid., no pages: virtually *all* of Lee's book is an exploration of this topic.

7   Carter Plymton Hydrick, *Critical Mass: How Nazi Germany Surrendered Enriched Uranium for the United States' Atomic Bomb* (Whitehurst and Company, 2004). See especially pp. 143–255. "K" also explains subsequently that the highest headquarters of this organization was in Paraguay. See "Exposing the Nazi International," p. 285.

8   Adventures Unlimited Press, 2005, 2006 and 2008 respectively. I greatly expand on the scientific implications of the Nazi Bell project and its postwar political and economic implications in my forthcoming book, *The Philosophers' Stone: The American "Gold," The Soviet "Mercury," and the Nazi "Serum,"* which will be published by Feral House in the

spring of 2009.

9   For the full story of Kammler's likely escape, see my *Reich of the Black Sun*, pp. 99–116. For the wider implications of Nazi scientists involved both in the Bell project and in NASA, see my *SS Brotherhood of the Bell*, pp. 114-128, 155–157.

10   Joseph P. Farrell, *Secrets of the Unified Field: The Philadelphia Experiment, the Nazi Bell, and the Discarded Theory* (Adventures Unlimited Press, 2008), p. 232. As far as the Bell and its survival in an independent Nazi project in South America goes, this will be one of the main subjects of a new book I am currently writing.

11   p. 278.

12   Perhaps it gave it a great deal of leverage, as the Bush family recently purchased a huge ranch in Paraguay, one of the friendliest of South American countries to postwar Nazis! Perhaps the Bush family just likes South American ranches. Perhaps they have "old friends" or relatives there and just wanted to "get away from it all." Or perhaps they, or someone *else*, knows something. There are endless speculative possibilities, but would the reader be willing to take a bet that it really *is* mere coincidence?

13   "Exposing the Nazi International," p. 279.

14   There is a slight inaccuracy in "K's" description of the German company involved, which might indicate that he was not a native German speaker. The company's actual name is Messerschmitt-Bölkow-Blohm, not Messerschmidt-Volkau-Blum.

15   "Exposing the Nazi International," p. 282.

16   Ibid., p. 283.

17   Ibid., p. 284.

18   Ibid., pp. 284–285, emphasis added.

19   Ibid., p. 285.

20   Many readers might have had occasion to receive an MRI or high dosage radioactive cancer therapy. Chances are good that the equipment they were in was built by Siemens. In the case of the MRI, we are in the presence of yet another technology involving resonance.

21   See Henry Stevens, *Hitler's Suppressed and Still-Secret Weapons, Science, and Technology* (Adventures Unlimited Press, 2007), pp. 209–211.

22   Joseph P. Farrell, *Reich of the Black Sun: Nazi Secret Weapons and the Allied Cold War Legend* (Adventures Unlimited Press, 2004), pp. 221–223, 349–350.

Lingering Questions About 9/11

by Harry Helms

Many questions linger, of course, concerning the infamous plane disasters of September 11, 2001, almost none of them having to do with the absence of a plane striking the Pentagon or the projection of holographic images of airliners on the Trade Towers as they were being demolished by explosive charges. It took three years for a head of steam to build up about the JFK assassination (until the publication of Mark Lane's seminal Rush To Judgment*); it took only hours after the 9/11 crashes for a plethora of competing and often inane conspiracy theories to emerge on the Internet. Just as Bill Cooper's well-known "driver-did-it" theory of JFK faded away after attracting a large audience to the topic, so too have the 9/11 "troofers" — the self-named Truth movement that posits so many demonstrably false 9/11 theories — begun to recede from limelight, leaving behind many still wondering exactly what did happen that day. If it's too much to suggest that Dick Cheney ordered a shoot-down of Flight 77, might he have ordered a stand-down, going with the flow of horrific events? If the whole thing wasn't personally bankrolled by George Bush, could one lower-level Western intelligence pay-off have led both to the resignation of the chief of Pakistan's covert police and the tragic beheading of journalist Danny Pearl? Like the Warren Commission, the government's blue-ribbon 9/11 Commission provided little and false information. JFK assassination researchers have been filling in the gaps for 45 years; the effort to really figure out this tragedy remains in its infancy. The following excerpts a coming book from author Harry Helms* (Top Secret Tourism). — Kenn Thomas

Did Vice President Cheney Order American Airlines 77 Shot Down Before It Hit The Pentagon?

According to then-Secretary of Transportation Norman Mineta, he did.

Mineta testified before the 9/11 Commission that he arrived at the White House at approximately 9:20 a.m., about 15 minutes after the South Tower of the World Trade Center was hit. He was taken immediately to the Presidential Emergency Operations Center, a reinforced bunker under the White House. Mineta said Vice President Cheney and National Security Adviser Condoleezza Rice were already in the Center. Mineta further testified that he learned an unidentified plane had been detected headed toward Washington. A young man Mineta could not identify entered the bunker and said to Cheney, "The plane is 50 miles out." Mineta conferred by phone with acting FAA Deputy Administrator Monte Belger, who was at FAA's Washington headquarters. Mineta said Belger told him the transponder of the plane had been turned off but they were able to track it on radar. After speaking with Belger, Mineta said the young man returned to the bunker and told Cheney, "The plane is 30 miles out." The young man left, but quickly returned and said to Cheney, "The plane is ten miles out. Do the orders still stand?"

Mineta testified that Cheney, in his words, "whipped his neck around," and said to the young man, "Of course the orders still stand, have you heard anything to the contrary?" Mineta told the 9/11 Commission he inferred from the situation that the orders being referred to were shoot-down orders against the incoming plane. American 77 crashed into the Pentagon at 9:37 a.m.

However, the 9/11 Commission concluded that the timeline of Mineta's account was wrong, that Cheney didn't arrive at the Presidential Emergency Operations Center until 9:58 a.m. — roughly 20 minutes after American 77 crashed — and therefore the discussion Mineta witnessed concerned United 93, not American 77. But the 9/11 Commission did qualify its conclusion by saying there was "conflicting evidence as to when the Vice President arrived in the shelter conference room."

There was a lot of that "conflicting evidence." Richard Clarke, counterterrorism coordinator for President Clinton and then President Bush, claimed he saw Vice President Cheney leave for the Presidential Emergency Operations Center around 9:10 a.m. He later speaks to Cheney before 10 a.m. by telephone, and says he learned Cheney had already issued a shootdown order, thus partially corroborating Mineta's account. David Bohrer, an official White House photographer, said Cheney left just after 9 a.m.. But the 9/11 Commission claimed Cheney did not leave for the Center until after 9:30 a.m. and then was almost carried there by Secret Service agents who entered his office, lifted him up by his arms, and took him to the bunker. Cheney repeated this account in television interviews.

In putting together the timeline of Cheney's actions and whereabouts on September 11, the 9/11 Commission apparently put greater emphasis on Cheney's account than the eyewitness testimony of Mineta, Clarke, and Bohrer when evaluating the "conflicting evidence." Mineta, Clarke, and Bohrer were disinterested observers, while Cheney could have had numerous reasons — such as concern over political repercussions over a failure to stop American 77 before it hit the Pentagon — to claim he arrived at the Center later.

The question of exactly when Vice President Cheney arrived at the Presidential Emergency Operations Center is still open and may never be resolved.

Why Did The Hijackers Make At Least Six Trips To Las Vegas In The Months Before The Attacks?

Las Vegas likes to use the slogan "What happens in Vegas stays in Vegas" to promote tourism. Ironically, that same slogan could be used to describe our knowledge of what the 9/11 hijackers were up to in Las Vegas in the months preceding their attacks. The FBI pursued over 3000 leads concerning the hijackers' activities in Las Vegas but came up empty. As the 9/11 Commission was forced to conclude, "Beyond Las Vegas' reputation for welcoming tourists, we have seen no credible evidence explaining why, on this occasion and others, the operatives flew to or met in Las Vegas."

But the hijackers were definitely in Las Vegas several times and were busy doing something (or some things). For example, Mohammed Atta made his first trip to Las Vegas on June 29, 2001, arriving from Boston via a connection in San Francisco. He rented a car, and put 110 miles on the car in the two days he was there. Where he went and what he did — and who, if anyone, he met with while there — is unknown.

What we do know is that none of the hijackers apparently spent time in any of the casinos, either on the Strip or elsewhere. When it became known shortly after the hijackings that the perpetrators had made several trips to Las Vegas prior to September 11, the FBI requested security camera videos from all casinos in the Las Vegas area for the dates of the hijackers' known visits. Despite intensive analysis, the FBI was unable to find any of the hijackers on the security videos.

The first hijackers known to have visited Las Vegas were Nawaf Alhazmi and Khalid Almihdar, who drove there several times in 2000 during the period they lived in San Diego. Beginning in late May of 2001, the hijackers began traveling to Las Vegas regularly, both individually and in groups. For example, Marwan Alshehhi was in Las Vegas May 24 to 27, as was Ziad Jarrah on June 7 to 10; Jarrah is known to have rented a car while in Las Vegas. The activities of the hijackers during their visits are unknown. In all, investigators have been able to identify at least six visits to Las Vegas by the hijackers in 2001; there may have been additional ones (such as by car) that investigators are unaware of.

The most significant visit was apparently on August 13 and 14. Mohammed Atta arrived in Las Vegas from Reagan National Airport in Washington and Hani Hanjour and Nawaf Alhazmi arrived from Dulles Airport in Washington via a connection in Los Angeles. Atta checked into the Econo Lodge at the north end of Las Vegas Boulevard (the Strip), an area populated by strip clubs and cheap souvenir shops instead of the glamorous casinos found on the south end. Alhazmi is known to have stayed at a Days Inn in Las Vegas; according to a hotel employee, his manner was "cold and abrupt." Alhazmi told the employee he was in Las Vegas on "important business" and asked for a list of Days Inns in the Los Angeles area, although he declined an offer by the employee to make a reservation for him in Los Angeles.

Many investigators believe the August 13–14 meeting was the final planning session for the 9/11 attacks and Las Vegas was selected because persons of all nationalities and ethnicities freely travel and mix there; a group of Arab men would not have warranted a second glance in August, 2001. However, some believe the hijackers were considering Las Vegas as a possible target. The 109-story Stratosphere Casino tower would've made a tempting target, and so would any of the glitzy Strip casinos; certainly Las Vegas represents all the decadence and hedonism of Western culture that Islamic fundamentalists are supposed to hate. Jerry Keller, the former sheriff of Clark County (where Las Vegas is located), said, "We had to be a collateral target or they wouldn't have been here."

In the aftermath of the attacks, the FBI vigorously pursued a flood of tips concerning the hijackers' activities in Las Vegas. There were numerous reports that some of the hijackers patronized various strip clubs, where the dancers remembered them as quiet, well-groomed, and poor tippers. Employees at a Starbucks said they remembered serving the hijackers coffee; librarians say they recall them using computers for internet access. Some of the reports were ridiculous on their face — such as Mohammed Atta being spotted driving a cab — while others, such as the hijackers requesting that ham be removed from slices at a pizza parlor, had the ring of truth. However, the FBI was unable to establish exactly what the hijackers were doing in Las Vegas or why they made so many visits there in the months just before the hijackings. It now seems unlikely that we will ever resolve those mysteries.

Did Actor James Woods Try To Alert The U.S. Government About The Planned Hijackings?

Yes he did. The mystery is what happened to his information.

Woods took a non-stop flight from Boston to Los Angeles sometime around August 1, 2001. He was one of five passengers in the first-class section; the other four were well-dressed young men who appeared to be Middle Eastern and were obviously traveling together. As he later told Seymour Hersh for an article in the June 3, 2002 of the *New Yorker*, "I watch people like a moviemaker... I thought these guys were either terrorists or FBI guys. The guys were in-synch dressed alike. They didn't have a drink and were not talking to the stewardess. None of them had a carry-on or a newspaper. Nothing." Woods told Hirsch he felt the men were "casing" the plane, like crooks "casing" a bank before a robbery, and he was so unnerved by them that he kept his cutlery after lunch was served.

In a February, 2002 Fox TV interview with Bill O'Reilly on *The O'Reilly Factor*, Woods elaborated on his suspicions. "I was on a flight, without going into the details of what made me suspicious of these four men, although it would have been blatantly obvious to the most casual observer. I took it upon myself to go the flight attendant and ask to speak to the pilot of the plane. The first officer came out.... I said, 'Can you look over my shoulder and see who I'm talking about?' And he said, 'Yeah.' I said, 'I think they're going to hijack this plane.' I mean, everything they're doing, and I explained to him these details, which I've been asked to keep private, until whatever jurisdiction, you know, whatever trials may take place, their behavior was such that I felt that they were going to hijack the plane. I also said I'm very much aware of how serious it is to say on an American aircraft in flight the word hijack."

Upon landing, a flight attendant told him that a report of the incident would be filed with the FAA. When his agent later asked him how his flight went, Woods jokingly replied, "Aside from the terrorists and turbulence, it was fine."

Woods telephoned the Los Angeles FBI office on the afternoon of September 11 and told an agent about his experience on the August 1 flight. The next morning, he received a phone call at 6:45 a.m. from the agent he had spoken to the previous day; the agent said the FBI urgently wanted to speak to him. Woods replied that he would come down to the FBI office as soon as possible. The agent replied that wouldn't be necessary — he and another FBI agent were waiting outside Woods' home.

Woods told the agents he couldn't recall the exact date of his flight, but he could clearly remember the men and their actions. Agents showed him various photographs, and Woods recognized Hamza Alghamdi (United 175) and Khalid Almihdar (American 77). As Woods told O'Reilly, "I said, 'Look, I'm dying to know, were these the guys?' And he (an FBI agent) said, 'Well, we've had 36,000 tips in one day. And there's two of us and we're going to be at your house all this morning. So you can do the math, but we can't tell you.' You know, so since then, I have identified for sure two of them as two of the terrorists." Woods paused, and continued, "Who actually were not on flight 11, but one was on flight 175 and one was on flight 77. And I've been told unofficially, not by the FBI, but by someone else in a, actually a higher level of government, believe it or not, just through a coincidence, through a mutual friend, that all four of them were terrorists involved." Later in the interview, Woods told O'Reilly, "But what's significant about this is that it was a rehearsal with four men. And I can't say it as a fact that they were the four, but I've been led to believe without going into the details of how, that they were on different flights."

Later in 2005, author Annie Jacobsen said a FBI agent told her one of the passengers observed by Woods was Mohammed Atta. However, Seymour Hersh reported in his *New Yorker* article that "a senior FBI official" told him the FBI had not been able to confirm any hijackers were on the flight Woods had taken. "We don't know for sure," said the unnamed official.

If the flight crew did file a report as they promised Woods, what happened to it? Prior to September 11, reports of "suspicious passengers" did not raise many alarms at the FAA and the report, if actually filed, triggered no action. The FAA did issue four "information circulars" between June 22 and July 31, 2001, warning of possible aviation-based terrorism, but these were only vague warnings. The FAA could have issued higher-priority warnings, known as "security directives," which would have forced the airlines to take additional precautions, but the FAA apparently did not consider the threats serious enough to justify the stronger warnings.

The totality of the evidence strongly indicates that James Woods indeed witnessed a "dry run" for the September 11 attacks. The September 11 hijackers took numerous airplane trips in the months before the attacks, and it is likely that many, if not all, of them were also "reconnaissance" flights. The big remaining question is whether the crew of Woods' flight filed a report and, if they did, what happened to it. Another troubling question is why Hersh's "senior FBI official" was so equivocal about Woods' report.

Did George W. Bush Really Watch American Airlines Flight 11 Hit The World Trade Center On Live Television?

On December 4, 2001, President George W. Bush held a "town meeting" in Orlando, Florida. The event was televised live nationally by CNN. One of the attendees, named Jordan, asked Bush how he felt when he learned of the attacks on the World Trade Center. He replied as follows:

> Well, Jordan, you're not going to believe what state I was in when I heard about the terrorist attack. I was in Florida. And my chief of staff, Andy Card... actually I was in a classroom talking about a reading program that works. And I was sitting outside the classroom waiting to go in, and I saw an airplane hit the tower... the TV was obviously on, and I used to fly myself, and I said, "There's one terrible pilot." And I said, "It must have been a horrible accident." But I was whisked off there.... I didn't have much time to think about it, and I was sitting in the classroom, and Andy Card, my chief who was sitting over here walked in and said, "A second plane has hit the tower. America's under attack."

On January 5, 2001, Bush participated in another town meeting, this time in Ontario, California. He was asked a question similar to the one he was asked in Orlando about his reactions to learning of the September 11 attacks, and his reply was also similar. According to the official White House press office transcript of the event, Bush replied:

Anyway, I was sitting there, and my Chief of Staff... well, first of all, when we walked into the classroom, I had seen this plane fly into the first building. There was a TV set on. And you know, I thought it was pilot error and I was amazed that anybody could make such a terrible mistake. And something was wrong with the plane, or... anyway, I'm sitting there, listening to the briefing, and Andy Card came and said, "America is under attack."

But there is a big problem with President Bush's answers in Orlando and Ontario; he didn't see, as he phrased it in Ontario, a "plane fly into the first building" on television. Neither did anyone else, for that matter. Television coverage of the World Trade Center attacks began *after* the "first building" (the north tower) was struck by American flight 11, not before. The only video of American 11 striking the World Trade Center — taken by a film crew making a documentary about a New York Fire Department company — did not surface until later in the evening on September 11.

In addition, the first plane struck the World Trade Center at 8:46 a.m.. At that time, President Bush was in a limousine traveling from the Colony Beach and Tennis Resort to Booker Elementary School in Sarasota, Florida. He was not, as he claimed in his Orlando and Ontario statements, "outside the classroom."

In other words, there is no way Bush could have observed the first strike against the World Trade Center on September 11, as he claimed, and the statements he made in Orlando and Ontario had no basis whatsoever in reality.

Some supporters of President Bush later claimed he became confused and inadvertently "confabulated" a memory based upon later seeing the second World Trade Center attack on television. But this explanation seems extremely unlikely, for reasons obvious to anyone who has seen footage of the second attack: the upper reaches of the north tower are in flames with large quantities of black smoke before the second airplane hits the south tower. The damage can't be overlooked or ignored; it's painfully clear the north tower has suffered catastrophic damage long before the second airplane hits the south tower. And Bush himself has made other, contradictory accounts of how he learned of the first attack. For example, he told the *Washington Post* in its January 27, 2002 issue that he learned about the first crash from his advisor Karl Rove, and Rove had told him a small airplane, not a jet airliner, had hit the north tower.

The real mystery here is why President Bush twice made a preposterous claim that could so easily be totally debunked.

Who Funded the 9/11 Plot And
Supported The Hijackers Financially?

The 9/11 Commission Report states, "To date, the U.S. government has not been able to determine the origin of the money used for the 9/11 attacks. Compelling evidence traces the bulk of the funds directly back to KSM [Khalid Sheikh Mohammed], but from where KSM obtained the money remains unknown at this time.' The Report further states, "No credible evidence exists that the operatives received substantial funding from any person in the United States. Specifically, there is no evidence that Mihdhar and Hazmi received funding from Saudi citizens Omar al Bayoumi and Osama Bassnan, or that Saudi Princess Haifa al Faisal provided any funds to the conspiracy either directly or indirectly."

The first statement — that the United States government has been unable to determine the origin(s) of the money used to finance the attacks — is true. But there is considerable evidence the 9/11 hijackers did receive financial and other support from persons in the United States as well as persons with connections to the government of Saudi Arabia and the Saudi royal family.

The exact amount of money spent to carry out the attacks is not known, although the 9/11 Commission estimated the total cost as from $400,000 to $500,000. The FBI determined that $303,481.63 was deposited into American checking accounts in the names of the hijackers. But only $193,200 of that was in the form of wire transfers from Middle Eastern banks; the remainder was in traveler's checks, third-party checks, and cash — all ideal vehicles for money laundering. There is dispute over how many bank accounts the hijackers had in the United States. In the July 10, 2002 issue of the *New York Times*, Dennis Lormel, part of the FBI unit investigating the hijackers' finances, stated the hijackers had 35 different accounts, including 14 with SunTrust Bank. But on September 26, 2002, FBI Director Robert Mueller told Congress, "In total, the hijackers opened 24 bank accounts at four different U.S. banks." On July 31, 2006, the FBI revised its estimates again and stated the hijackers had opened ay least 25 accounts with six different banks. The 9/11 Commission Report did not state how many bank accounts the hijackers used. Further complicating matters is the possibility the hijackers and their associates may have opened accounts using forged identification and stolen Social Security numbers.

Despite the 9/11 Commission's conclusion that the hijackers received no direct or indirect financial assistance from persons in the United States or representatives of the Saudi Arabian government, there is abundant evidence that is not true. Senator Bob Graham (D-Fla), the former chairman of the Senate Intelligence Committee and co-chair of the Congressional 9/11 Inquiry, told reporters on September 7, 2004, "I find that the actions in San Diego present a compelling case that there was Saudi assistance." Senator Graham was referring to the activities of Omar al Bayoumi and Osama Bassnan, both of whom he said were linked to the Saudi government.

Omar al Bayoumi helped hijackers Nawaf Alhazmi and Khalid al-Midhar get settled in the San Diego area and provided them with financial assistance. According to al Bayoumi, he overheard the two hijackers conversing in Arabic in a restaurant at the Los Angeles International Airport and quickly befriended them. He drove them to San Diego, found them an apartment and paid the first two months of rent ($1550) for them, introduced them to local Muslims, helped them get Social Security cards and open bank accounts, and assisted them in enrolling at local flight schools. While he did all this, al Bayoumi was employed by Dallah Avco, a firm having numerous contacts with the Saudi Ministry of Defense and Aviation. The Ministry was headed by Saudi Prince Sultan, the father-in-law of Princess Haifa al Faisal, the wife of the Saudi ambassador to the United States and daughter of King Faisal.

Beginning in January 1999, Princess al Faisal began sending a series of cashier's checks for $2000 to a San Diego woman named Majeda Ibrahim Dweikat, a Saudi national. The checks were supposedly to help her pay for medical treatments for a thyroid condition. But in early 2000 Dweikat began endorsing those checks over to a woman named Manal Ahmed Bagader.

Bagader is the wife of Omar al Bayoumi. They left San Diego for England in July, 2001. After their departure, the FBI examined their San Diego telephone records and found al Bayoumi made frequent telephone calls to the Islamic Affairs department at the Saudi embassy in Washington. The Islamic Affairs department regularly provides financial support to radical mosques and madrassahs (religious schools) in the United States, including several attended by the 9/11 hijackers and otherwise linked to terrorist activities.

According to Senator Graham, al Bayoumi used those extra funds to assist and support Alhazmi and al-Midhar. "From these two sources, al Bayoumi was funneled in excess of $40,000 above his usual salary — somewhere between one-sixth and one-twelfth the estimated total amount needed to fund the September 11 attacks."

Princess al Faisal issued a statement saying, "I find that the accusations that I contributed funds to terrorists outrageous and completely irresponsible." And on August 27, 2002, Princess al Faisal and her husband were guests of President George W. Bush at his ranch in Crawford, Texas.

Maybe Princess al Faisal was telling the truth, and she had no idea Dweikat was redirecting her checks to Bagader. Maybe al Bayoumi had no idea what Alhazmi and al-Midhar were up to, and he spent so much time, and money, to assist them out of nothing more than simple kindness toward strangers. Maybe al Bayoumi's repeated calls to the Saudi embassy were innocent, and the departure of he and his wife to England two months before the attacks was just a coincidence.

Maybe. But to assume all the activities of al Bayoumi and those linked to him were nothing more than mere coincidences takes a lot of assuming. There is still much unknown about how the 9/11 plot was financed, who financed it, and how the routes by which the funds made their way to the hijackers.

How Did Hani Hanjour Suddenly Become Such A Good Pilot?

According to the 9/11 Commission Report, "Among the five hijackers aboard American Airlines Flight 77, Hani Hanjour was the sole individual who FAA records show completed flight training and received FAA pilot certification. Hanjour received his commercial multi-engine pilot certificate from the FAA in March 1999. He received extensive flight training in the United States including flight simulator training, and was perhaps the most experienced and highly trained pilot among the 9/11 hijackers."

Most observers consider Hanjour's flying on September 11 to have been the most impressive of any of the hijacker's pilots. Hanjour's American 77 was five miles west-southwest of the Pentagon when it initiated a 330-degree turn in which it descended 2200 feet; this was a maneuver that required a high degree of pilot skill. When it had been completed, Hanjour then pointed American 77 toward downtown Washington and the Pentagon, opened the throttle to maximum, and plunged the jet into the Pentagon. Unlike the World Trade Center towers, the Pentagon was not an easy target. While easy to spot from the air, it was not very tall and the pilot of American 77 had to carefully bring in the jet at the proper angle to strike the building. Film of the crash from Pentagon security cameras show American 77 coming in like a well-executed runway landing, albeit at a very high rate of speed (the consensus estimate is that American 77 was traveling at 530 miles per hour when it struck the Pentagon). Flying at such speed at low altitudes also takes an uncommon degree of pilot skill.

But there's a problem. According to many who observed Hanjour when he was undergoing pilot training in the United States, Hanjour wasn't a very good pilot at all.

According to the May 4, 2002 *New York Times*, a Phoenix-area flight school called JetTech contacted the Federal Aviation Administration (FAA) in January 2001 about Hanjour. Hanjour held a FAA commercial pilot's license since 1999 but, according to the JetTech staff, did not have the flying skills or English language proficiency required for the license. (The FAA requires all holders of pilot licenses to be fluent in English.) One JetTech employee was quoted as saying, "I'm still to this day amazed that he could have flown into the Pentagon. He could not fly at all." JetTech employees remembered that when he tried to use a flight simulator, he had little understanding of the cockpit instruments and what they were used for. Other JetTech employees remembered Hanjour as "a weak student: who was 'wasting our resources.'" *CBS News* reported on May 10, 2002 that how Hanjour managed to get a commercial pilot's license "remains a lingering question that FAA officials refuse to discuss."

While the 9/11 Commission Report termed Hanjour "perhaps the most experienced and highly trained pilot among the 9/11 hijackers" in one section, it seemed to contradict itself in another section when it noted about his time at JetTech, "By early 2001, he was using a Boeing 737 simulator. Because his performance struck his flight instructors as sub-standard, they discouraged Hanjour from continuing, but he persisted."

Examinations for pilot licenses are not conducted by FAA employees but instead by private contractors authorized by the FAA to test prospective pilots. The private contractor gives a written test using questions provided by the FAA and sits next to the examinee during the flight check. The fee for the examination when Hanjour took it in 1999 was around $300, and the examiner who administered the test to Hanjour had a reputation for being an "easy grader" who passed many marginal students. After the 9/11 attacks, both the FAA and FBI investigated the examiner, including a polygraph test, but were unable to uncover any evidence of deliberate fraud on the examiner's part.

Regardless of whether or not he obtained his commercial pilot license legitimately, it is clear that Hanjour was not an accomplished pilot in early 2001. So how did his skills become so much better in just a few months?

One possibility is that Hanjour was pretending, for some reason, to have less flying and English proficiency than was the case. Concerning the latter, Hanjour was the first hijacker to visit the United States, in 1991, and spent substantially more time in the country than any other hijacker; he also took English as a second language classes at the University of Arizona. However, it is hard to understand why Hanjour would feign a lack of flying or English capability, as this only attracted suspicion of the JetTech employees and endangered his mission.

Another possibility is that Hanjour received additional flight training that investigators have not uncovered. As the 9/11 Commission Report notes, "the FBI's Phoenix office believes it is plausible that Hanjour return[ed] to Arizona for additional training" in June and August of 2001. However, there was only one flight school witness who claims to have remembered seeing Hanjour at that time, and she was only "fairly certain" it was Hanjour. No record has been discovered indicating Hanjour ever enrolled in a flight school or used a flight simulator in Arizona during the summer of 2001. If he did, his flying and English skills did not attract attention from flight school employees.

While it may initially seem farfetched, there is the possibility that the "Hani Hanjour" who crashed American 77 into the Pentagon was not the same "Hani Hanjour" who demonstrated poor flying and English skills a few months earlier. The September 27, 2001 *Los Angeles Times* reported that during the second week of August 2001, Hani Hanjour attempted on three separate occasions to rent an airplane at Freeway Airport in Bowie, Maryland. Each time, a flight instructor took Hanjour on a brief check flight and deemed him too incompetent to fly solo and the rental was denied. Yet a month later, "Hani Hanjour" demonstrated considerable flying skills when he hit the Pentagon with American 77.

Hani Hanjour was a Saudi national, and, as the 9/11 Commission Report notes, "There were significant security weaknesses in the Saudi government's issuance of Saudi passports in the period when the visas to the hijackers were issued. Two of the Saudi 9/11 hijackers may have obtained their passports legitimately or illegitimately with the help of a family member who worked in the passport office." The possibility of irregularities in the issuance of a passport to Hani Hanjour can not be discounted. We do know there were irregularities in the issuance of U.S. visas to Hanjour. Again quoting the 9/11 Commission Report, "The applications of Hani Hanjour, Saeed al Ghamdi, and Khalid al Mihdhar stated that they had not previously applied for a U.S. visa when, in fact, they had. In Hanjour's case the false statement was made in an earlier application for a visit, in 1997, not his final visa application in 2000. Hanjour and Mihdhar also made false statements about whether they had previously traveled to the United States." Once in the United States, Hanjour obtained a Virginia's driver's license on August 2, 2001 — an odd behavior for someone who was planning to die in less than six weeks. Making this behavior even odder, Hanjour had previously held other driver's licenses in the United States.

It is very tempting to jump to the conclusion that there were two or more persons using the name "Hani Hanjour" in 2001 and that the pilot of American 77 and the inept pilot recalled by JetTech instructors were two different people. The evidence currently available does not conclusively prove that, but it does indicate a big discrepancy between the skills Hanjour demonstrated to flight instructors and those he exhibited on September 11. The reason for that difference is unknown.

Paranotes

by Al Hidell

Ohio Vote-Rigging Convictions

On January 5, 2007, the Associated Press reported that two Ohio election workers were convicted of rigging a recount of the 2004 presidential election. You may recall that Ohio gave President Bush the electoral votes he needed to defeat John Kerry. The rigging took place in Cuyahoga County, Ohio's most populous county. Apparently willing to let bygones be bygones, U.S. media virtually ignored the news.

Elections coordinator Jacqueline Maiden and ballot manager Kathleen Dreamer were each convicted of a felony count of negligent misconduct of an elections employee. Prosecutors accused Maiden and Dreamer of secretly reviewing ballots before the public recount, and screening out any ballots that might be questionable. (Recounts are supposed to be based on randomly-selected ballots.) Prosecutor Kevin Baxter was careful to downplay any political ramifications, portraying the women as bureaucrats trying to avoid the work of a long drawn-out recount. Disturbingly, given the many credible allegations of 2004 election improprieties throughout Ohio, defense attorney Roger Synenberg said the election workers did nothing out of the ordinary. "They just were doing it the way they were always doing it."

The Green Scare

On November 9, 2006, four environmental activists facing up to life in prison negotiated non-cooperating plea agreements which reduced their recommended sentences to five to eight years. After a ten-year FBI investigation known as "Operation Backfire," these individuals, along with eleven others, were indicted in several arson fires for which the Earth Liberation Front or the Animal Liberation Front claimed responsibility. The fires damaged property, but no one was hurt. The FBI defined the activists as "terrorists," and clearly sought the draconian prison sentences to send a message to domestic dissenters: crimes based on a strong political or social viewpoint — even non-violent crimes — are "terrorism," and will be treated accordingly. After all, life in prison is unheard of for arsons in which no one is hurt, and (non-political) arsonists in the U.S. generally face five years in prison from the get go. [*greenscare.org*]

Thought-crime and Punishment

Sometimes an idea or viewpoint will get you locked up, even if all you do is express it. Until recently, America's relatively free society has provided refuge for historians and researchers who question aspects of the official history of the Holocaust (sometimes labeled inaccurately as "Holocaust denial"). During 2006, however, three of the most prominent revisionists, each of whom was at least partly resident in the U.S., found themselves imprisoned in European jails.

The best known is British historian David Irving, who spends part of each year in Florida and organizes "Real History" conferences in Ohio. Irving was released from an Austrian prison in January 2007 after serving one year of a three-year sentence. On February 15, 2007, another key revisionist, Ernst Zundel, was sentenced to five years in prison by a German court for his nonviolent thought-crime. Zundel, who is married to an American, has already spent four years in a German jail, ever since he was arrested and deported by U.S. authorities in 2003. Lastly, Germar Rudolf, an associate of David Irving, was seized by U.S. authorities on November 14, 2005 and deported to Germany, where he was imprisoned and placed in solitary confinement. Prior to his arrest, Rudolf — who has an American wife and child — had unsuccessfully applied for U.S. political asylum.

The criminalization of the non-violent expression of ideas is unjust, no matter how unpopular or offensive the ideas may be. It is nothing more than a club wielded by those in power to beat people whose beliefs are judged too extreme and too dangerous. A similar club was used against the victims of "Operation Backfire." Whether dealing with "environmental terrorism" or "hate crimes," governments should stick to punishing actions — fairly — and stay out of the business of policing our thoughts. [*americanfreepress. net, zundelsite.org, germarrudolf.com*]

This Apple Isn't Green

Despite its cachet among hip and progressive consumers, Apple's environmental policies are surprisingly lackluster. So says Greenpeace in a December 2006 report, which ranked the iPod gurus dead last when it evaluated the overall environmental policies of America's high-tech companies [see *greenmyapple.org*]. In a January 30, 2007 article on the Greenpeace ranking ("Apple Computers: Fun for You, Toxic for the Environment," *alternet.org*) Jess Hemerly took Apple to task: "Companies like Dell and Nokia have made great strides to eliminate the most toxic chemicals from their products and offer strong recycling programs," while "Apple has not."

Responding to its low ranking, Apple spokesperson Kristin Huguet stated, "We disagree with Greenpeace's rating and the criteria they chose. Apple has a strong environmental track record and has led the industry in restricting and banning toxic substances such as mercury, cadmium, hexavalent chromium, as well as many brominated flame retardants." She also cited the fact that several Apple products scored "best in class" in a new EPA ranking system known as EPEAT. In addition, she proclaimed Apple had "completely eliminated CRT monitors, which contain lead," from its product line. (No great hardship there, since consumer demand for CRTs has plummeted since the introduction of flat-panel monitors.) Responding to similar criticism from the Silicon Valley Toxic Coalition in 2005, Apple CEO Steve Jobs was more succinct: he said Apple was being "singled out" and called the charges "bullshit."

Big iPod is Tracking You

Speaking of iPods, if you're a runner who uses the cool new Nike+iPod Sport Kit, you may be making it easier for people to track your movements. The high-tech pedometer uses Nikes with RFID capability and a small receiver that plugs into an iPod to give runners real-time updates of their workouts. Citing the work of four University of Washington researchers, Annalee Newitz of *wired.com* reported that "security flaws" in the kit "make it easy for tech-savvy stalkers, thieves and corporations to track your movements. ... [S]omeone could even plot your running routes on a Google map without your knowledge." Essentially, the kit turns your running shoe into a beacon that transmits your whereabouts up to 60 feet away. The University of Washington researchers proved the signal — which is unique for each kit — can be recorded by a small $79 device, and also transmitted to a nearby wi-fi access point. Attorney Lee Tien of the Electronic Frontier Foundation warns, "We're going to see more devices like this in the next few years," though he believes the surveillance capability of the Nike/iPod combo was unintentional.

Tougher Nuke Plant Security Standards Nixed

In this post-9/11 world, one would assume that security standards for nuclear power plants have been enhanced, right? Well, in December 2006, the Nuclear Regulatory Commission (NRC) decided not to institute tougher requirements on new nuke plants. The rule that's been in place for decades — that plants should be able to withstand a well-armed attack by three people and a plant insider — seems rather quaint these days. Yet the NRC apparently thinks the scenario (inspired, perhaps, by a 1980s action movie) is still the most dangerous threat a nuclear plant might face. The NRC's December (in) action came despite an April 2006 Government Accountability Office (GAO) report that criticized the Commission for its lax attitude toward security standards. Indeed, the report essentially (though not literally) accused the NRC of being a bunch of lackeys for the nuclear power industry. As an April 4, 2006 *Christian Science Monitor* article by Alexandra Marks put it, the GAO found the NRC "[had] not increased standards enough to ensure plants are genuinely secure, but only as much as industry officials believed was necessary."

The industry's response to the GAO report was strangely refreshing due to its lack of PR spin. According to the *Monitor*, industry officials complained that plant security requirements were already too burdensome. As for the possibility of terrorists plowing a commercial jet into a nuclear plant, the industry appears to be placing its faith in Uncle Sam. "Through the FAA and the North American [Aerospace] Defense Command, they do have procedures and protocols in place now for interdicting flights much better than they did prior to 9/11," noted Stephen Floyd of the industry's Nuclear Energy Institute (NEI). "There's a fair amount of increased protection there." Floyd acknowledged that nuke plants were potential targets, but suggested there are lots of other, less-fortified, targets available, such as chemical plants. "There's nobody who's stronger than we are," Floyd declared. The rest of the nation's critical infrastructure, he explained, "hasn't done a tenth of what we have done." [*csmonitor.com, nei.org*]

Bloggers Behind Bars

Reuters, citing the Committee to Protect Journalists [*cpj.org*], reports that the number of jailed journalists worldwide rose from nine in 2005 to 134 in 2006, with Internet bloggers and online reporters now constituting one-third of those incarcerated. American freelance journalist and blogger Joshua Wolf is one of them. He videotaped a San Francisco protest rally in July 2005 and posted excerpts on his weblog. In January 2006, the Federal Joint Terrorism Task Force issued a subpoena ordering him to testify before a federal grand jury investigating the protest. The subpoena also ordered him to hand over his unused video footage. Wolf refused, and was jailed by Judge William Alsup for contempt of court August 1, 2006. "This great country which has allowed you to be a journalist — sometimes your country asks for something back," the Judge bellowed. As Josh Wolf's father commented, "Aside from its fragmentary grammar, it's an interesting statement with a flawed, if commonly accepted, premise: that the U.S. 'allows' the existence of the press. It doesn't. Freedom of speech and press is not a right granted by the state," but rather an inalienable right. Perhaps Judge Alsup missed that lecture during law school. [*JoshWolf.net*]

Cell Phone Genocide

Much has been written about the role oil plays in the violence of the Middle East. When it comes to other natural resources and regions, though, decision-makers in both government and the media are often silent. It's as if there is a tacit agreement that discussion of naked greed and aggression on the part of corporations and governments starts and stops at the gas pump. Case in point: The Democratic Republic of the Congo (DRC), where the humanitarian aid organization International Rescue Committee [*theirc.org*] estimates 3.9 million people have died since 1998 as a direct or indirect result of that nation's brutal "civil war." Most died from easily-treated diseases; the violence and chaos has caused a breakdown of the healthcare infrastructure and made it extremely difficult for aid workers to reach the sick and dying.

While the IRC's work in the region is laudable, its characterization of the problem as a humanitarian crisis caused by "civil war" obscures a key fact: the violence in the DRC has been the result of coups, invasions and wars sponsored by Washington, London, and Tel Aviv, and has involved up to nine African nations at various times. At stake is control of the region's mineral wealth — diamonds, tin, copper, gold, uranium, cobalt, coltan, and niobium. Coltan, in particular, is vital for the manufacture of cell phones and other electronic gadgets, and the DRC is home to 80% of the world's supply, as well as 60% of the world's cobalt. Needless to say, when U.S.-sponsored Rwandan and Ugandan forces entered the DRC in 1996, gaining control of the mineral mines was a top priority.

Two years earlier, the Rwandan Patriotic Front (RPF) had destabilized and then taken over Rwanda, in a U.S.-backed "regime change" that was largely overlooked in coverage of the "Rwanda Genocide." Keith Harmon Snow, a journalist cited by *Project Censored* for his work covering the DRC, has stated, "What played out in Rwanda in 1994 is now playing out in Darfur, Sudan; regime change is the goal, 'genocide' is the tool of propaganda used to manipulate and disinform." Indeed, Africa's problems are almost always presented as inexplicable humanitarian tragedies, while the political and economic forces behind them remain in the shadows. Conversely, the politics and economics behind the Iraqi conflict are widely discussed, while the humanitarian crisis receives scant attention. It's time to bring both issues out from behind their respective curtains. [For sources and more information, see "High-Tech Genocide in Congo" at *projectcensored.org*]

Timothy McVeigh: Lost and Found

A video has emerged that appears to show alleged Oklahoma City bomber Timothy McVeigh at a U.S. military base over a year after the government says he was discharged from the military. The footage was released in 2006 by Bill Bean, a film producer who toured Camp Grafton, North Dakota on August 3, 1993. According to Paul Joseph Watson and Alex Jones of *prisonplanet.com*, Bean "has suffered intense surveillance and harassment since the taking of the footage."

"The FBI states the only time they lose track of McVeigh, in his entire life, is the late summer of 1993," Bean explains, "They think he was probably ... at gun shows, meeting antigovernment right-wing militia types. But he wasn't, he was at Camp Grafton, in uniform, learning explosives and demolition!" (According to the North Dakota National Guard, Camp Grafton contains a Demolition Range where "shaped charges, C4, and Bangalore torpedoes can be used," though the footage described by *prisonplanet.com* does not show McVeigh on that range.) The North Dakota National Guard denies that McVeigh was ever at Camp Grafton.

Lobbying "Reform" Sham

Cynics don't put much faith in the periodic efforts to "clean up" Congress. Lobbying money, like water, always seems to find a way around new obstacles. Even some cynics, though, were likely surprised by the speed with which Congress' latest reform effort fizzled. In a February 11, 2007 *New York Times* article, David D. Kirkpatrick reported the "sweeping new rules intended to curb the influence of lobbyists," passed with much fanfare the previous month, had already been bypassed. Yes, the lobbyists are still helping to pay for such things as lawmaker birthday parties, California wine-tasting tours, hunting and fishing trips, and even tickets to concerts by the Who and Bob Seger. "Instead of picking up the tab directly," Kirkpatrick wrote, "lobbyists pay a political fundraising committee created by an individual politician and, in turn, the committee pays the lawmaker's way."

Turns out the ethics rules ban personal gifts (but not political contributions) and restrict lawmakers' use of money donated to their re-election campaigns (but not to their political fundraising committees, also known as PACs). Tellingly, only about one-third of the money raised by lawmaker PACs in the past two years was used to make campaign contributions, the ostensible purpose of the PACs. The rest was spent on "travel and miscellaneous expenses." So, did the new ethics rules change anything? Kind of. According to Kirkpatrick, the rules now "bar lobbyists from treating lawmakers to less-expensive amusements" like meals. This will, presumably, result in lobbyists treating lawmakers to more-expensive amusements.

The Real U.S. Attorney Scandal

A man suing Novation, LLC, a company connected to both Attorney General Alberto Gonzales and Jeb Bush, has raised suspicions about the deaths and firings of federal prosecutors involved in cases against the firm. In 2004, Thelma Quince Colbert, Fort Worth's lead assistant U.S. Attorney for civil enforcement, was found floating face-down in her swimming pool. She had been investigating Medicare fraud and money laundering cases involving Novation and others. Two months later, Dallas Assistant U.S. Attorney Shannon K. Ross was found dead in her home. She had issued subpoenas to Novation as part of a "criminal investigation of the medical-supply industry," according to the *New York Times*.

Samuel Lipari is president of Missouri company Medical Supply Chain, which is suing Texas-based Novation for alleged anticompetitive practices and Medicare fraud. Novation is the nation's largest medical supply broker. The President's brother Jeb Bush serves on the board of its subsidiary Tenet Healthcare, though he was not associated with the firm at the time of the U.S. Attorney deaths. In addition, prior to becoming U.S. Attorney General, Alberto Gonzales was a partner with the law firm of Vinson & Elkins LLP, which counted Novation among its clients. More significantly, the first prosecutor fired by the Office of the Attorney General in December 2006 was Carol Lam of San Diego. She had been prosecuting Medicare fraud at Tenet Healthcare's Alvarado hospital.

In April 2007, Lipari told investigative reporter Tom Flocco, "The news blackout and lack of a public investigation regarding two dead senior assistant U.S. attorneys leads me to believe that foul play was involved." Referring to additional personnel changes at Attorney Ross' office one month after her death, he added, "Two attorneys just don't turn up dead and three more in the same unit either resign or get fired all at once."

Coroners ruled the deaths of Ross and Colbert by natural causes and accident, though Flocco disputes this. Lipari's factual assertions were confirmed in a November 2005 article in the *Fort Worth Weekly*. Reporter Pablo Lastra wrote Novation was "a target of a Dallas-based investigation by the U.S. Attorney's office into massive allegations of Medicare fraud — a probe that has been hampered by the deaths, within the last 18 months, of two of the prosecutors involved in it."

["Texas Assistant U.S. Attorney Deaths Raise Foul Play Questions," Tom Flocco, April 30, 2007, *tomflocco.com*; "Wide U.S. Inquiry Into Purchasing For Health Care," Mary Williams Walsh, *New York Times*, August 21, 2004; "Hijacking at the Hospital," Pablo Lastra, *Fort Worth Weekly*, November 23, 2005]

TB-Infected Lawyer Evaded Homeland Security

The case of Andrew Speaker — an Atlanta personal injury lawyer infected with an often fatal form of tuberculosis (TB) — has raised concerns about the effectiveness of the government's multi-billion dollar effort to protect the homeland. Speaker knew he had multiple-drug resistant TB (MDR-TB) before he flew to Europe for his wedding in May 2007, but doctors said he wasn't contagious. After he arrived in Europe, the Centers for Disease Control and Prevention (CDC) told him he had extensively drug-resistant TB (XDR-TB), a much deadlier strain. CDC officials told him not to fly commercial aircraft home and to check into a Rome treatment center. In' fact, a "no-fly" order was issued, according to CNN. Nevertheless, Speaker was able to board a flight to Montreal. He admitted to ABC News he flew to Canada to sidestep the "no-fly" order, which apparently pertained only to direct flights to the United States.

At the border crossing, Speaker's passport produced an alert — including instructions to don a protective mask, detain him, isolate him, and call health authorities. Nevertheless, Speaker was allowed through. According to a Department of Homeland Security (DHS) official quoted by the Associated Press, the border agent thought the warning was "discretionary." So much for "Homeland Security."

Furthermore, Speaker's new father-in-law is a CDC microbiologist and TB researcher. At this time, it appears to be a coincidence. "As part of my job, I am regularly tested for TB. I do not have TB, nor have I ever had TB," Dr. Robert Cooksey said in a statement released by his employer. "My son-in-law's TB did not originate from myself or the CDC's labs." On June 1, 2007 federal health officials said Dr. Cooksey had helped to find Speaker and diagnose his condition, and that his role in the matter was under investigation. Is there more to the case? Dr. Cooksey himself told reporters the situation was "complex," but provided no details. As MSNBC anchor Alison Stewart said in her intro to the story, "Conspiracy theorists, start your engines..."

Commenting on this case, Drs. Lawrence Broxmeyer and Alan Cantwell told *PARANOIA* that cases of MDR-TB and XDR-TB have been increasing for the past several decades worldwide, with little media attention. "Many people carry TB bacteria,". they warn, "and TB bacteria mutate — and with bacterial mutations comes inevitable drug resistance." [Sources as indicated; Dr. Broxmeyer: *medamericaresearch.org*; Dr. Cantwell: *ariesrisingpress.com*]

Homeland InSecurity, Part II

OK, so they dropped the ball on Andrew Speaker, but the Department of Homeland Security is catching lots of terrorists, right? In actuality, terrorism charges represented only .0015 percent of charges filed in immigration courts by the DHS, according to May 2007 report by a government watchdog group. The Transactional Records Action Clearinghouse (TRAC) said that of the 814,073 people charged by DHS in immigration courts during the past three years, 12 faced charges of terrorism. "The DHS claims it is focused on terrorism. Well, that's just not true," said David Burnham, a TRAC spokesman. "Either there's no terrorism, or they're terrible at catching them. Either way it's bad for all of us." In response, Russ Knocke of the DHS said the agency's general immigration enforcement efforts have made it difficult for terrorists to come to the United States. ["Group: Terrorism Not Focus of Homeland Security," Scott Bronstein, May 27, 2007, *cnn.com*; TRAC: *trac. syr.edu*]

Brits Caught Up in "Shadowy War"

Iran's March 2007 capture of 15 British sailors was widely condemned, while U.S. detentions and kidnappings of Iranian officials in the months before received scant attention. Richard Walker of the *American Free Press* believes the Iranian action was a "tit-for-tat" in a "shadowy war being waged by the United States against Iran."

On December 20, 2006, U.S. soldiers in Iraq stopped a car and arrested its four occupants — three Iranians and one Iraqi. Two of the Iranians were diplomats who were in Iraq at the invitation of Iraqi President Jalal Talibani. The next day, U.S. forces arrested two senior Iranian military officials in the home of Hadi al-Ameri, chairman of the Iraqi parliament's security committee. Similarly, on January 11, 2007, American Special Forces raided a de facto Iranian consulate in Abril, Kurdistan (northern Iraq) and seized five low-level officials. The previous captures were based on assertions that the Iranians were directly involved in support for the insurgency. This time, in a relatively tentative allegation, U.S. officials said the Iranians were "suspected of being closely tied" to anti-coalition activities.

In the April 3, 2007 London *Independent*, Patrick Cockburn suggested the January 11 operation was actually a botched attempt to hook much bigger fish. Cockburn quoted a high-level official of the Kurdistan government as saying, "They were after [Mohammed] Jafari. Americans thought he was there." Jafari is the deputy head of Iran's National Security Council. At the time of the raid, Jafari and General Minojahar Frouzanda — intelligence chief of the Iranian Revolutionary Guard — were in Kurdistan for an official meeting with Iraqi President Jalal Talabani. Cockburn likened the planned capture of Jafari to Iran kidnapping a high-level U.S. official during an Iraqi visit. [*americanfreepress.net* and *independent.co.uk*]

"Wal-Mart Paid Me to Be Paranoid"

A Wal-Mart security worker has revealed a sophisticated surveillance operation that targeted Wal-Mart employees, critics, and stockholders. Bruce Gabbard, who worked for Wal-Mart's Threat Research and Analysis Group (TRAG), was fired in March 2007 for intercepting phone calls to a news reporter. Gabbard told *The Wall Street Journal* he recorded the calls on his own, but that most of his spying activities were sanctioned by corporate management. "I used to joke that Wal-Mart paid me to be paranoid, and they got their money's worth," Gabbard said.

However, it wasn't just paranoia that motivated company spying. Gabbard says Wal-Mart increased its surveillance of employee phone calls as part of the battle against terrorism. Citing Gabbard, the *Journal* reported the company increased such surveillance after 9/11 "in response to government requests to employers in general to help ·find terrorist cells." Indeed, the TRAG operation sounds like something out of the NSA playbook. Group members "enter a separate glass-enclosed structure by holding the palm of their hand to a biometric reader that grants them access to a dimly lit work area" known among employees as "the Bat Cave."

In a 2006 covert op, the TRAG selected a male "long-haired" employee to infiltrate an anti-Wal-Mart group, which suggests the Wal-Mart's activism mindset is stuck in the 1960s. In addition, Wal-Mart security teams were asked to "assess" the "potential threat" posed by shareholders whose resolutions the company was trying to block. The list included an 85-year-old retired teacher and his 93-year-old sister. The "threat" was unfounded, as it appears the pair did not cause a ruckus at the company's annual shareholders meeting. ["Inside Wal-Mart's 'Threat Research' Operation," Ann Zimmerman and Gary McWilliams, *Wall Street Journal*, April 4, 2007]

Global Pedophile Ring Broken

British and U.S. authorities have rescued 31 children, some only a few months old, from an international pedophile ring. The investigation netted over 700 suspects, and involved agencies from 35 countries. The ring's hub, an Internet chat room called "Kids the Light of Our Lives," featured images and live videos of "children being subjected to horrific sexual abuse," according to an Associated Press report. Investigators found 75,960 child porn images on the computer of the alleged ringleader, known online as "The Son of God." They also found evidence he distributed 11,491 images to other site users.

In such cases, the suspected pedophiles are rarely identified. The arrest of the Who's Pete Townshend in 2003 was a notable exception (Townshend said he was downloading the photos for research purposes, and was exonerated). Were any powerful or famous people involved this time? If so, they likely used their influence to avoid arrest — or gave in to blackmail. ["Police Smash Global Pedophile Ring," D'Arcy Doran, Associated Press, June 18, 2007]

Washington Pedophile Ring Intact

Investigative reporter Tom Flocco and others believe elite involvement in the sexualization of children goes far beyond internet downloads. On October 6, 2006, he reported allegations by an unnamed senior intelligence agent and national security expert that Washington, D.C. hotels were recently being used to compromise House and Senate members who "had sex with children" at the hotels.

Flocco says the operation was organized by convicted Republican lobbyist Jack Abramoff. As with the U.S. Attorney firings, official "scandals" — in this instance, the 2006 Rep. Mark Foley page scandal and 2007 D.C. Madam story — might be what intelligence agents call a "limited hangout." That is, relatively minor scandals revealed in order to satisfy investigators and the public while the real scandals remain obscured.

Apparently, the Abramoff sex ring took on all comers. Flocco says "male and female heterosexuals, homosexuals, lesbians, bisexuals and underage children provided sexual services to numerous congressmen, senators, national media hosts, top military officers and other federal officials who were compromised and made susceptible to blackmail." ["Agents Say Foley Scandal Tip Of Iceberg," Tom Flocco, October 5, 2006, tomflocco.com]

The Price of Loyalty

Even if you're not the subject of an NSA wiretap, you probably have one of the lesser-known threats to your privacy in your wallet or purse. It can involve chips (of the corn rather than RFID variety). Increasingly, stores and supermarkets are offering customers discounts in exchange for using a plastic card when they make a purchase. These so-called "loyalty cards" — which are generally linked to the customer's name and address — enable marketers and retailers to keep a detailed record of your purchases: what, when, how much, and how you paid for it.

The fact is, most consumers appear willing to give up some privacy in order to save money. In and of itself, it seems relatively benign. However, as with other privacy issues, it is the potential use (and misuse) of our personal data that is raising concerns. Writing in *New York* magazine, Reed Tucker suggests loyalty card data could be used to do more than make you a marketing target. He cites a court case where such data was used as evidence, and raises the specter of insurance companies buying the data to learn more about a person's health and lifestyle. (That gallon-a-week ice cream habit may cost you.)

In February 2007, a bill was introduced in the Maryland legislature to prohibit retailers from sharing or selling the information gleaned from the cards. At this writing, no action had been taken on the bill. However, if it passes, Maryland will join California and Connecticut as states that have acted to restrict the use of loyalty card consumer data. ["A Swipe at Store Loyalty Cards," Lisa Rein, *Washington Post*, February 5, 2007; "Self-Incrimination in the Supermarket Checkout Line," Reed Tucker, *New York* magazine, March 13, 2006]

The "Gay Bomb"

Did the Pentagon consider developing a "Gay Bomb" that would turn enemy soldiers into sex-crazed homosexuals? The charge, dismissed as an internet hoax a couple of years ago, has proven to be true. In June 2007, Pentagon officials confirmed to a California news channel that military leaders had considered developing a so-called "Gay Bomb."

According to a 1994 Air Force proposal on non-lethal weaponry, "One distasteful...example would be strong aphrodisiacs, especially if the chemical also caused homosexual behavior." Edward Hammond, of bioweapon activist group the Sunshine Project, used the Freedom of Information Act to obtain a copy of the proposal. "The Ohio Air Force lab proposed that a bomb be developed that contained a chemical that would cause enemy soldiers to become gay, and to have their units break down because all their soldiers became irresistibly attractive to one another." The Pentagon apparently decided not to "make love, not war," and the $7.5 million proposal was ultimately rejected. ["Pentagon Confirms It Sought To Build A 'Gay Bomb'," Hank Plante, *cbs5.com*, June 8, 2007; *sunshine-project.org*]

Subprime Scapegoats

Subprime mortgages, housing loans made to borrowers with poor credit, don't have much to do with the current economic downturn, at least not directly. As of September 2007, only about five percent of U.S. mortgages were subprime, and only a fifth of those were at risk of default. "Defaulting middle-class U.S. homeowners are blamed, but they are merely a pawn in the game," derivatives expert Satyajit Das told financial writer Jon D. Markman. Derivatives — financial schemes that transfer the risks of investments from one entity to another — are the key to understanding the so-called "subprime mess."

Markman says we need to think about mortgages not as a loan to buy a house, but rather as a way for lenders to make money. Essentially, the bankers made money up front by making risky loans, packaged them into derivatives, and sold them (along with the accompanying risk) to pension funds, insurance companies and hedge funds. Enticed by record low interest rates, many of these buyers purchased the derivatives with borrowed funds — and in turn used them as collateral to obtain new loans. In other words, it was an old-fashioned Ponzi scheme. Much of that money fueled the stock market boom, and now it's time for the bust.

Das predicts a stock market collapse that could last for ten years or more. Indeed, finance author Robert Kuttner warned Congress in October 2007 that the market crash of 1929 was caused by — you guessed it — banks making, repackaging, and selling "highly speculative" (i.e., risky) loans. And we all know what happened after that speculation shuffle came to an end. ["The Credit Crisis Could Be Just Beginning" Jon D. Markman, *thestreet.com*, 9/21/07; "1929 Redux: Heading for a Crash?," Robert Kuttner, *alternet.org*, 10/8/07]

Fuzzy Math

Talk about burying the news. A major September 15, 2007 antiwar rally in Washington, D.C. produced this *New York Times* website headline: "Dozens Arrested in Antiwar Protest Near Capitol." The subheadline transformed "dozens" into "at least 150 people." Finally, the article itself provided the number given by Capitol police: 189 arrests. Likewise, when it came to the head count, the *Times* only managed a vague "thousands." The ANSWER Coalition, which organized the rally, estimates that 100,000 people participated. Even if the organizers' estimates err on the high side, it's clear the supposedly "liberal" *New York Times* downplayed a major expression of anti-war sentiment. (The subheadline was later updated to read "189 people," but nothing else was changed.) [*answer.pephost.org*]

More Fuzzy Math

Another figure that's been underreported: 1.2 million. That's the latest estimate of how many Iraqis have died violently since the 2003 invasion. Non-violent deaths — such as those due to the decimation of Iraq's healthcare system — weren't included. The estimate comes from British pollster ORB, which surveyed over 1,700 Iraqi adults in 15 of Iraq's 18 provinces. Previously, the highest estimate of Iraqi deaths from all causes had been 650,000, based on a peer-reviewed Johns Hopkins' study. Meanwhile, most mainstream media sources still place the total at 70,000–80,000. Even so, the most disturbing number may be much smaller: 9,890. That's the median answer given by Americans when asked in an AP poll how many Iraqi civilians had been killed as a result of the invasion and occupation. ["Iraq Death Toll Rivals Rwanda Genocide," Joshua Holland, *alternet.org*, 9/17/07]

Dollar Collapse Danger

Over the past few years, Iran has been quietly selling more of its oil in euros and yens. According to Reuters, as of October 2007, about 85 percent of Iran's oil exports were in non-dollar currencies. The move is part political (the U.S. and Iran are currently in a standoff over its nuclear program) and part practical (the weakening dollar is simply worth less). Indeed, Iraq's Saddam Hussein had planned doing likewise before he was deposed.

It's not just America's enemies who are abandoning the greenback. In April 2007, the Gulf nation of Qatar announced it had cut the dollar holdings of its key $50 billion investment fund from 99% to 40%. Ambrose Evans-Pritchard of *The Telegraph* described the shift as "a warning that petro-dollar powers ... may pull the plug on the heavily indebted U.S. economy." More significantly, China recently threatened what state media termed "the nuclear option": a major sell-off of its hundreds of billions of U.S. dollar currency reserves. The ominous words came amid increasing U.S. pressure to allow the "free market" to determine the price of its currency, the yuan.

Why should we care? "OPEC and Asia have been the two blocks funding the U.S. current account deficit," Hans Redeker, currency chief at BNP Paribas, told *The Telegraph*. In other words, the world has been bankrolling Washington's profligate spending, and the spigot is starting to tighten. Matters weren't helped when former Federal Reserve Chairman Alan Greenspan told Germany's *Stern* magazine that the euro could replace the U.S. dollar as the reserve currency of choice because the dollar "doesn't have all that much of an advantage" anymore.

Despite all this, the Bush administration has never intervened in the currency markets to support the dollar, preferring to let the "free market" determine its value (no wonder China is reluctant to do likewise). ["Iran gets over 85 pct oil income in non-U.S. currencies," *reuters.com*, 10/2/07; Ambrose Evans-Pritchard, "Dollar's double blow from Vietnam and Qatar"; "China threatens 'nuclear option' of dollar sales," *telegraph.co.uk*, 4/10/07–10/8/07; "Greenspan: Euro Gains As Reserve Choice," Associated Press, 9/17/07]

Chinese Embrace Conspiracy

A recent book has made conspiracy theory fashionable in Beijing. The author of *Currency Wars*, Song Hongbing, claims many world events — from the deaths of six U.S. presidents to the 1997–1998 Asian financial crisis — can be traced back to the Rothschild international banking dynasty. The tome is being read "at senior levels of government and business," according to a report in the UK's *Financial Times*. "I never imagined it could be so hot and that top leaders would be reading it," Hongbing said during a book tour in Shanghai. "People in China are nervous about what's going on in financial markets... This book gives them some ideas."

America has been pressuring China to "open its financial system," i.e., give Western banks greater power and influence. *Currency Wars* — issued by a state-owned publisher — may be part of a high-stakes government PR campaign to maintain control of its banking system. On the other hand, it may be an effort by pro-Western Chinese officials to portray their opponents as anti-Semitic conspiracy kooks. Jon Benjamin, chief executive of the Board of Deputies of British Jews, told the *Financial Times* the book played to discredited anti-Semitic "canards." Mayer Amschel Rothschild himself may have had the last word on the subject. "Give me control of a nation's money," he declared in the 18th century, "and I care not who makes her laws." ["Chinese buy into conspiracy theory," Richard McGregor, *Financial Times*, 9/25/07]

Subliminal Science

Until recently, evidence for the influence of subliminal messages has been largely circumstantial. For example, in 2006 researchers at the University of Nijmegen found that thirsty people subliminally exposed to the phrase "Lipton Ice" were more likely to choose Lipton Ice Tea. Now, University College London (UCL) researchers have produced the first physiological evidence that the brain perceives subliminal images. Researchers found that images caused activity in the visual cortex of subjects' brains, even when they were not conscious of having seen them. Dr. Bahador Bahrami of the UCL Institute of Cognitive Neuroscience concluded "that your brain does log things that you aren't even aware of and can't ever become aware of." The findings did not prove subliminal messages influences decision-making, but Bahrami speculates such influence is "likely." The study also suggests the brain does not pick up subliminal stimuli if occupied by a complex task. This may explain the prevalence of dumb TV shows. ["Subliminal advertising leaves its marks on the brain," *ucl.ac.uk*, 3/9/07]

Air Force Official Found Dead

In October 2007, Charles Riechers, the Air Force's principal deputy assistant secretary for acquisition, was found dead at his home in an apparent suicide. The branch's number-two procurement official, he had been "working on the Air Force's highest priority weapons" projects, according to a Reuters report.

Riechers' predecessor did jail time in 2005 for taking a job with Boeing while still overseeing its Air Force contracts, prompting Congress to end a $23.5 billion tanker deal with the firm. At the time of Riechers' death, the service had still not decided who would be awarded the new contract. "Whatever the reason for the suicide, this is going to contribute to a widespread perception that something is not right about the Air Force acquisition system," said Loren Thompson of the Lexington Institute, a military policy think-tank. While Riechers had been the subject of a relatively minor *Washington Post* exposé on October 1, Thompson believes that "it certainly didn't rise to the level of a serious scandal, so his apparent suicide is hard to explain." ["Air Force's No. 2 weapons buyer found dead," Andrea Shalal-Esa, *reuters.com*, 10/15/07]

A Billion Here, A Billion There...

Of the $12 billion delivered to Iraq in 2003 and 2004, at least $9 billion cannot be accounted for. The 360 tons of cash was dispensed by Paul Bremer's Coalition Provisional Authority (C.P.A.) As Donald L. Barlett and James B. Steele of *Vanity Fair* magazine put it, "The entire nation of Iraq needed walking-around money, and Washington mobilized to provide it. What [it] did not do was mobilize to keep track of it."

Wasn't anyone keeping tabs? On October 25, 2003, the C.P.A. did award a $1.4 million contract to a company called NorthStar Consultants "to provide accountant and audit services" for its giant ATM. NorthStar President Thomas Howell told *Vanity Fair* he discovered the opportunity while browsing the Web. According to California business records, Howell wore two other hats: business consultant and home remodeling contractor. One thing he is not is a certified public accountant. Nor is anyone else employed by NorthStar, which is based out of a private home in San Diego. The C.P.A., it seems, could not find any C.P.A.s to audit Bremer's billions. ["The Spoils of War: Billions Over Baghdad," Donald L. Barlett and James B. Steele, *Vanity Fair*, Oct. 2007; *truthout.org*]

Microchip Health Hazard

Even if you're not concerned about mind control issues, you might want to think twice before hosting a microchip. A series of mid-1990s studies found chip implants "induced" malignant tumors in some lab mice. Todd Lewan of the Associated Press uncovered the research, never made public, in September 2007. Cancer specialists interviewed by AP cautioned that animal results don't necessarily apply to humans. Still, some said they said they would not allow family members to receive implants, and all urged further research.

Since FDA approval, some 2,000 radio frequency identification devices (RFID) have been implanted in humans, according to RFID manufacturer VeriChip Corp. Company CEO Scott Silverman notes that millions of pets also have been implanted with microchips. Further, he assured AP that VeriChip had "received no complaints regarding malignant tumors caused by our product." ["Chip implants linked to animal tumors," Todd Lewan, Associated Press, 9/9/07; *antichips.com*]

"Welcome to Islamberg"

Is there a Jihadist training camp in upstate New York? It sounds far-fetched, but some people living on the western edge of the Catskill Mountains, near Hancock, NY, say it's true. There you'll find a sign welcoming you to "Islamberg," a 70-acre community run by Muslims of the Americas, a tax-exempt organization the Feds say is linked to the Sufi Islamic sect Jamaat ul-Fuqra (JF). Several sources say both groups were founded by Pakistani cleric Sheik Mubarak Ali Shah Gilani, though the Sheik has denied any association with JF, as well as its existence.

After committing a series fire-bombings and murders of rival religious figures in the 1980s, JF appears to have ended its violent ways after the conviction of a member in the 1993 WTC bombing. Nevertheless, at a 2001 bond hearing for a different JF member, BATF Special Agent Thomas Gallagher testified that JF members "are trained in Hancock, NY, and if they pass the training in Hancock they are then sent to Pakistan for [more] training..."

In 2006, Douglas J. Hagmann, director of the Northeast Intelligence Network (NIN), released the results of an NIN field investigation of the Hancock site. Investigators observed a "weapons firing range" and "a military-style training area" including ropes hanging from trees and an obstacle course. (In response, Sheik Gilani has said the latter was for recreational use by the Muslim Boy Scouts.)

Certainly, Islamberg (and 16 other Muslims of the Americas communities in the U.S.) are a potential security threat, but this threat has been greatly overstated. First of all, residents of Islamberg say they are not members of JF, and none have ever been arrested for or charged with terrorist activities. In addition, the State Department removed JF from its list of Foreign Terrorist Organizations in 2000. What about the gunfire and explosions reported by local residents? As a June 12, 2007 Fox News report noted, "The region is a hunter's paradise, practice shooting is a nearly universal hobby in the area, and the sounds of explosions most likely come from a very nearby quarry."

Even Hagmann's NIN report says that, with the exception of "armed sentries guarding the perimeter" of the facility, "no activity of extreme significance was observed."

Still, Hagmann and area residents are concerned about the seeming indifference of law enforcement, and have urged further investigation of the Hancock site. Circumstantial evidence, however, suggests the group has been sufficiently investigated. A New York State Police official told Fox News that they had "a file" on the Hancock group. In addition, the Feds have pursued cases against Muslims of the Americas members in other states (the FBI also alleged — but did not prove — D.C. sniper John Mohammad was a JT member associated with at least one Muslims of the Americas community.) Lastly, there is Sheik Gilani's own statement that "many individuals from both the FBI and CIA...over the last ten years have kept open relations with the Muslim of the Americas."

Indeed, it's possible the Feds have infiltrated the organization with informers and agent provocateurs, which would explain why no attempts have been made to shut down its alleged terrorist training camps. Or perhaps the Sheik is correct when he says allegations against himself and Muslims of the Americas are more smoke than fire. [*Foxnews.com*; Northeast Intelligence Network, *homelandsecurityus.com*; Muslims of the Americas, iqou-moa.org]

McCain and Hillary's Occult Connections

While all five-pointed stars are technically pentagrams, it is the inversion that is considered Satanic. What does this have to do with John McCain and Hillary Clinton? Well, the official symbol of the Republican Party contains inverted pentagrams/stars, as opposed to the much more common "single point up" depiction. Meanwhile, Hillary Clinton chose a large American flag with the unusual inverted pentagrams/stars as a backdrop for a major campaign rally prior to her "must-win" 2008 New Hampshire primary.

The Republican nominee and former Democratic candidate have also been linked to another occult symbol, the Phoenix. Since 1999, Hillary Clinton and her supporters have worn unusual lapel pins depicting a Phoenix. Occultist Manly Hall has written, "The Phoenix is one sign of the secret orders of the ancient world, and of the initiate of those orders..." In addition, "Most occultists believe that the Phoenix is a symbol of Lucifer who was cast down in flames and who they think will one day rise triumphant. This, of course, also relates to the rising of Hiram Abiff, the Masonic 'christ'." (Dr. C. Burns, *Masonic and Occult Symbols Illustrated.*)

Oddly, despite the Phoenix pin's association with Hillary Clinton, John McCain's wife Cindy has worn the same pin, most notably after her husband's "must-win" New Hampshire primary victory in 2000. More recently, in February 2008, *Time* magazine did a cover story on McCain headlined, "The Phoenix: Can McCain Keep Rising?" Around that time, CBS news anchor

Katie Couric likewise described McCain as having "risen like a Phoenix" against his Republican rivals. Between the inverted pentagrams and Phoenix pins, McCain seemed to have all his occult bases covered. This may all be coincidental. However, it is interesting to note that although Barack Obama, like McCain, overcame long odds and early setbacks to become his party's nominee, he was not described as a Phoenix by the corporate media. [Cutting Edge Ministries, *cuttingedge.org*]

Obama's Cousin Accused of Ethnic Cleansing

If Barack Obama loses the November election, let's hope he doesn't turn to his cousin for advice. Kenyan officials have charged opposition leader Raila Odinga, who claims to be Obama's cousin, with ethnic cleansing following his loss of that nation's December 2007 presidential election. Justice Minister Martha Karua told the BBC that the government had suspected Odinga's ODM party was "planning mayhem if they lost" but they had not expected "the magnitude [of the violence] and for it to be ethnic cleansing."

More than 600 people have died in unrest since the disputed election, including up to 50 men, women and children who were burned alive in a church. Another quarter of a million have been driven from their homes. The victims have mostly been members of President Mwai Kibaki's tribe, while those committing the atrocities have mostly been supporters of Mr. Odinga. He told the BBC he had done everything he could to prevent the violence, and characterized it as a response to attacks by Kenyan police on his supporters.

However, another Obama relation — a distant eighth cousin — is responsible for death on a scale that dwarfs the Kenyan violence. He is Vice President Dick Cheney. Mr. Obama's spokesman, Bill Burton, responded to this genealogical shocker by saying, "Every family has a black sheep." [Daniel Johnson, "The Kenya Connection," *nysun.com*, 1/10/08; "Cheney, Obama 'distant cousins'," *bbc.co.uk*, 10/17/07]

The Next Bubble

The record surge in the prices of oil, foodstuffs, and other commodities has little to do with supply and demand. So says commentator Mike Whitney, who says investment banks and hedge funds are using billions in subprime mortgage bailouts to create the commodities boom. "Oil is just another mega-inflated equity bubble — like housing, corporate bonds and dot.com stocks — that is about to crash to earth as soon as the big players grab a parachute," he explains.

There are three things that are driving up the price of oil: the falling dollar, speculation and buying on margin. These factors, not the so-called law of supply and demand, are the real reason oil has rocketed from roughly $30 per barrel in 2001 to $128 today. Whitney quotes author F. William Engdahl: "A conservative calculation is that at least 60% of today's $128 per barrel price of crude oil comes from unregulated futures speculation by hedge funds, banks and financial groups..." This is encouraged by the U.S. Commodity Futures Trading Commission (CFTC), which allow speculators to buy crude oil futures contracts by paying only 6% of the value of the contract and borrowing the other 94%. These sweet terms encourage speculation and keep the prices rising, just as the easy availability of no-money-down and low interest loans inflated housing prices. And we all know what happened after that. [Mike Whitney, "The Great Oil Swindle," *informationclearinghouse.info*, 5/30/08]

The Doomsday Seed Vault

In February 2008, the Norwegian government opened the Svalbard Global Seed Vault in a mountain on Spitsbegen, a remote Arctic island. Operational costs are being funded by, among others, Bill Gates and agribusiness giant Monsanto Corporation. Behind its blast-proof doors and steel-reinforced concrete walls, it will hold approximately 4.5 million seed samples from around the world.

It's scary enough to think that we need to protect existing crop lines in the event of nuclear war or catastrophic climate change, but is there more to the story? Monsanto is a leading promoter of genetically-modified (GMO) crop farming, as are two other doomsday vault sponsors, DuPont/Hi-Bred and Swiss-based Syngenta, two of the largest owners of patented GMO seeds and related agrichemicals.

Could these seeds be used for GMO or even biowarfare research, as some fear? For its part, the Norwegian Ministry of Agriculture and Food has stated, "Each country or institution will still own and control access to the seed they have deposited." On the question of whether GMO seeds will be stored in the Vault, the Ministry's rather cryptic answer leaves open the possibility: "Import and storage of GMO seeds according to Norwegian legislation will require advance approval. Certain other criteria will apply to 'sealed internal use' for research purposes..."

Ironically, while the Global Seed Vault project purports to protect and preserve crop seeds for future generations, Monsanto's so-called "Terminator" technology causes seeds to "commit suicide" after one harvest, forcing farmers to buy new seeds each year. Perhaps that's the point. Even if the Seed Vault's contents are never used for GMO or biowarfare research, it will still serve its agribusiness backers as a public relations offensive to divert attention from their more nefarious endeavors. [F. William Engdahl, "Doomsday Seed Vault in the Arctic," *globalresearch.ca*; Norwegian Ministry of Agriculture and Food: *regjeringen.no/en/dep/lmd.html*]

"Smiley-Face" Serial Killings?

At least 40 young men found drowned may have actually been victims of a national gang that has left smiley-face markings at the scenes, a team of retired New York City police detectives and criminal justice investigators stated in April 2008. In what may be a chilling true case of *Revenge of the Nerds*, the task force believes the gang has killed popular college students — often with high grades and impressive athletic records — in about ten different states.

The team investigated 89 separate cases dating back a decade and said it had connected 40 of them through a variety of evidence, aside from the smiley-faces. The death of University of Minnesota student Chris Jenkins in 2003 was particularly suspicious. According to Fox News, "His body was found encased in ice in the Mississippi, his hands folded across his chest in an odd pose that was inconsistent with a chance drowning." Investigators believe the killers have been roaming interstates from New York to Wisconsin, staging the drownings. They suspect the men were drugged and possibly tortured, then tossed into the water to make it appear as if they'd drowned. The FBI and most local police authorities do not see a connection among the deaths. ["Detectives: 40 Drowning Victims May Have Been Murdered by 'Smiley Face Gang'," *foxnews.com*, 4/29/08]

Deaths of Tens of Thousands Covered Up

When it comes to conspiracy theories, one will often hear that a cover-up is impossible because "someone would have said something." Apparently, this wasn't the case with the mass slaughter of Korean civilians in the summer of 1950. As reported by the Associated Press, "With U.S. military officers sometimes present...the southern army and police emptied South Korean prisons, lined up detainees and shot them in the head, dumping the bodies into hastily dug trenches. Others were thrown into abandoned mines or into the sea. Women and children were among those killed. Many victims never faced charges or trial." The mass killings of potential supporters of Communist North Korea "were carried out over mere weeks and were largely hidden from history for a half-century." A South Korean commission estimates at least 100,000 people were executed, but one official said the estimate is "very conservative" and could be over 200,000. American military reports of the South Korean slaughter were simply stamped "Secret" and filed in Washington. Meanwhile, Communist accounts of the atrocities were always dismissed as lies and propaganda. [Charles J. Hanley and Jae-Soon Chang, "Thousands killed in 1950 by U.S.'s Korean ally," Associated Press, 5/19/08]

Iraq Commander Details Bush Rant

A *Washington Post* article about former White House press secretary Scott McLellan's tell-all book discussed a lesser-known Bush Administration exposé. A new autobiography by retired Lt. Gen. Ricardo S. Sanchez, former commander of U.S. troops in Iraq, charges that George Bush "led America into a strategic blunder of historic proportions." In *Wiser in Battle: A Soldier's Story*, Sanchez relates the response of an apparently out-of-control Bush to the killings of four U.S. contractors in Fallujah in 2004.

During a videoconference, Sanchez writes, Bush launched into a disturbing rant — what Sanchez charitably describes as a "confused" pep talk: "Kick ass!" he quotes the President as saying. "If somebody tries to stop the march to democracy, we will seek them out and kill them! We must be tougher than hell! This Vietnam stuff, this is not even close. It is a mind-set. We can't send that message. It's an excuse to prepare us for withdrawal. There is a series of moments and this is one of them. Our will is being tested, but we are resolute. We have a better way. Stay strong! Stay the course! Kill them! Be confident! Prevail! We are going to wipe them out! We are not blinking!" [Michael Abramowitz, "McClellan Recounts Administration's Missed Chances After '04 Election," *Washington Post*, 6/2/08]

Electronic Votescam

by Robert Sterling

"It doesn't matter who casts the ballots. What matters is who counts the ballots." — Joseph Stalin

Say what you will about the 2000 election, but at least we have a paper trail proving that George W. Bush swindled the election. That may no longer be the case.

Where to begin? Start in Nebraska: in 1996, Chuck Hagel, a Republican, won the race for the U.S. Senate, the first Republican Senate victory in the state in 24 years. The *Washington Post* declared his "victory against an incumbent Democratic governor was the major Republican upset in the November election." His stunning win included many black communities that had never before voted Republican, made more remarkable by Hagel's right-wing political views. In 2002, he won by an astounding 83% of the vote.

Hagel is the former chairman and chief executive of ES&S, the company that made all the vote-counting equipment in the state of Nebraska during both elections. ES&S is a heavy contributor to the Republican Party. Hagel failed to disclose his relationship to and continuing ownership of the company on his FEC disclosure statements and Senate ethics investigators.

In 2002, Republican Saxby Chambliss upset incumbent Max Cleland in the Georgia Senate race by a 53–46% margin. Polls showed Cleland leading 49–44%, understandable after Chambliss attacked the war hero (Cleland lost three limbs in a grenade explosion) on his supposed lack of patriotism. Republican Sonny Perdue also defeated incumbent Roy Barnes in the governor's race by a margin of 52–45%. The most recent poll showed Perdue trailing by nine points.

In January 2003, a folder — cleverly named "rob-georgia" — was discovered at Diebold Election Systems, the company which built and programmed all of the Peach State's voting machines. There were three more folders inside it: one had instructions to place new files in the election management folder, the second had files which were to replace existing ones in the management folder, and the third instructed users to replace Windows with its contents and run a program. The Georgia Secretary of State's Office admits a patch was administered to all 22,000 voting machines in the state before the election.

Diebold is the main competitor of ES&S in the electronic voting field, and is also a heavy contributor to the Republican Party. Diebold's then CEO Walden O'Dell was a major fund-raiser for the Bush 2004 election campaign. (He would leave the company in 2005 under a cloud of scandal over allegations of security fraud and insider trading by the corporation.) In 2003, he wrote a letter declaring he was "committed to helping Ohio deliver its electoral votes for the president next year." When a controversy ensued in the Buckeye State over his statement, he explained he wasn't talking about rigging the state's machines. For some reason, his explanation didn't sound particularly reassuring, especially after Diebold's home state became ground zero for the 2004 election battle.

Back in Florida, some voters who pressed the touch-screen button for Jeb's opponent in the 2002 election noticed something strange: their vote was registered for Bush. Meanwhile, in Texas, Jeff Wentworth won his state Senate seat, Carter Casteel her state House seat and Judge Danny Scheel won re-election. Nothing necessarily suspicious about that — except they all won with exactly 18,181 votes. All three are from Comal County, and both Wentworth and Casteel are Republicans while Scheel is a conservative.

That two of the most predominant electronic voting machine makers are heavily tied to the GOP is a pretty disturbing fact (as they would be if tied to the Democratic Party). Adding to the disturbing facts: a chief financial backer of both companies was California multimillionaire Howard Ahmanson Jr. Ahmanson is a Christian Reconstructionist, the ultra-right religious movement to remake the U.S.A into a Old Testament-based religious theocracy, complete with a return of public stonings for adultery and sodomy.

There is usually no paper trail left by electronic machines, and they use source codes which are proprietary — which means they're the corporation's private property unavailable for public inspection, including losing candidates.

Dan Spillane was a software engineer for *VoteHere*, an electronic machine company that included former CIA director Robert Gates and Dick Cheney's former assistant as directors. After uncovering holes in their security system, he was fired, and he filed a whistle-blower lawsuit. He described their vote integrity program "very much like Arthur Andersen in the Enron case."

On the subject of Arthur Andersen, they changed the name of Andersen Consulting to Accenture, and incorporated offshore in Bermuda. Besides other schemes, Accenture landed the fat contract for a new Pentagon online voting system in the 2004 presidential election to help American soldiers vote. Now that's supporting our troops.

Even without these blatantly dubious examples, voting with no paper trail is a terrible idea. So is privatizing the power to count votes. Even if the companies involved in these activities weren't corrupt, the influence they would have on democracy would likely turn them corrupt quickly. Electronic voting is what is known as "a bad idea."

The controversy surrounding electronic voting (which has mainly been thanks to brave isolated efforts by Beverly Harris of BlackBoxVoting. com and Internet magazines such as *Online Journal*) slowly started receiving mainstream coverage in 2004. However, even then establishment mouthpieces tried desperately to minimize the dangers involved, all in a predictable attempt to sanction a potential criminal reign as legitimate (a hallmark of the years of George W. Bush). Courts followed in kind: in late October 2003, a federal appeals court dismissed a suit over electronic voting machines, bizarrely justifying the machines by stating that "electoral fraud can never be completely eliminated no matter which type of ballot is used." Left unmentioned by the judges was why it would then be okay to use a system that seems to maximize the potential for abuse and fraud.

The one public official who did the most to battle electronic voting was Kevin Shelley, elected California's Secretary of State in 2002. On March 2005, Shelley resigned from office under threats of criminal investigation and a cloud of supposed scandal. Three years later, he still hasn't been charged with a single crime, which supports the belief he was hounded from office in a politically motivated vendetta. Shelley, a Democrat, decertified the usage of certain machines, demanded a verifiable paper trail for all electronic machines in use and launched an investigation of machine manufacturer Diebold for criminal prosecution. (In an October 2002 interview with this writer, which perhaps sparked Shelley's concern over the issue, a Shelley camp rep conceded if someone like Katherine Harris was in charge of insuring the integrity of electronic voting machines, "We'd be screwed.")

His replacement, appointed by the specially-elected Governor Schwarzenegger after the ouster of Gray Davis, is Arnold's fellow Republican Bruce McPherson, who unsurprisingly (in true Kat Harris style) recertified the Diebold machines, publicly opposed a paper trail for electronic machines and launched a computerized "Voter Registration Database" for new voters (who are more liberal than previous voters) that rejected 43 percent of all Los Angeles County applicants through March 15 of this year.

Meanwhile, temp-worker Stephen Heller leaked to reporters transcripts of audiotapes he received from Diebold lawyers, in which they admitted the company violated a $12 million contract with the state by changing its voting machine software. His reward: prosecution by right-wing Republican Los Angeles District Attorney Steve Cooley, for theft (though he stole nothing) and violation of attorney-client privilege (though he isn't an attorney). As for Diebold itself, it has yet to be prosecuted, though it did pay $2.6 million to settle the lawsuit (filed by Shelley) charging it had given false information to the state about the security and reliability of its machines (less than a quarter it received in the contract Heller provided whistle-blowing evidence on).

The end results in 2004: Democratic candidate John Kerry won the exit polling in both Ohio and nationally, but lost the actual official voting to

Bush. Exit polls are the most accurate kind, and any results which don't match their results should logically be met with suspicions of fraud. With the mainstream press, public courts and politicians of both stripes avoiding the disturbing evidence of malfeasance already involving electronic voting, the future of so-called democracy in America doesn't look too promising. Already with the perversion of money and media access controlling the terms of debate in mainstream politics to a tight margin, there is reason to suspect even this controlled charade won't be decided by the American public.

Robert Sterling is the editor of The Konformist *at Konformist.com*

Sources:

Some of this article was adapted from Mr. Sterling's book *50 Reasons Not to Vote for Bush* (Feral House, 2004) and various articles from *Konformist.com*

Al-Aqeel, Tamadhur. "Whistle-Blower Protection Depends On Who Hears Whistle." *Los Angeles Daily Journal,* 21 April 2006.

Black Box Voting. *www.blackboxvoting.com.*

BuzzFlash. "Will Electronic Voting Machines Steal the 2004 Election?" *AlterNet,* 1 October 2003. *www.alternet.org/story.html?StoryID=16874.*

Byrne, John. "Diebold CEO Resigns After Reports of Fraud Litigation, Internal Woes." *Raw Story* 12 December 2005. *rawstory.com/news/2005/Diebold_CEO_resigns_after_reports_of_1212. html.*

Conover, Bev. "Computerized Voting Systems Cannot Be Made Secure." *Online Journal,* 20 October 2003. *www.onlinejournal.com/Commentary/102003Conover/102003conover.html.*

Friedman, Brad. "California Voters File Lawsuit Against State's Use, Purchase of Diebold Voting Systems!" *The Brad Blog,* 21 March 2006. *www.bradblog.com/?p=2583.*

Friedman, Brad. "Democracy Crumbling: New Electronic Voter Registration Database Rejects 43% of New Los Angeles Voter Applications!" *The Brad Blog,* 29 March 2006. www.bradblog. com/?p=2621.

Hartmann, Thom. "Evidence Mounts That The Vote May Have Been Hacked." *Common Dreams,* 6 November 2004. www.commondreams.org/headlines04/1106-30.htm.

Hartmann, Thom. "If You Want To Win An Election, Just Control The Voting Machines." *Common Dreams,* 31 January 2003. www.commondreams.org/views03/0131-01.htm.

Hartmann, Thom. "Now Your Vote Is the Property of a Private Corporation." *Online Journal,* 13 March 2003. www.onlinejournal.com/Commentary/031303Hartmann/031303hartmann. html.

Hartmann, Thom. "The Theft of Your Vote Is Just a Chip Away." *AlterNet,* 30 July 2003. *www. alternet.org/story.html?StoryID=16474.*

Jacobs, Alan. "Apocalyptic President?" *Boston Globe,* 4 April 2004. www.boston.com/news/ globe/ideas/articles/2004/04/04/apocalyptic_president/.

Keating, Dan. "New Voting Systems Assailed." *Washington Post* 28 March 2003.

Kravets, David. "Federal Appeals Court Dismisses Electronic Voting Machine Lawsuit." *SF Gate,* 29 October 2003. *www.sfgate.com/cgi-bin/article.cgi?f=/news/archive/2003/10/29/ state0331EST0005.DTL.*

Landes, Lynn. "2002 Elections: Republican Voting Machines, Election Irregularities, and "Way-off" Polling Results." *Online Journal,* 8 November 2002. *www.onlinejournal.com/Special_ Reports/Landes111402/landes111402.html.*

Landes, Lynn. "Internet Voting: The End of Democracy?" *Online Journal,* 4 September 2003. *www. onlinejournal.com/Special_Reports/090403Landes/090403landes.html.*

Landes, Lynn. "Offshore Company Captures Online Military Vote." *Online Journal*, 21 July 2003. *www.onlinejournal.com/Special_Reports/072103Landes/072103landes.html.*

Landes, Lynn. "Voting Machines Violate Constitution." *Online Journal*, 15 April 2003. *www.onlinejournal.com/Commentary/041503Landes/041503landes.html.*

Leopold, Jason. "Electronic Voting Minus Paper Trails Makes It Easy to Rig Elections." *Online Journal*, 4 September 2003. *www.onlinejournal.com/Special_Reports/090403Leopold/090403leopold.html.*

Levy, Steven. "Black Box Voting Blues." *Newsweek*, 3 November 2003. *www.msnbc.com/news/985033.asp.*

McGowan, David. "Newsletter #75." *The Center for an Informed America*, 2 November 2005. *www.davesweb.cnchost.com/nwsltr75.html.*

Otter, Faun. "Vote Fraud — Exit Polls vs. Actuals." *Scoop*, 4 November 2004. *www.scoop.co.nz/stories/HL0411/S00072.htm.*

Palast, Greg. *The Best Democracy Money Can Buy.* New York: Plume, 2003.

Parry, Robert. "Evidence of a Second Bush Coup?" *ConsortiumNews.com*, 6 November 2004. *www.consortiumnews.com/2004/110604.html.*

Partridge, Ernest. "Are American Elections Fixed?" *Online Journal*, 3 April 2003. *www.onlinejournal.com/Commentary/040303Partridge/040303partridge.html.*

Punpirate. "Did Your Vote Count?" *Democratic Underground*, 15 February 2003. www.democraticunderground.com/articles/03/02/15_vote.html.

Vankin, Jonathan. "Call Me Hal." *Metro* 21, December 2000. *www.metroactive.com/papers/metro/12.21.00/cover/election-0051.html.*

"Voting Machines: Vote Tampering in the 21st Century." *WhoseFlorida.com*, 2003. *www.whoseflorida.com/voting_machines.htm.*

"Voting Security." *Populist*, 2003. *www.populist.com/voting.html.*

Winograd, Marcy. "Congressional Contender Winograd Calls on McPherson to Scrap New Voter ID Rule That Disengages Electorate, Disenfranchises New Voters and Sends Wrong Message about Democracy." *Marcy Winograd for Congress*, 2006. *www.winogradforcongress.com/mcpherson.htm.*

Zetter, Kim. "Did E-Vote Firm Patch Election?" *Wired*, 13 October 2003. *www.wired.com/news/politics/0,1283,60563,00.html.*

The Culling

A Speculative Look into the Global Apocalypse

by Jay Weidner

I've seen The Future: it is murder. — "The Future," Leonard Cohen

There is a Plan. It's been operational for decades and possibly for over a hundred years.

I call it "The Culling," and its final stages are upon us.

The Plan was born long ago, signaled by the writings of Thomas Malthus that were eagerly taken up by the British aristocratic class.

In his travels for the East India Trading Company in the early 1800s, Malthus examined "savage" populations and population growth. According to his calculations, too many people on earth would trigger massive famines wiping out most of the Earth's inhabitants.

This wasn't prophecy, this was science.

One of the biggest bestsellers of the '60s was the non-fiction scare *The Population Bomb,* by Paul Ehrlich. Due primarily to the book's influence, many people voluntarily agreed to have fewer or no children.

The Population Bomb predicted that overpopulation would bring on a famine that would bring down the world. This famine would start, said Ehrich, in the late 1970s, and by the late 1980s, there would be hardly anyone left.

In 1980, a strange granite monument, the Georgia Guidestones, was built in the small town of Elberton, Georgia that addressed some of the same issues that Ehrlich touched upon in his book.

Financed by an anonymous gentleman who called himself R.C. Christian, the Georgia Guidestones seem to have been created to give people of the future a new set of rules for proper government. Mr. Christian gave the owner of a local granite company a large sum of money and a blueprint for the granite monument. Mr. Christian also instructed the builder as to what the words chiseled into the monument, would say. These Commandments were written in eight different languages.

Moving clockwise around the structure from due north, are sayings in

English, Spanish, Swahili, Hindi, Hebrew, Arabic, Chinese, and Russian. The message in English reads:

* Maintain humanity under 500,000,000 in perpetual balance with nature.
* Guide reproduction wisely — improving fitness and diversity.
* Unite humanity with a living new language.
* Rule passion — faith — tradition — and all things with tempered reason.
* Protect people and nations with fair laws and just courts.
* Let all nations rule internally resolving external disputes in a one world court.
* Avoid petty laws and useless officials.
* Balance personal rights with social duties.
* Prize truth — beauty — love — seeking harmony with the infinite.
* Be not a cancer on the earth — Leave room for nature.

As in the ten Bill of Rights to the U.S. Constitution and the Ten Commandments of the Old Testament, the first Commandment is the most important of the ten. The other Rights back that very important initial Right.

With the Georgia Guidestones the same rule applies. The last nine Commandments would only go into effect after Commandment Number One is followed. With Guidestones, the last nine Commandments could only occur when world's population is reduced from the current six billion to 500 million.

When I was producing the feature documentary *2012: The Odyssey*, we interviewed Gary Jones, editor of the *Elberton Star*, the local newspaper in the town near the Guidestones. Mr. Jones informed us that local Masons were behind the Guidestones. Yoko Ono, Ted Turner, Mikhail Gorbachev and many others have commented about how much they admire the Georgia Guidestones and their message.

During the shooting of the *2012* film we also explored the strange murals, plaques and rumors that surrounded Denver Airport. Begun in the late '80s and finished in the mid-'90s, the Denver Airport was the top project for Denver Mayor Fredrico Pena and other civic leaders from the Rocky Mountains.

The strangeness begins with the notion that a new airport in Denver was actually necessary. The old airport, Stapleton, was a perfectly adequate international facility. The new airport took years longer than expected to be finished, going more than a billion dollars over budget.

During the new airport's lengthy construction rumors arose about a purported secret military base also being built beneath the new Denver Airport. Locals reported hearing deep underground noises. Thousands of truckloads of dirt were removed from the area over the years according to nearby neighbors. Painters and drywall installers talked of elevators that go down 30 to 40 stories and ex-intelligence spooks spoke of underground trains traveling into the bowels of the Rockies.

Other stories were getting around, some concerned with a secret government plan to avert the government's destruction in the advent of a disaster, either man-made or natural. This plan was called COG, for Continuity of Government.

We know COG exists in part due to Richard Cheney's report to the press that his odd actions during Sept. 11 were due to following COG rules. President Bush's flight to Offutt Air Base in Omaha on that day may also have been part of the COG plan.

Is it possible that the rumored underground base built under the Denver Airport was part of COG operations? With its high altitude and proximity to the center of the country could serve Denver as a last-ditch escape hatch for the elites of our country. Since it would take just about the same time to get to Denver from the farthest reaches of the 48 contiguous states and because there were already underground bunkers under Pikes Peak at NORAD, the choice of Denver and the nearby Rockies would be an obvious choice for COG headquarters.

There are other odd things about the new Denver airport that merit examination.

The first is the odd plaque and monument that sits at the south end of the airport. This stone monument capstone has a dedication to the airport from the Grandmaster of the Freemasons and thanks Colorado luminaries like Fredrico Pena and others.

The artist Leo Tanguma, who painted the strange airport monuments, has changed his story. His first story was that the murals were commissioned and he was told exactly what to paint, but according to *Westword* magazine, he now claims that he simply decided what to paint. Does it sound like normal operating procedure to just pay an artist to paint what he likes in a public airport, an airport that has a Masonic influence?

There are four murals located between the baggage claims area and the center under the giant towering tent that makes up the central building of the airport.

The first mural has the children of the world beating a sword into a plowshare. The second mural depicts the children of the world surrounding a psychedelic cactus of some kind, and their faces are filled with jubilation.

The third mural shows three people — two children and a native American woman — lying in coffins. Behind these three dead people are animals that have gone extinct in the last past few hundred years. Behind the extinct animals is an immense forest fire which appears to be burning up the world.

The mural also shows a Nazi-like figure wearing a gas mask and carrying a huge rifle. He walks down the streets of a haunted deserted town apparently looking for victims. Hiding in the floors and walls of the town are poor people who are frightened and crying. The Nazi-like figure is piercing the breast of a white dove with the bayonet on his rifle. Why does this disturbing mural sits prominently in a major airport?

The Denver Airport murals seem to tell us that if we go one way all the children of the world will be united. But if we go the other way, Nazis will exterminate us.

The Georgia Guidestones and the Denver Airport are both recent creations and both possess a deep Masonic influence. Both are concerned with overpopulation. Both project a message of what we can expect to come. By looking at the two monuments together, we can see an opening into the Plan. And they seem to do it in a symbolic language that is obvious to brothers on the inside and obscure to cowans on the outside.

If we become a world of only five hundred million people, as the first commandment of the Georgia Guidestones tells us, then the children of the world will beat their swords into plowshares, and live in peace, with no war.

On the other hand, if the population is properly culled, then we face certain extinction, or Nazis in the street killing us one by one.

We can see that these two monuments both helped in their construction by Freemasons, but it's likely that only the upper rank of the Freemasonic order dreams of a world with a substantial population loss. Population reduction appears to have been a major preoccupation of the ruling elite for quite a while.

Elite groups have been pursuing the problem of overpopulation for decades. Club of Rome, the Trilateralists, the Crown. George Soros, Karl Popper and others were part of a research group devoted to examining methods of depopulation. The Rockefellers were also heavily involved with financing the eugenics movements of the early 20th century. The Bush family has always been interested in population control, abortion and eugenics.

Some conspiracy theorists on both the left and right believe that population control is the number one concern of the elites.

It is as if the elites, sometime after Darwin published his book on evolution, began designing philosophies based on a warped version of Darwinism. Perhaps the most famous "Social Darwinist" was Adolf Hitler, who rose to power riding a wave of racial Darwinist concepts. A major driving factor of this emerging "evolutionary" meme was that, once the rules of Darwinian evolution were properly understood, the real truth of Nature is that only one group can be at the top. This emerging new philosophy believed that survival of the fittest is the *only* rule of nature.

This new polity served to destroy the last vestiges of the ancient values of the old initiatory bodies of Europe and America. Traditional beliefs in Liberty, Fraternity and Equality gave way to a more selfishly derived ethos. Ideas like freedom and equality were quaint but had no place in a world ruled by dominance and by the fierce reality borne out of a superficial understanding of evolution.

Darwinism gave rise, inadvertently, to a self-centered philosophy that professed that it was in one's interest to wipe out everyone who is not of your kind. This line of reasoning also held that you and your race must pursue its own survival interests as completely as possible, or else another race or culture will remove your kind as part of the war of the selfish gene.

In a Darwinist sense, moral values and ethics had become antiquated artifacts that inhibit the natural racial desire to conquer and become the dominant species, culture or race.

The idea of racial superiority had been around a long time before Darwin, but Darwinian thought empowered the elites with an intellectual reason to spring into action.

It is within this idea of racial and cultural superiority, carried out with technology, that The Culling was born.

The eugenics movement, the large world wars, the spread of disease, the destruction of the environment, some theorists argue, is the elites attempting to curtail population growth.

If this is true, why is the population fast approaching seven billion people?

Here, the theories of Malthus and Ehrlich appear to be wrong. It is easy to see that the world did not disappear from famines brought on by overpopulation. Many historians, and others, will tell you that advancements in farming techniques have created a vast food supply. These experts argue that man's ingenuity has steadily kept the food supply rising with the growing population.

Financed by the Rockefellers, the "Green Revolution" was put into place by the United Nations to teach the farmers of the third world modern agricultural methods. These farmers, who in many cases had been tilling the same soil as their fathers and grandfathers, were encouraged to exchange their ancient farming practices for modern methods. The peasant farmer, with his animal-driven plows, was replaced by gigantic machines and combines that vastly increased food production all over the world.

Always an easy target for conspiracy buffs, the Rockefellers were one of the major financiers of the Green Revolution that fed millions of hungry people every day. Didn't this prove that the elites were actually assisting the world in finding new ways to grow food and feed themselves? The elites talk of free trade, globalization and the spreading of democracy.

Have the aristocratic classes changed their minds about Malthus? Is that why they were encouraging the poor of the world to abandon ancient farming methods in favor of the modern methods?

Why would these same elites, who only a few years ago were openly talking of plans for depopulation, have now changed their minds? Why would these wealthy people now also be spreading the idea of a Green Revolution, a Global economy, free trade, essentially a world government some have called the New World Order?

Why bother going on with the pretense that they are going to create a great future for all of humanity if the ultimate game plan is the opposite?

There is one thing that the creators of the Green Revolution have seemed to overlook. It will only work if the farmers have access to cheap oil.

The same thing can be said about the advocates of free trade. The only way that the global economy can work, and power the processing and shipping of goods and services, is by having endless amounts of cheap oil.

Is there a disconnect among the elites? Is it one side against another?

Have they stopped their grandiose ideas concerning depopulation of the Earth? Did they grow benevolent somehow in the last 30 years?

The answer to that important question is that the two memes are working together to achieve the real goal.

The central idea is this: globalization will lead to depopulation.

The elites have funded studies examining the population explosion. Many have argued that war, AIDS, drugs, easy access to weapons are all policies that governments are implementing to reduce certain undesirable populations.

But given the notion that depopulation is the desired goal, it's still not working, even after a hundred years of wars, famines, and diseases.

The elites have discovered that people are tenacious.

An answer to the dilemma had to be found. The Plan would have to be twofold: it had to kill those they wanted to die and there had to be insurance that the elite would survive whatever occurred.

We know from Congressional testimony in the 1970s that biological solutions were tried and discarded. AIDS, which may have come out of this research at Fort Dietrich, was devastating but proved to be difficult to spread. The problem with viruses and other biological attack schemes was the possibility that they could backfire and spread into the very populations that they wished to survive. That path was deemed too risky for the elites.

I believe the final Plan was hatched in the mid 1970s. With the first oil shock from OPEC tripling the price of gas in a few weeks' time, the leaders of the world began to consider what the world would look like without cheap oil.

The leaders came to the startling conclusion that it would be the industrialized north, the United States, Canada, and Europe, that would be the most devastated by the end of cheap oil. Because these countries were considered "advanced" economies they had an overdependence on cheap oil. These men realized that the entire economy would fail if there were no more cheap oil.

But they also saw that the third-world countries, where they still farmed like they had done for millennia, would survive. These countries, mostly non-white, might even thrive in the event of an oil shortage. They saw that abundant supplies of oil had caused the people of the Western world to forget how to grow their own food without oil.

It was with this realization that they began to hatch the Plan. The people involved were all in the oil business and they knew where and how much oil lay in the ground for the most part. There were a few renegade countries that produced oil but they would all be targeted for control.

If they could control the world's oil supply then the Final Plan could work. But first they had to do something that would ensure that The Culling would happen on schedule, and with all of the possible problems solved.

This is the true reason for the mad rush toward globalization in the last 20 years. A key part of the Plan was to globalize the economies of the world and shove NAFTA and GATT down our throats.

With this particular Plan they would be able to finish off the flotsam and survive themselves. A great Darwinian finish would then be at hand and the elite would win in the end.

But first, flood cheap oil onto the world's population for several decades, and after addicting the world to petroleum, take it away, leaving everything to fall into chaos.

The most damaging part of the Plan to the third world was to use oil and mass chemical fertilizer to seduce it into forgetting how to grow food without oil, without chemicals and without huge machinery. When the Rockefellers and the Trilateralists financed the "Green Revolution," people throughout the world started to abandon old farming practices.

Is the "Peak Oil" scenario a scam? Since the Rockefellers made their billions owning Standard Oil, and Bush and Cheney are both "oil men," a scam would not be beyond the imagination. If Dr. Thomas Gold's abiogenic petroleum origin theory can be believed, then oil is formed from deep carbon deposits, and supplies are continuously replenishing themselves. But even if oil is not a fossil fuel, it's going to get more and more difficult to capture it.

Looking at most of the available data on oil, it does appear that we are running out of sweet crude. The Saudis will not let anyone audit their fields and we do know that they are pumping 10 million gallons of sea water a day into their biggest fields. That tells us that they have used up the light crude and are now hitting the bottom of the barrel where the oil is like tar and they need the sea water to loosen it up to be able to pump it out.

The first thing the U.S. did when it got Marines into Iraq was to audit the fields and find out how much crude was down there. I have heard that they were shocked at how much Saddam had pumped out.

There was only one other country that had a lot of oil and was not allowing an audit: Iran.

If there is a Plan then it would be logical that the next place of tension will be Iran. For the Plan to work the playmakers must be in control of the oil.

The argument here is not whether there is a Peak Oil scam or not. The argument is whether this entire ordeal is being put into place to create a situation of sudden population reduction.

But what is The Plan? Industrious countries like the U.S. had to lose their ability to do everything for themselves. The world must become interdependent. The leaders of the World Trade Commission, the Trilateralists and others told us this was being done to help create a more neighborly world, a place where we would know each other better because we now traded freely.

Considering the character of the men who devised the Plan it all sounds rather dubious. The hidden agenda of Globalization is to weaken the strong so that they would not be able to save themselves.

Advocates of Globalization — the World Trade Commission, the Council on Foreign Relations — argued that the new economies' products would be created in an multinational environment relying on plastics and cheap transportation.

Once cheap oil is removed from the transaction, the entire apparatus will crumble. And it will be a spectacular failure. An All-Fall-Down that takes everything, or almost everything, with it.

It will start with the advent of expensive gasoline which will lead to huge losses in the food supply. China and India will be the first to get hit. The U.S., Argentina and Europe will send rice and food there and to other famine-wracked countries but soon they will discover their own supplies beginning to run down.

With much of the valuable farming land now going to grow corn for ethanol coupled with the increase in gas prices, food prices are going to skyrocket.

When gas hits ten dollars a gallon, or more, the food supply chain will probably fall completely apart. You will only be able to get what you eat locally.

The entire world economy, now knitted together by the New World Order, will also all fall together.

The first signs of real danger will be when the people in the inner cities figure out that there is no work, no jobs. Mass transit systems will begin to fail as they have to keep raising their prices because of increasing energy costs. This will freeze out the poorer who will no longer be able to afford bus fare.

Simple maintenance of roads and infrastructures will soon become so costly that they will simply not be done. Roads and highways will fall apart soon after the maintenance stops.

The cities will explode when the food supply chain is so disrupted that the food is too expensive to transport from the country to the cities. Many factions — mostly of an ethnic nature — will explode, warring against each other as the fight for survival begins.

Those with the most guns and best organization will win. Those who are not prepared will face an endless series of disasters. War lords will emerge from the cities and break out into the countryside where there will still be food. The people in the country will have to prepare for attacks from the city folk who will be desperate, hungry and pissed.

Those in the country, especially those who have land and animals, will be better off than their cousins in the cities. But still there will be huge problems. Due to globalization we face the uneasy dilemma that few today knows how to successfully feed themselves. How many of us know how to raise chickens, milk a goat or a cow, or even plant a big enough garden just to feed ourselves?

We have been cut off from the knowledge that our ancestors had from a couple generations ago. We have forgotten how to feed ourselves.

In their citadels, inside their underground bunkers, the Chosen Ones will wait it out. Each person who has a seat on these modern Noah's Arks will have done something to deserve being saved.

Perhaps they owned a bank, or a newspaper, or a television network.

Perhaps they sold their soul in some other way.

This is The Plan.

This is how The Future happens.

"I've seen The Future: it is Murder."

About the Authors

Mike Bara ("The Secret History of NASA") is, with Richard Hoagland, a co-author of the book, *Dark Mission, the Secret History of NASA*. His blogs can be read at *www.darkmission.net*.

Mark Bruback ("Who Was Adam Weishaupt?"), also known as Sir Mark the Poet, is a Seattle resident, videographer, painter and member of the Knight Templar brotherhood. His website is *www.sirmarkthepoet.com*.

Mae Brussell's prodigious research on political conspiracies found radio broadcast through KLRB and KAZU California FM readio stations. Material and photos of Brussell can be found online at *www.maebrussell.com*, *www.prouty.org/brussell* and *www.newsmakingnews.com/mblinks.htm*, a site curated by Virginia McCullough. Mae Brussell died on October 3, 1988.

Joan D'Arc ("The Darwin Wars") is the publisher of *HunterGatheress Journal* (huntergatheress. com) and the co-publisher of *PARANOIA: The Conspiracy & Paranormal Reader* (paranoiamagazine. com). She is the author of *Space Travelers and the Genesis of the Human Form*, and *Phenomenal World*, both published by The Book Tree (*www.thebooktree.com*). Joan also founded BIPED: Beings for Intelligent Purpose in Evolutionary Design, the Website of Darwinian Dissent (*www.biped.info*) about the separation of science and state.

Joseph P. Farrell ("Exposing the Nazi International: An Analysis") is the author of *The Giza Death Star, Reich of the Black Sun: Nazi Secret Weapons and the Cold War Allied Legend*, *The SS Brotherhood of the Bell: NASA's Nazis, JFK, and Majic-12*, *The Cosmic War: Interplanetary Warfare, Modern Physics and Ancient Tests*, and the forthcoming *The Philosopher's Stone* from Feral House.

William W. Flint ("The Bussard Fusion Reactor and Its Detractors") is a Physics professor and researcher on innovative forms of energy. He lives in Port Angeles, Washington.

Adam Gorightly ("Tiffany Overtakes Tuesday Weld") is the author of books on Kerry Thornley (*The Prankster and the Conspiracy*) and Charles Manson (*The Shadow Over Santa Susana*). His website is *www.adamgorightly.com*.

Douglas Hawes ("Tiffany Overtakes Tuesday Weld") is a resident of Santa Cruz, Ground Zero of the Tuesday Weld pagan movement.

Craig Heimbichner ("An Idiots Guide to the Cryptocracy" and "The Brotherhood of the Gun") is the author of *Blood on the Altar*, a book about the occult fraternity, the OTO. His work can be seen on *www.heimbichner.tripod.com*.

Harry Helms ("Lingering Questions About 9/11") is the author of *Top Secret Tourism* and *The Shadow Government*.

Al Hidell ("Paranotes") is co-founder of *Paranoia* magazine.

Jim Hougan ("Jonestown") is the author of *Spooks*, about the private use of secret agents by multinational corporations and the rich, and *Secret Agenda: Watergate Deep Throat and the CIA*. Mr. Hougan has also worked for *60 Minutes* and under the pseudonym John Case published six thriller novels.

ABOUT THE AUTHORS277

Paul Krassner ("The Mind of Mae Brussell") is the publisher of the famed freethought magazine, *The Realist*, and the author of a dozen books.

Jim Marrs ("Occult Nashville") is the author of eight books about fraternal orders, UFOs, 9/11, intelligence agencies, and the assassination of John F. Kennedy, which was used as the basis of the Oliver Stone film, *JFK*. Mr. Marrs' website is *www.jimmarrs.com*.

David Martin ("Seventeen Techniques for Truth Suppression") also goes by the sobriquet "DC Dave" and his website is *www.dcdave.com*.

Adam Parfrey (co-editor) is publisher of Feral House, and co-publisher, with Jodi Wille, of Process Media. He is also the author of *Cult Rapture*, co-author (with Maja D'Aoust) of *The Secret Source*, *Extreme Islam*, *It's a Man's World*, and editor of the two volumes of *Apocalypse Culture*.

Fletcher L. Prouty was a colonel in the United States Air Force and the author of books critical of American intelligence agencies, including *The Secret Team: The CIA and its Allies in Control of the United States and the World* and *JFK: The CIA, Vietnam, and the Plot to Assassinate John F. Kennedy*.

Lady Queenborough ("Occult Theocrasy"), also known as Edith Starr Miller, was the daughter of the New York Industrialist, William Starr Miller. Though accused of relying on anti-Masonic material of dubious validity, "Occult Theocrasy" also contained copies of actual correspondence between occultists Theodore Reuss, Aleister Crowley, William Wynn Wescott and John Yarker. "Occult Theocrasy" was Lady Queenborough's primary life's work, and is often quoted as the source for material of both pro and anti-Masonic perspectives.

Richard Sauder ("Are Aliens and Their Technology Underground and Undersea") is the author of *Underground Bases and Tunnels*, *Kundalini Tales* and *Underwater and Underground Bases*. Sauder's interviews on radio program can be heard here: *www.redicecreations.com/specialreports/rsauder.html*

Jerry E. Smith ("Secret Weather Wars") is the author of three books, including *HAARP: The Ultimate Weapon of the Conspiracy*, *Spear of Destiny*, and *Weather Warfare*. His website is *www.jerryesmith.com*.

Robert Sterling ("Electronic Votescam") is the author of *50 Reasons Not to Re-Elect George Bush* and the founder of *The Konformist* at *www.konformist.com*.

Kenn Thomas (co-editor) publishes Steamshovel Press, a magazine with the motto "All conspiracy. No Theory." His most recent books include Conspiracy Files and Parapolitics. Thomas' previous work includes NASA, Nazis & JFK; Maury Island UFO about possible JFK assassin Fred Crisman; and The Octopus: Secret Government and the Death of Danny Casolaro, about the Inslaw affair, updated in a new edition by Feral House in 2004. A sample copy of Steamshovel costs $10, from POB 210553, St. Louis, MO 63121 (checks payable to "Kenn Thomas," not "Steamshovel Press").

Jay Weidner ("The Culling") is a filmmaker (*Secrets of Alchemy*, *2012: The Odyssey*, *Quantum Astrology*), and with Sharron Rose runs the production company Sacred Mysteries. His websites can be found here: *www.jayweidner.com* and here: *www.sacredmysteries.com*.

Robert Anton Wilson ("Weishaput Meets Wilson"), who died in January 2007, wrote 35 books, including *The Illuminatus Trilogy* (co-authored with Robert Shea), and *Cosmic Trigger*. RAW also contributed an Introduction to the Feral House book, *Sex and Rockets: The Occult World of Jack Parsons*. A website of Robert Anton Wilson's ideas can be seen at: *www.maybelogic.com*.

Also Available from Feral House
www.FeralHouse.com

Top Secret Tourism Your Travel Guide to Germ Warfare Laboratories, Clandestine Aircraft Bases, and Other Places in the United States You're Not Supposed to Know About
by Harry Helms
277 pages • photos and maps • $14

Dark Mission The Secret History of NASA
by Richard C. Hoagland and Mike Bara
560 pages • color and black and white photographs • $24.95

War is a Racket The Antiwar Classic by America's Most Decorated General
by Smedley D. Butler
84 pages • photos • $9.95

Secret Agent 666 Aleister Crowley, British Intelligence and the Occult
by Richard B. Spence
300 pages • photos • $24.95

The Octopus Secret Government and the Death of Danny Casolaro
by Kenn Thomas and Danny Casolaro
237 pages • photos • $15

The Secret King The Myth and Reality of Nazi Occultism
by Stephen E. Flowers and Michael Moynihan
320 pages • illustrated • $16.95